Volume 5

Ema Toyama

**Translated and adapted by
Alethea Nibley and Athena Nibley**

Lettered by Paige Pumphrey

Missions of Love
Ema Toyama

Character

Shigure Kitami

The ever-popular, yet black-hearted, student body president. He made a game of charming all the girls and making them confess their love to him, then writing it all down in his student notebook, but Yukina discovered his secret!

Yukina Himuro

A third-year junior high student who strikes terror in the hearts of all around her with her piercing gaze, feared as the "Absolute Zero Snow Woman." Only Akira knows that she is also the popular cell phone novelist Yupina.

Akira Shimotsuki

Yukina's cousin and fellow student. He loves to eat. As Yukina's confidant, he can always be found nearby, watching over her. There's a good-looking face hiding behind that hair.

me!

It is time for love.
Secret cell phone novelist vs. the most popular boy in school.
A mission of love for absolute servitude.

Mami Mizuno

A childhood friend of Shigure's. A sickly girl, she had been taking time off from school, but now she has returned. The teachers love her, and she's very popular with the boys. She's a beautiful young girl who always wears a smile, but....

Story

By blackmailing Shigure into holding her hand and holding her in his arms, etc., Yukina's romantic experience is growing nicely. But have Akira's confession of love and Mami's return to school changed their relationship? And why is Mami really getting close to Yukina!?

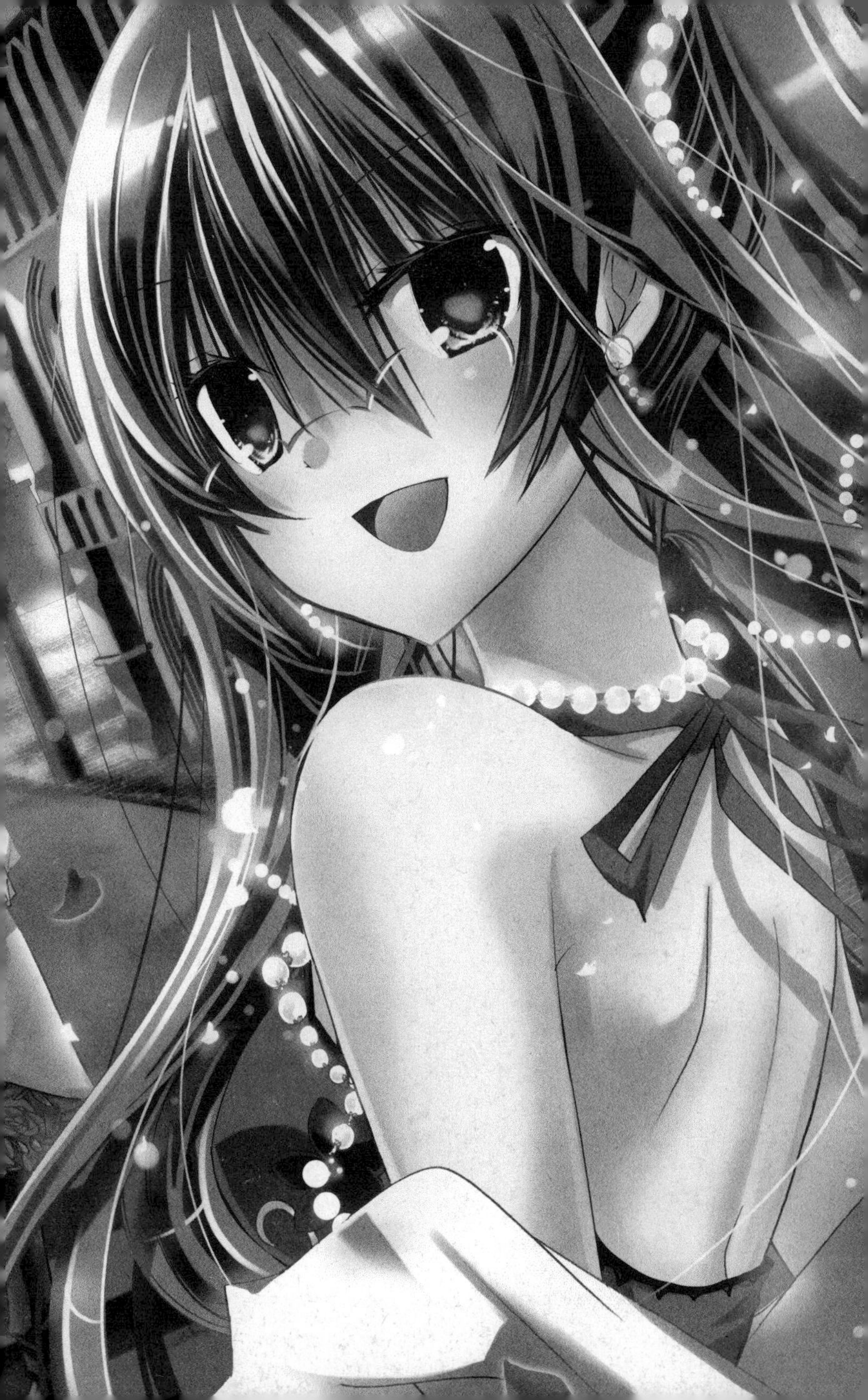

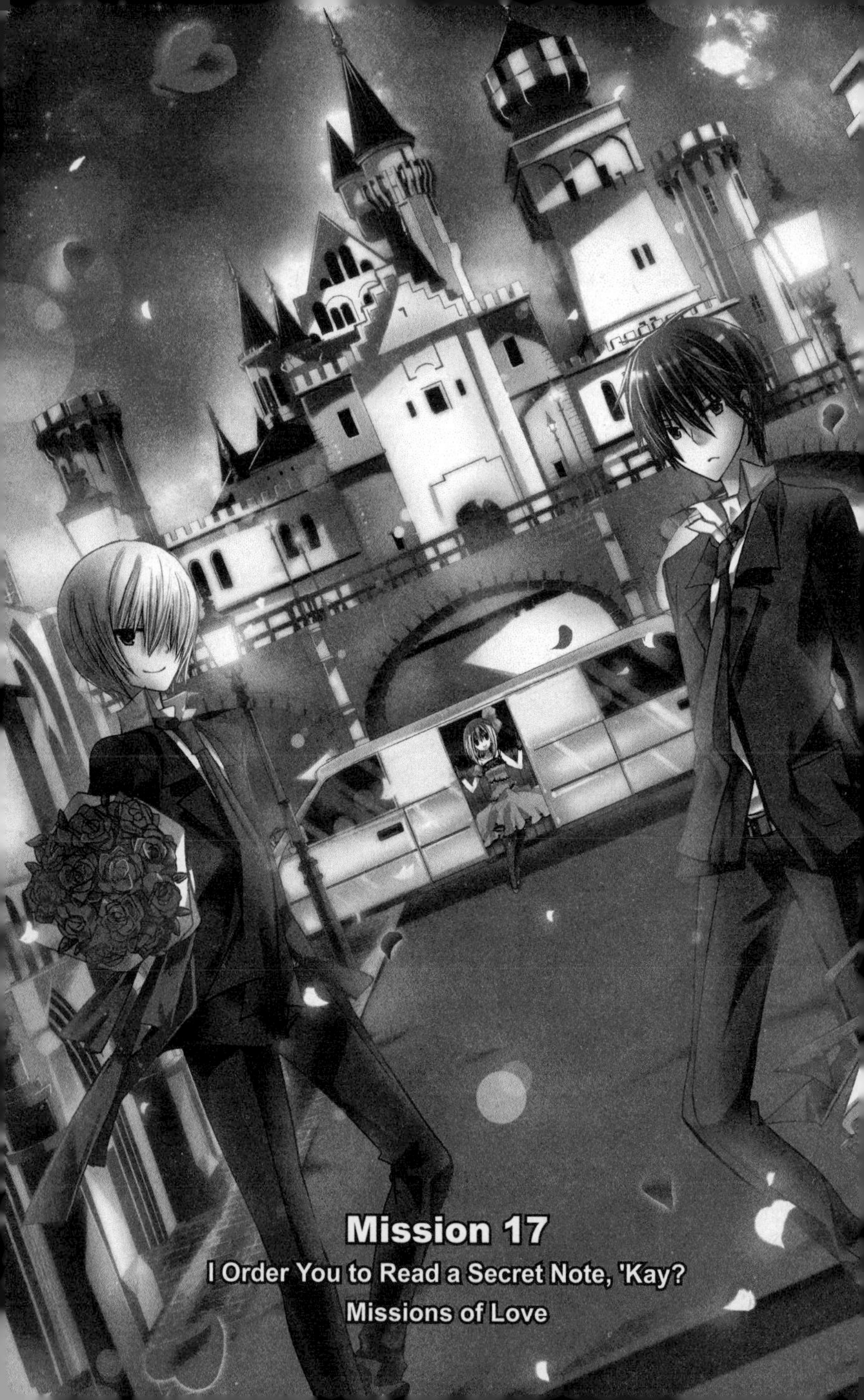
Mission 17
I Order You to Read a Secret Note, 'Kay?
Missions of Love

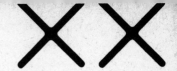

Missions of Love

It is time for love.
Secret cell phone
novelist vs. the most
popular boy in school.
A mission of love for
absolute servitude.

ne!

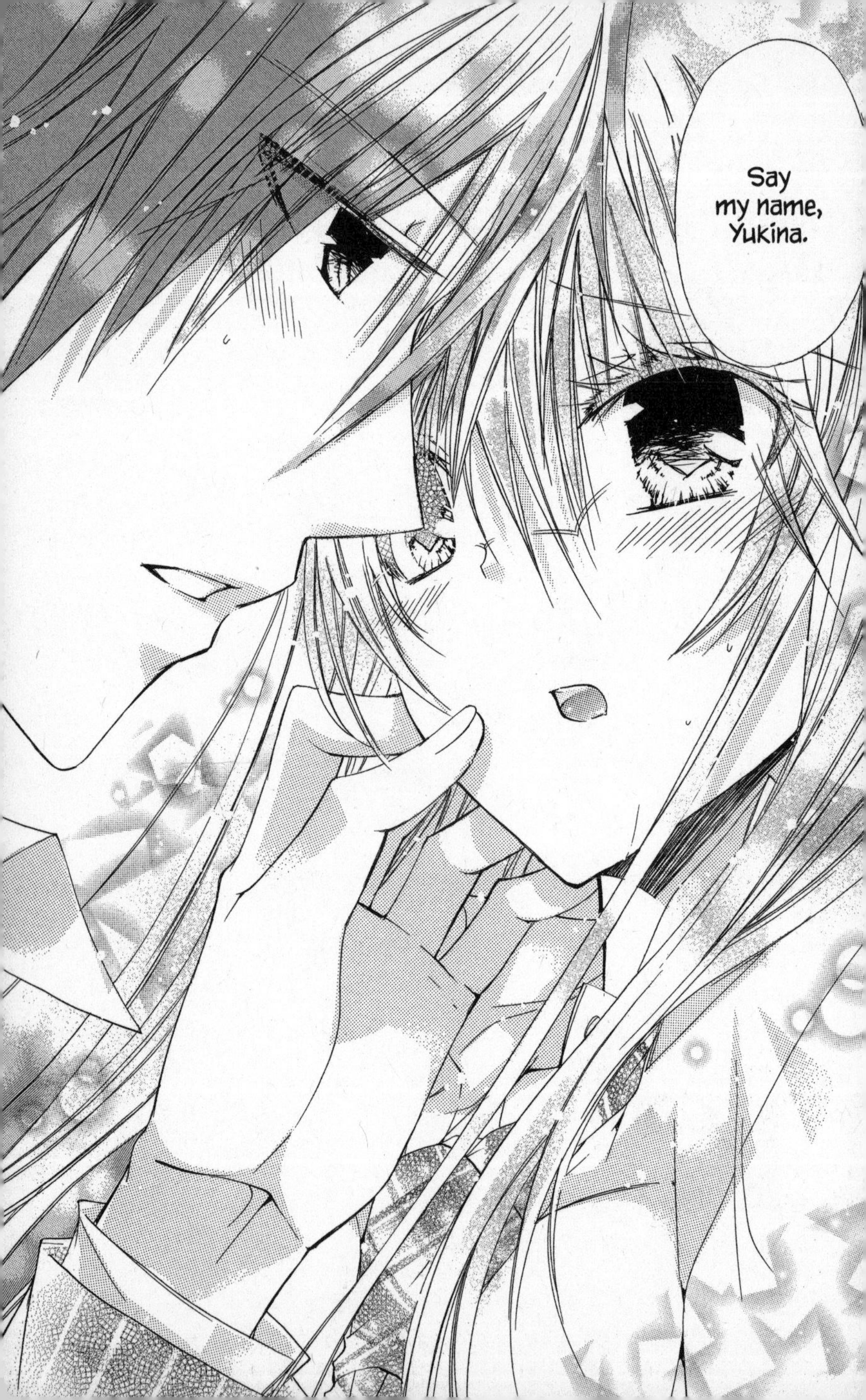
Say my name, Yukina.

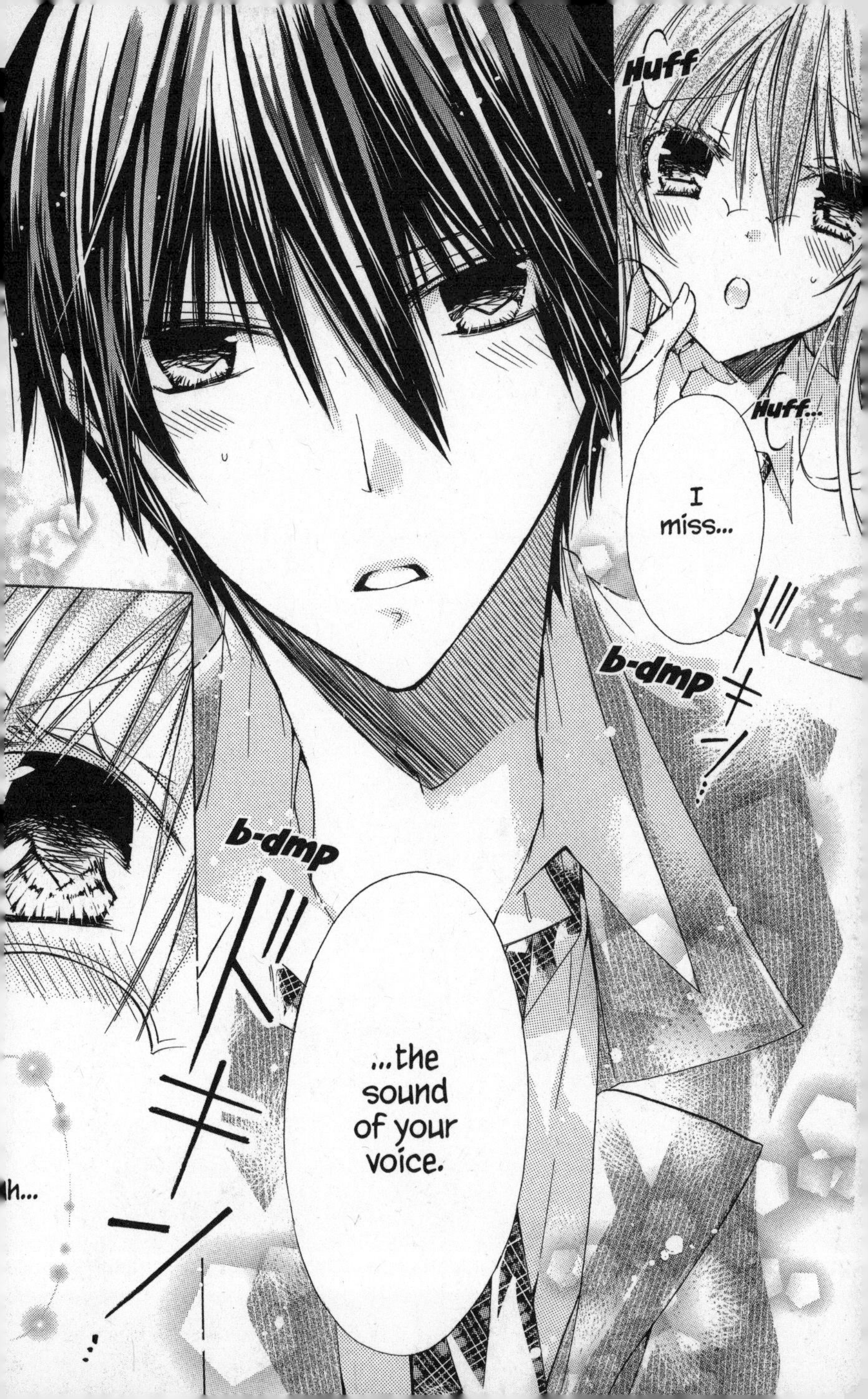
Huff
Huff...
I miss...
b-dmp
b-dmp
...the sound of your voice.

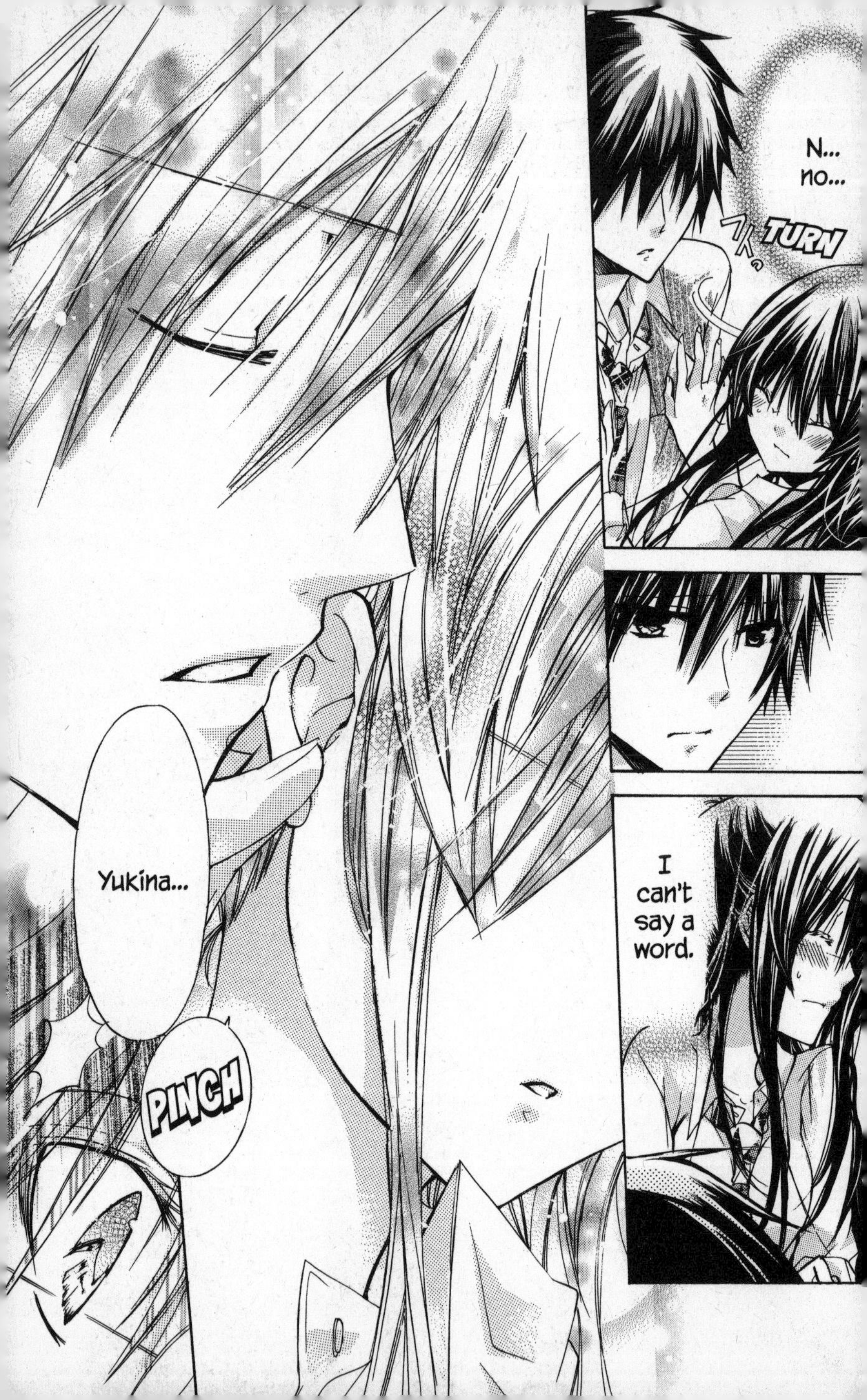

N... no...
TURN
I can't say a word.
Yukina...
PINCH

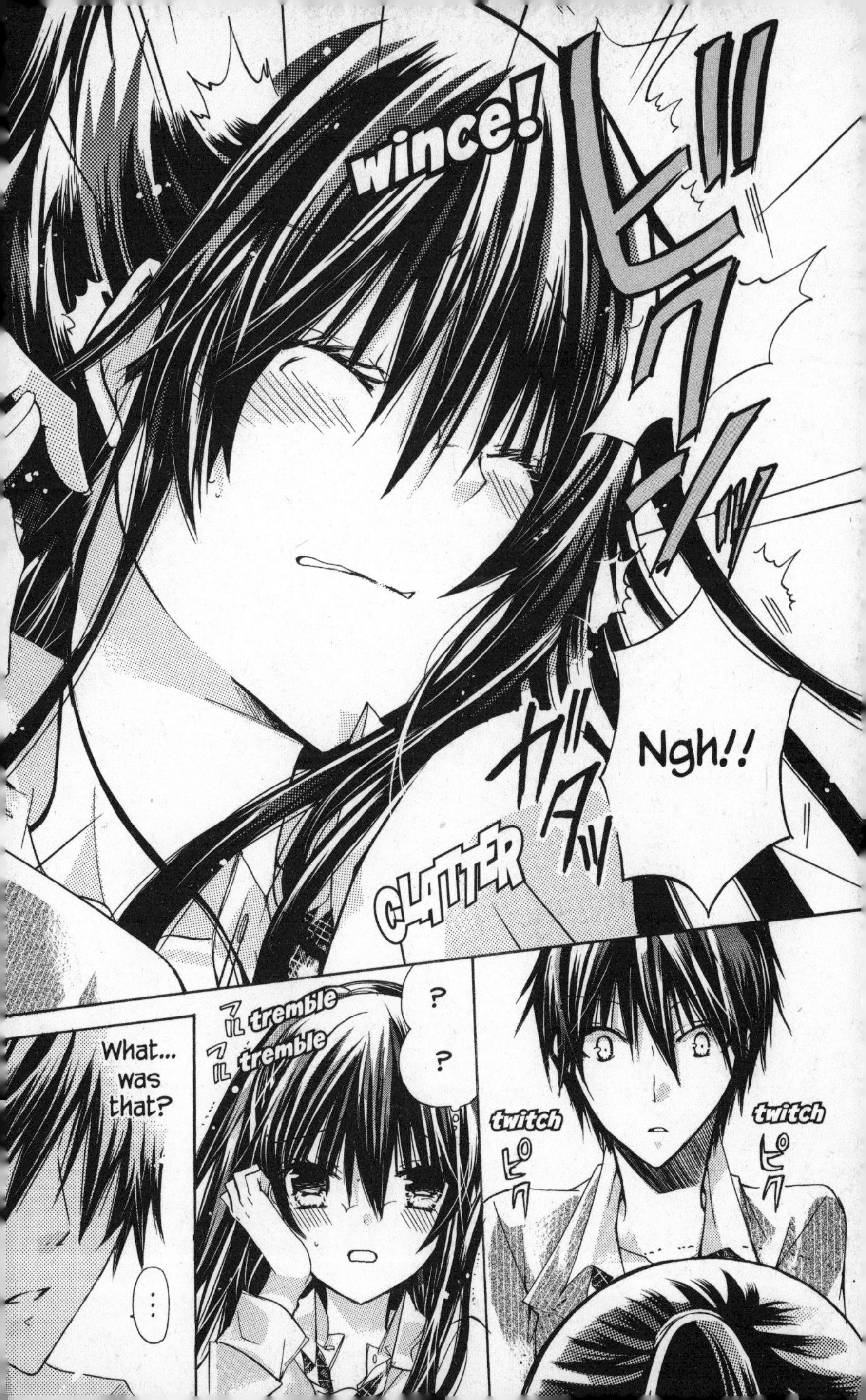

ビクッ
wince!
Ngh!!
ガタッ
CLATTER
ピク
twitch
ピク
twitch
?
?
フル
tremble
フル
tremble
What... was that?
...

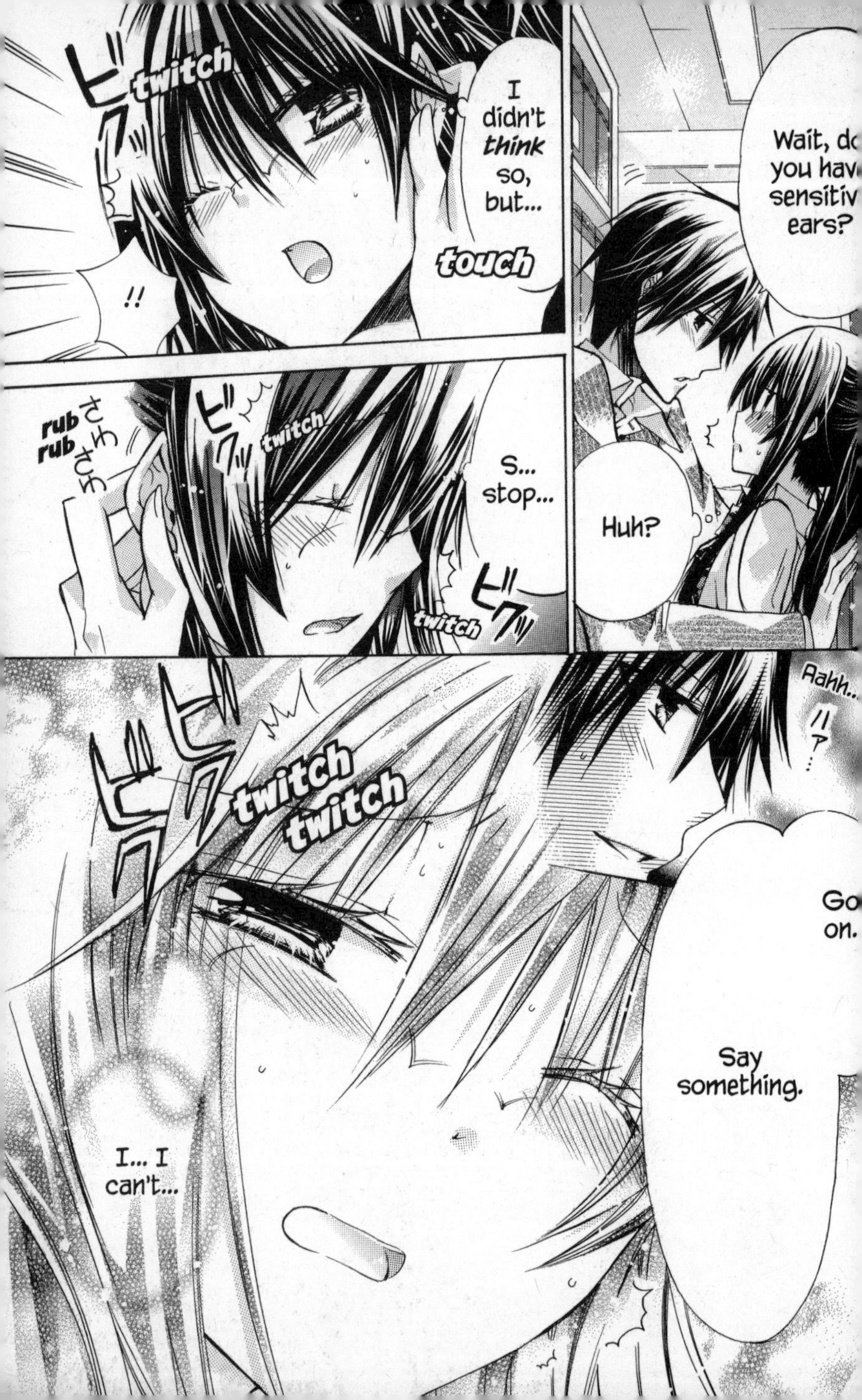
Wait, do you hav sensitiv ears?
Huh?
I didn't *think* so, but...
touch
ビクッ
twitch
!!
S... stop...
ビクッ
twitch
ビクッ
twitch
さわさわ
rub rub
Aahh...
ハァ...
Go on.
Say something.
ビクビク
twitch twitch
I... I can't...

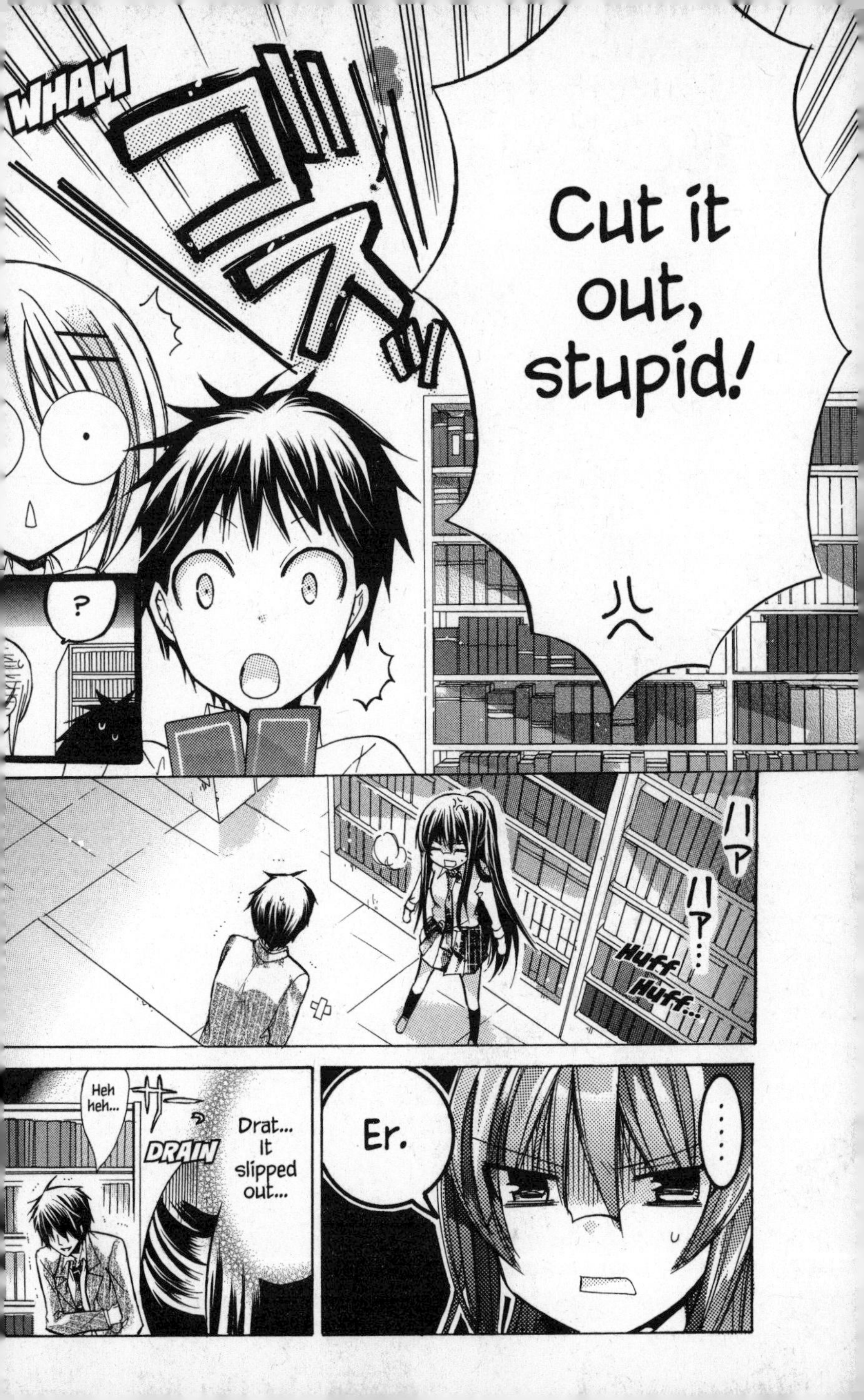
Cut it out, stupid!
WHAM
?
ハア ハア…
Huff Huff…
…
……
Er.
Heh heh…
DRAIN
Drat… It slipped out…

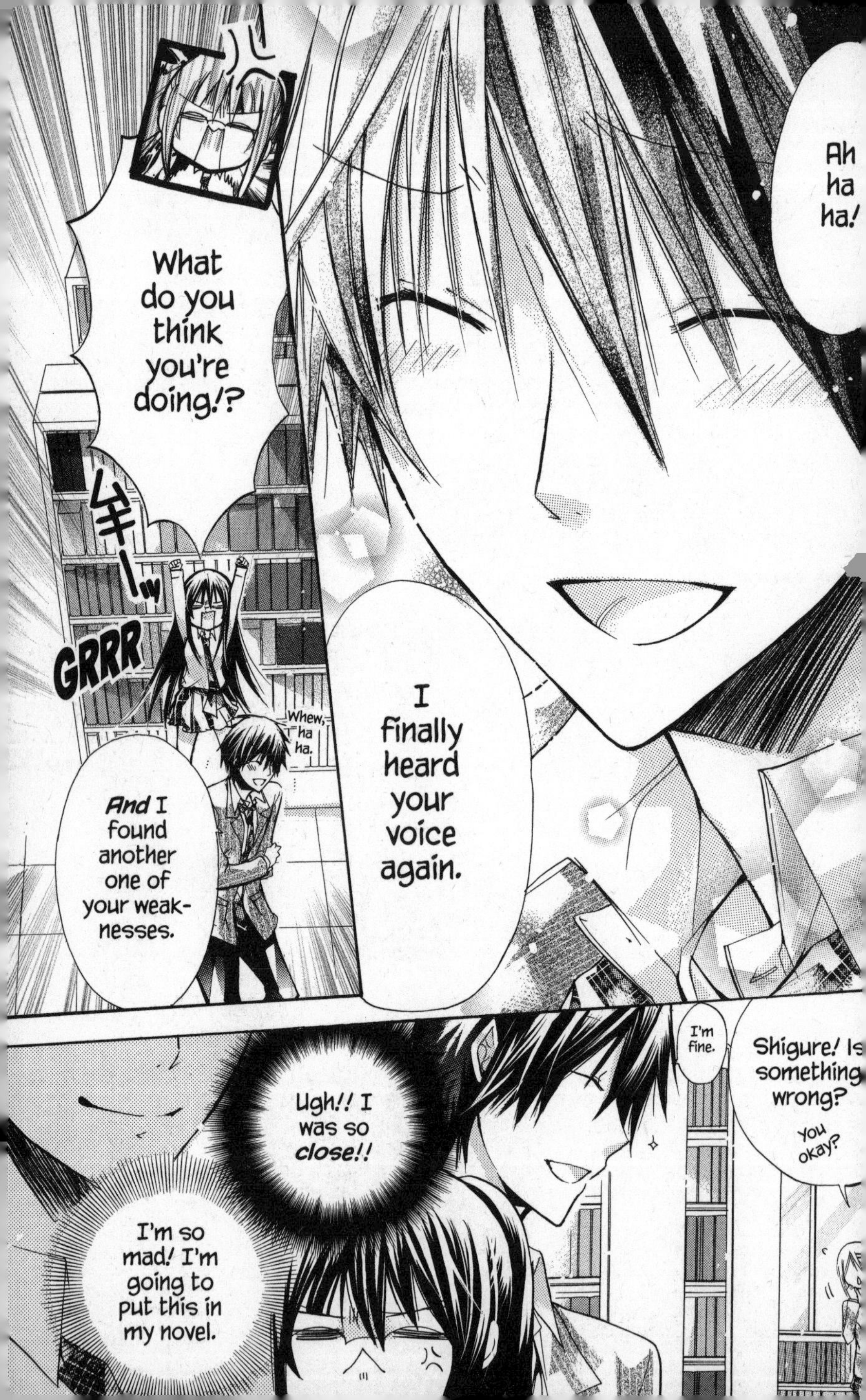

Ah ha ha!
I finally heard your voice again.
And I found another one of your weaknesses.
Whew, ha ha.
What do you think you're doing!?
GRRR
Shigure! Is something wrong?
You okay?
I'm fine.
Ugh!! I was so close!!
I'm so mad! I'm going to put this in my novel.

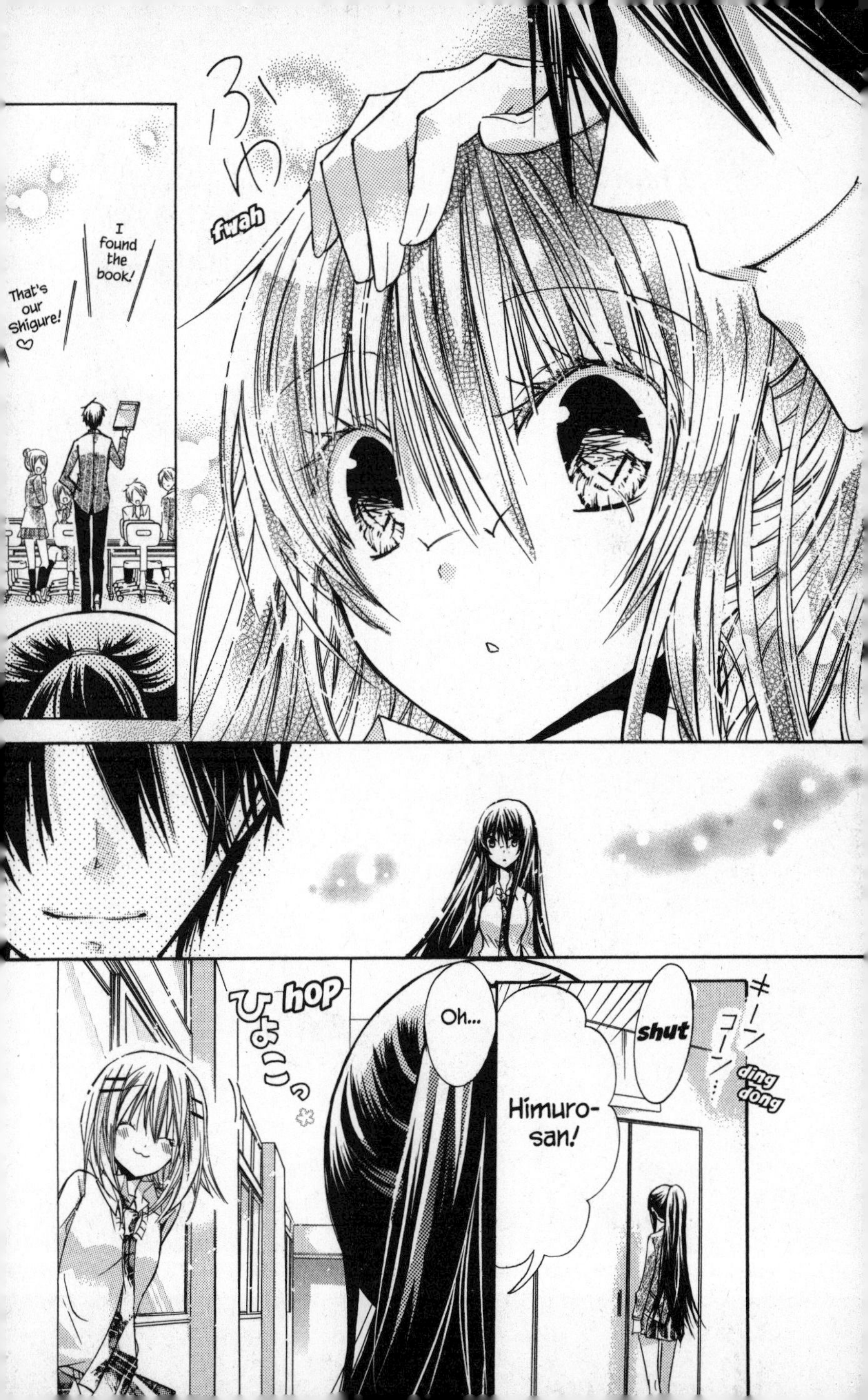
ふわ
fwah
I found the book!
That's our Shigure! ♡
キーンコーン…
ding dong
shut
Oh...
Himuro-san!
ひよこっ
hop

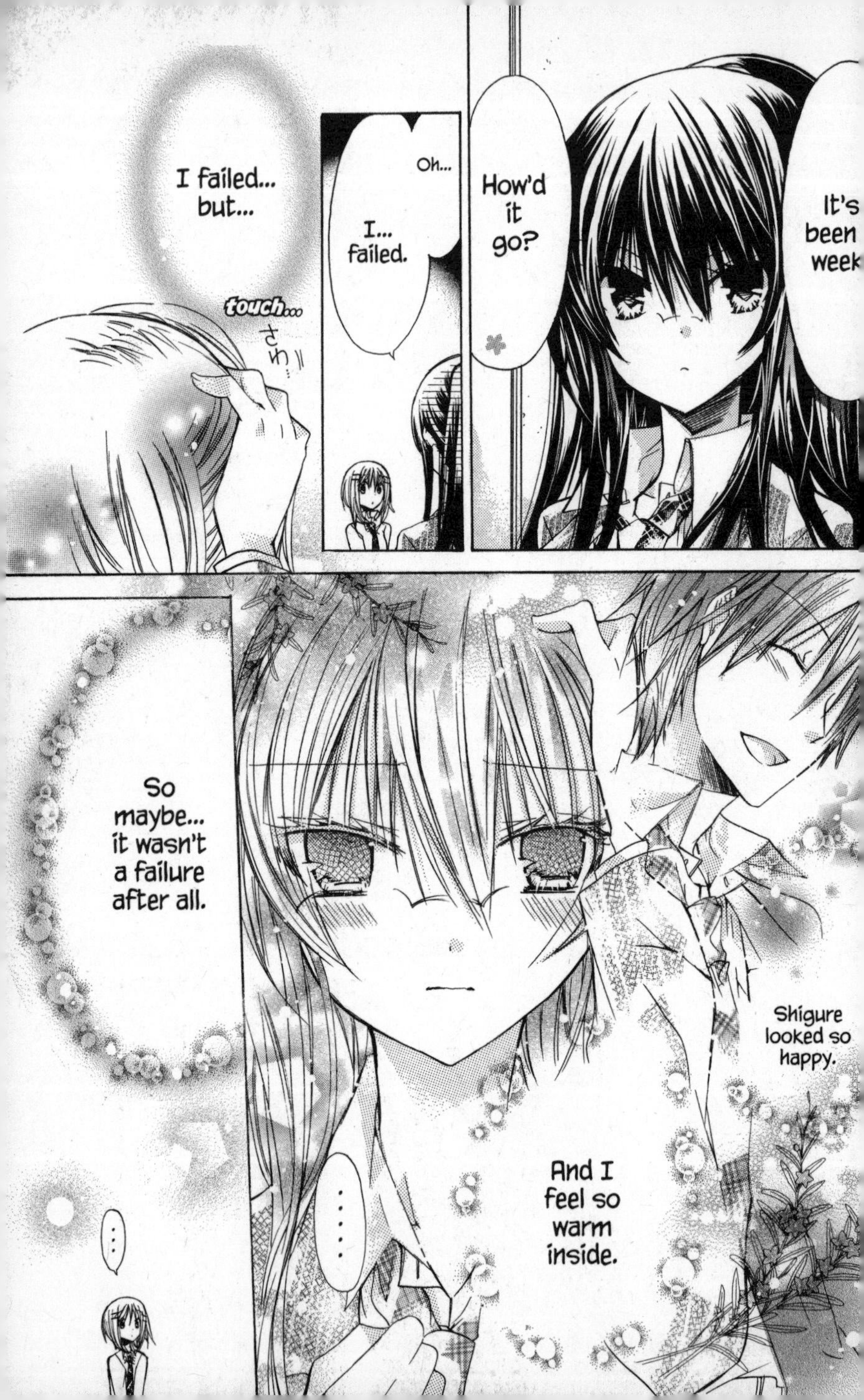

It's been week
How'd it go?
Oh...
I... failed.
I failed... but...
touch...
さわ
Shigure looked so happy.
And I feel so warm inside.
......
So maybe... it wasn't a failure after all.
...

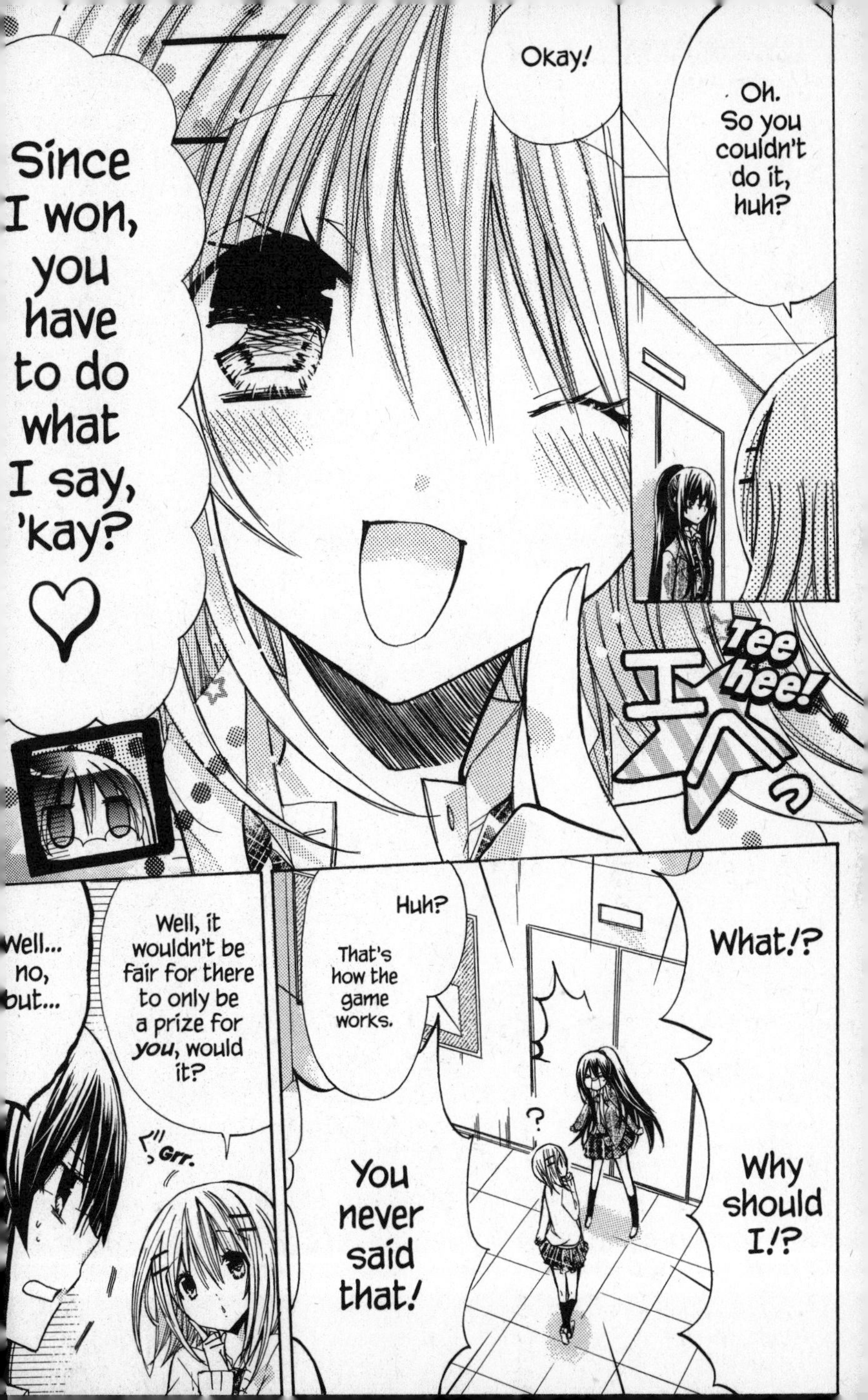
Oh. So you couldn't do it, huh?
Okay!
Tee hee!
Since I won, you have to do what I say, 'kay? ♡
What!?
Why should I!?
Huh?
That's how the game works.
You never said that!
Well, it wouldn't be fair for there to only be a prize for *you*, would it?
Well... no, but...
Grr.

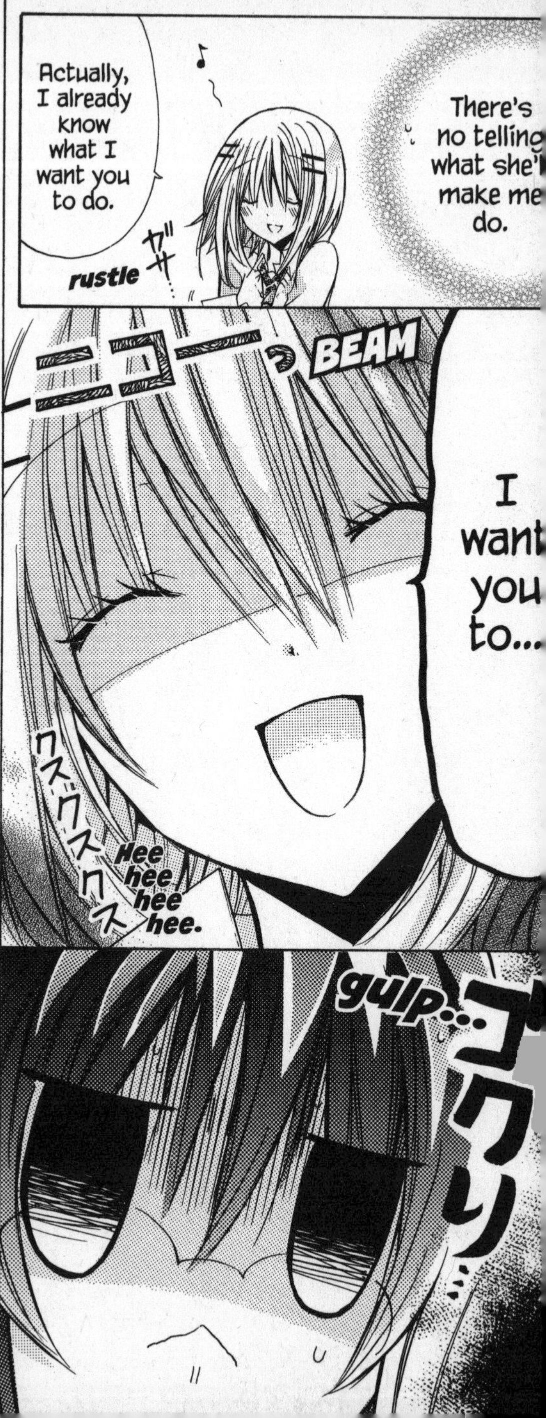
There's no telling what she'
make me do.
Actually, I already know what I want you to do.
rustle
BEAM
I want you to...
Hee hee hee hee.
gulp...

Snow Yukina 1

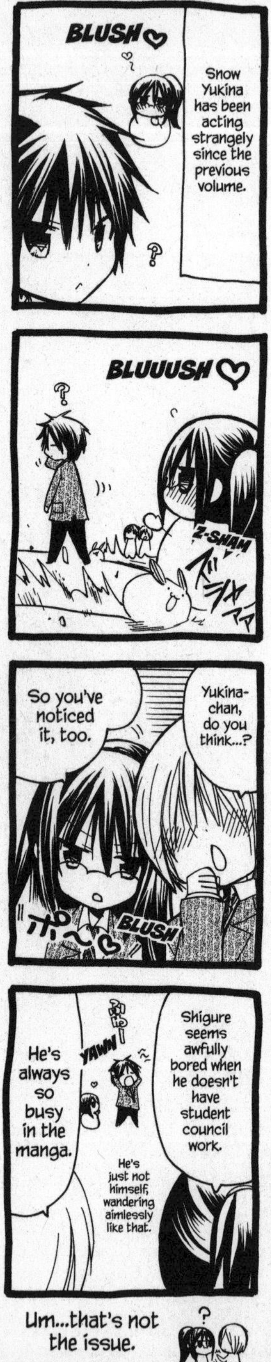
Snow Yukina has been acting strangely since the previous volume.
BLUSH
BLUUUSH
Z-SHAM
Yukina-chan, do you think...?
So you've noticed it, too.
BLUSH
Shigure seems awfully bored when he doesn't have student council work.
YAWN
He's always so busy in the manga.
He's just not himself, wandering aimlessly like that.
Um...that's not the issue.

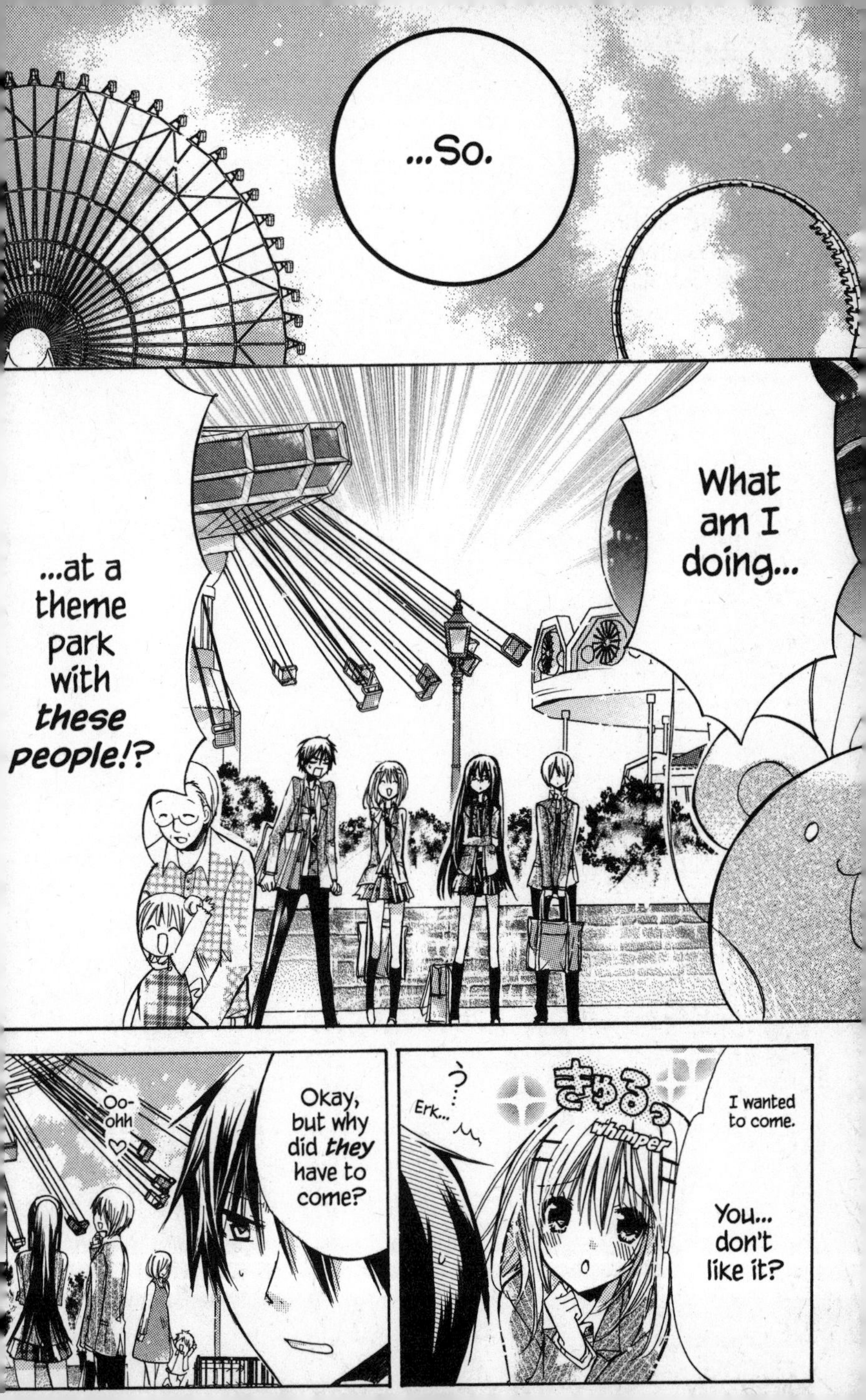
...So.
What am I doing...
...at a theme park with *these* people!?
I wanted to come.
きゅるっ
whimper
う…
Erk...
You... don't like it?
Okay, but why did *they* have to come?
Oo-ohh ♡

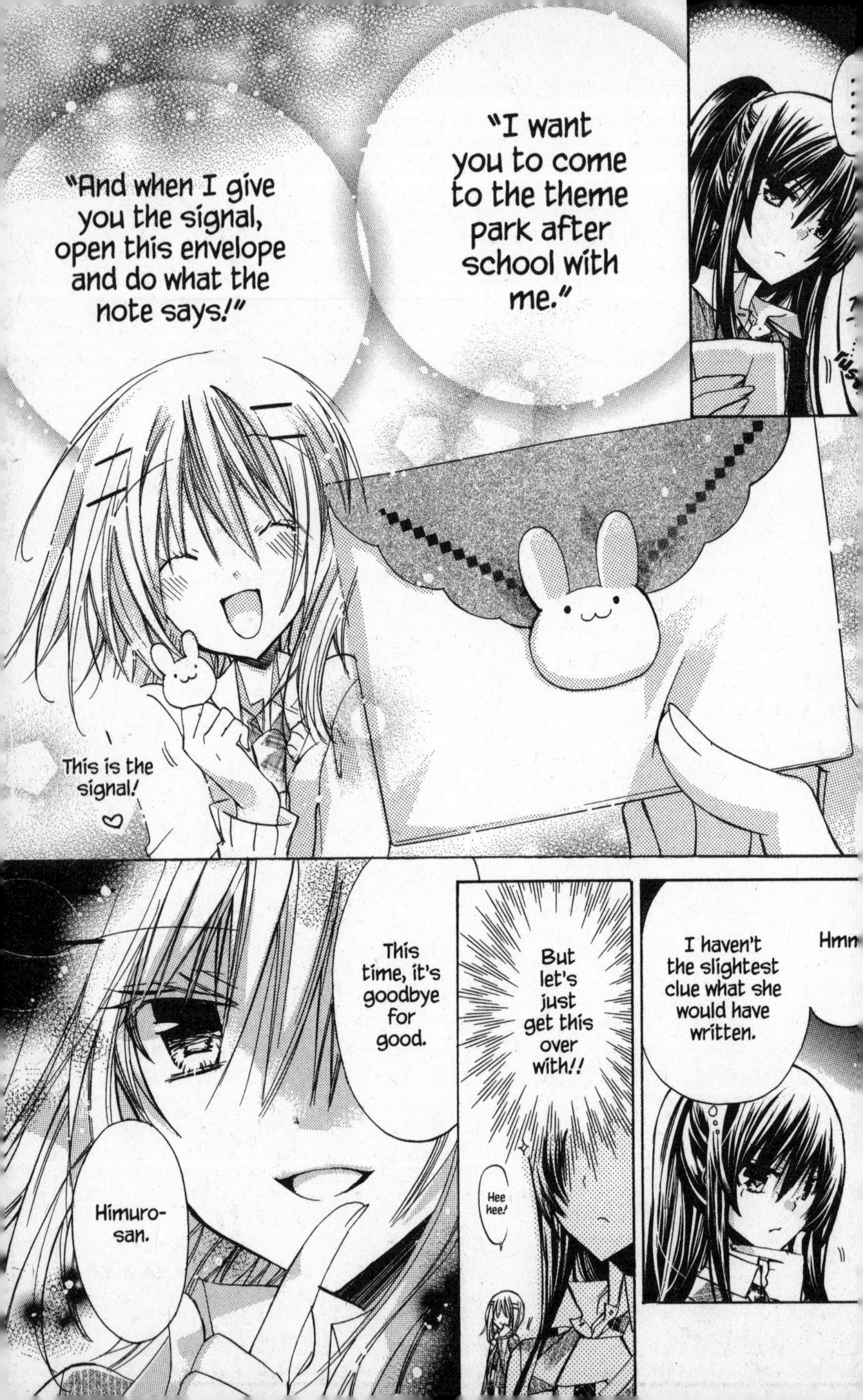
"I want you to come to the theme park after school with me."
"And when I give you the signal, open this envelope and do what the note says!"
This is the signal!
Hmn
I haven't the slightest clue what she would have written.
But let's just get this over with!!
Hee hee!
This time, it's goodbye for good.
Himuro-san.

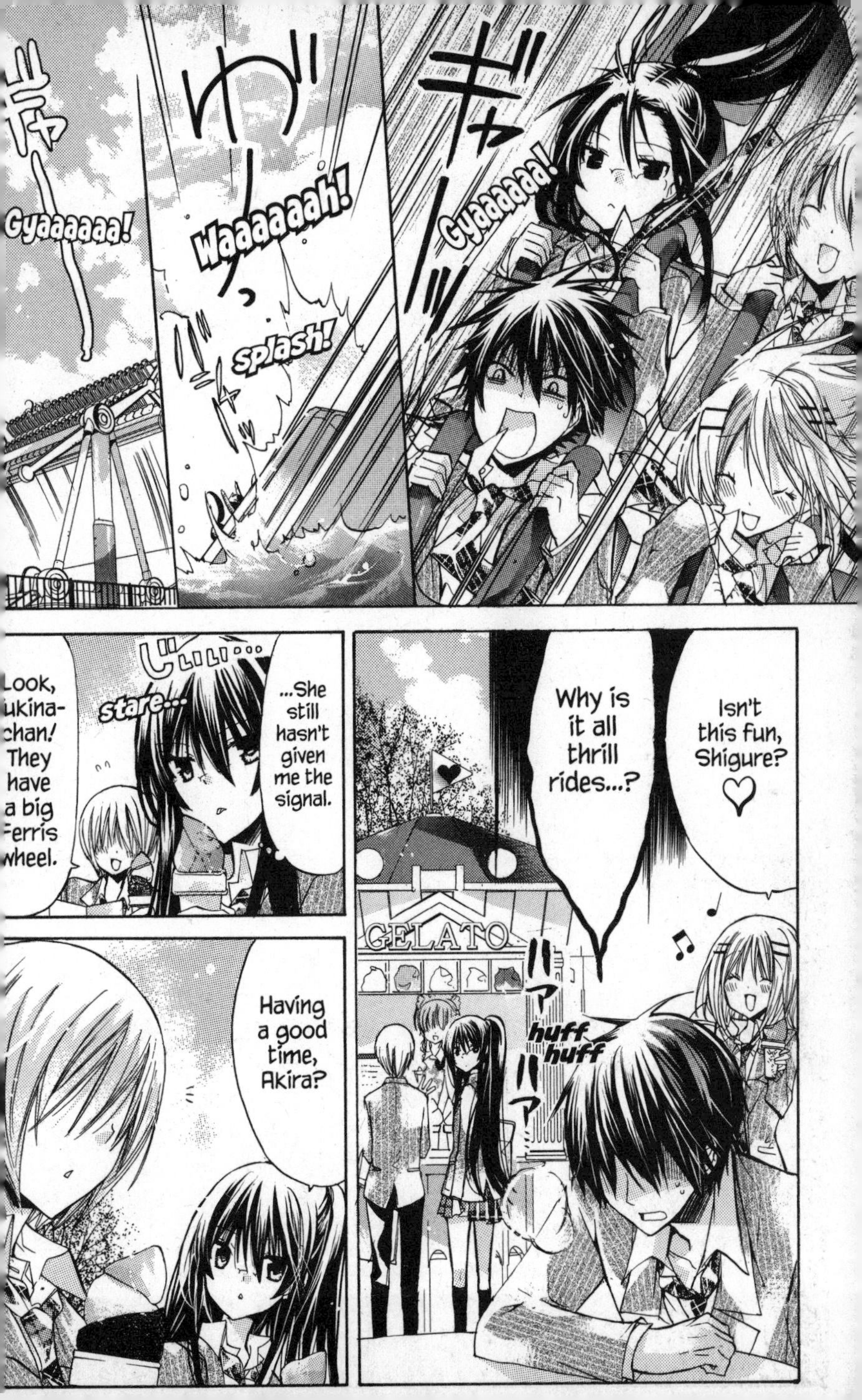
Gyaaaaaa!
Waaaaaah!
Splash!
Gyaaaaaa!
Isn't this fun, Shigure? ♡
Why is it all thrill rides...?
GELATO
huff huff
...She still hasn't given me the signal.
stare...
Look, ukina-chan! They have a big Ferris wheel.
Having a good time, Akira?

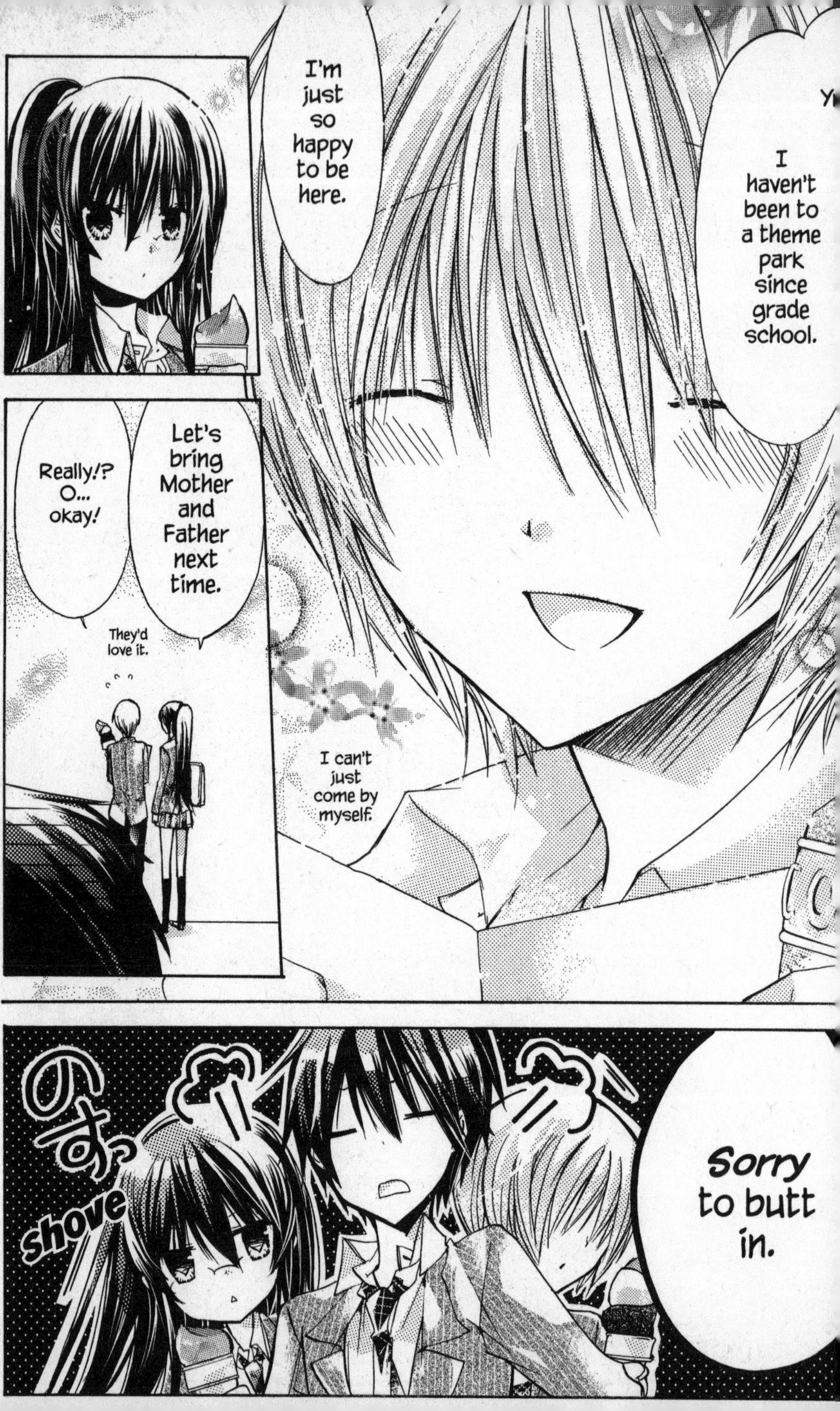
I haven't been to a theme park since grade school.
I'm just so happy to be here.
I can't just come by myself.
Let's bring Mother and Father next time.
Really!? O... okay!
They'd love it.
Sorry to butt in.
のすっ
shove

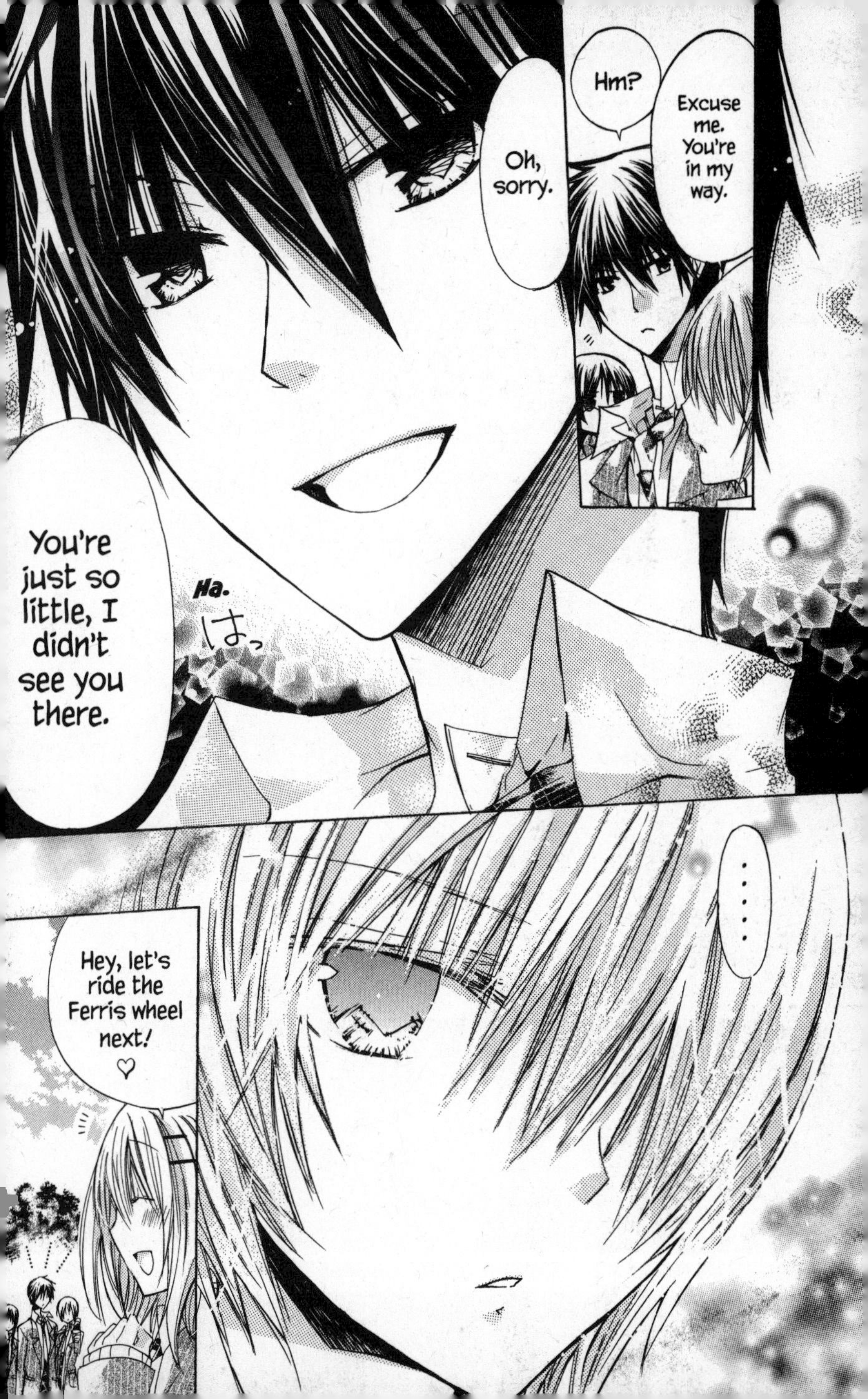
Excuse me. You're in my way.
Hm?
Oh, sorry.
Ha.
はっ
You're just so little, I didn't see you there.
......
Hey, let's ride the Ferris wheel next! ♡

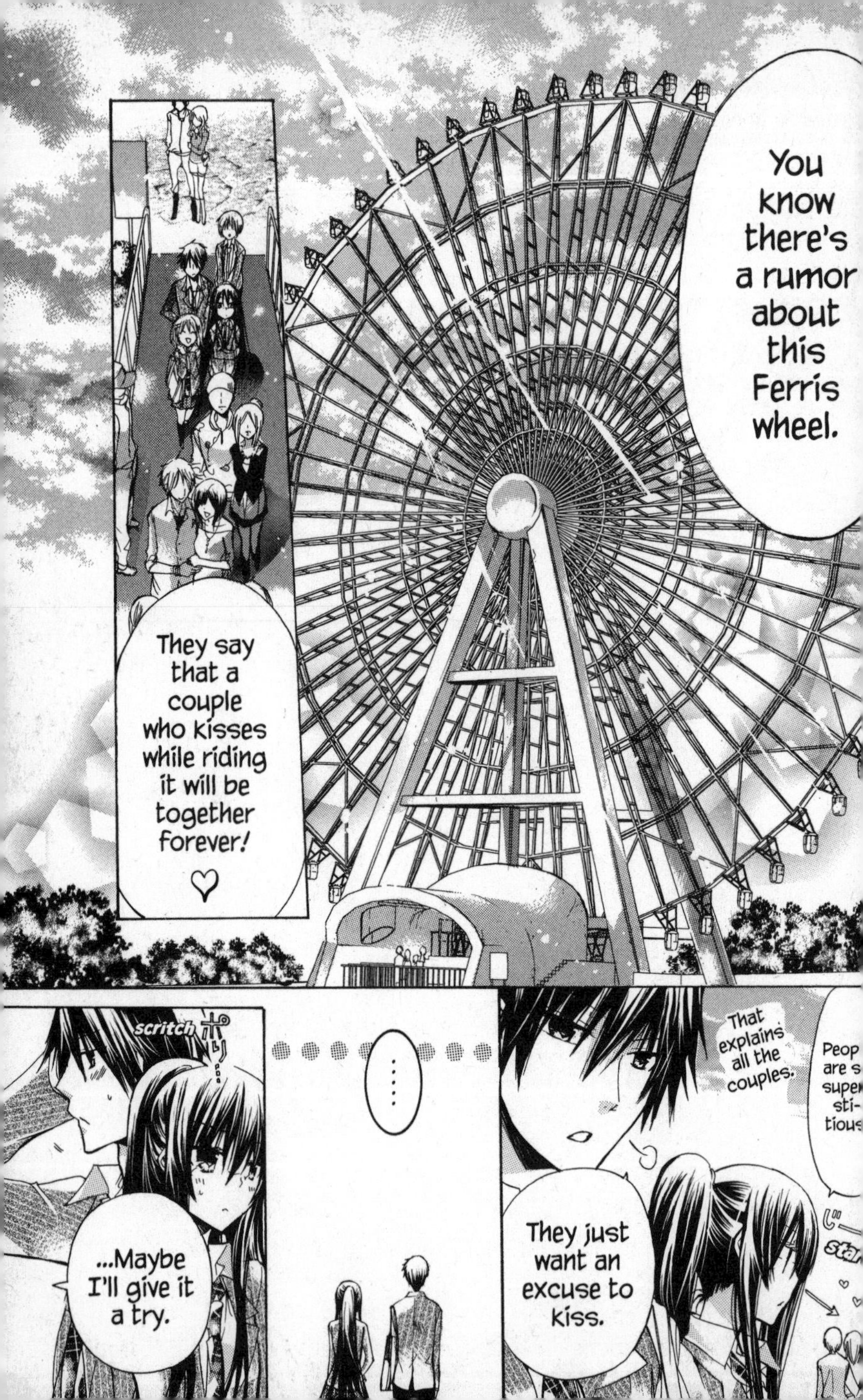
You know there's a rumor about this Ferris wheel.
They say that a couple who kisses while riding it will be together forever! ♡
Peop are s supe sti- tious
That explains all the couples.
They just want an excuse to kiss.
.....
scritch
...Maybe I'll give it a try.

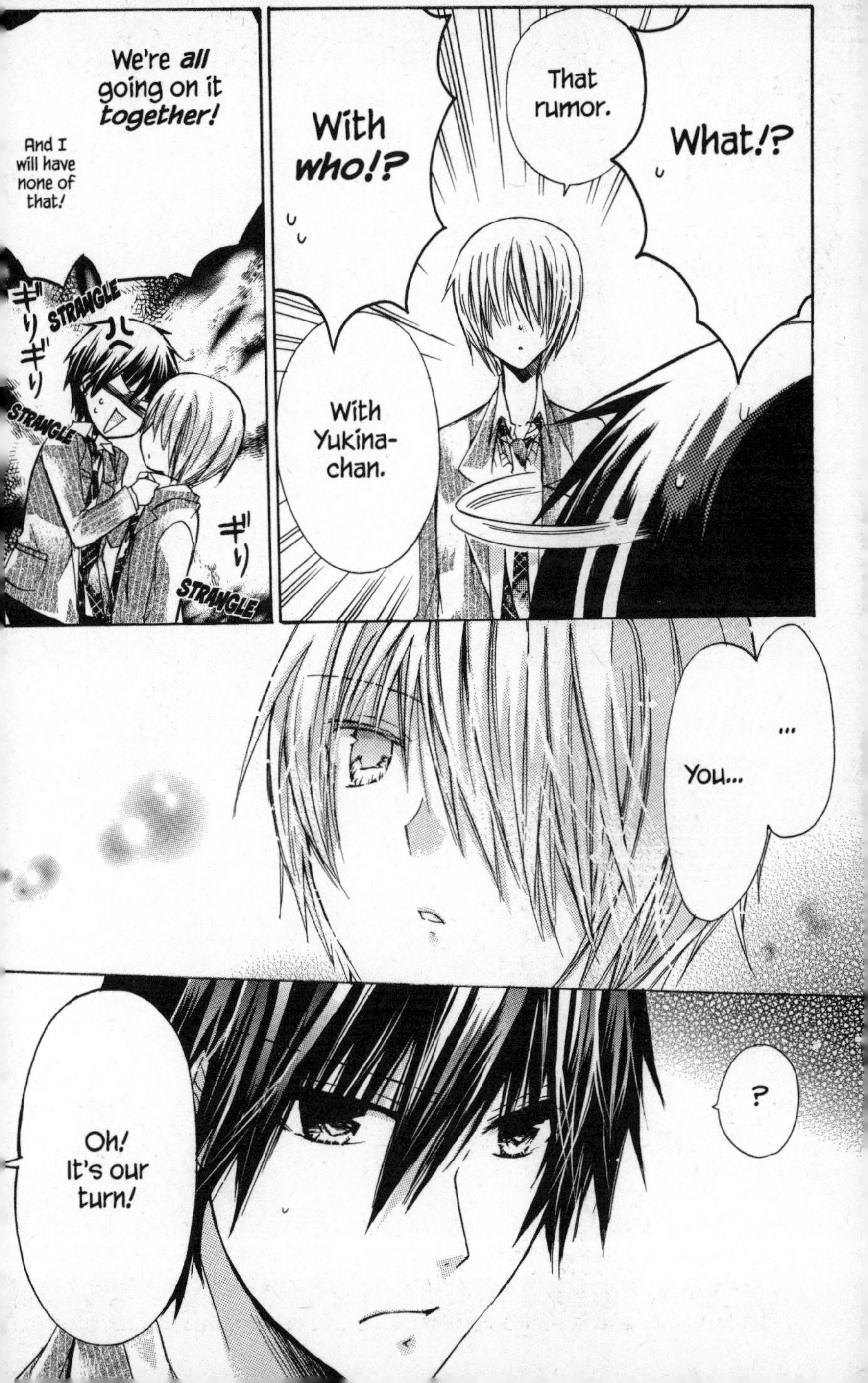

That rumor.
What!?
With who!?
With Yukina-chan.
We're all going on it together!
And I will have none of that!
ギリギリ
STRANGLE
STRANGLE
ギリ
STRANGLE
...
You...
?
Oh! It's our turn!

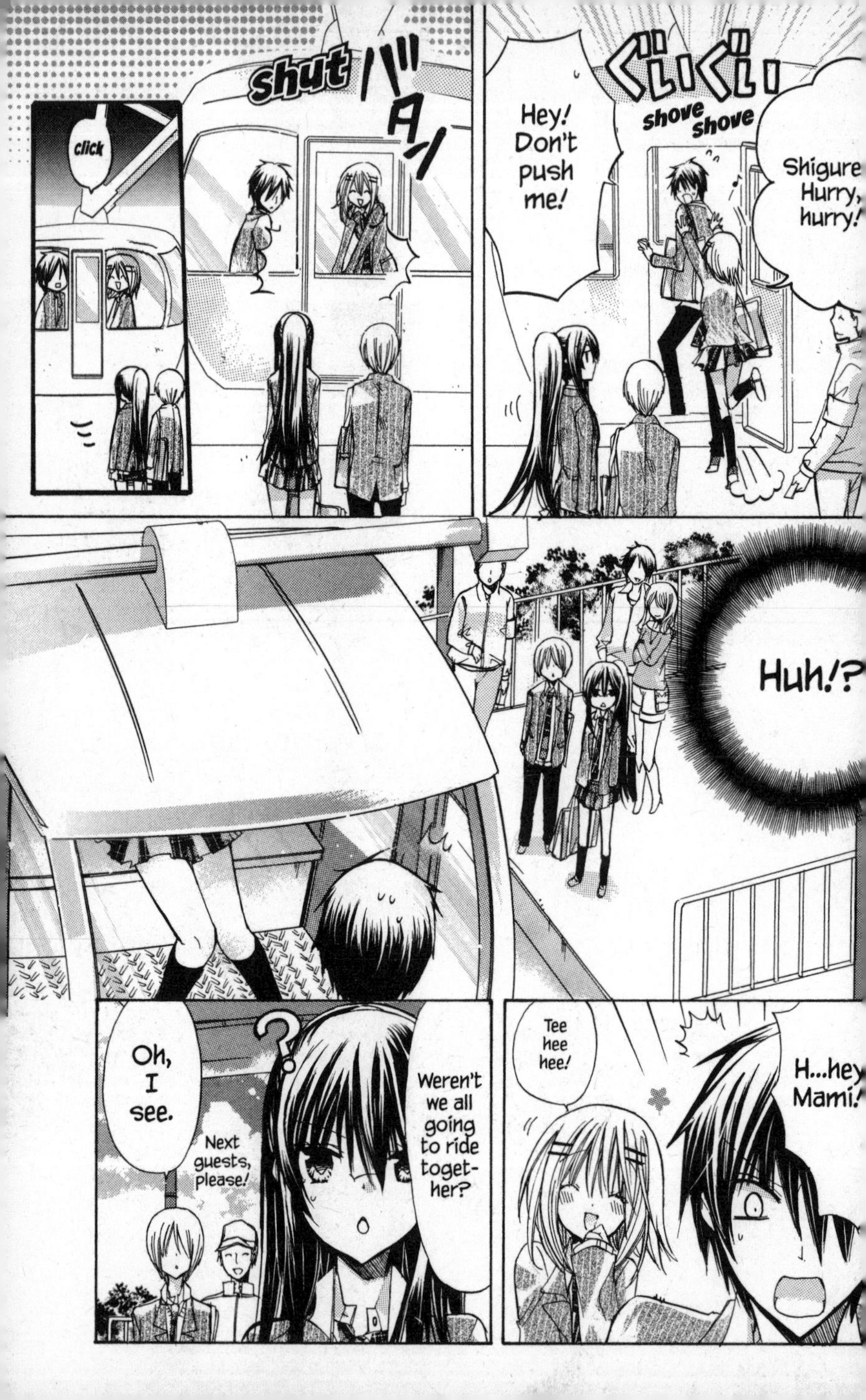
Shigure Hurry, hurry!
ぐいぐい
shove shove
Hey! Don't push me!
バタン
shut
click
Huh!?
H...hey Mami!
Tee hee hee!
Weren't we all going to ride toget-her?
Next guests, please!
Oh, I see.

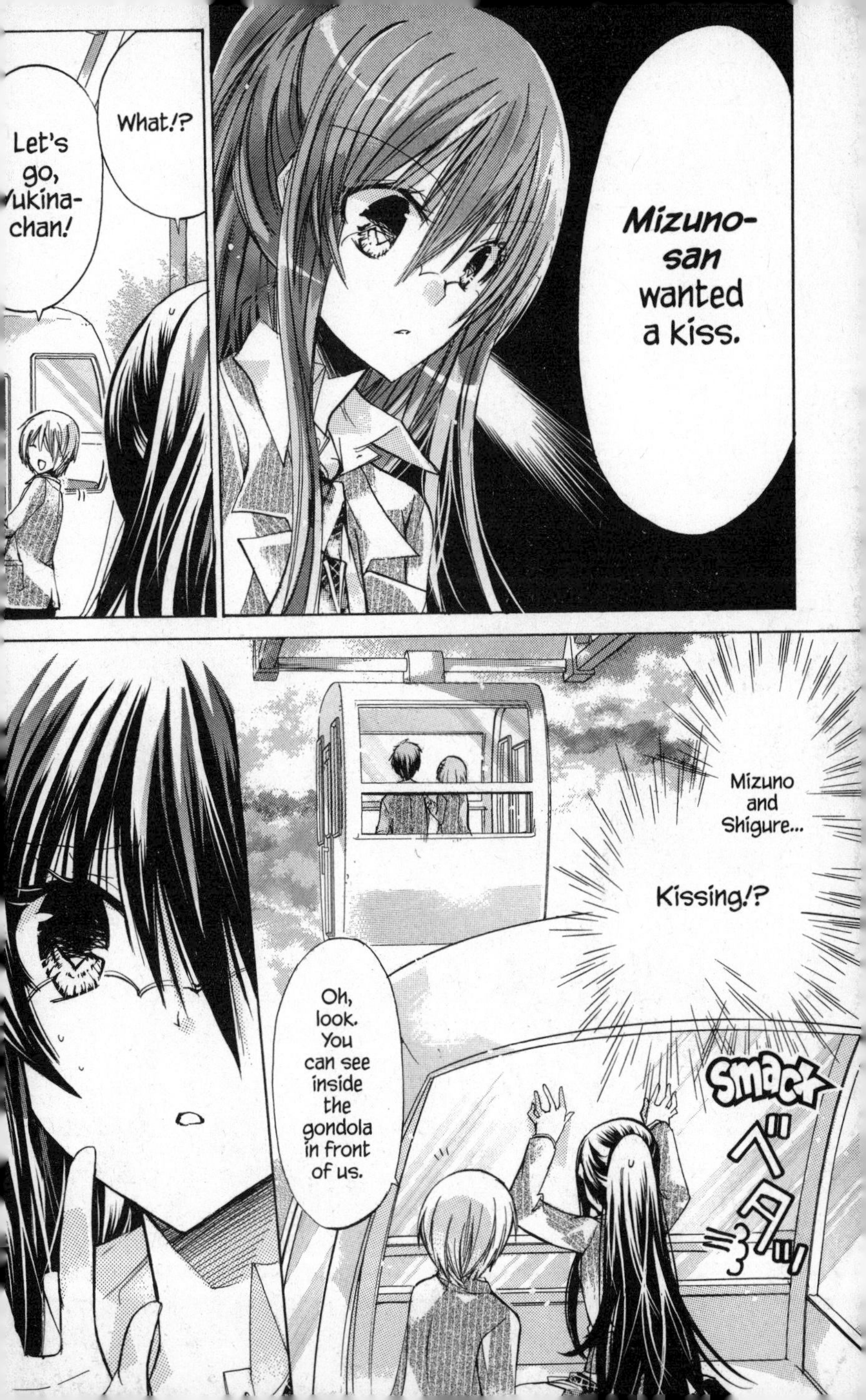
Mizuno-san wanted a kiss.
What!?
Let's go, Yukina-chan!
Mizuno and Shigure...
Kissing!?
Smack
Oh, look. You can see inside the gondola in front of us.

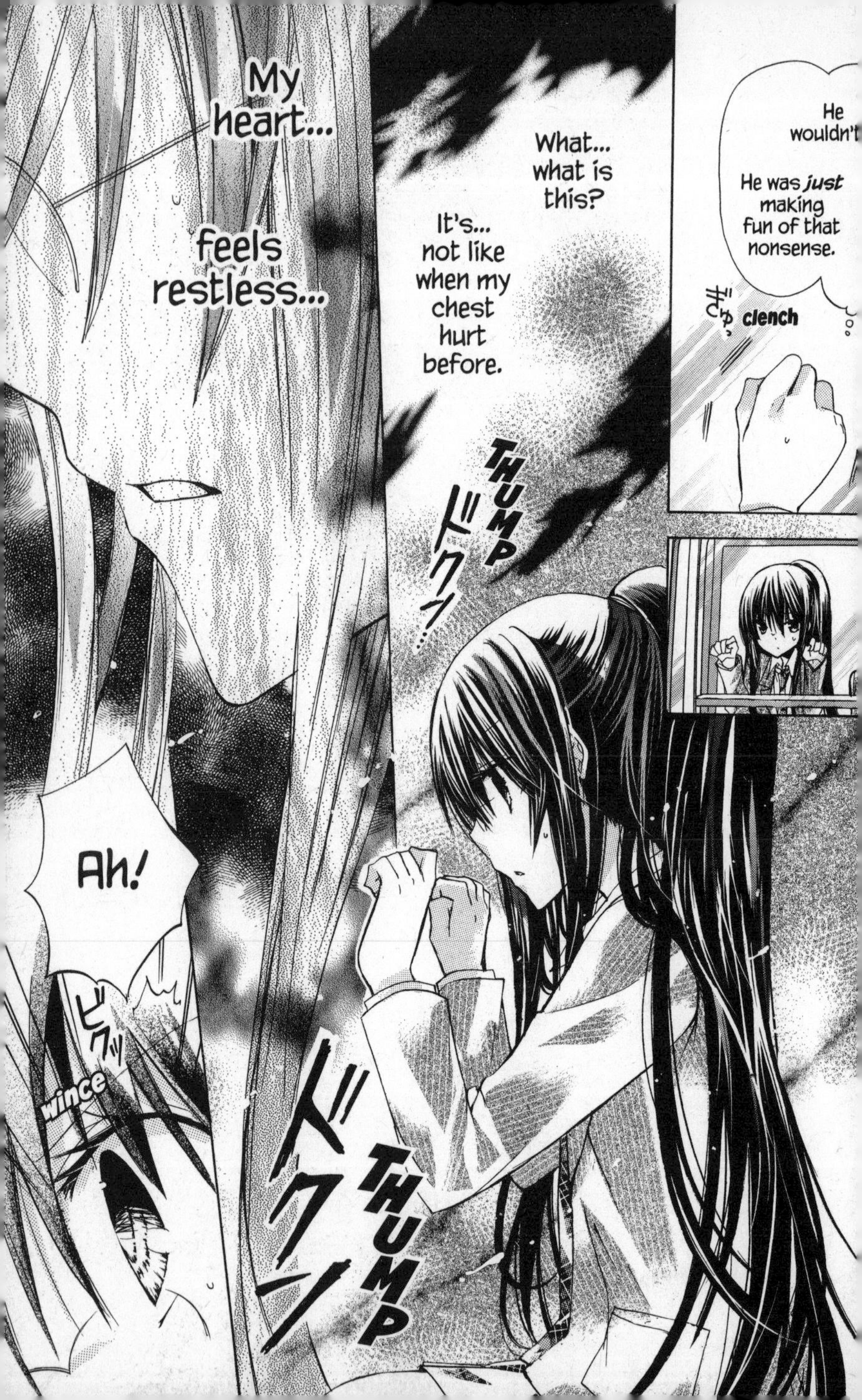
He wouldn't
He was *just* making fun of that nonsense.
ぎゅ clench
What... what is this?
It's... not like when my chest hurt before.
THUMP
My heart... feels restless...
Ah!
ビクッ wince
THUMP

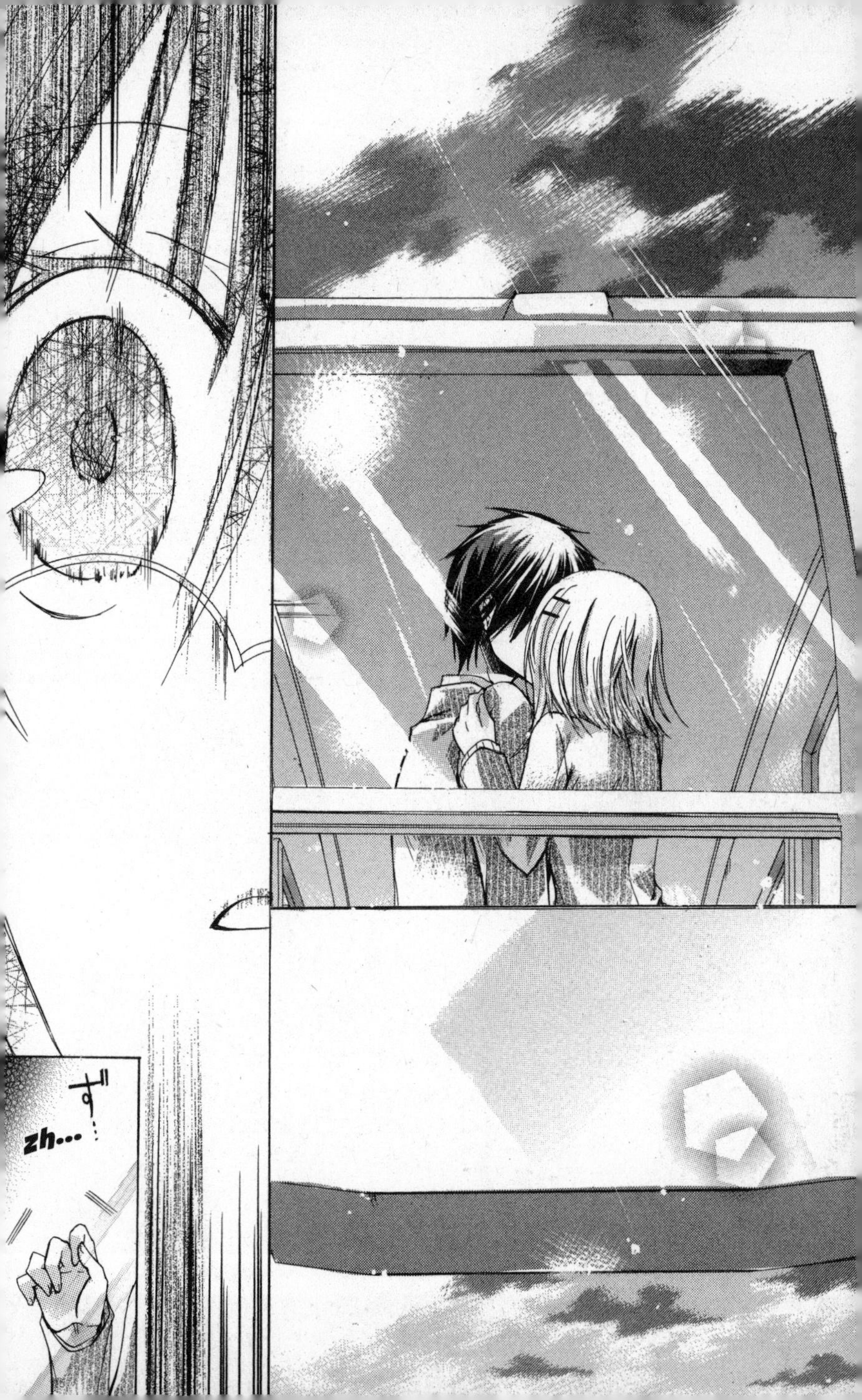
ず…
zh...

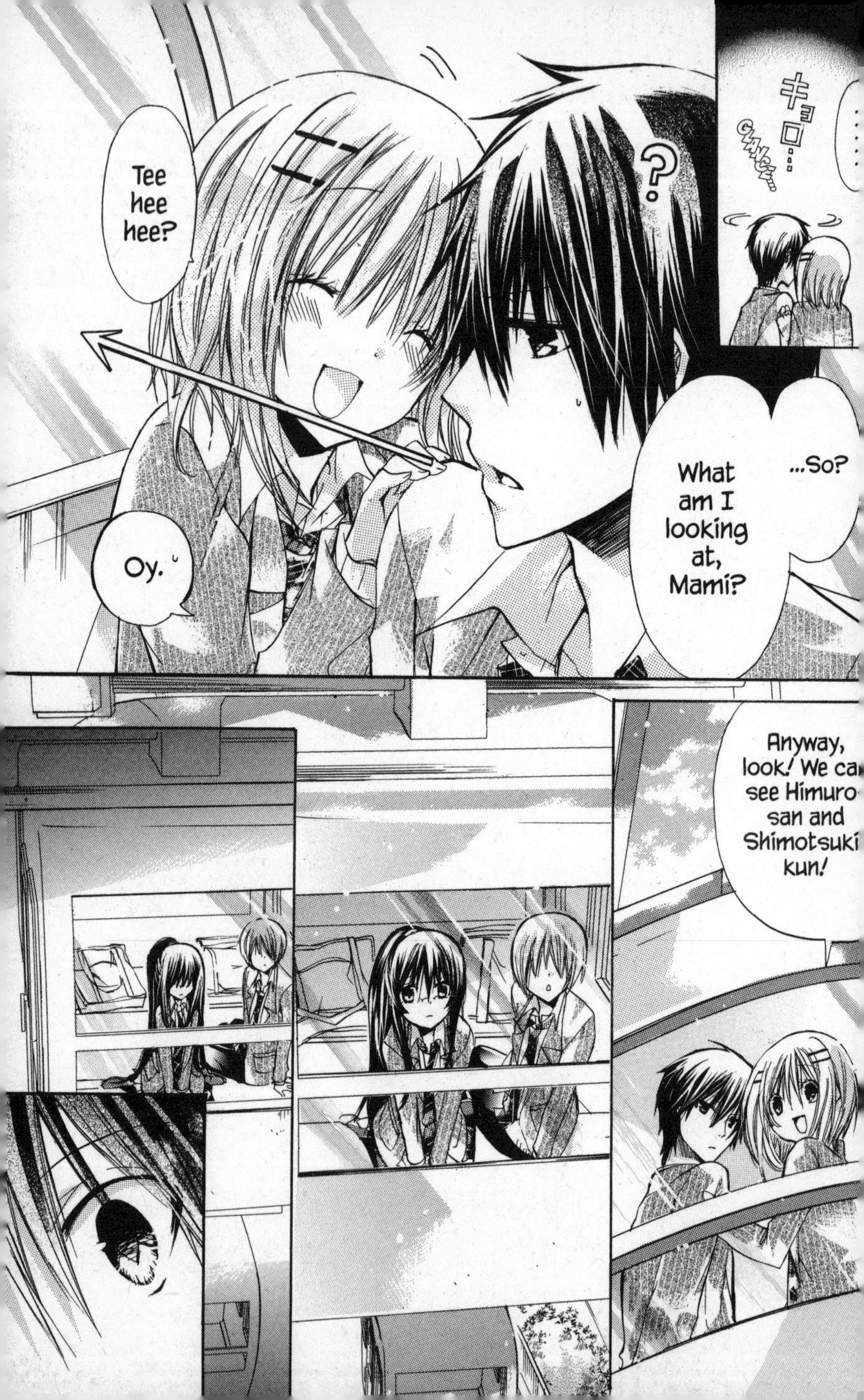
…
キョロ…
GLANCE…
?
…So?
What am I looking at, Mami?
Tee hee hee?
Oy.
Anyway, look! We ca see Himuro san and Shimotsuki kun!

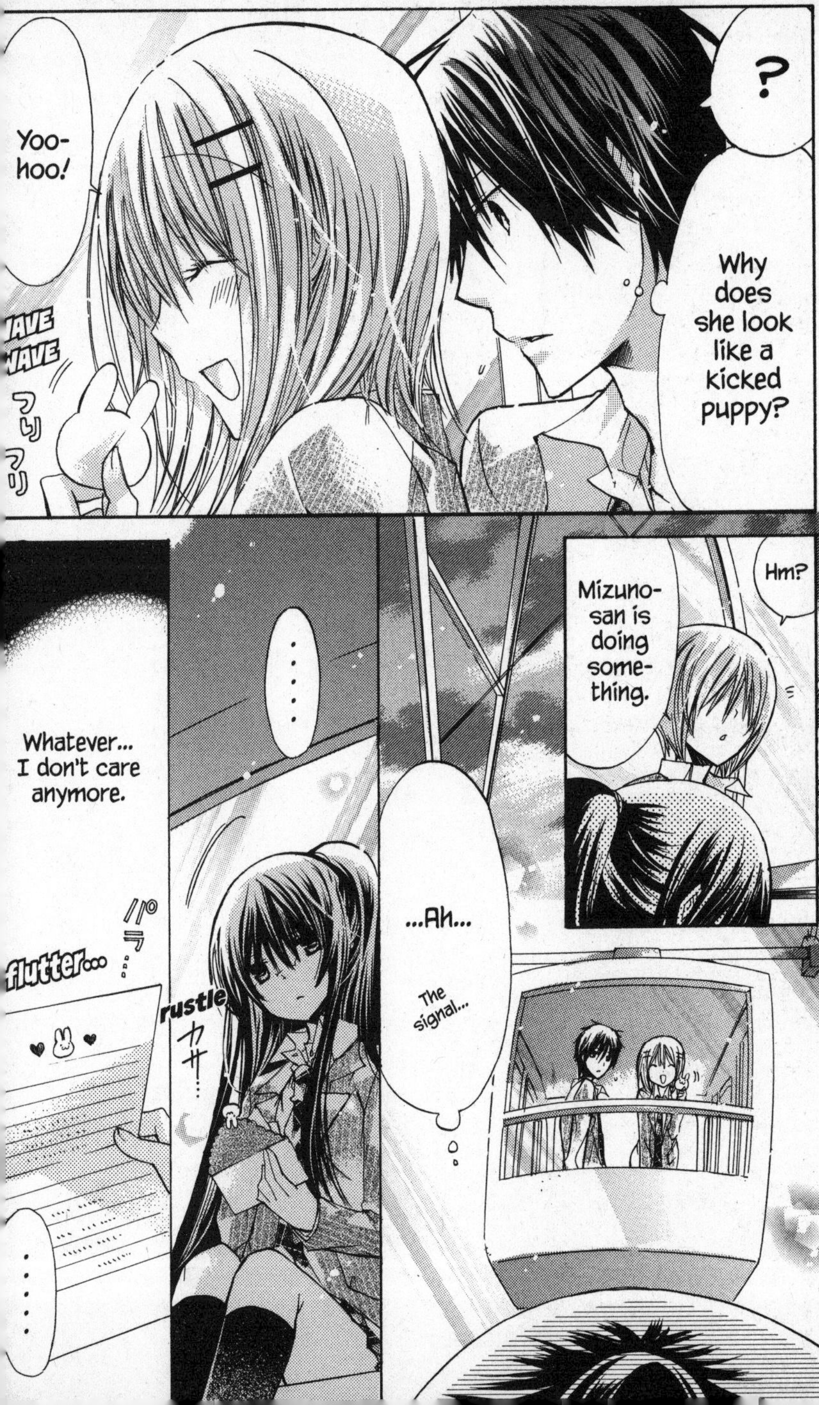
?
Why does she look like a kicked puppy?
Yoo-hoo!
フリフリ
Hm?
Mizuno-san is doing something.
...Ah...
The signal...
......
Whatever... I don't care anymore.
パラ...
flutter...
rustle
カサ...
......

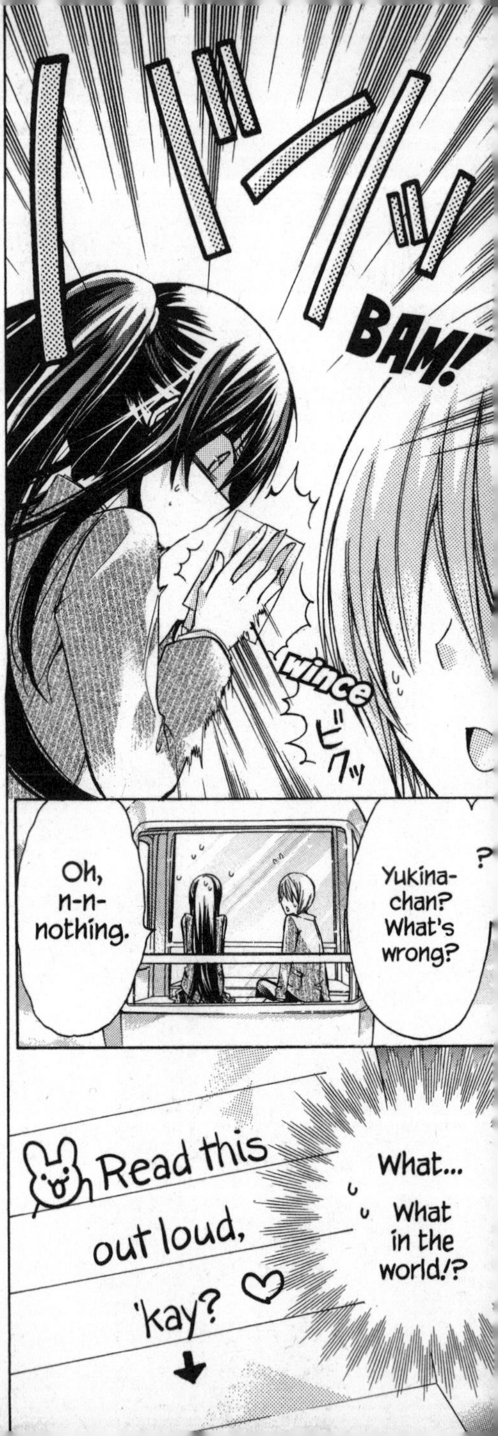
BAM!
wince
ビクッ
Yukina-chan? What's wrong?
?
Oh, n-n-nothing.
What... What in the world!?
Read this out loud, 'kay?

Snow Yukina 2

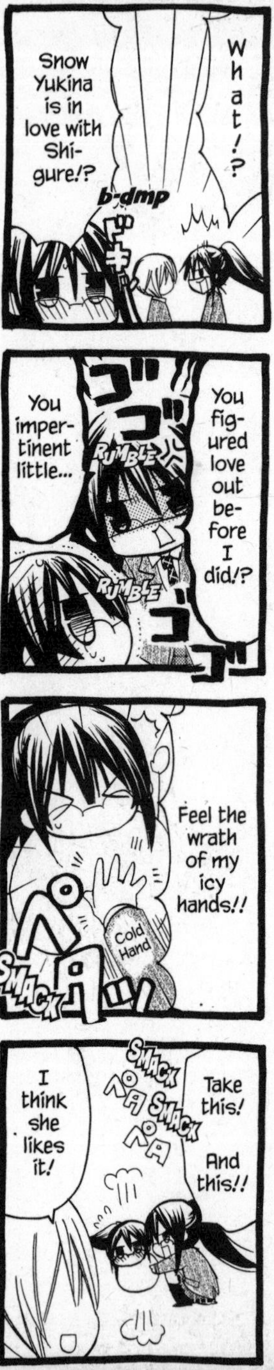
What!?
Snow Yukina is in love with Shigure!?
b-dmp
ドキッ
You figured love out before I did!?
You impertinent little...
RUMBLE
RUMBLE
ゴゴゴ
Feel the wrath of my icy hands!!
Cold Hand
SMACK
ペタッ
Take this!
And this!!
SMACK
ペタ
SMACK
ペタ
I think she likes it!

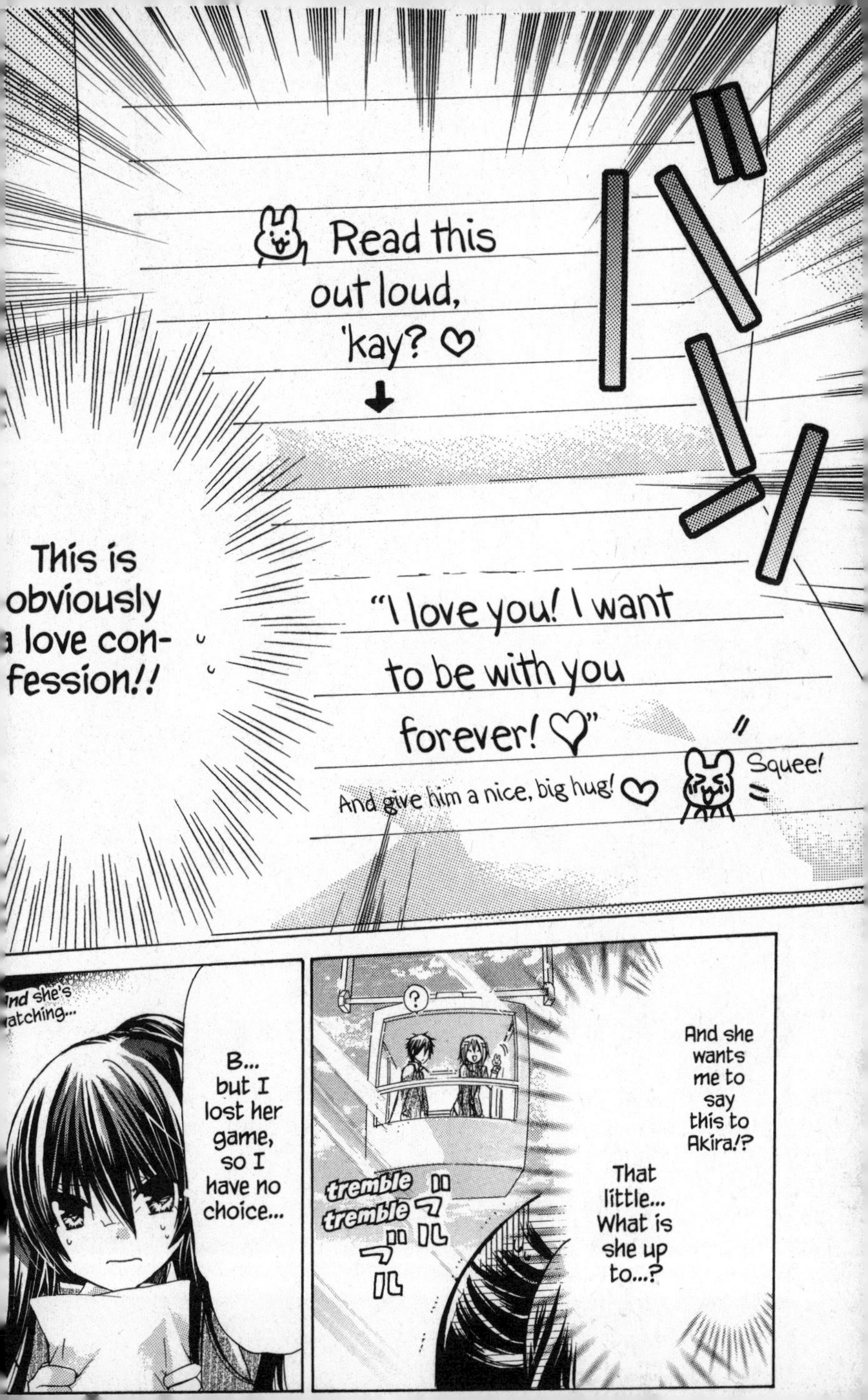
Read this out loud, 'kay? ♡
"I love you! I want to be with you forever! ♡"
And give him a nice, big hug! ♡
Squee!
This is obviously a love confession!!
And she wants me to say this to Akira!?
That little... What is she up to...?
tremble tremble
nd she's atching...
B... but I lost her game, so I have no choice...

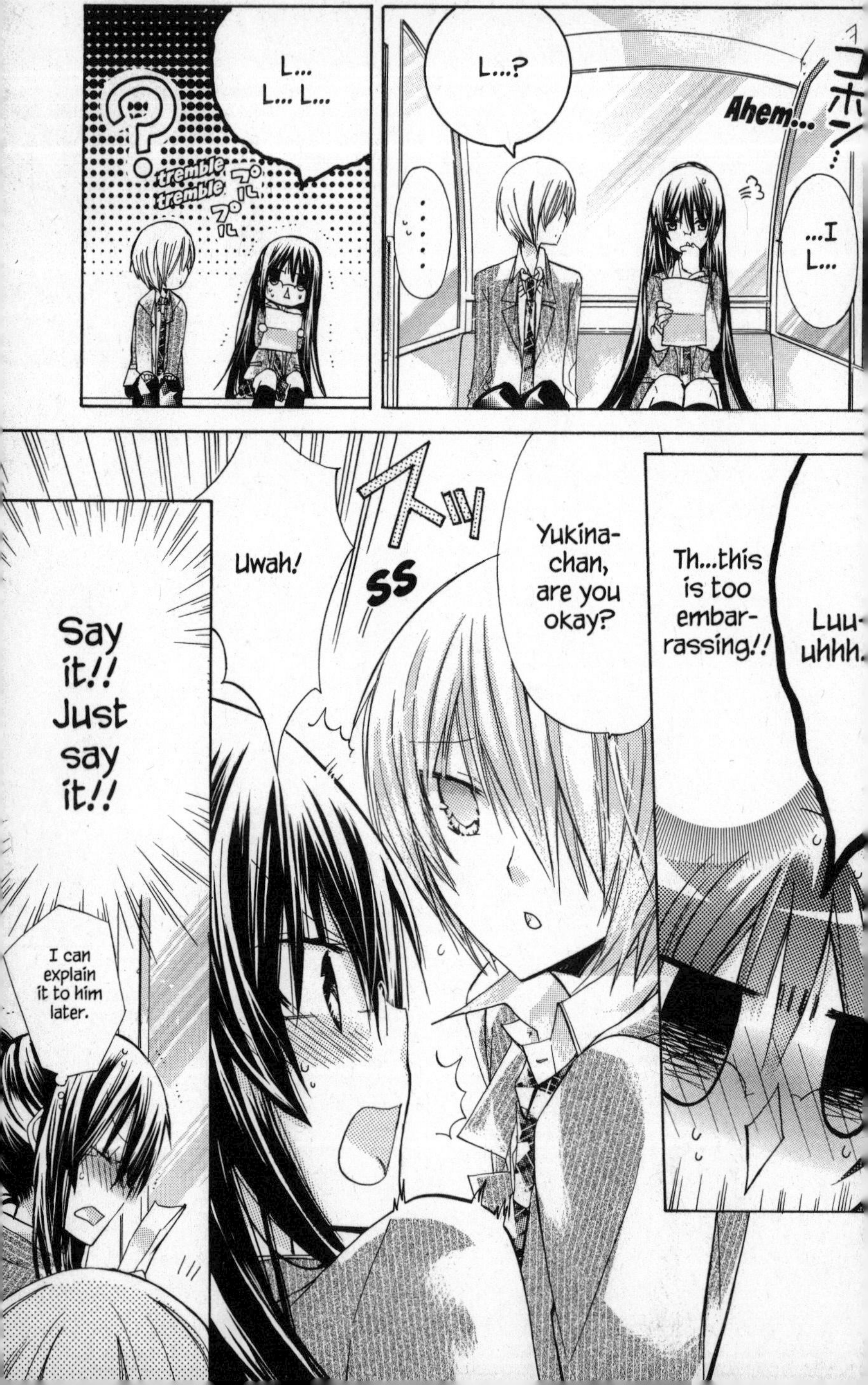
コホン…
Ahem...
...I L...
L...?
......
L... L... L...
tremble tremble
プルプル
Luu-uhhh.
Th...this is too embar-rassing!!
Yukina-chan, are you okay?
スッ
SS
Uwah!
Say it!! Just say it!!
I can explain it to him later.

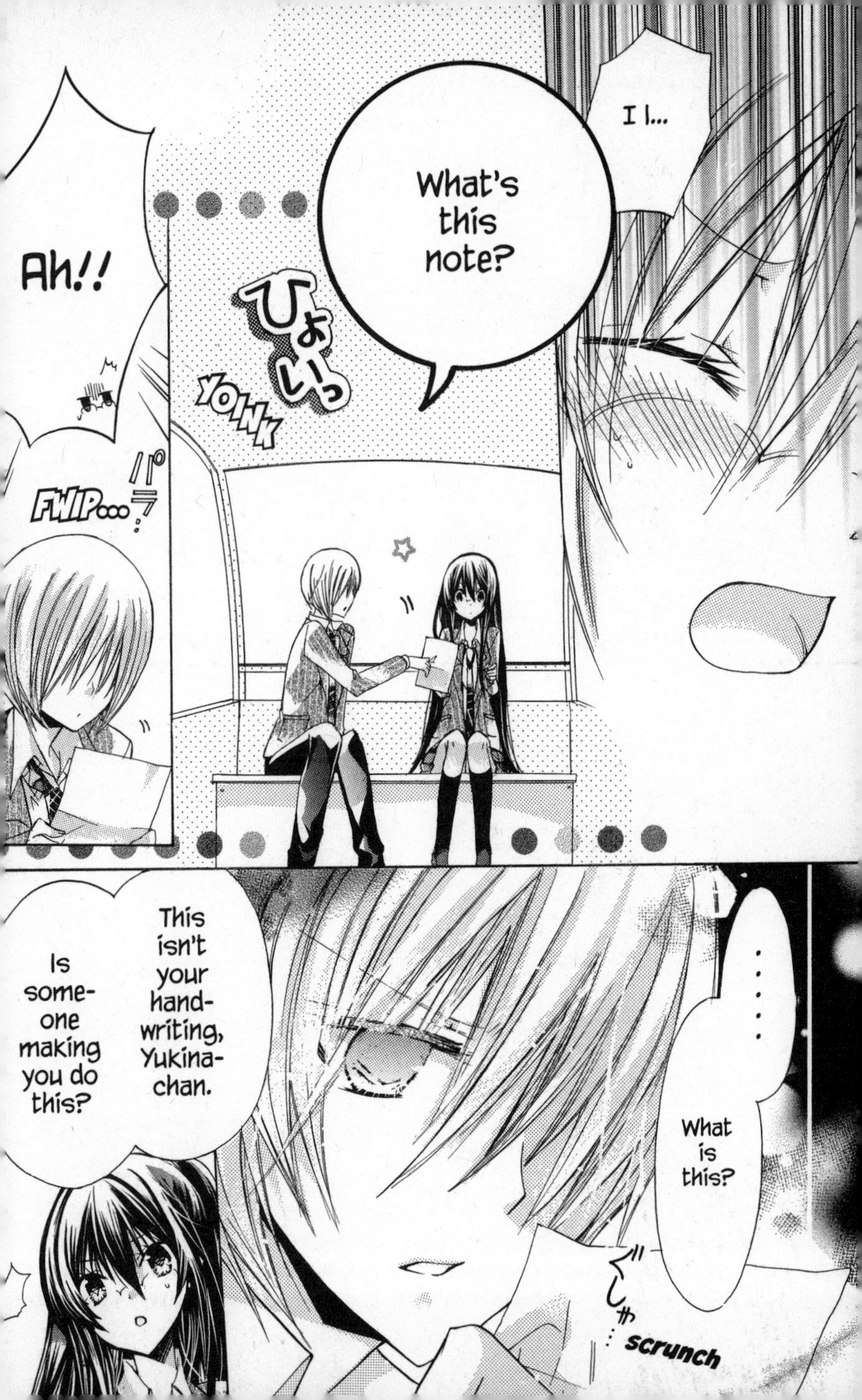
I I...
What's this note?
ひょいっ
YOINK
Ah!!
パラ
FWIP...
......
What is this?
ぐしゃ
scrunch
This isn't your handwriting, Yukina-chan.
Is someone making you do this?

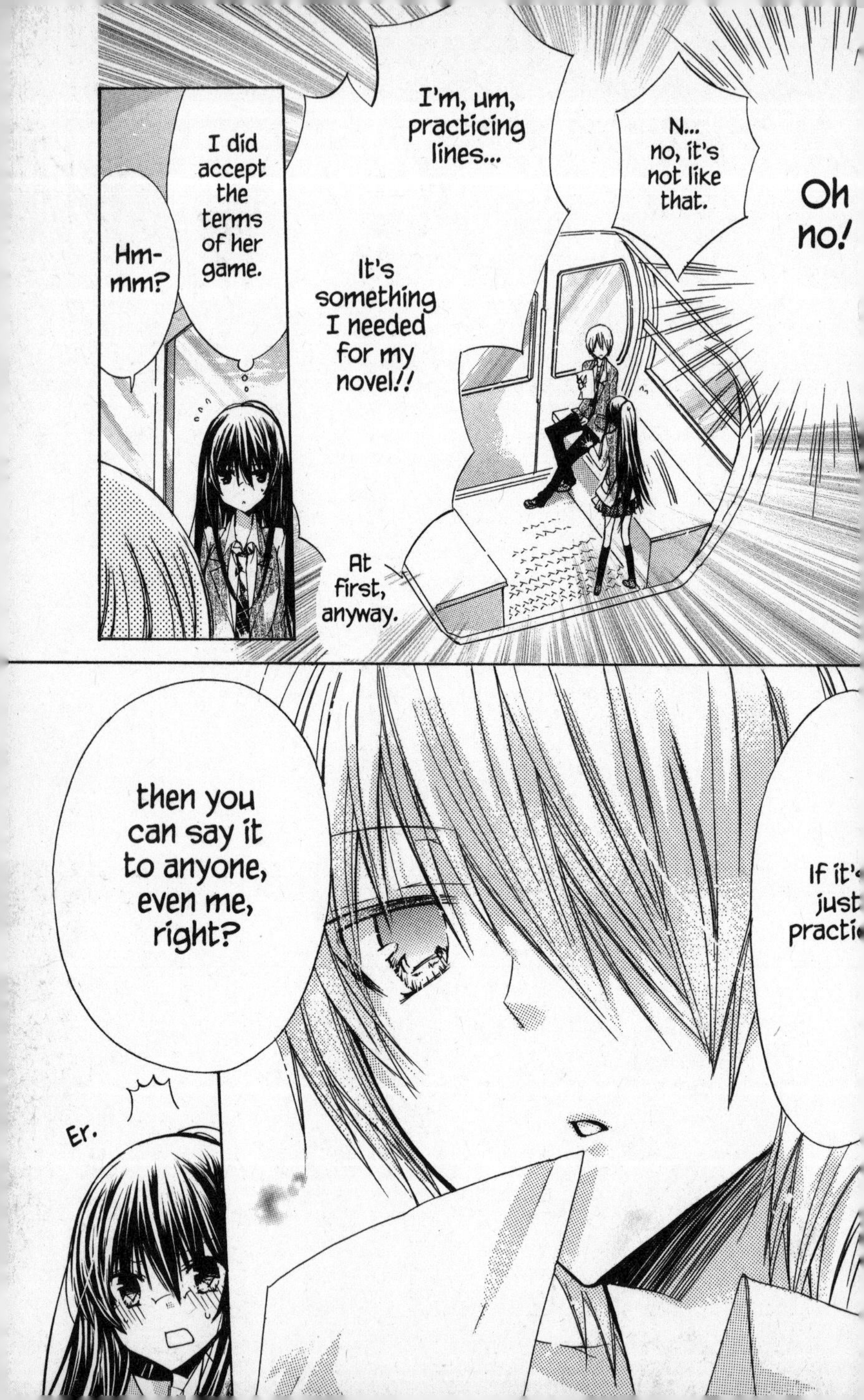

Oh no!
N... no, it's not like that.
I'm, um, practicing lines...
It's something I needed for my novel!!
At first, anyway.
I did accept the terms of her game.
Hm-mm?
If it' just practi
then you can say it to anyone, even me, right?
Er.

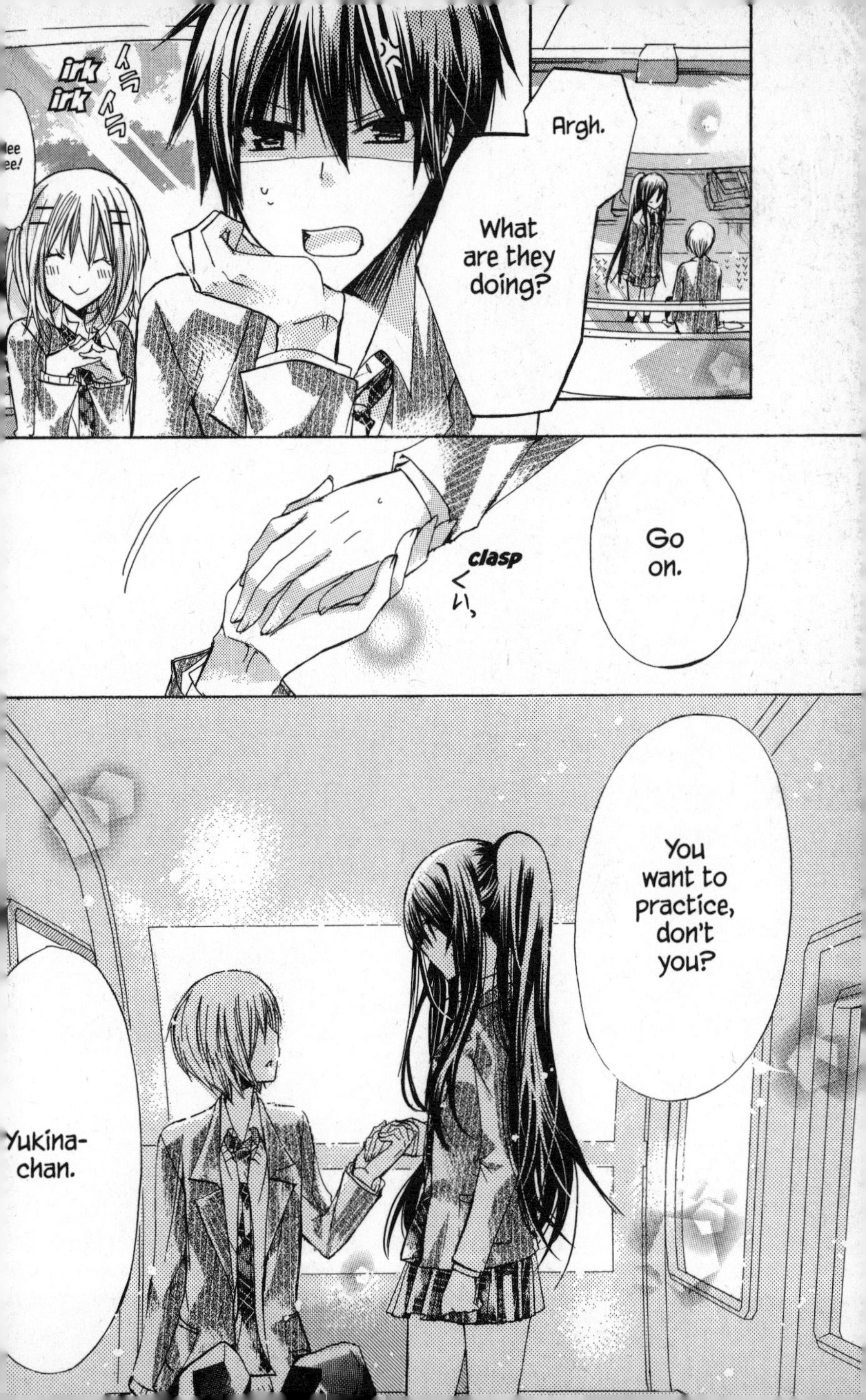
Argh.
What are they doing?
irk irk
イラ イラ
Go on.
clasp
くい
You want to practice, don't you?
Yukina-chan.

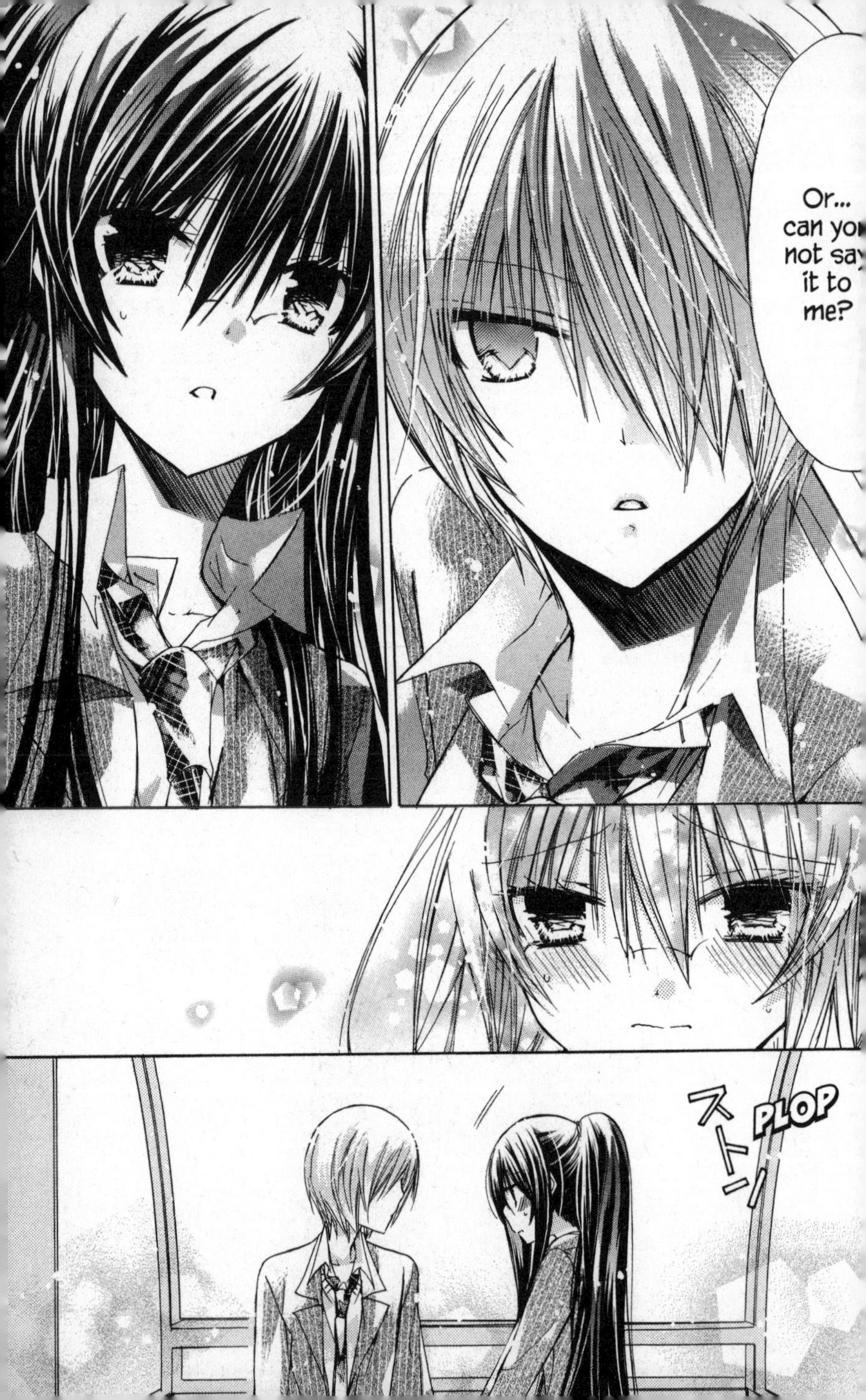
Or... can you not say it to me?
ストーン
PLOP

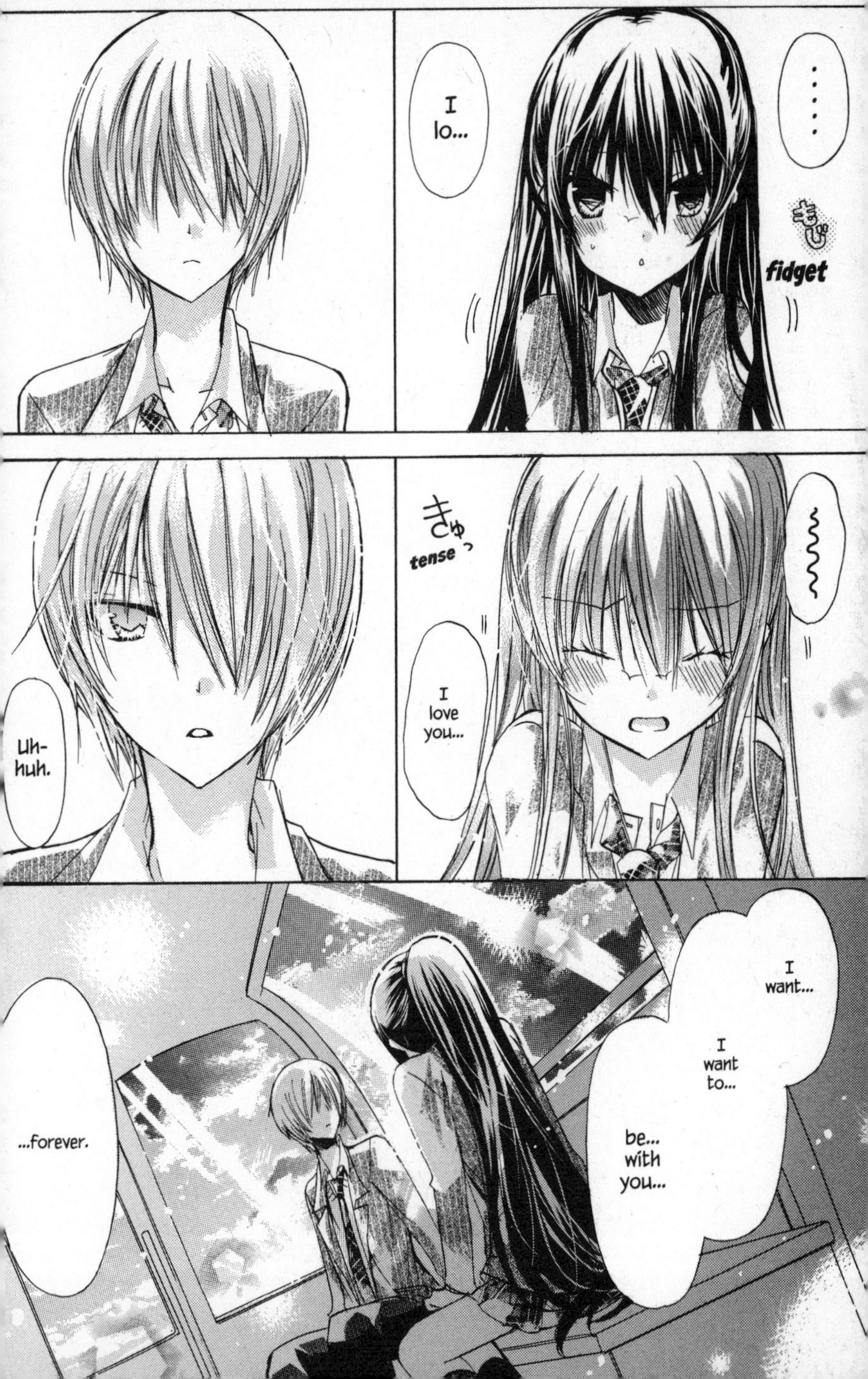
.....
fidget
I lo...
きゅっ
tense
I love you...
Uh-huh.
I want...
I want to...
be... with you...
...forever.

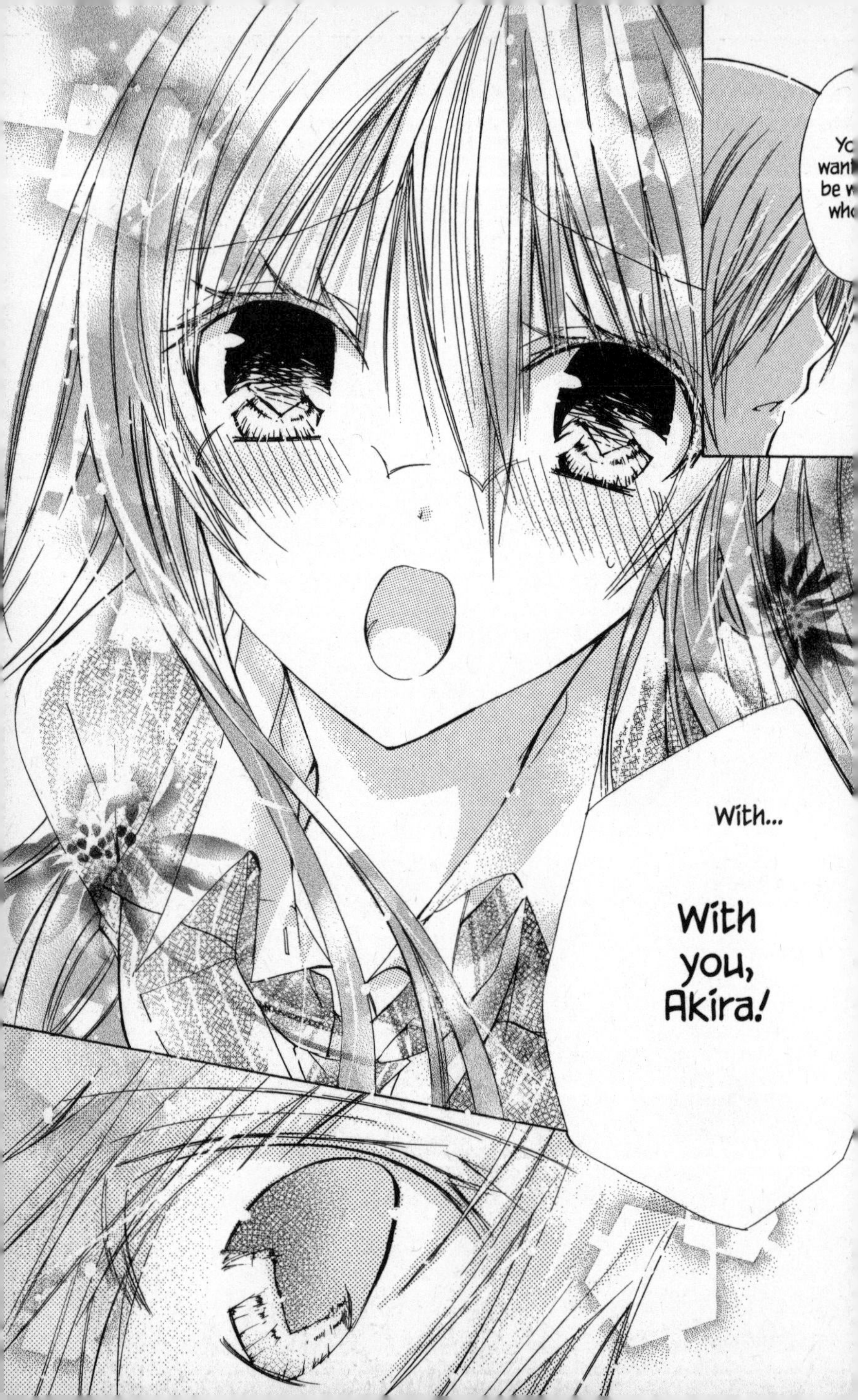
With...
With you, Akira!

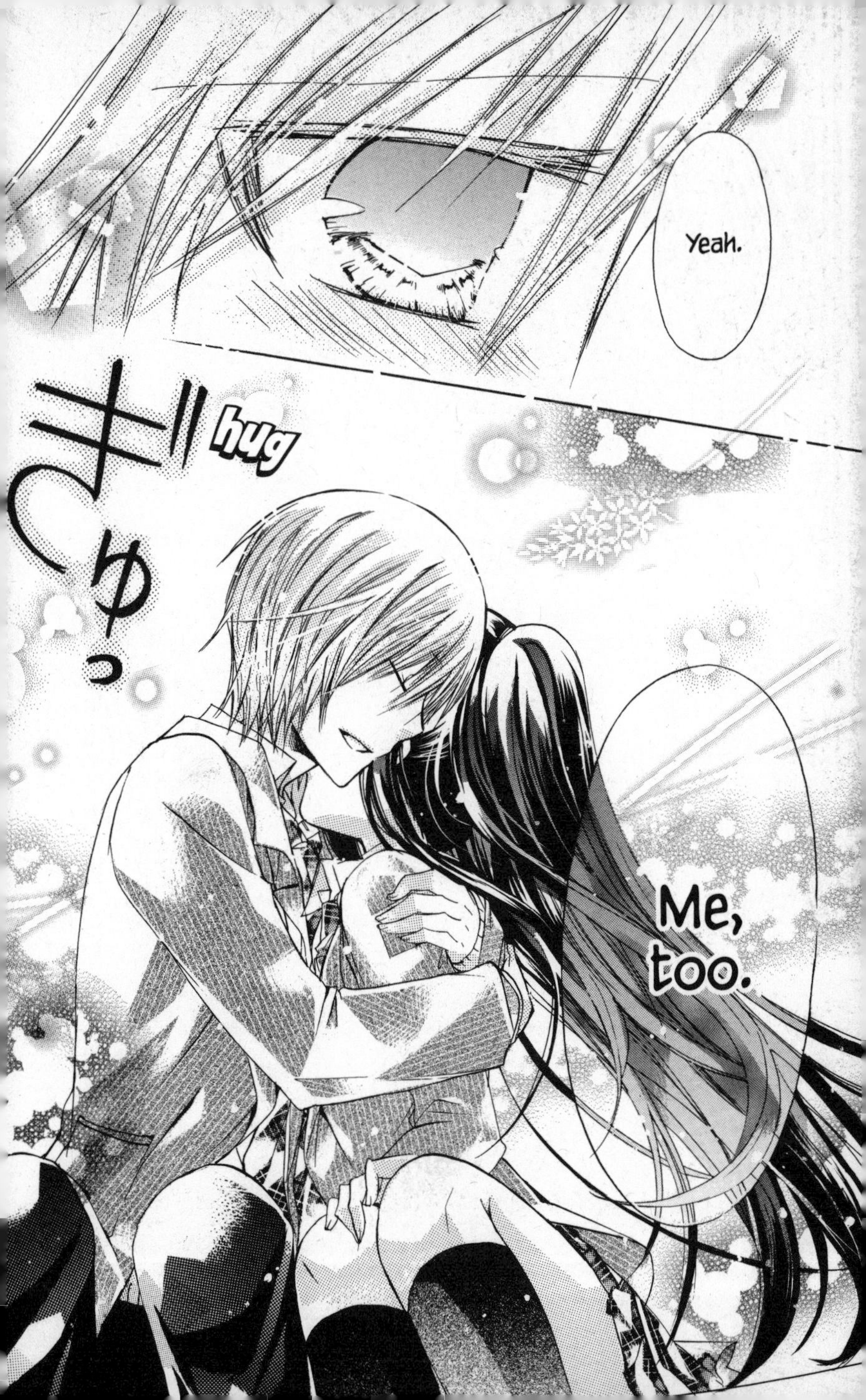
Yeah.
きゅっ
hug
Me, too.

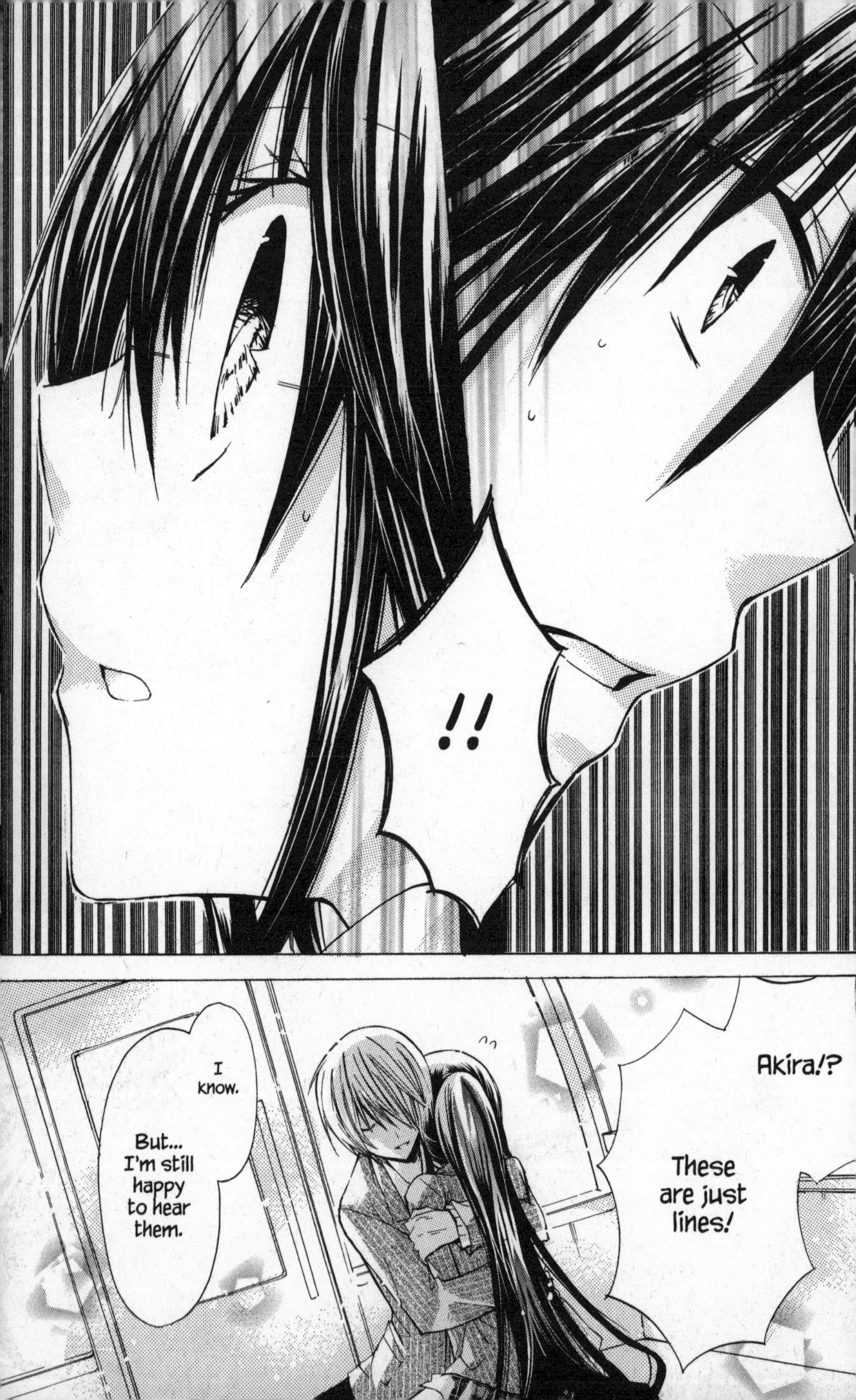
!!
Akira!?
These are just lines!
I know.
But... I'm still happy to hear them.

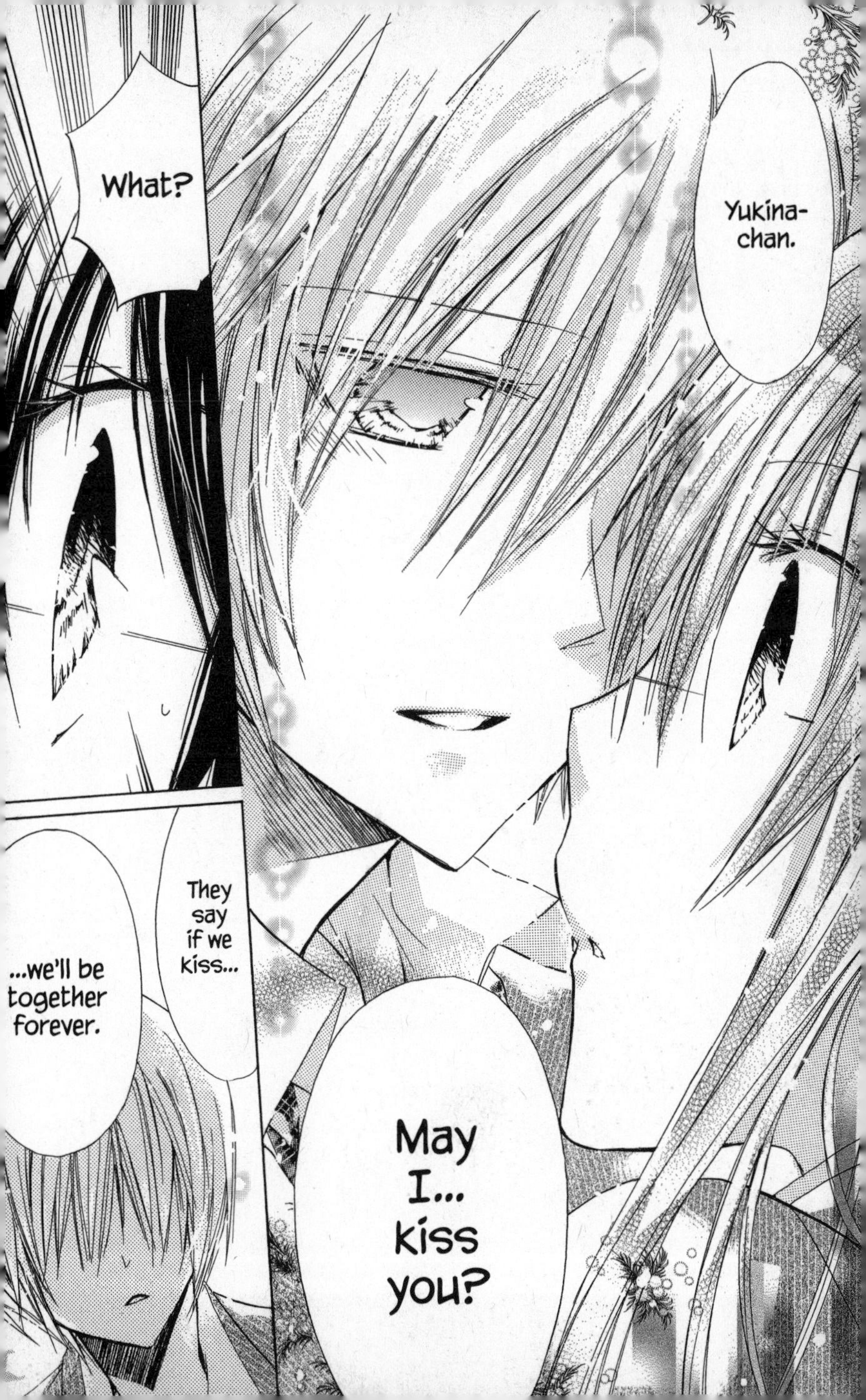
Yukina-chan.
What?
They say if we kiss...
...we'll be together forever.
May I... kiss you?

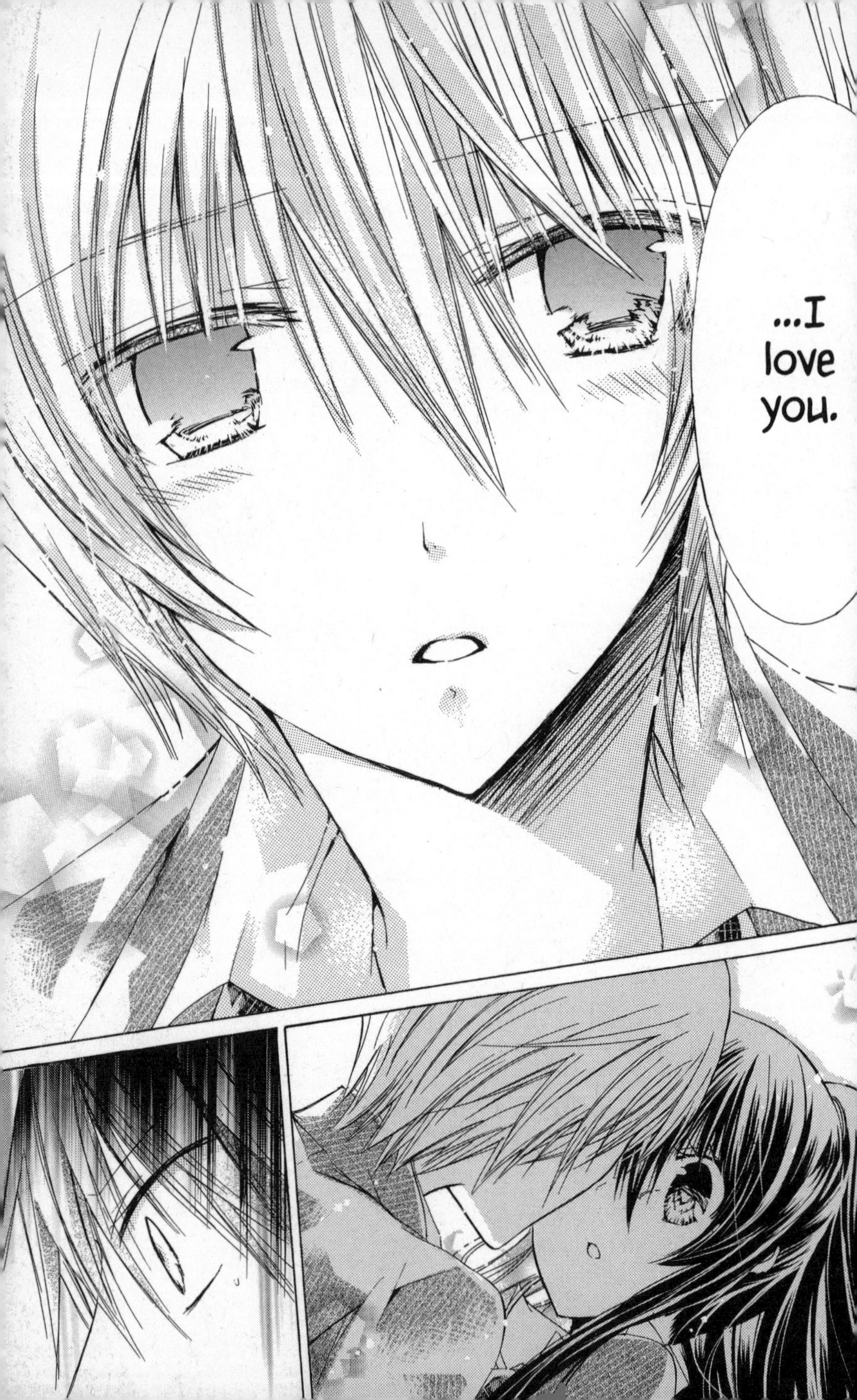
...I love you.

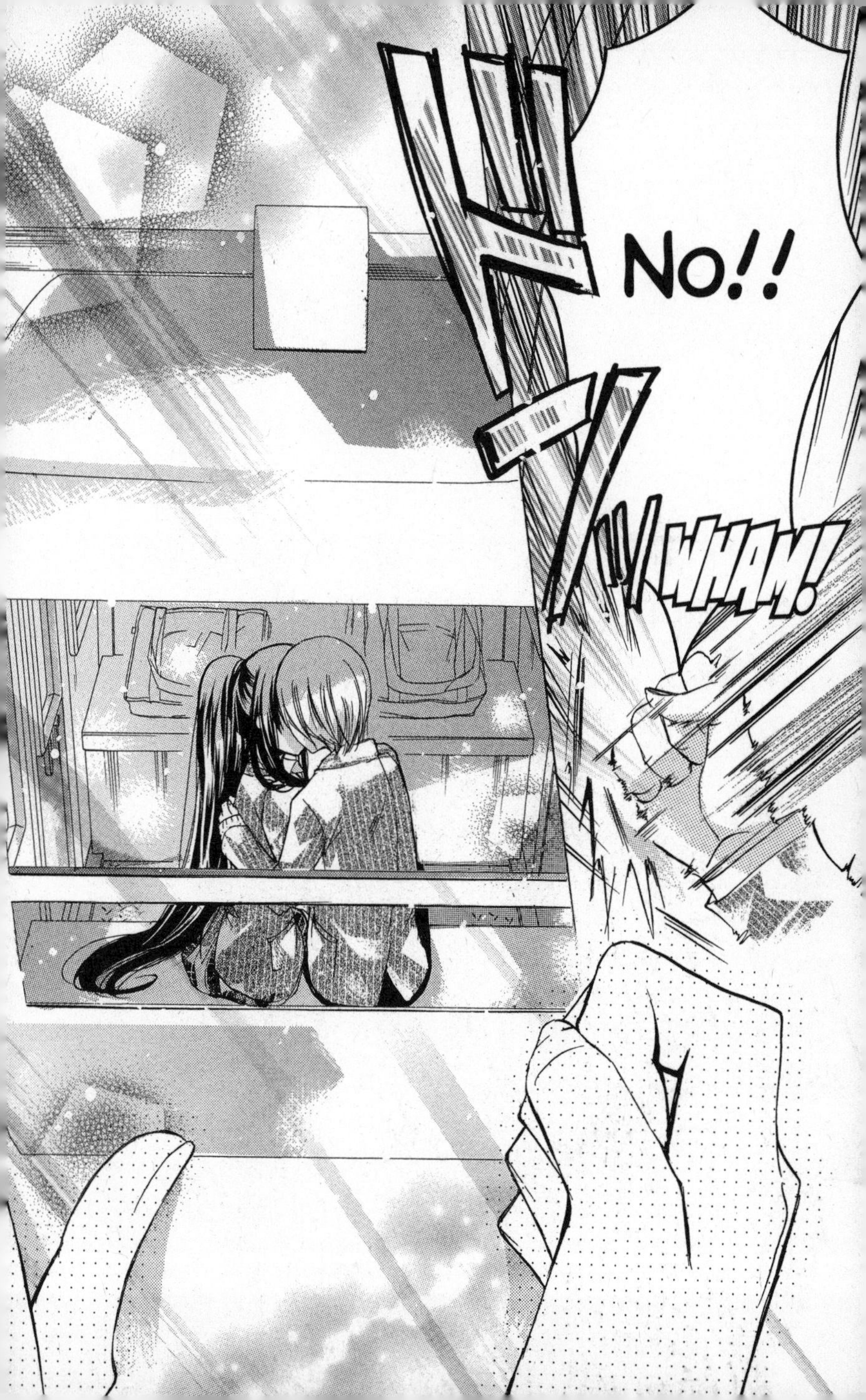
No!!
WHAM!

Missions of Love

It is time for love.
Secret cell phone
novelist vs. the most
popular boy in school.
A mission of love for
absolute servitude.

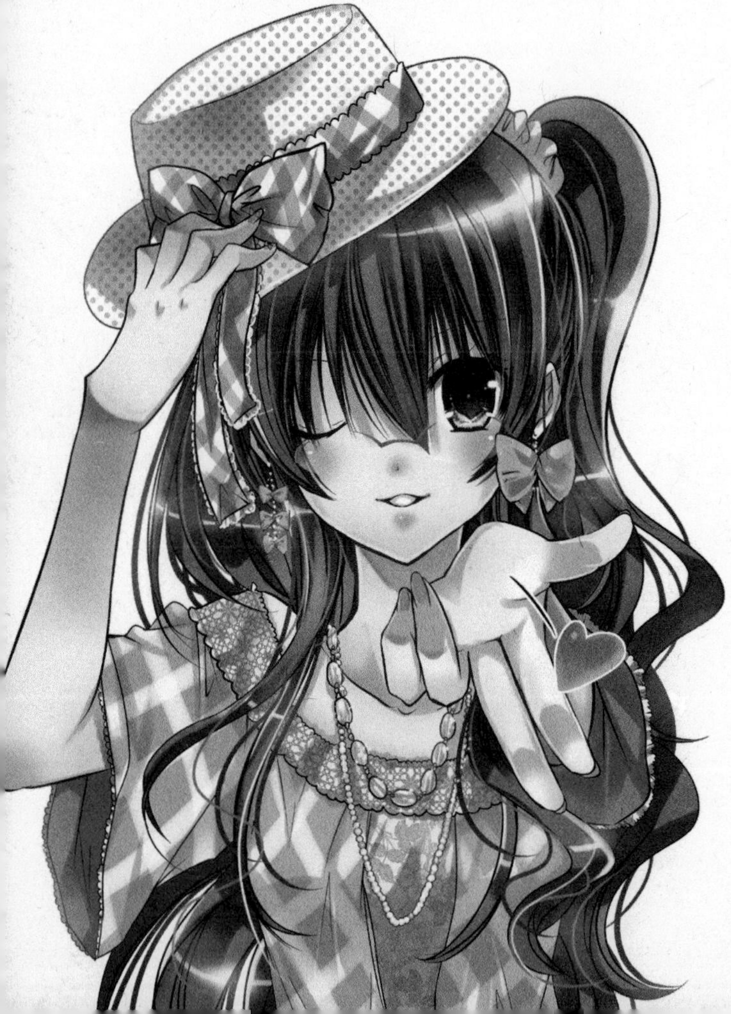

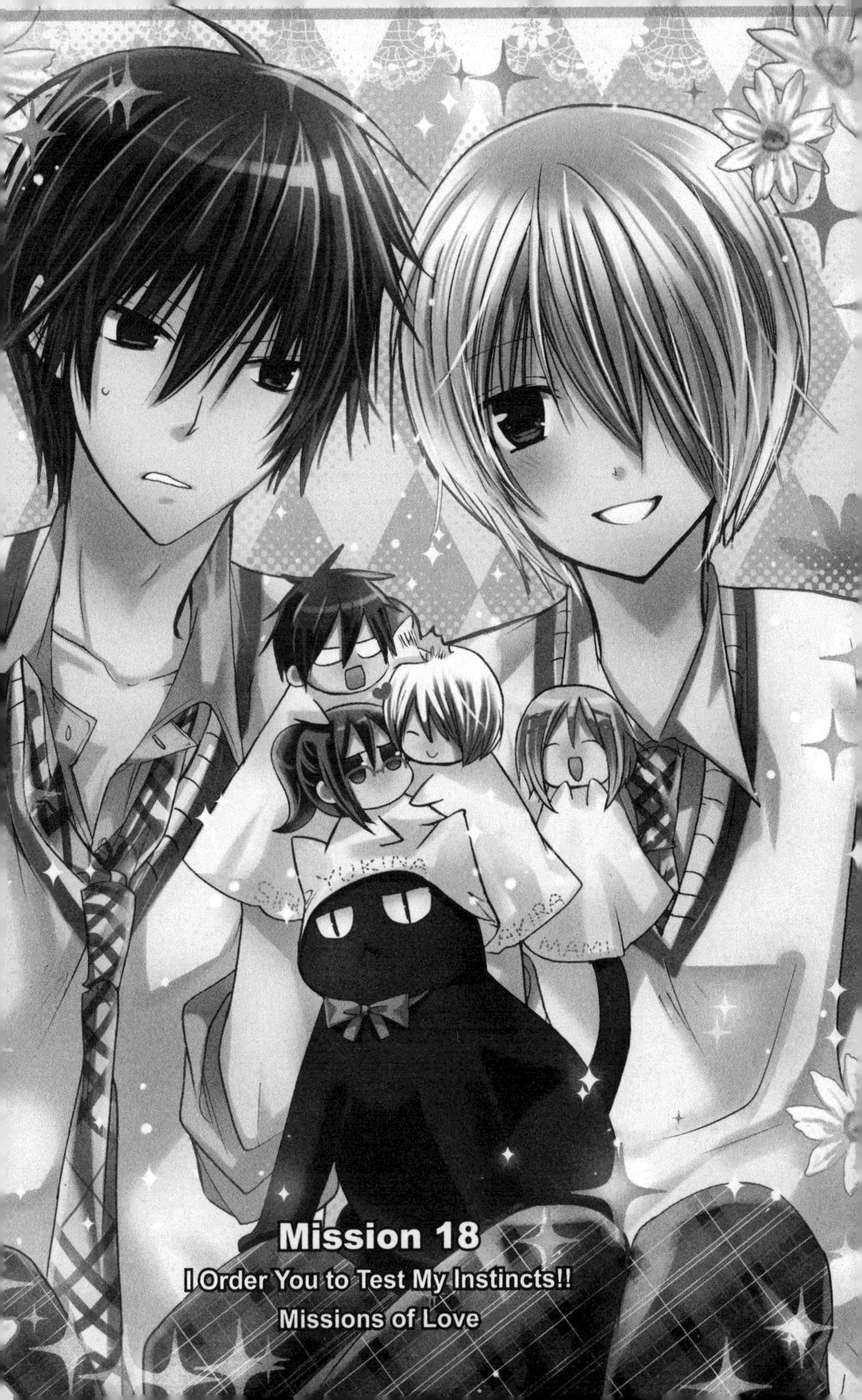
Mission 18
I Order You to Test My Instincts!!
Missions of Love

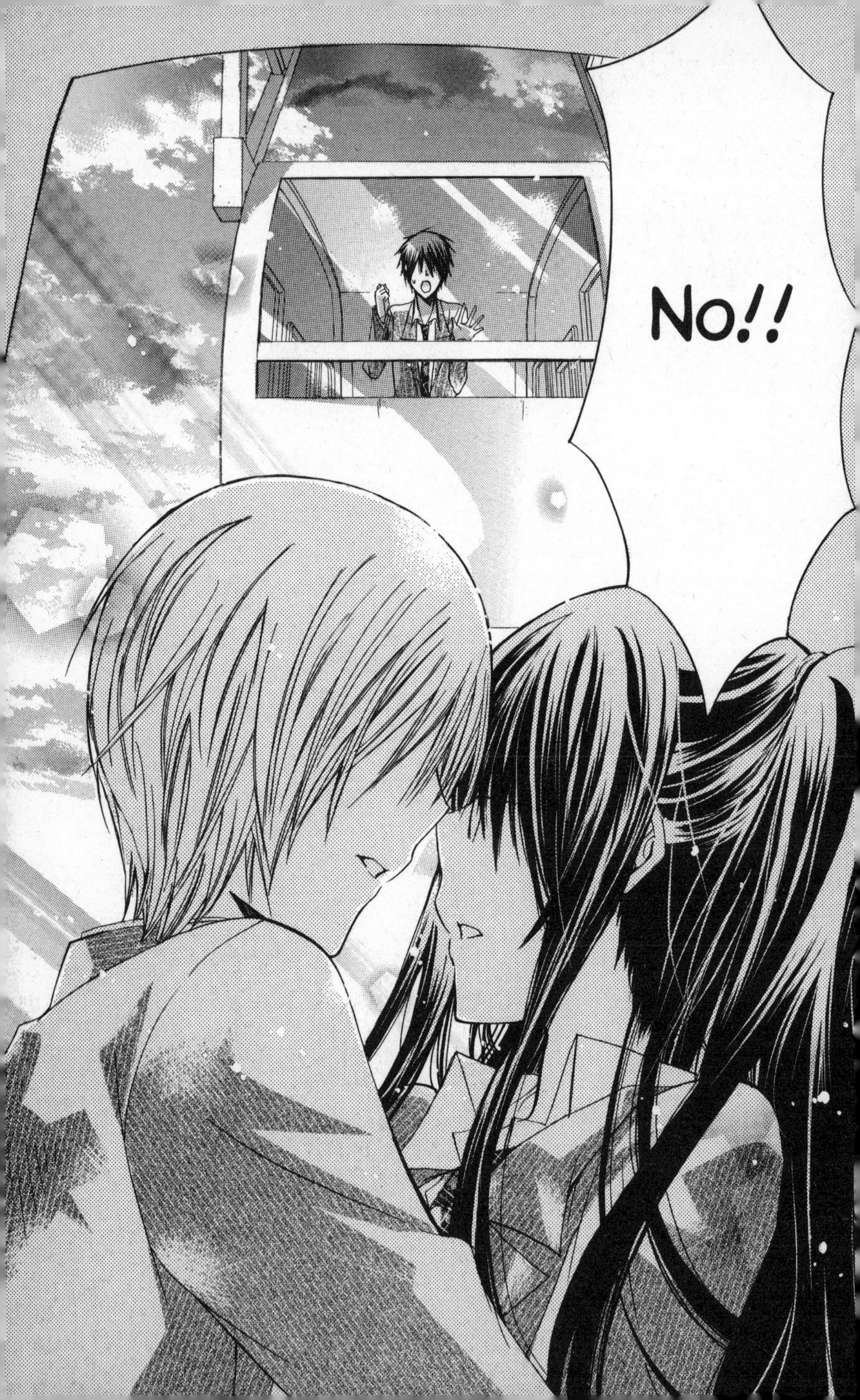
No!!

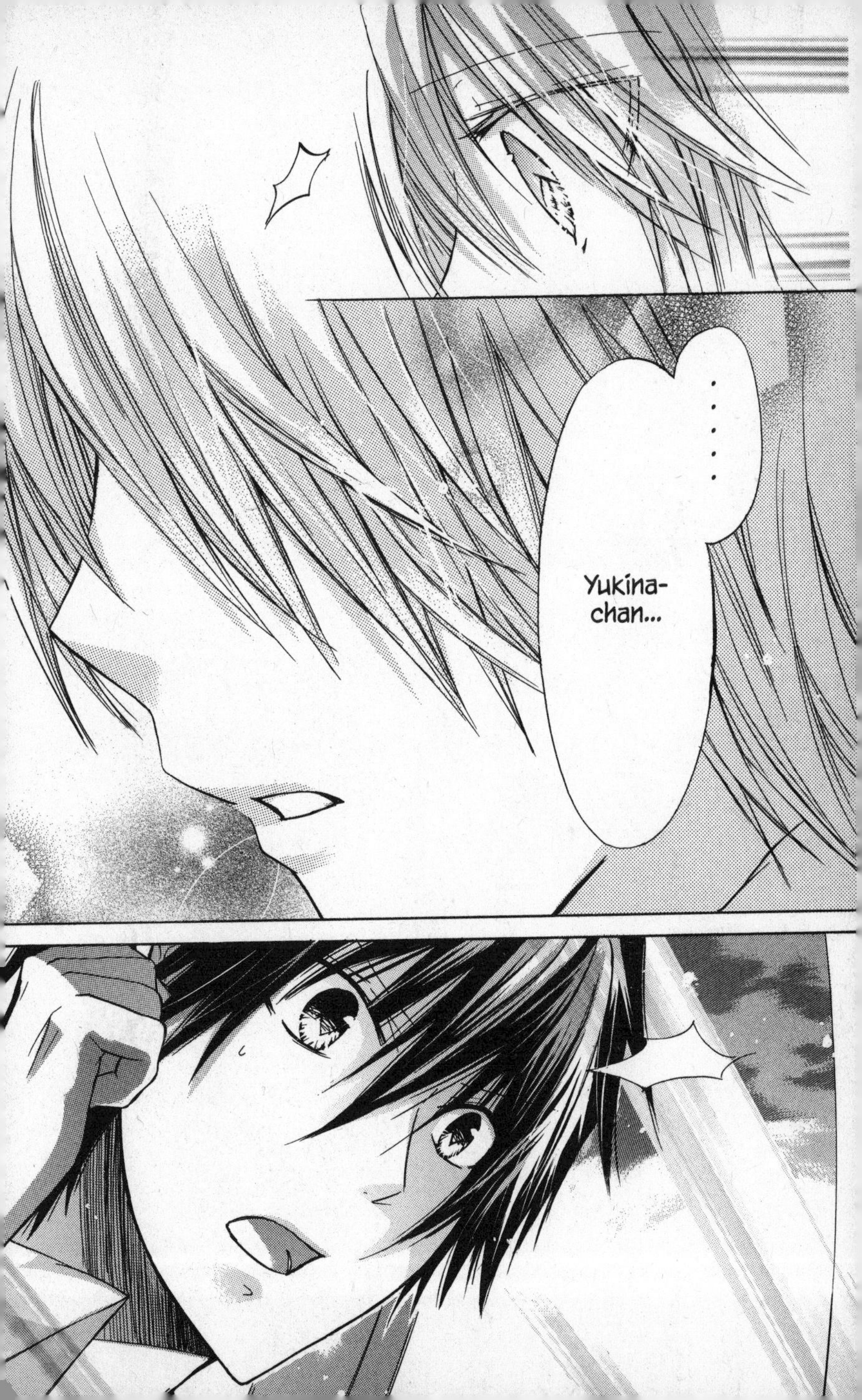
.....
Yukina-chan...

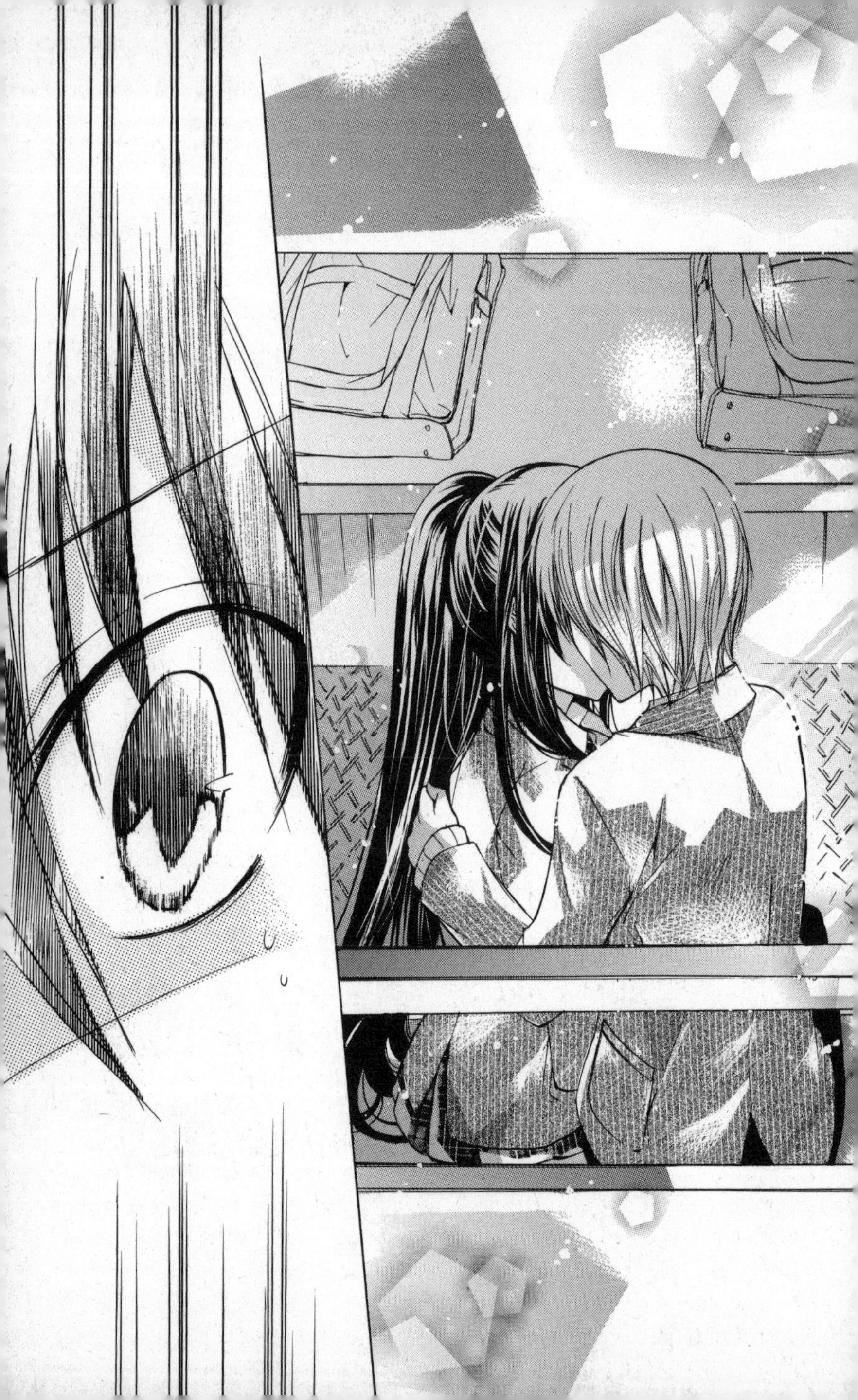

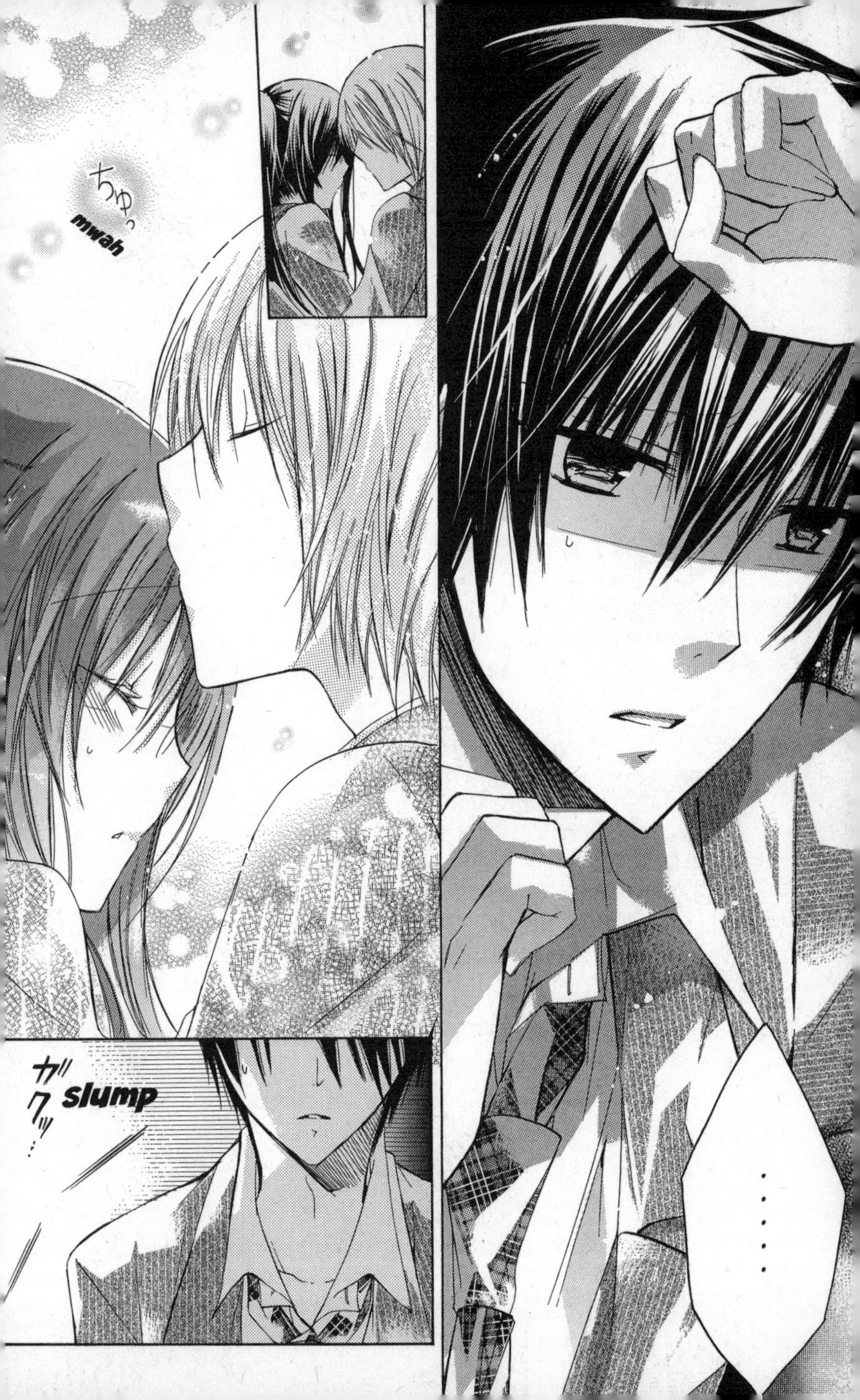
……
ちゅっ
mwah
ガクッ…
slump

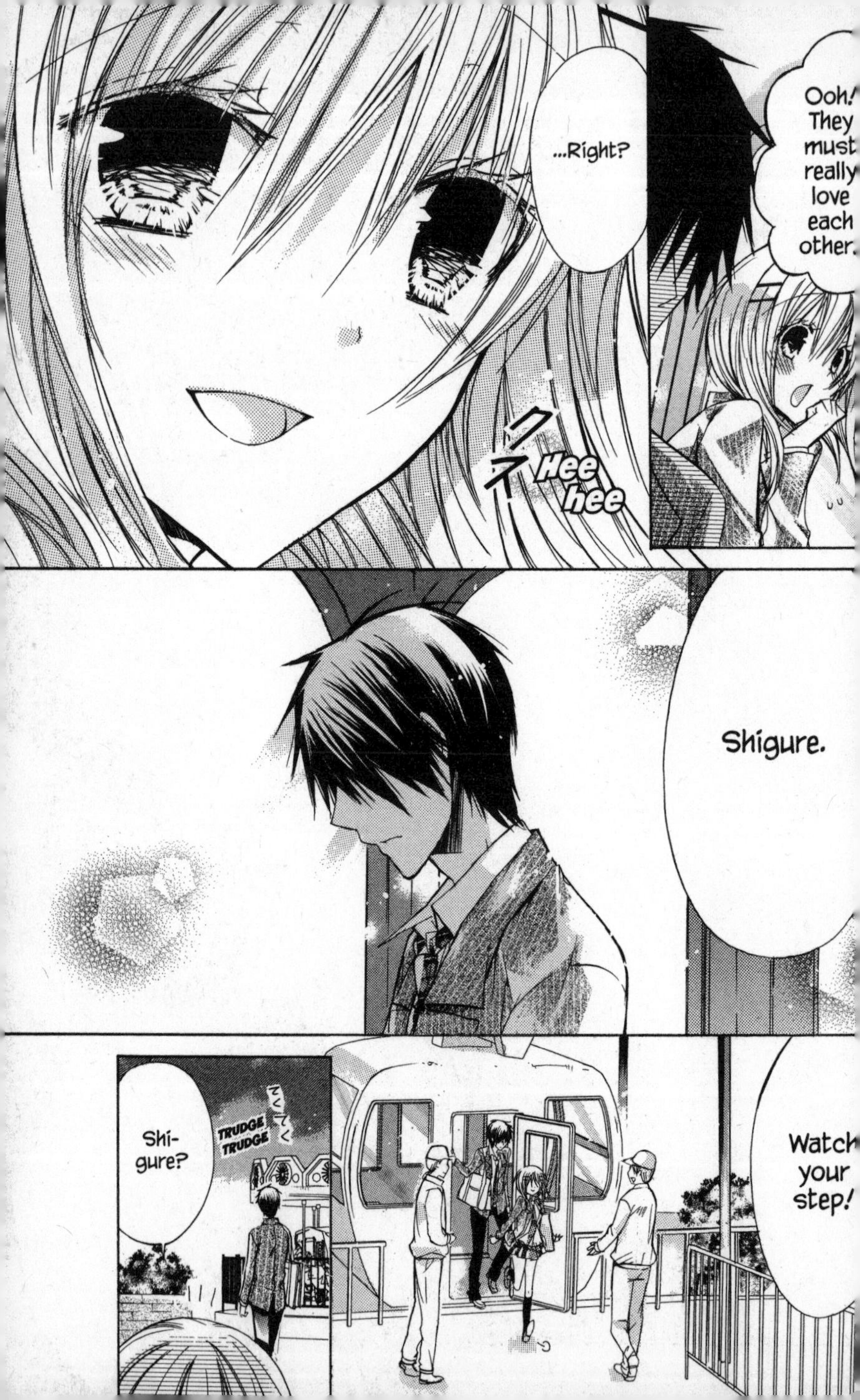
Ooh! They must really love each other.
...Right?
Hee hee
Shigure.
Watch your step!
Shi-gure?
TRUDGE TRUDGE

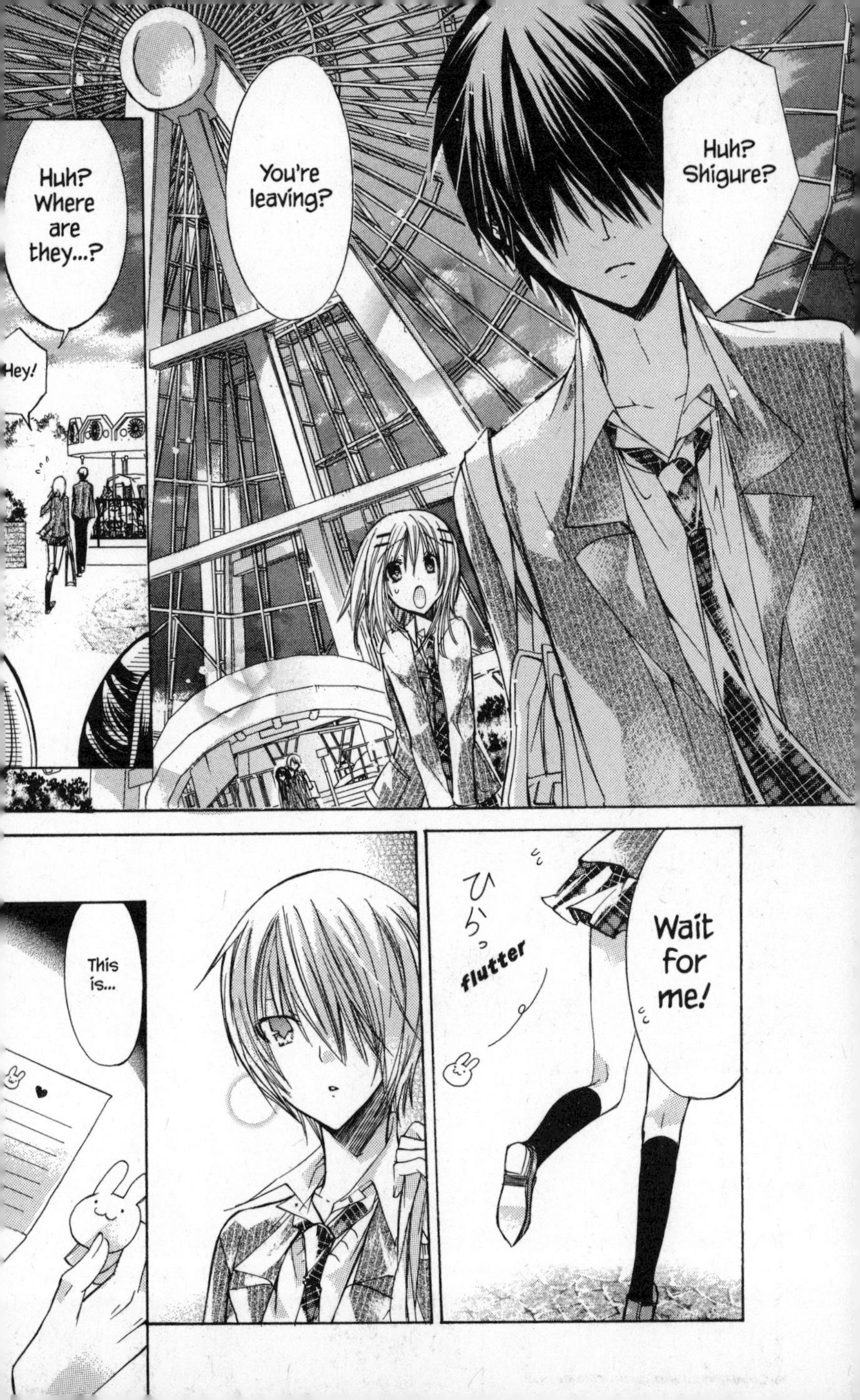
Huh? Shigure?
You're leaving?
Huh? Where are they...?
Hey!
Wait for me!
ひらっ
flutter
This is...

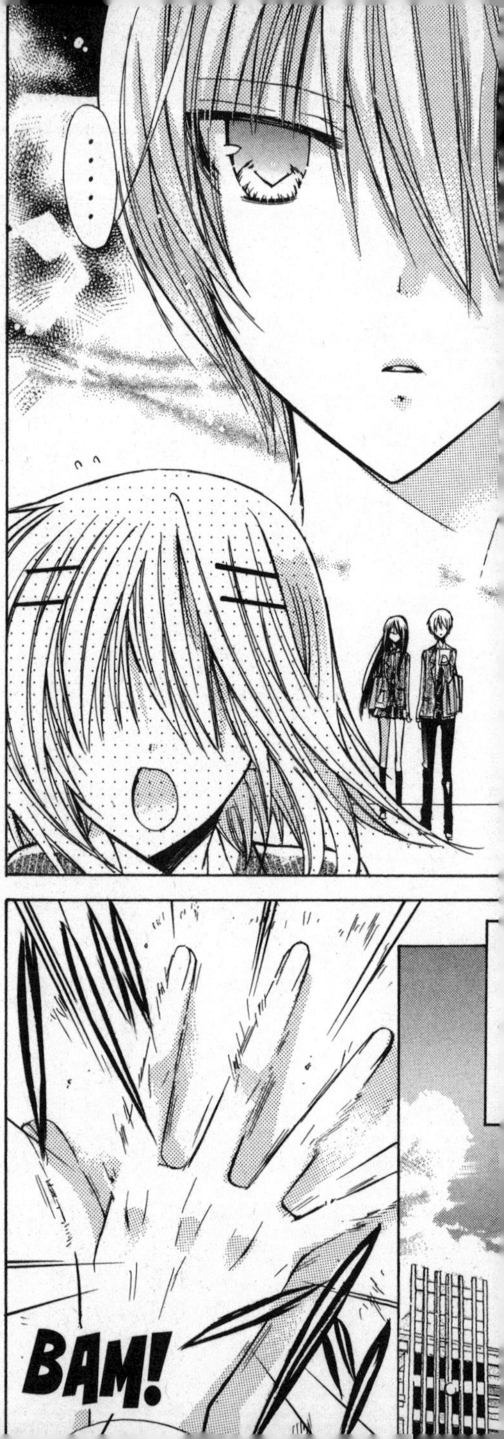
.....
BAM!

Snow Yukina 3

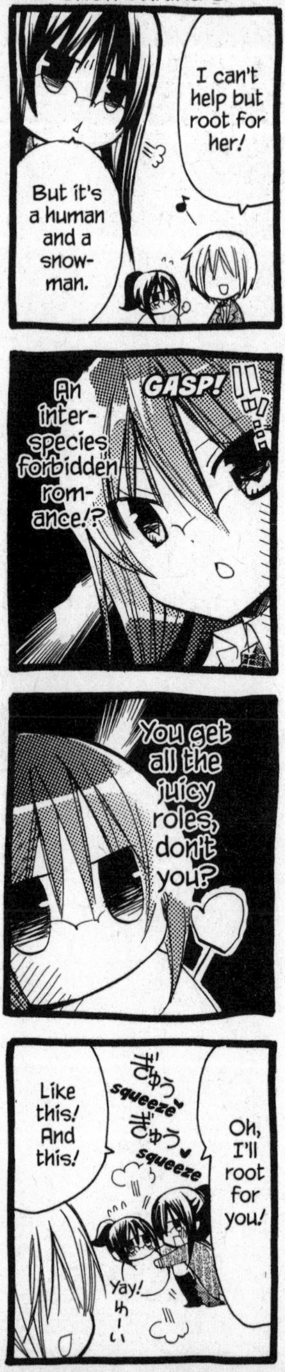
I can't help but root for her!
But it's a human and a snow-man.
GASP!
An inter-species forbidden rom-ance!?
You get all the juicy roles, don't you?
Oh, I'll root for you!
ぎゅう squeeze
ぎゅう squeeze
Like this! And this!
Yay!

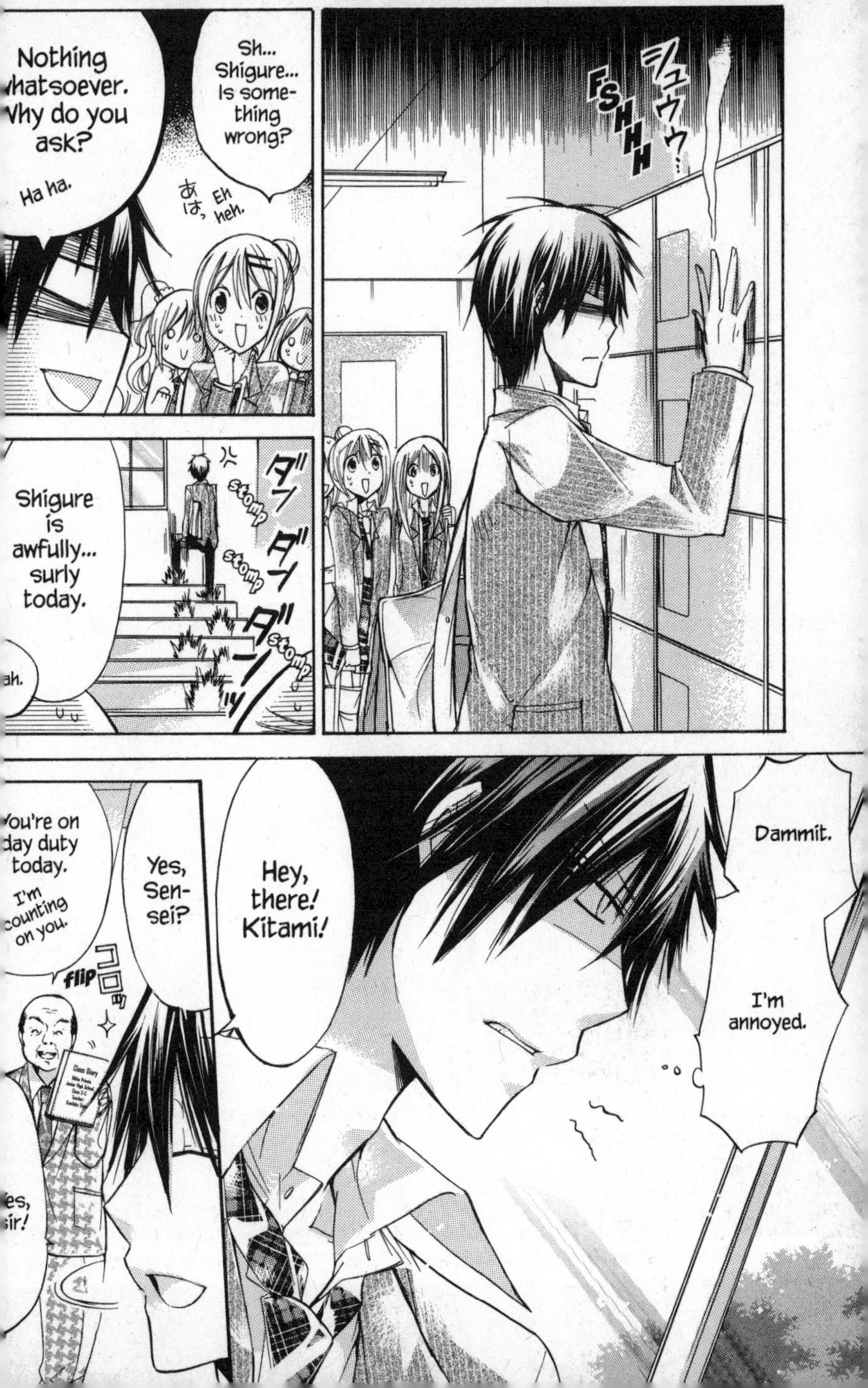
FSHHH
Sh... Shigure... Is some-thing wrong?
Eh heh.
Nothing whatsoever. Why do you ask?
Ha ha.
stomp
stomp
stomp
Shigure is awfully... surly today.
ah.
Dammit.
I'm annoyed.
Hey, there! Kitami!
Yes, Sen-sei?
You're on day duty today.
I'm counting on you.
flip
es, sir!

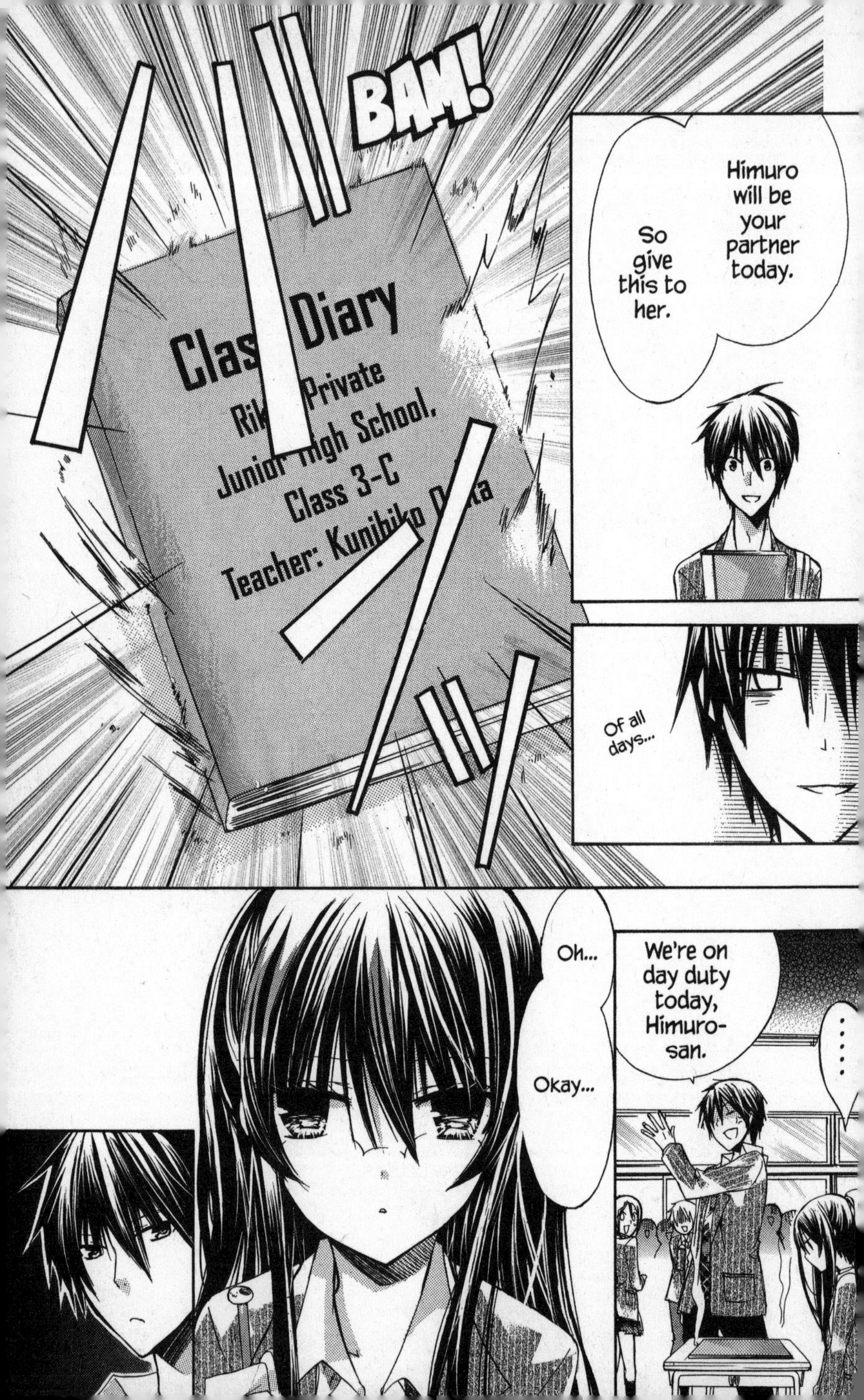
Himuro will be your partner today.
So give this to her.
Of all days...
BAM!
Clas Diary
Rik Private
Junior gh School,
Class 3-C
Teacher: Kunihi
......
We're on day duty today, Himuro-san.
Oh...
Okay...

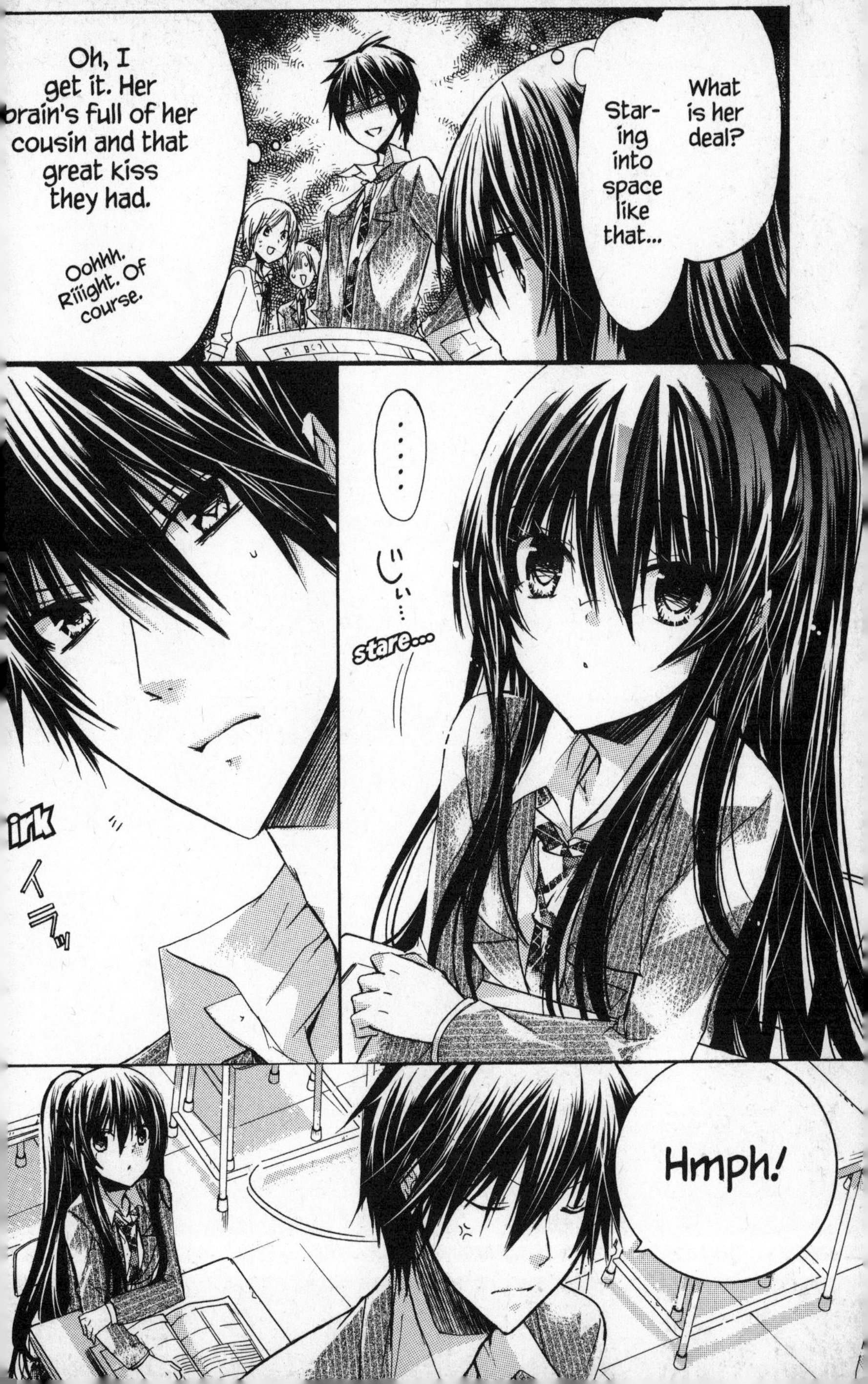
What is her deal?
Staring into space like that...
Oh, I get it. Her brain's full of her cousin and that great kiss they had.
Oohhh. Riiight. Of course.
......
じぃ…
stare...
irk
イラッ
Hmph!

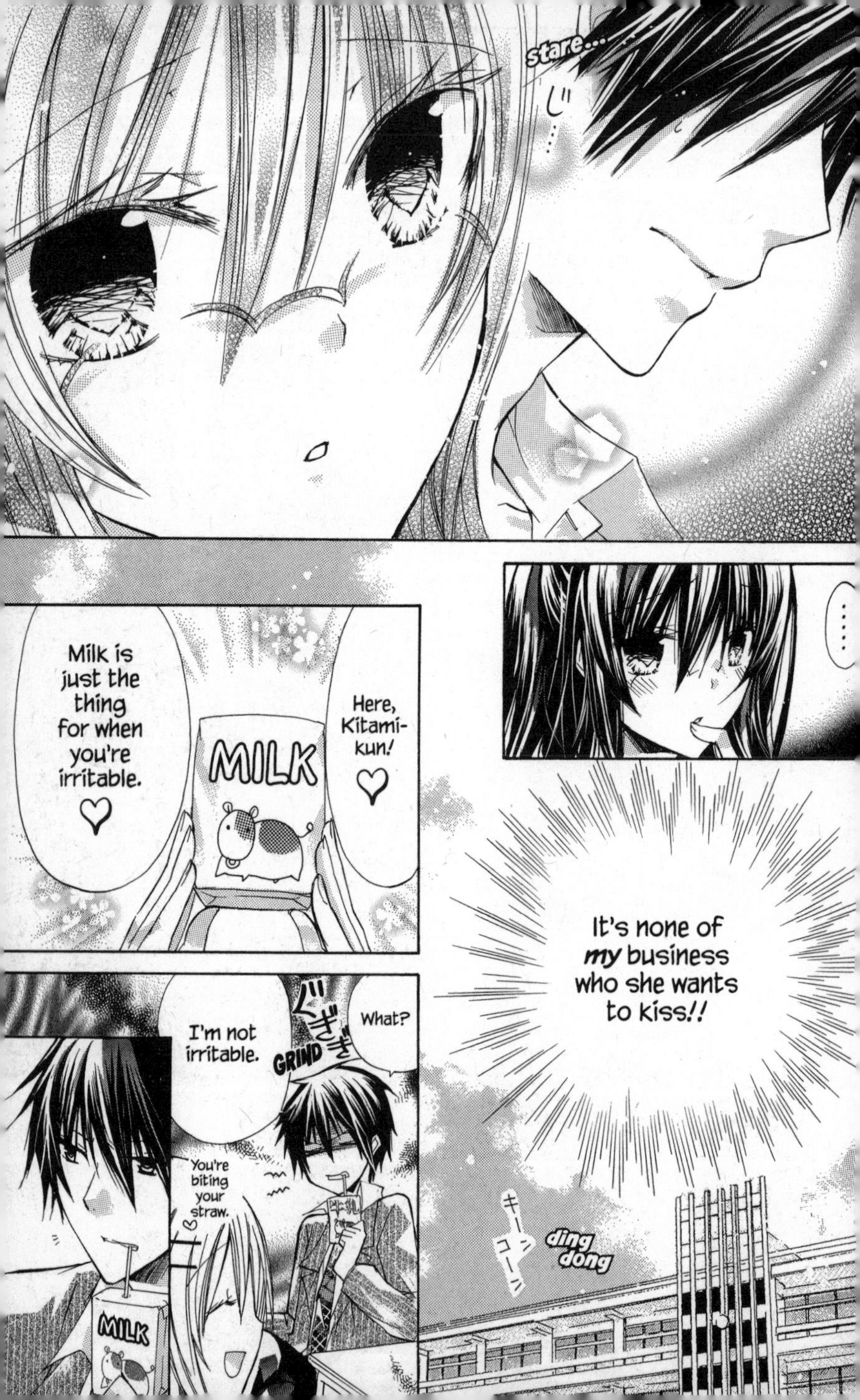

stare...
じ…
.....
It's none of *my* business who she wants to kiss!!
キーンコーン
ding dong
Here, Kitami-kun! ♡
MILK
Milk is just the thing for when you're irritable. ♡
What?
ぐぎぎ
GRIND
I'm not irritable.
You're biting your straw. ♡
MILK

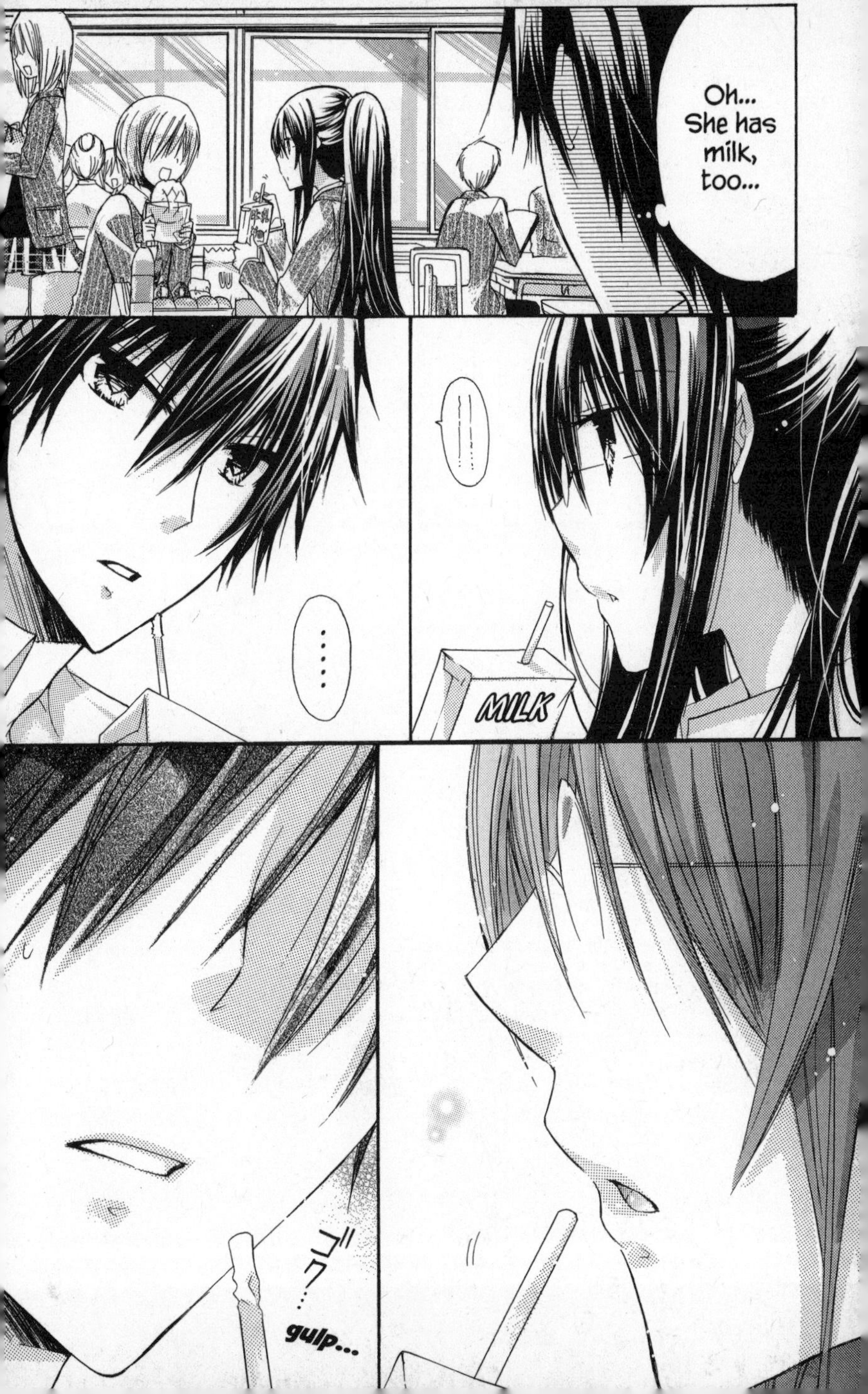

Oh... She has milk, too...
...!!
......
MILK
ゴク...
gulp...

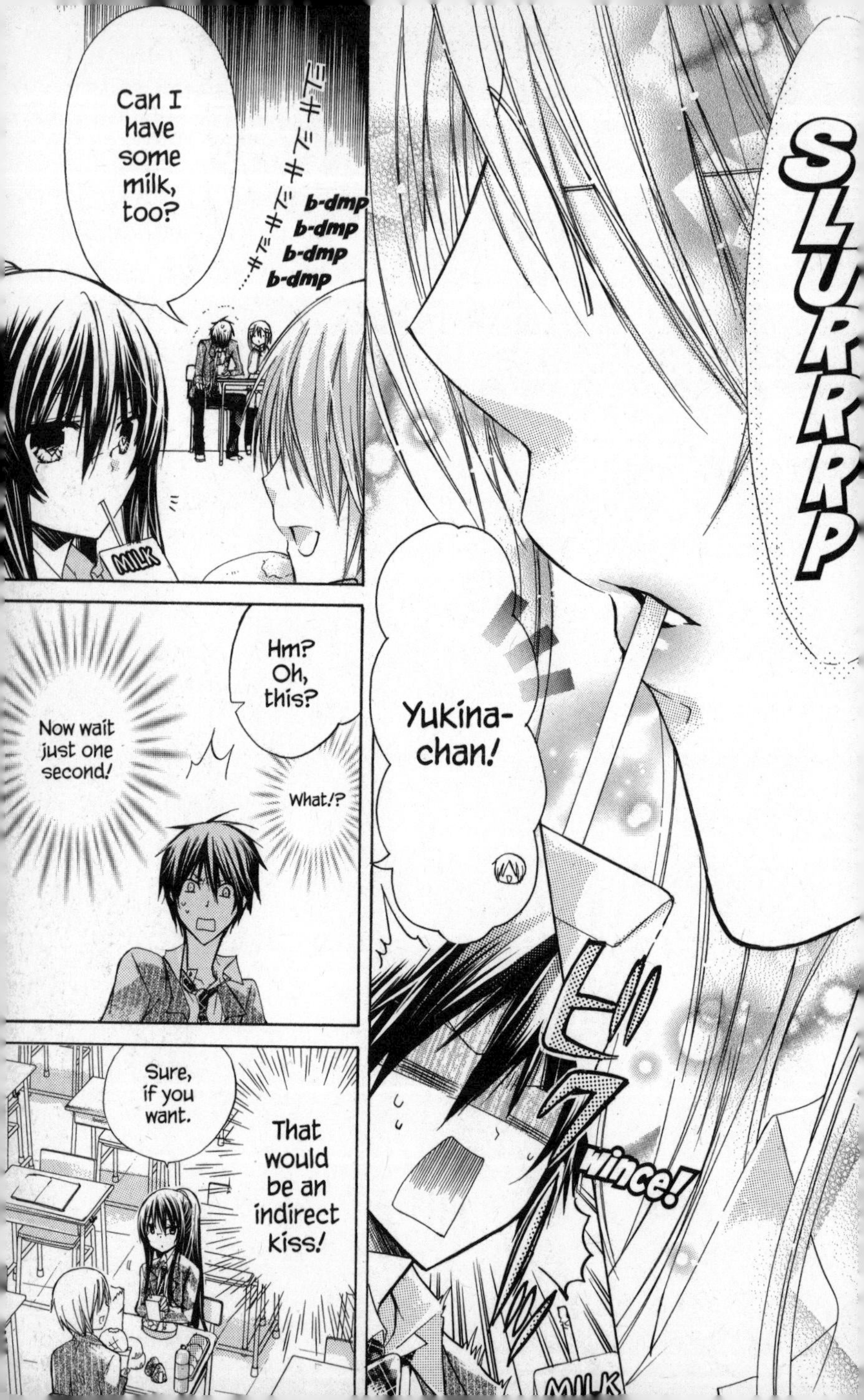
SLURRP
Yukina-chan!
wince!
MILK
Can I have some milk, too?
b-dmp
b-dmp
b-dmp
b-dmp
MILK
Hm? Oh, this?
What!?
Now wait just one second!
Sure, if you want.
That would be an indirect kiss!

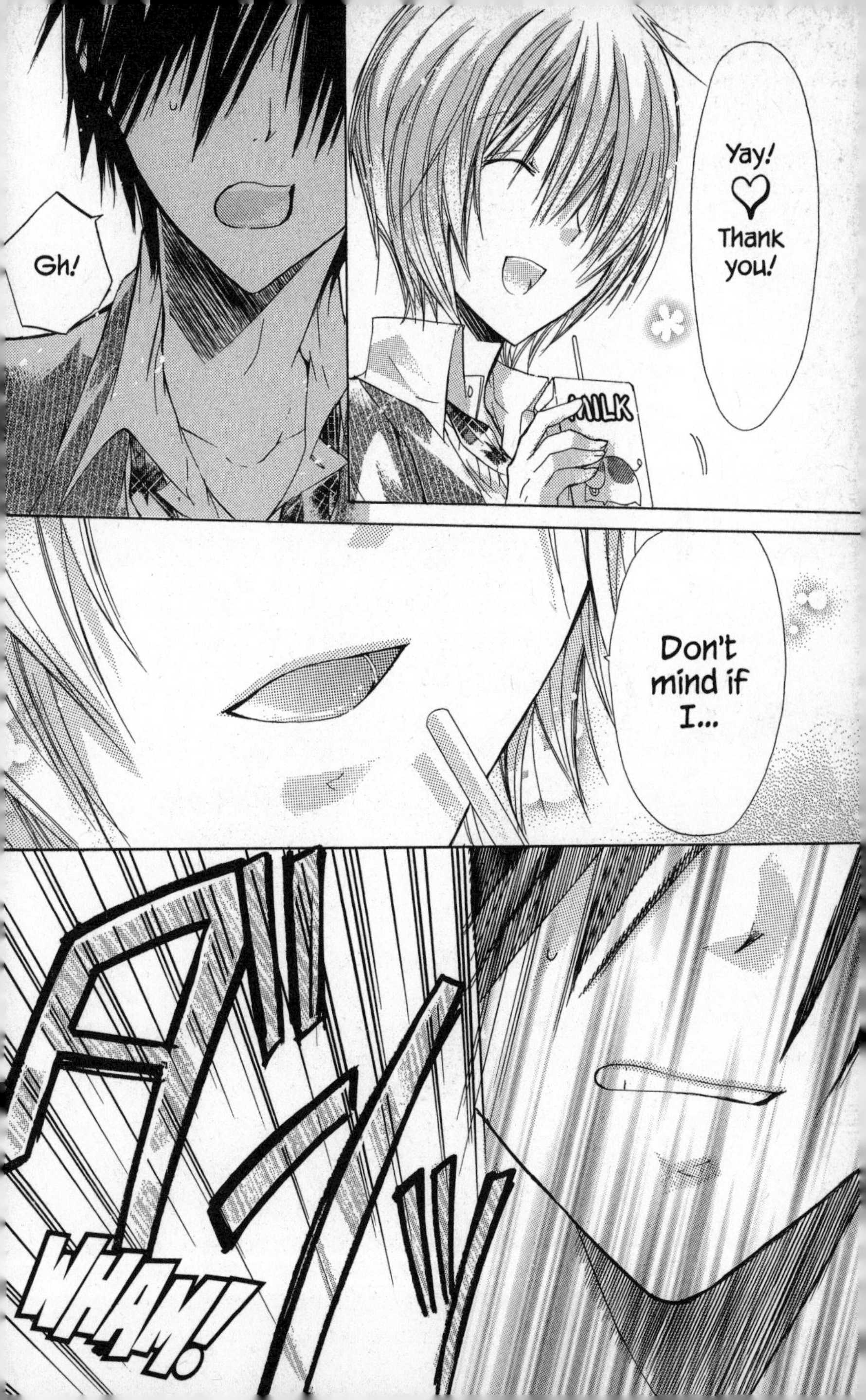
MILK
Yay! ♡ Thank you!
Gh!
Don't mind if I...
WHAM!

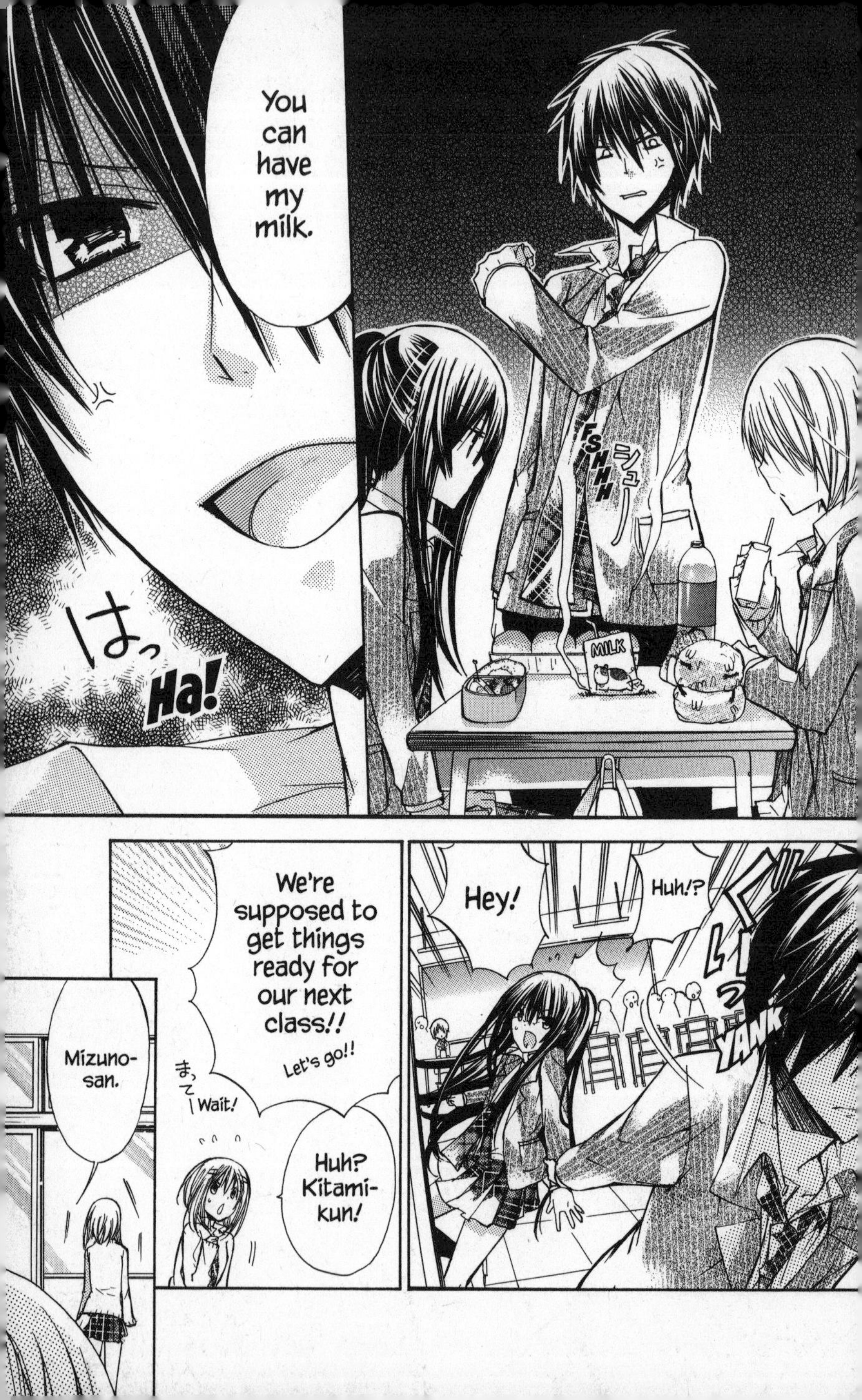
FSHHH
シュー
MILK
You can have my milk.
はっ
Ha!
Hey!
Huh!?
YANK
We're supposed to get things ready for our next class!!
Let's go!!
Huh? Kitami-kun!
まって
Wait!
Mizuno-san.

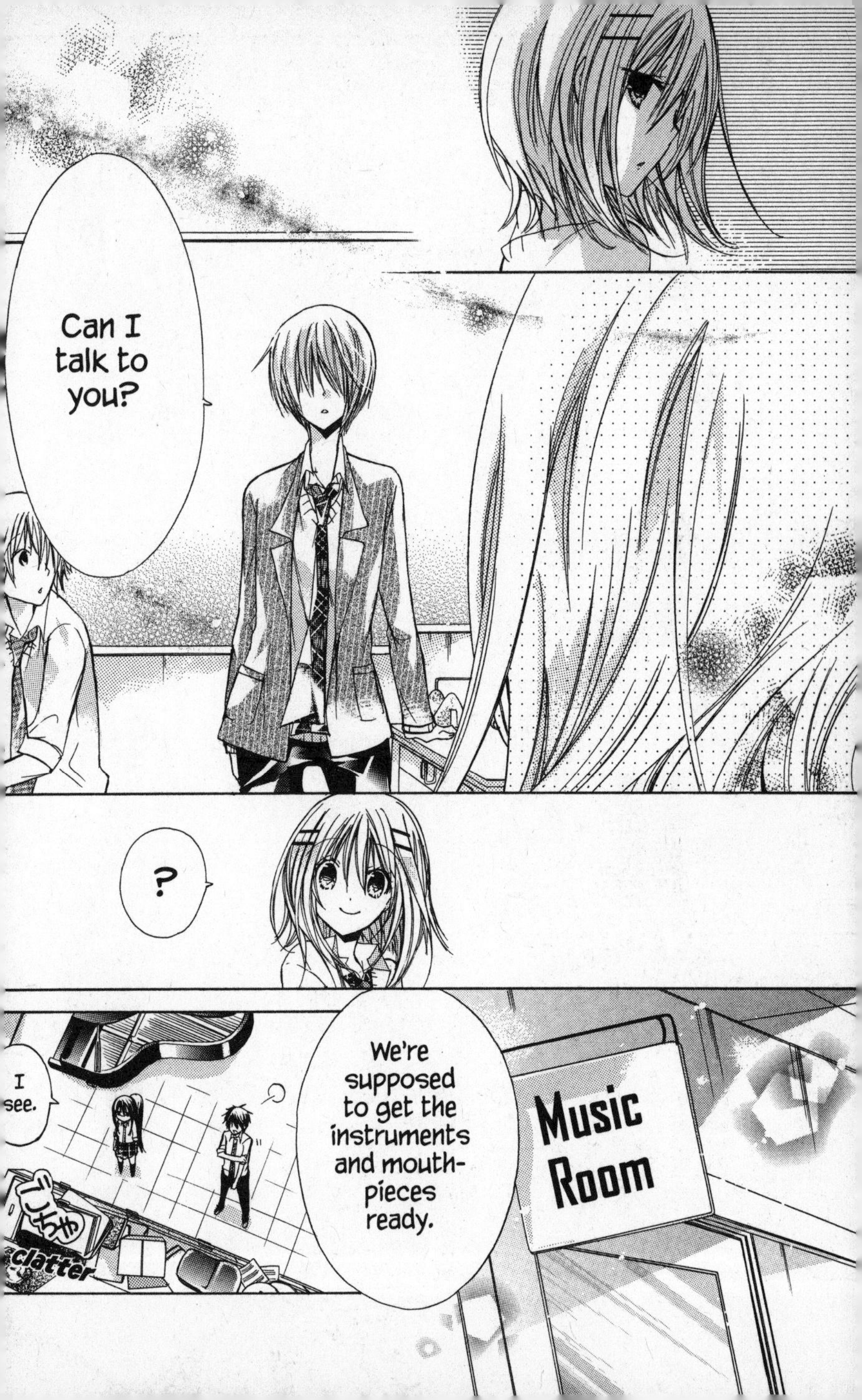
Can I talk to you?
?
Music Room
We're supposed to get the instruments and mouth-pieces ready.
I see.
ごちゃ
clatter

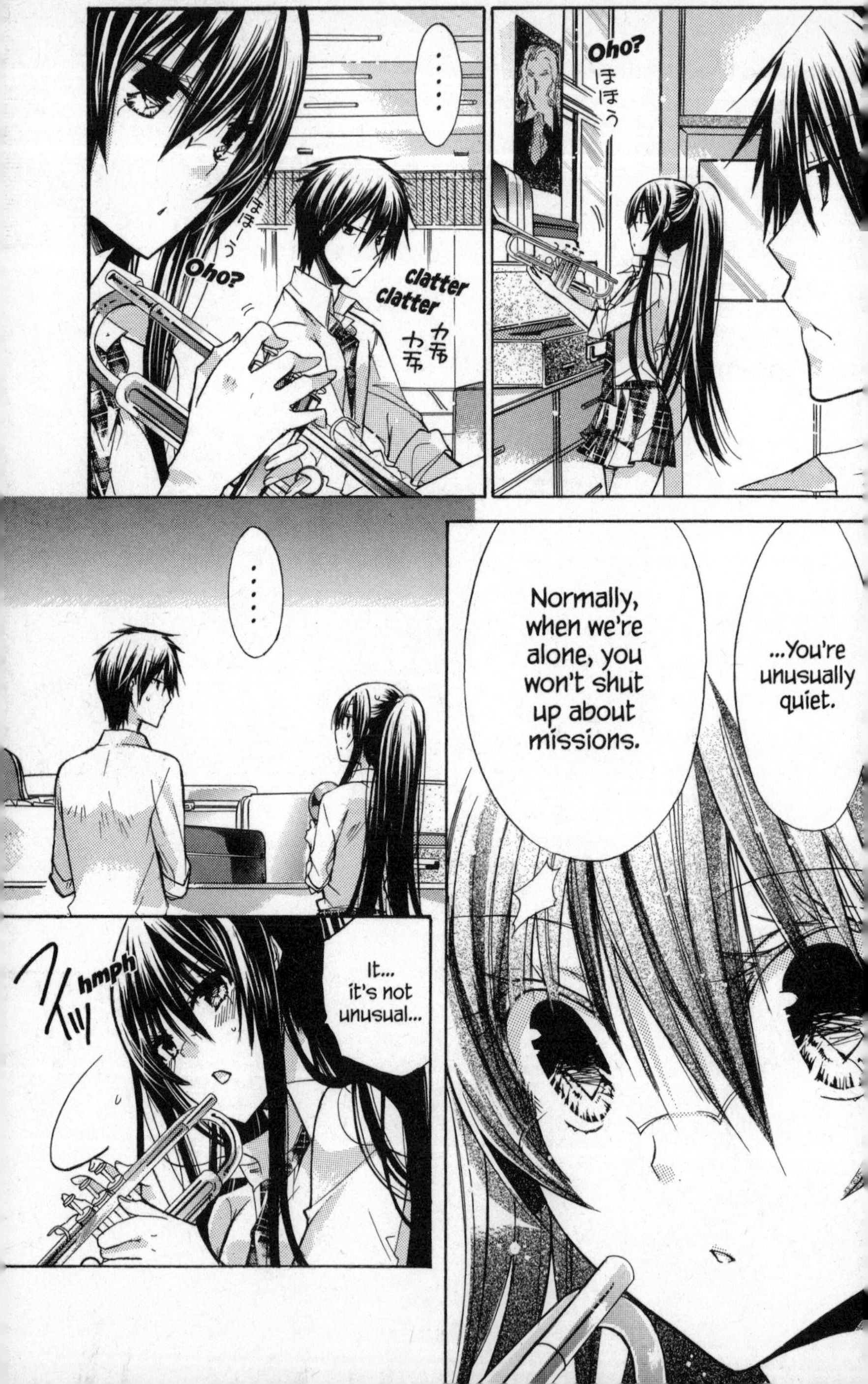
Oho?
ほほう
.....
ほほーう
Oho?
clatter clatter
カチャカチャ
...You're unusually quiet.
Normally, when we're alone, you won't shut up about missions.
.....
It... it's not unusual...
hmph
フイッ

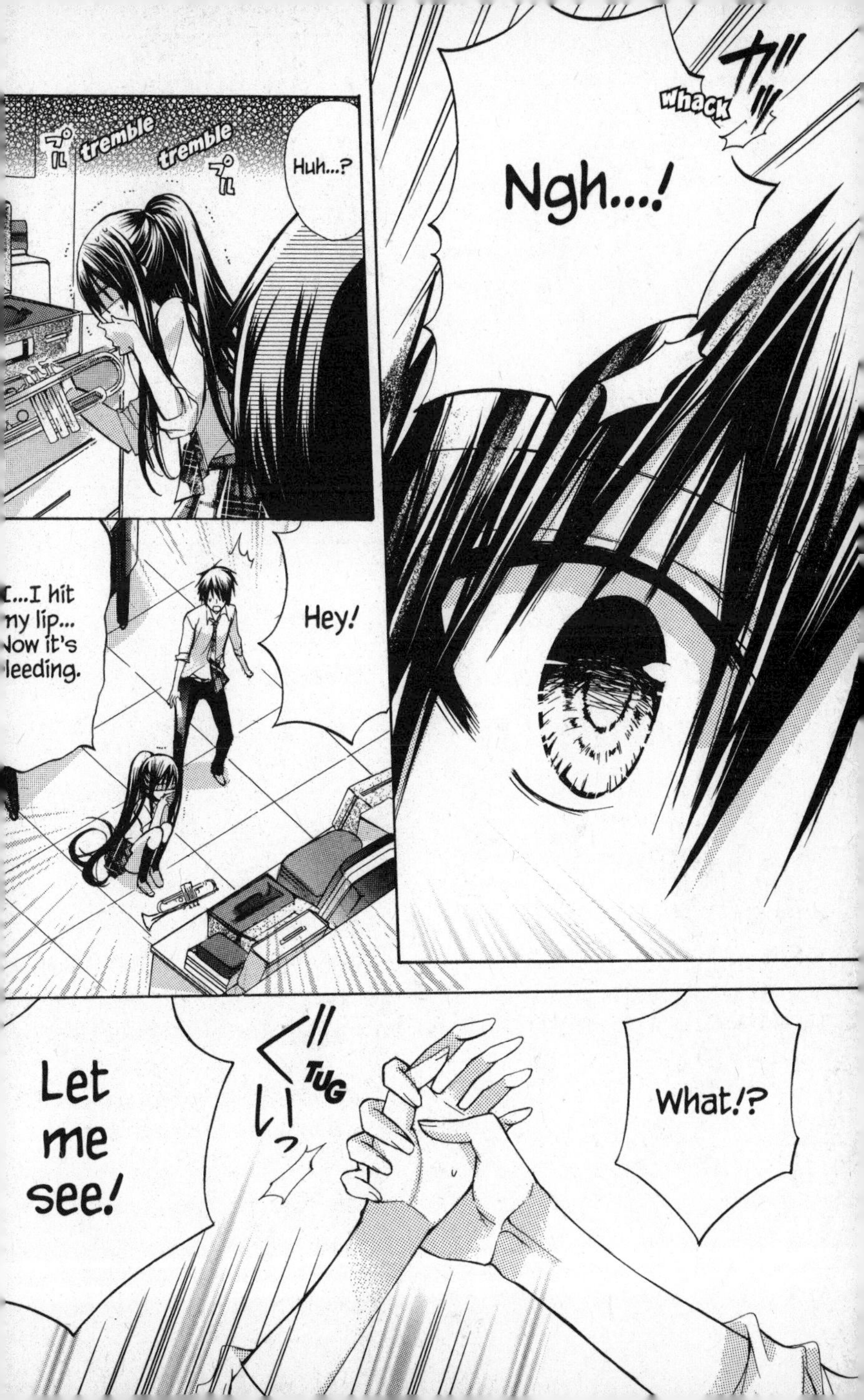

whack
Ngh...!
tremble
tremble
Huh...?
Hey!
...I hit ny lip... ow it's leeding.
What!?
TUG
Let me see!

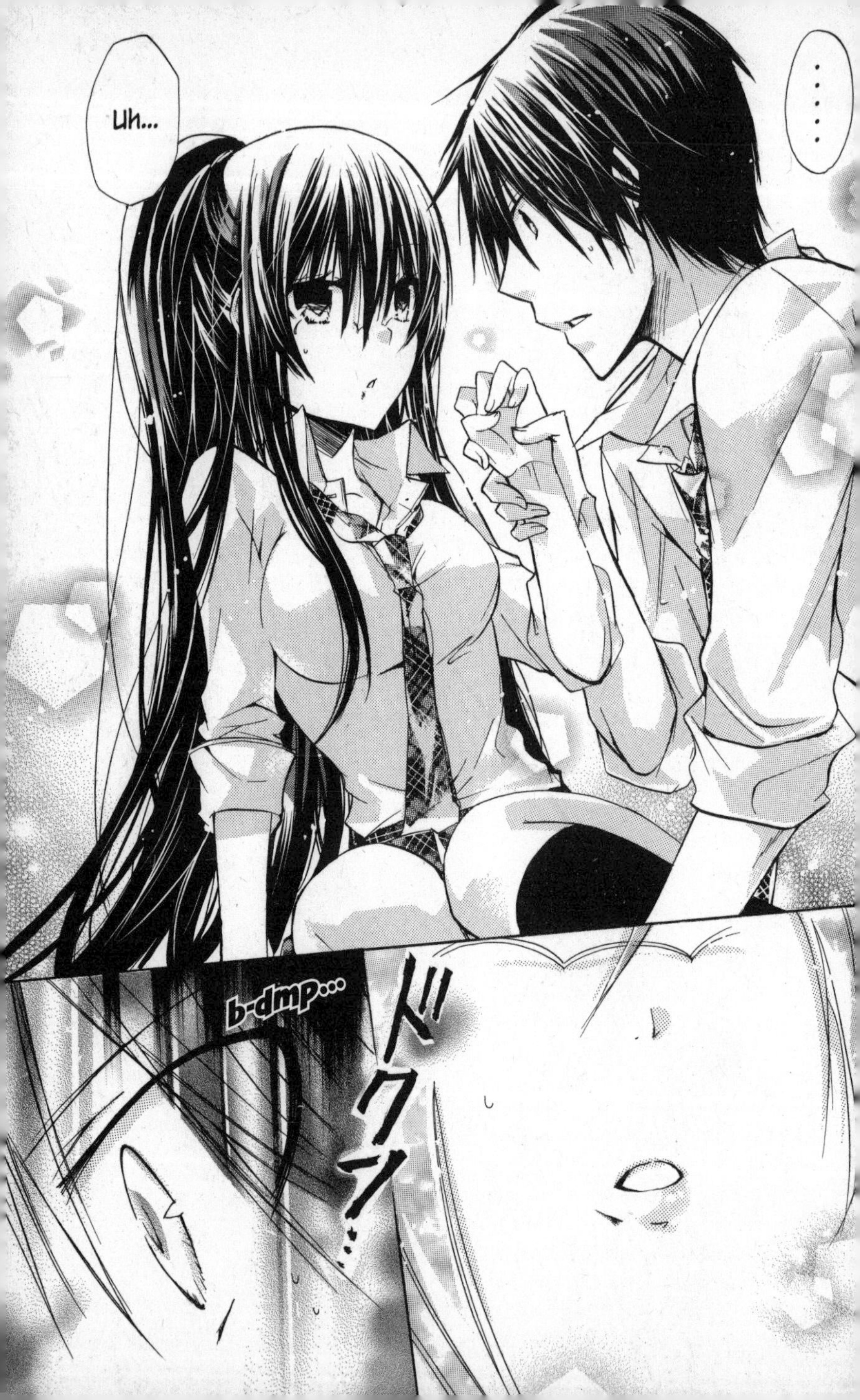

.....
uh...
b-dmp...
ドクン…

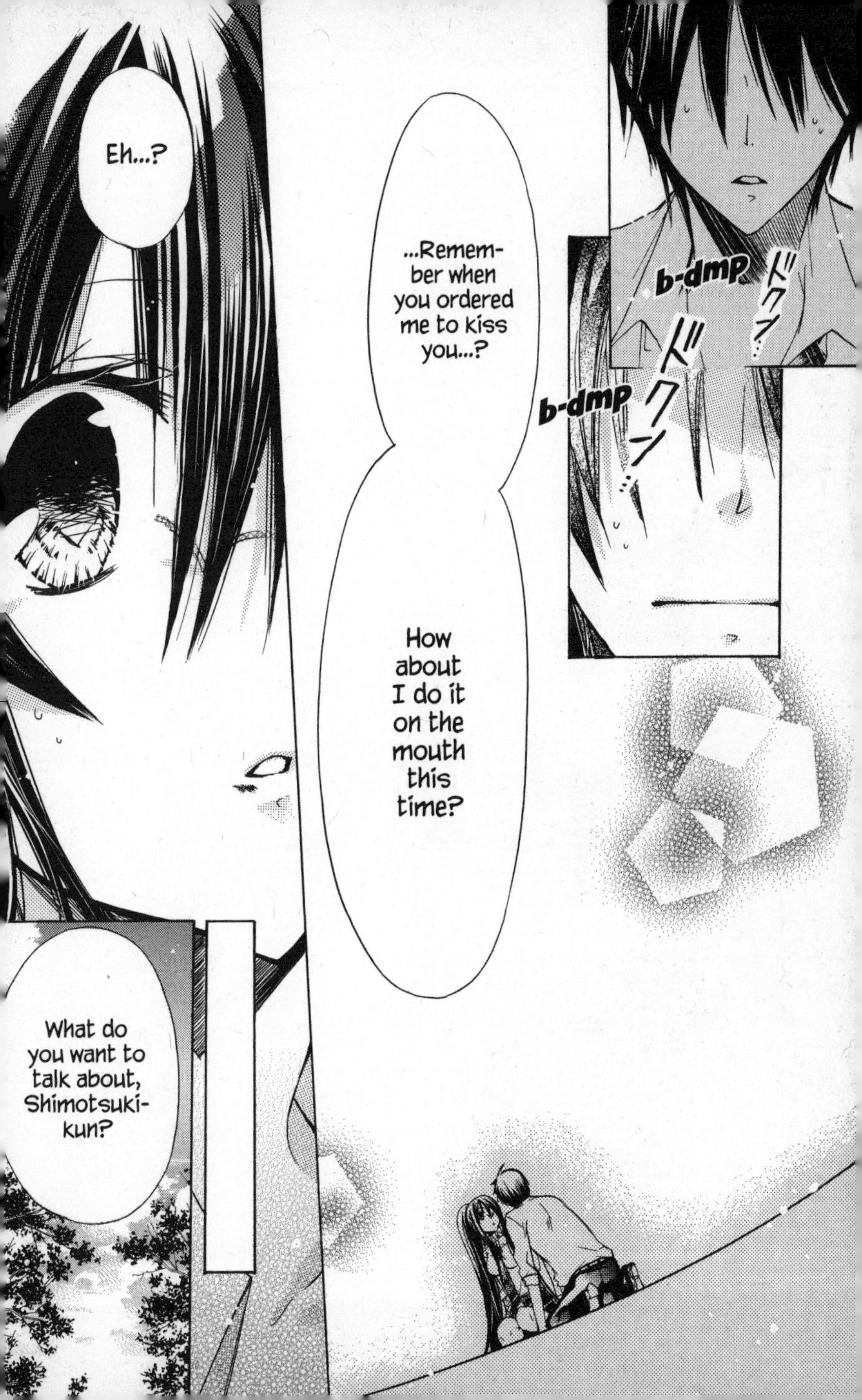
b-dmp
ドクン…
b-dmp
ドクン…
...Remember when you ordered me to kiss you...?
How about I do it on the mouth this time?
Eh...?
What do you want to talk about, Shimotsuki-kun?

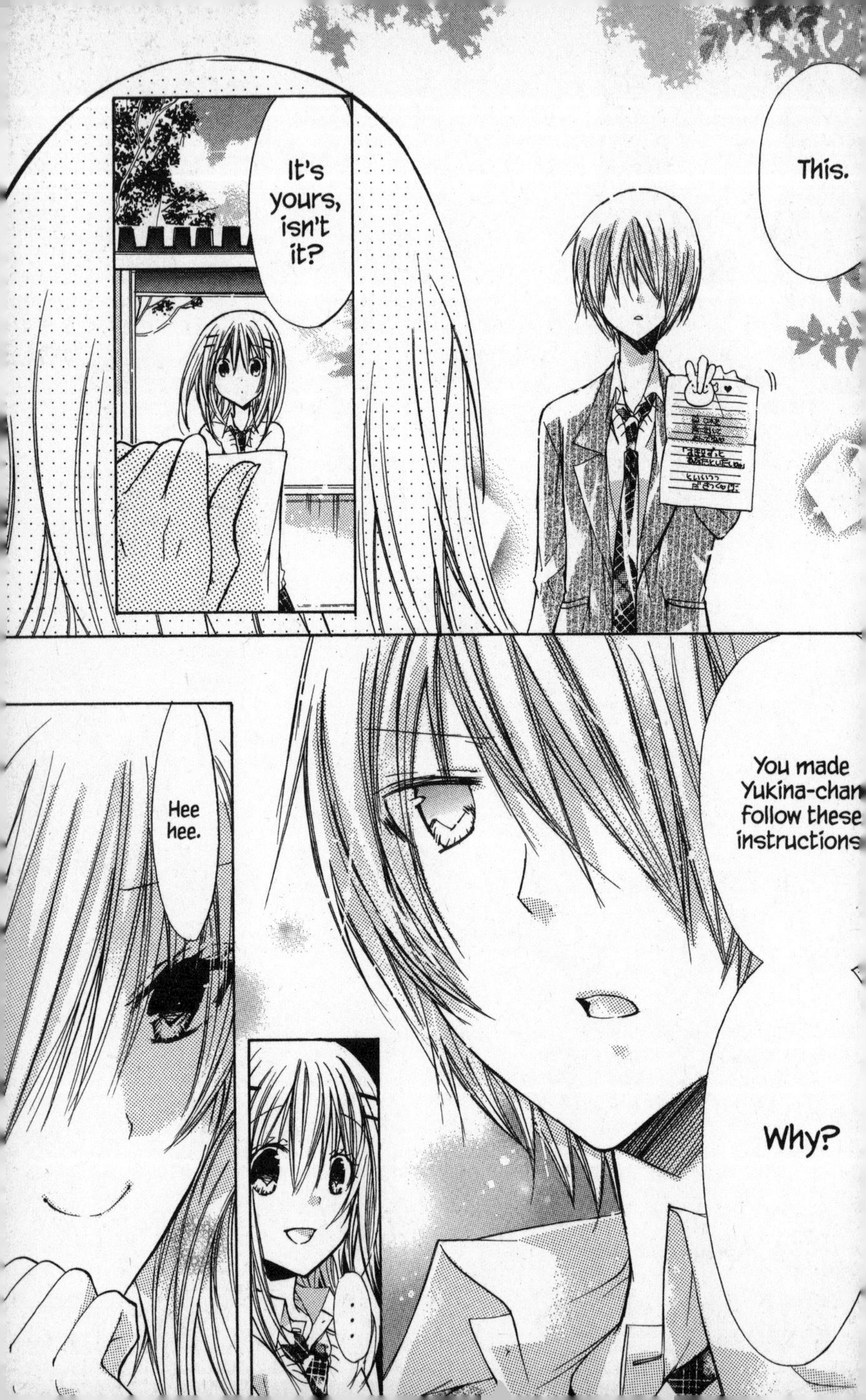
This.
It's yours, isn't it?
You made Yukina-chan follow these instructions
Why?
Hee hee.
...

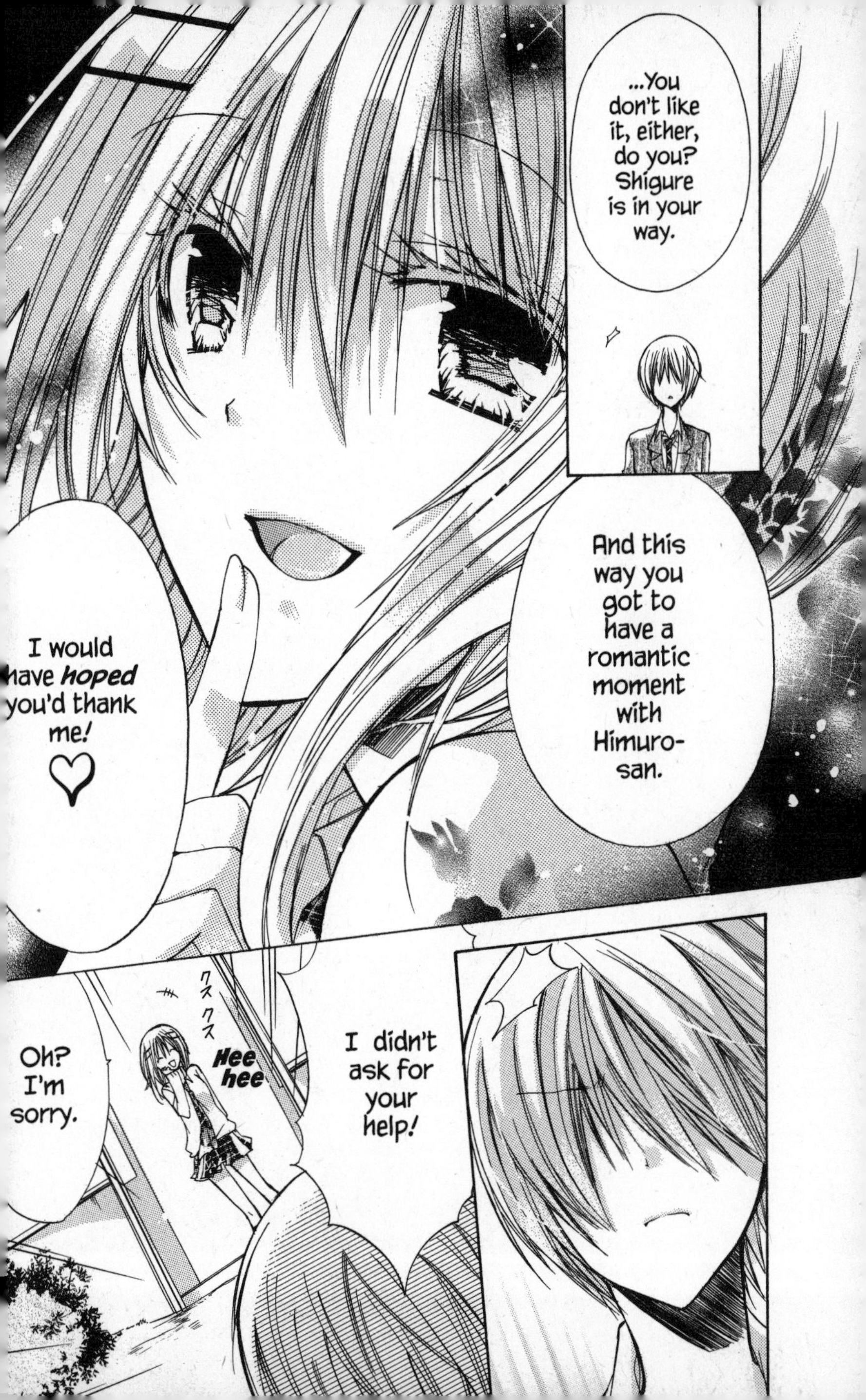
...You don't like it, either, do you? Shigure is in your way.
And this way you got to have a romantic moment with Himuro-san.
I would have *hoped* you'd thank me! ♡
I didn't ask for your help!
クスクス
Hee hee
Oh? I'm sorry.

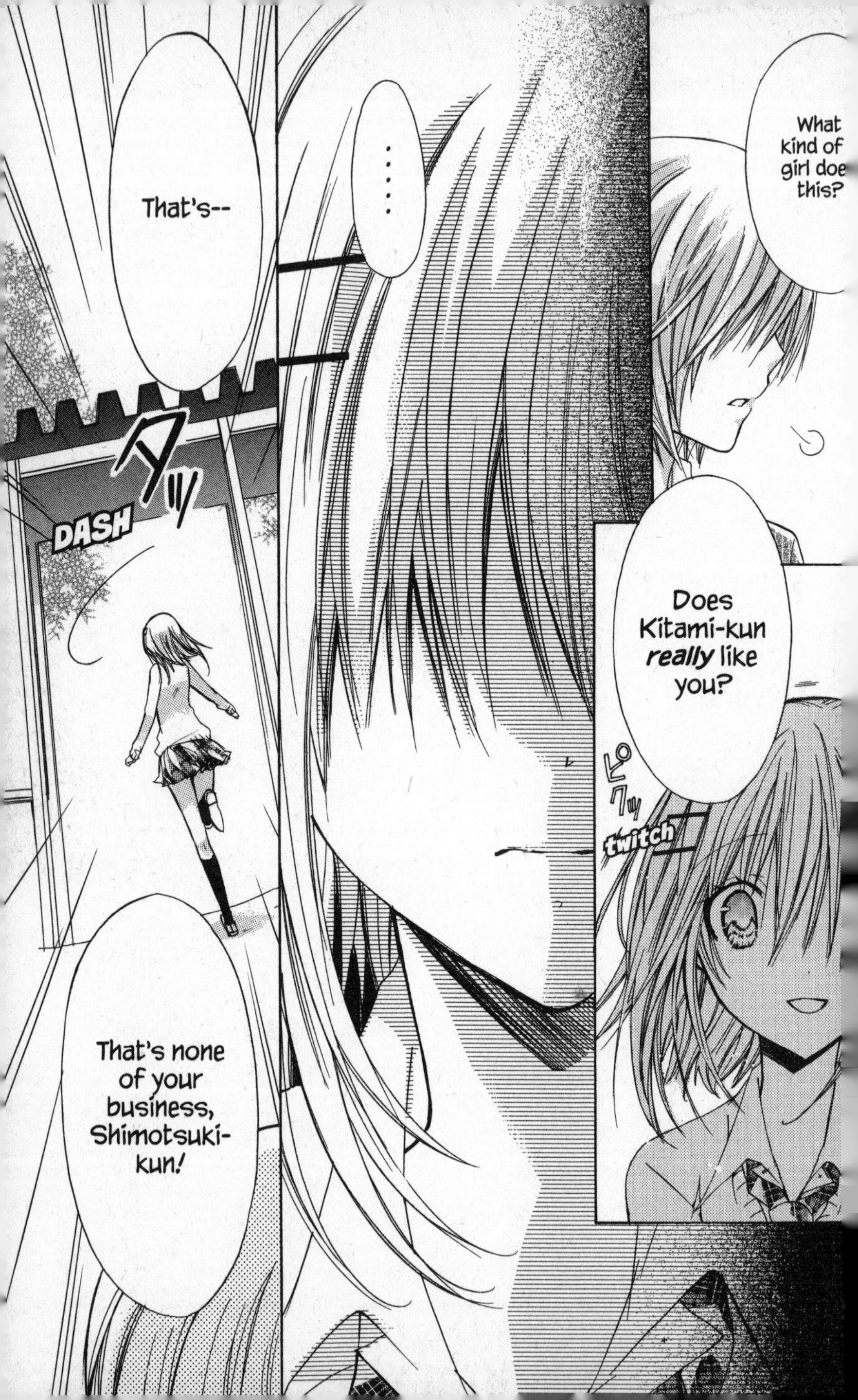
What kind of girl doe this?
Does Kitami-kun *really* like you?
twitch
.....
That's--
DASH
That's none of your business, Shimotsuki-kun!

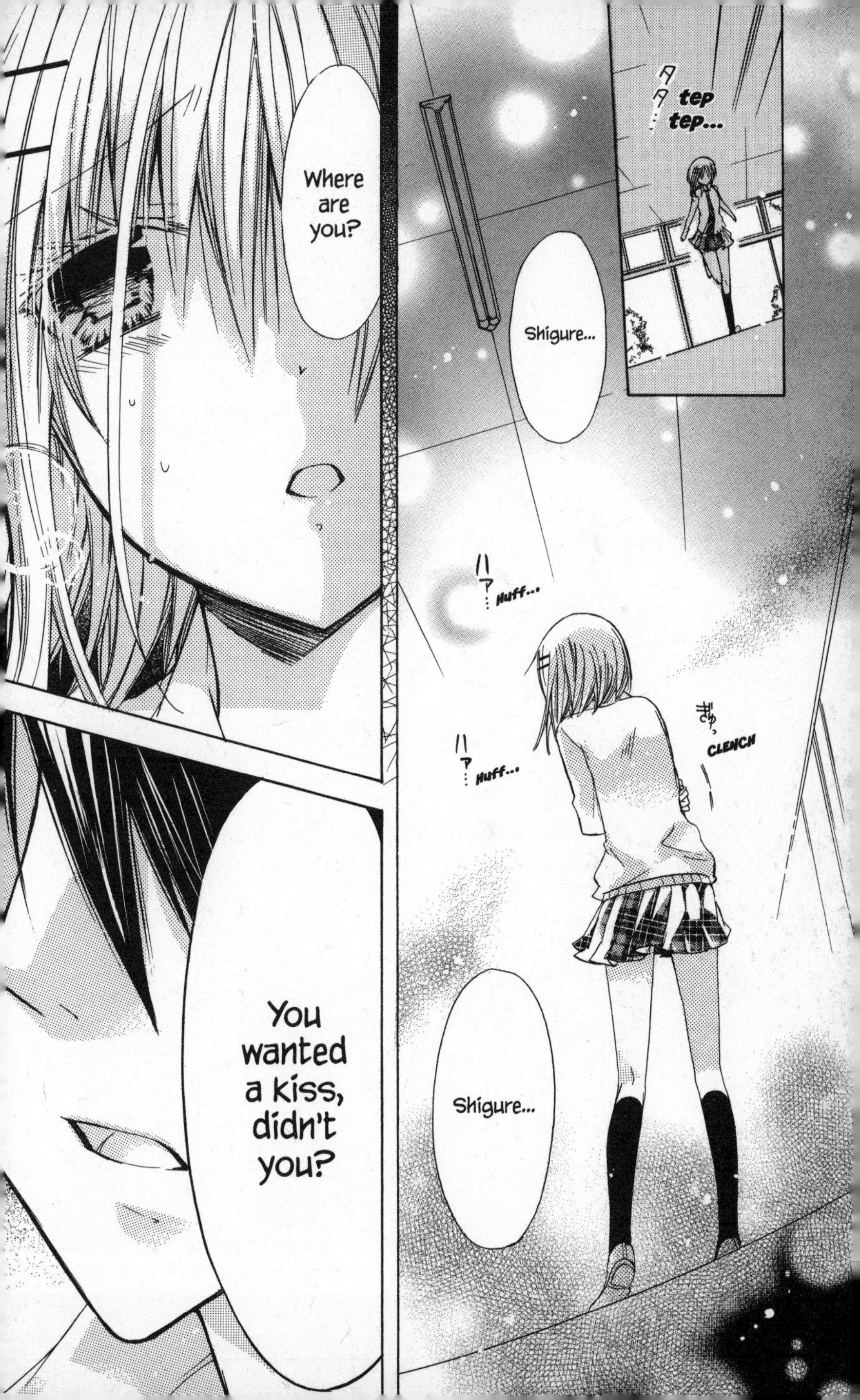
タタ…
tep tep...
Shigure...
ハァ…
Huff...
ぎゅっ
CLENCH
ハァ…
Huff...
Shigure...
Where are you?
You wanted a kiss, didn't you?

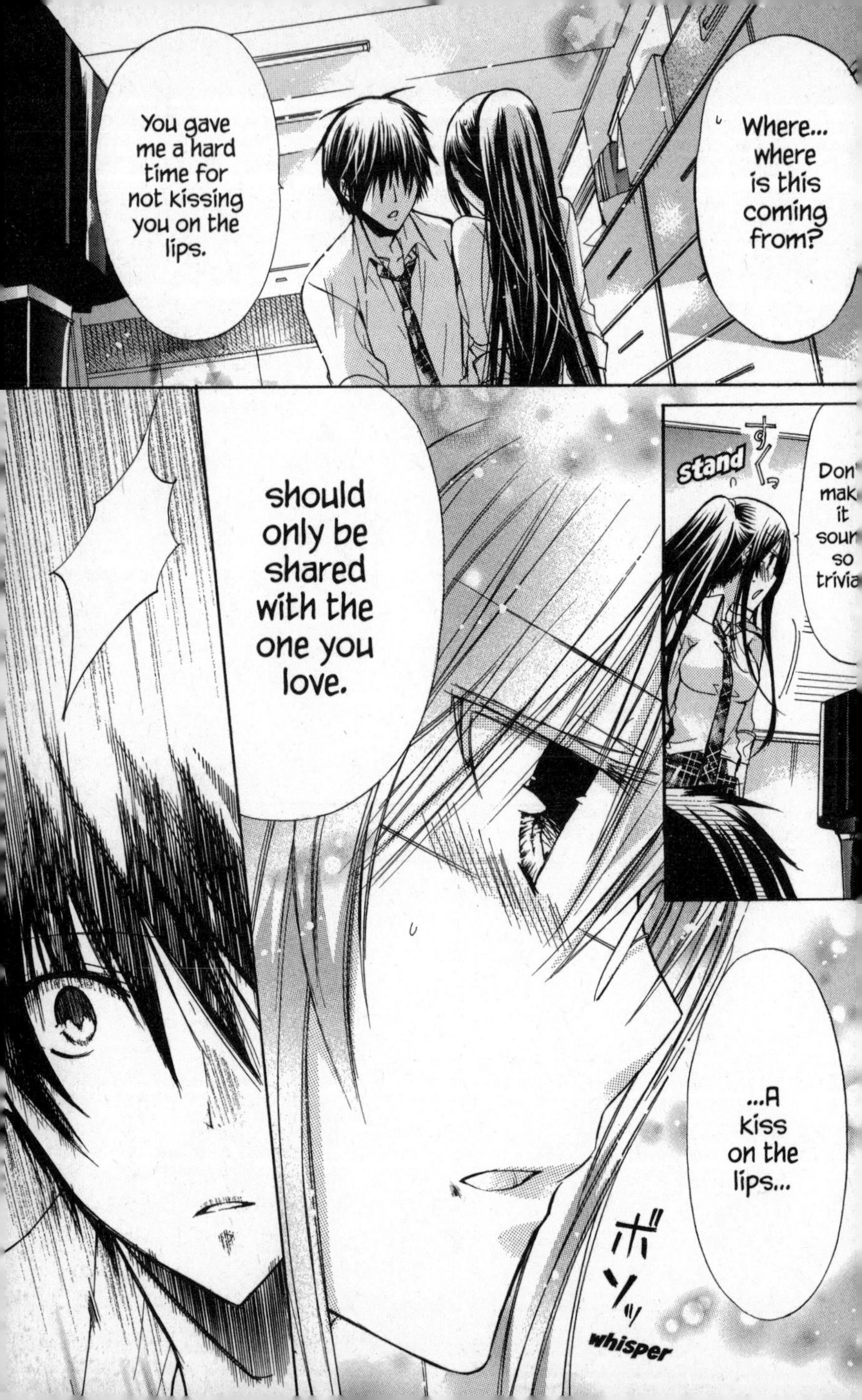
Where... where is this coming from?
You gave me a hard time for not kissing you on the lips.
すくっ
Stand
Don' mak it soun so trivia
...A kiss on the lips...
ボソッ
whisper
should only be shared with the one you love.

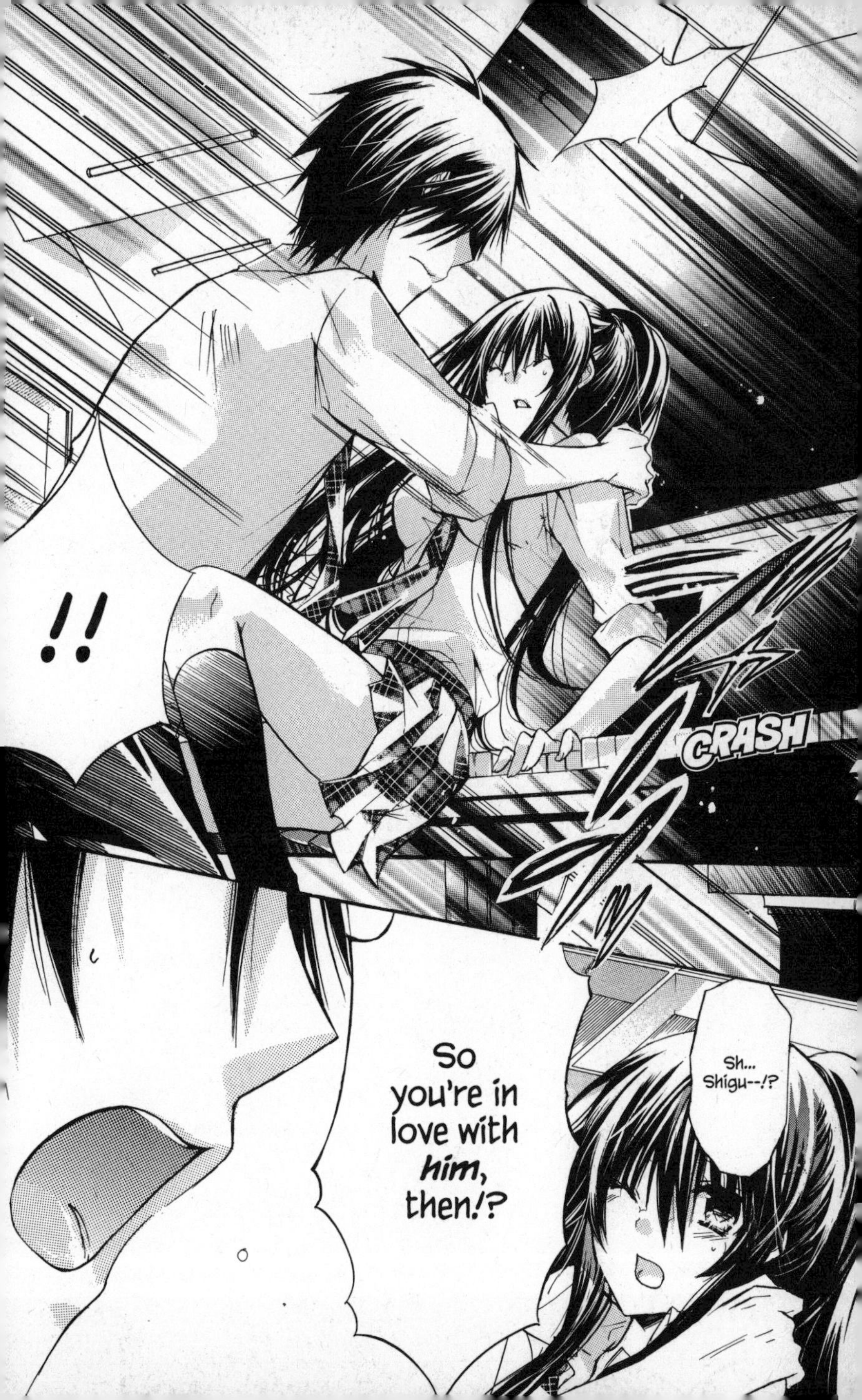
CRASH
!!
Sh... Shigu--!?
So you're in love with *him*, then!?

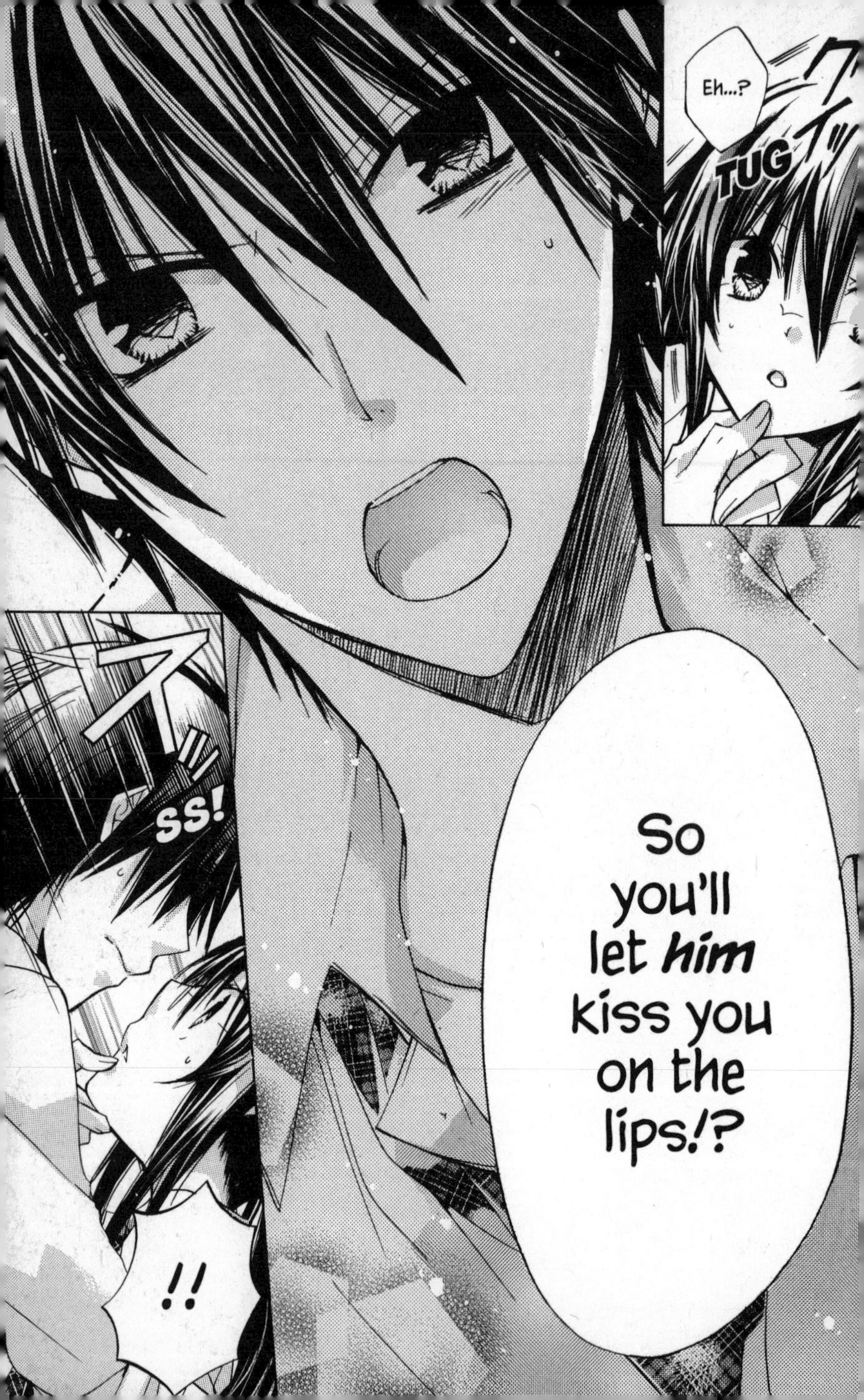
Eh...?
TUG
So you'll let *him* kiss you on the lips!?
SS!
!!

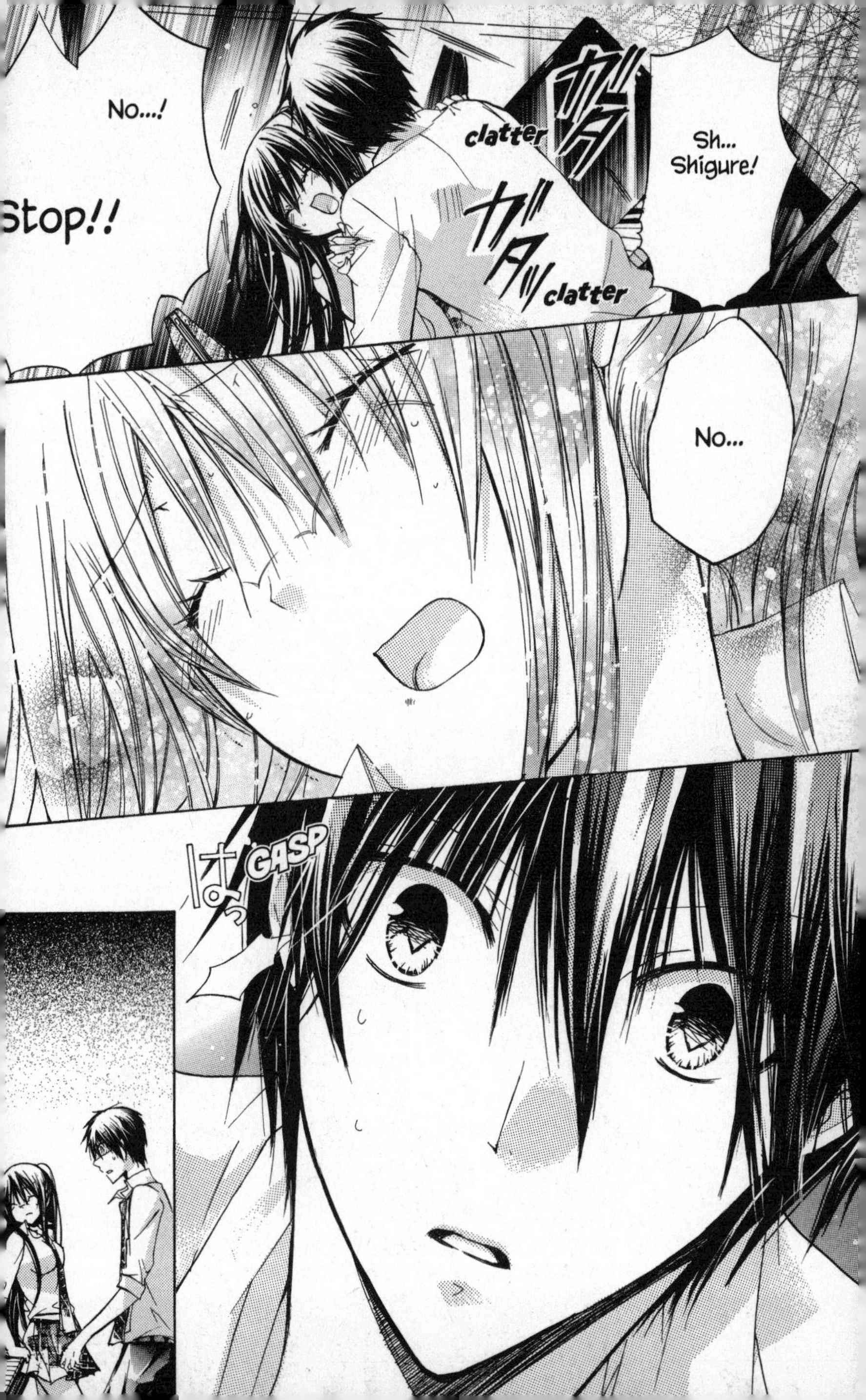
Sh... Shigure!
ガタ
clatter
ガタッ
clatter
No...!
Stop!!
No...
はっ
GASP

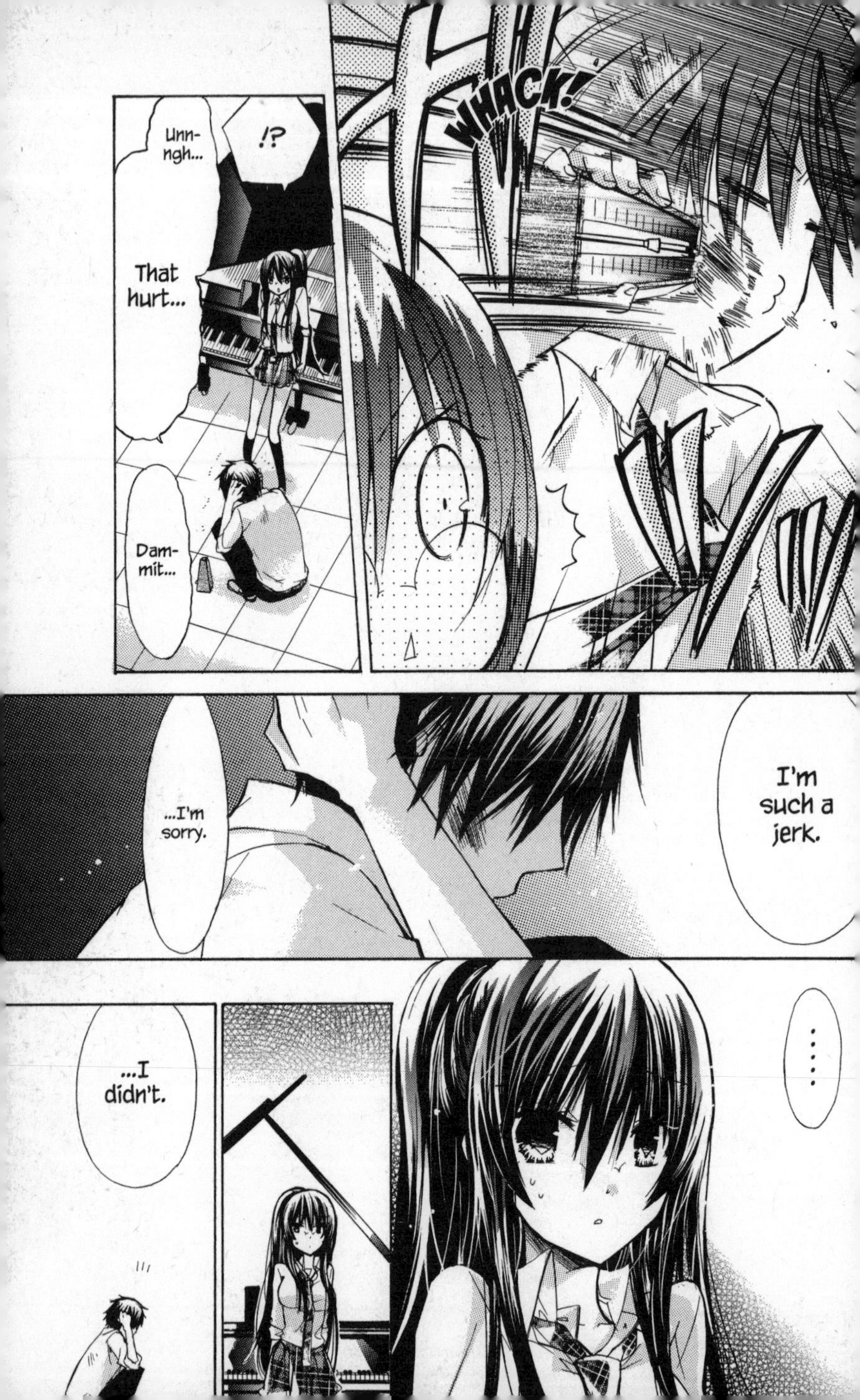
WHACK!
!?
Unn-ngh...
That hurt...
Dam-mit...
I'm such a jerk.
...I'm sorry.
.....
...I didn't.

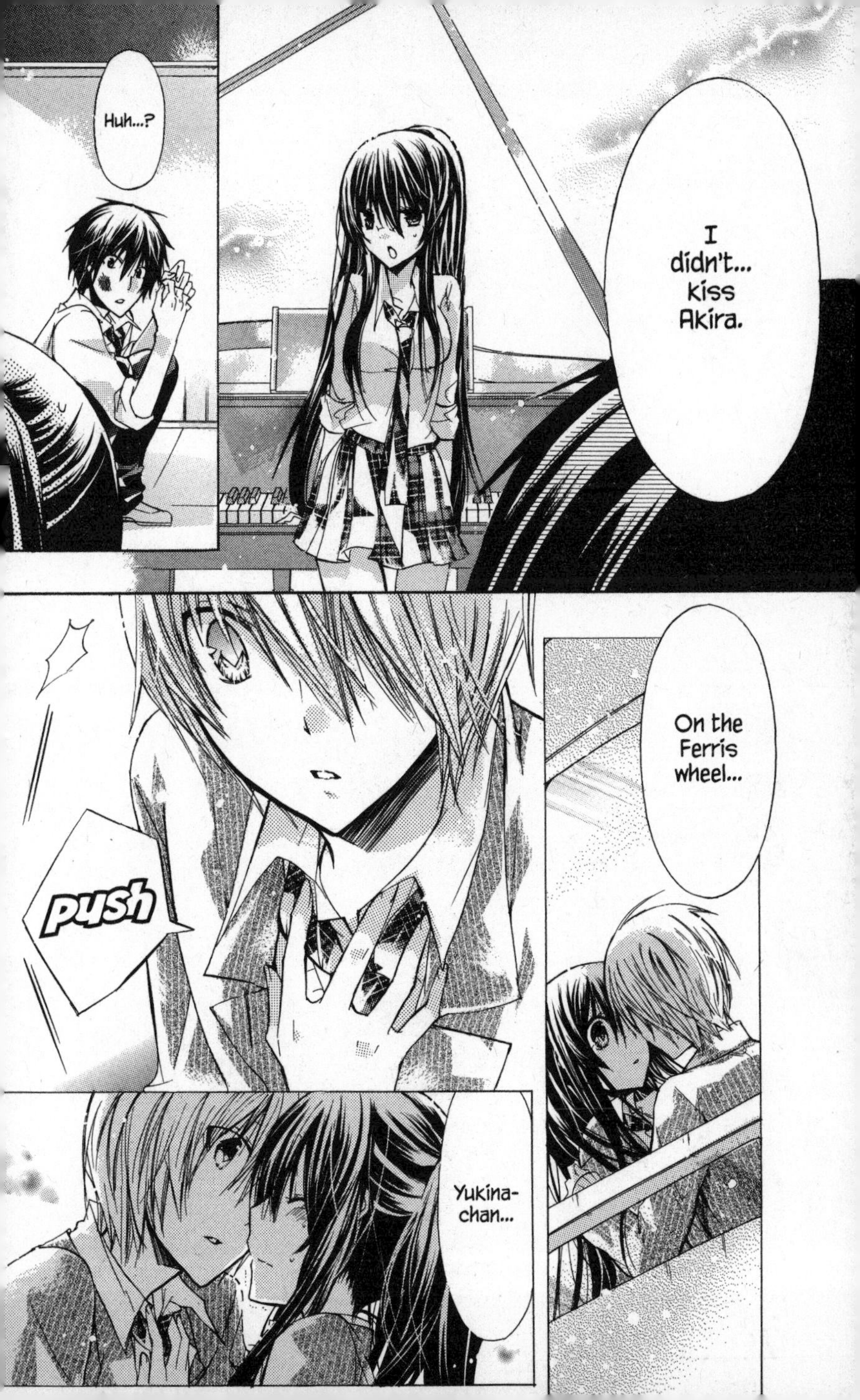
I didn't... kiss Akira.
Huh...?
On the Ferris wheel...
push
Yukina-chan...

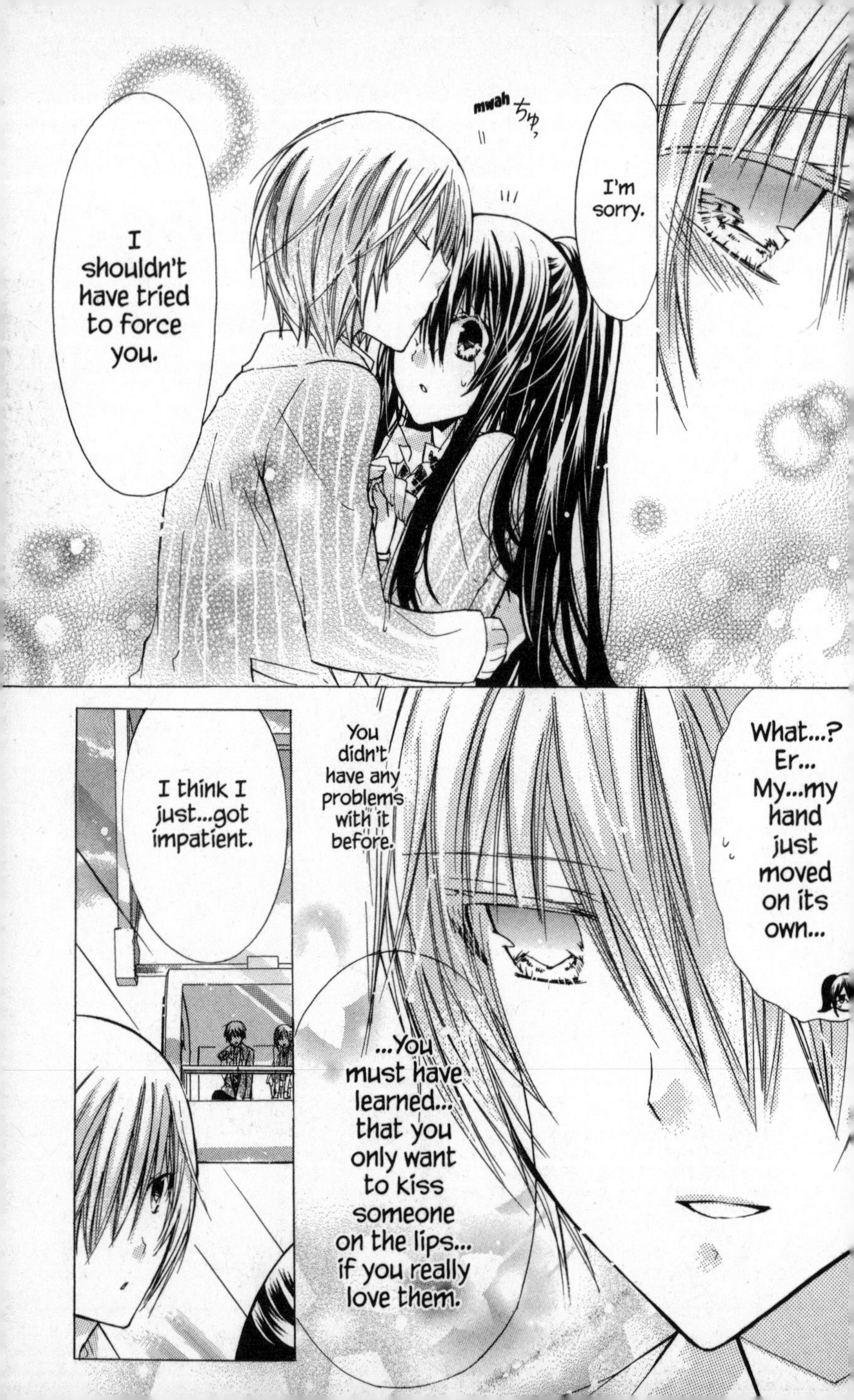
I'm sorry.
mwah ちゅ
I shouldn't have tried to force you.
What...? Er... My...my hand just moved on its own...
You didn't have any problems with it before.
...You must have learned... that you only want to kiss someone on the lips... if you really love them.
I think I just...got impatient.

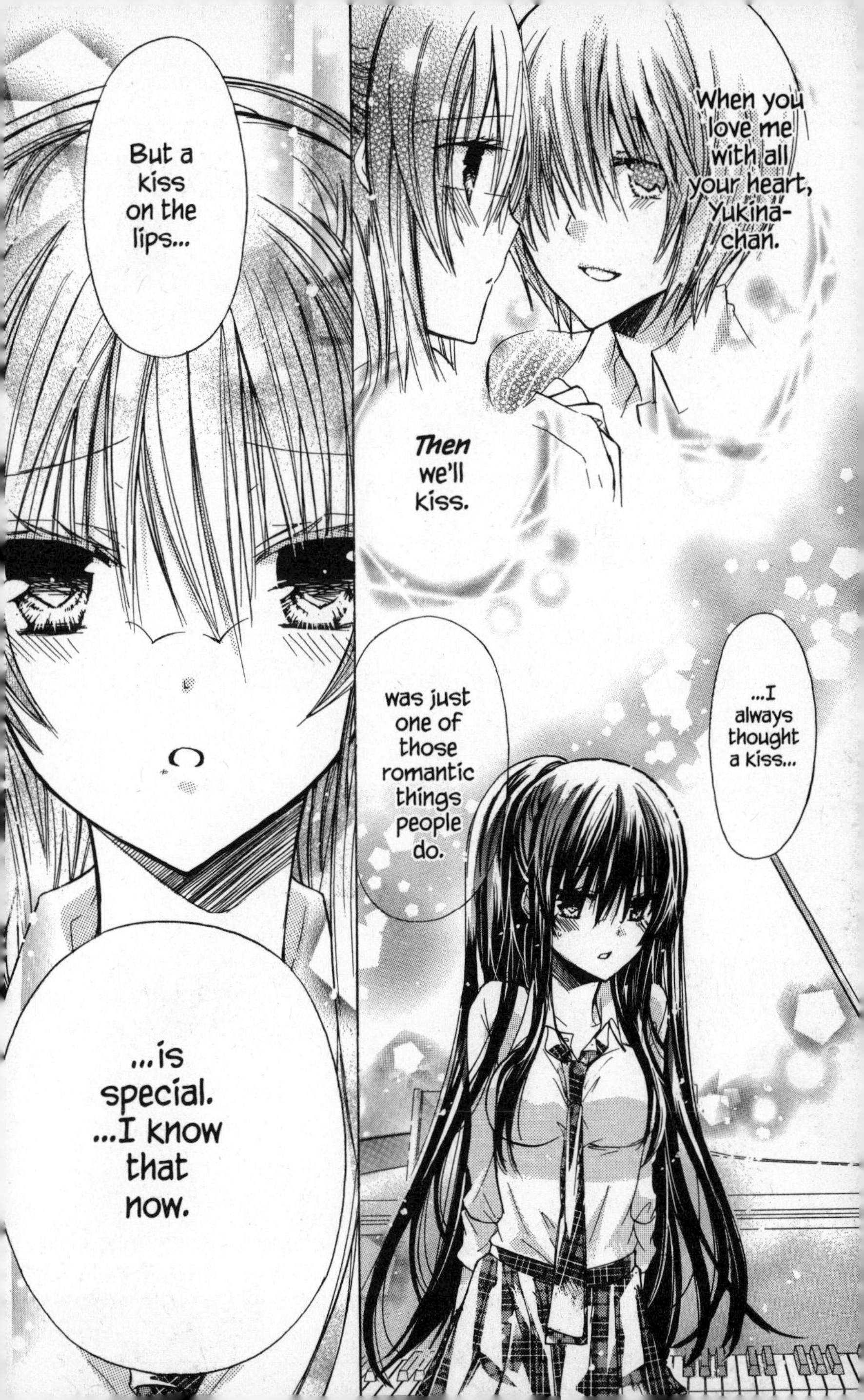
When you love me with all your heart, Yukina-chan.
Then we'll kiss.
...I always thought a kiss...
was just one of those romantic things people do.
But a kiss on the lips...
...is special. ...I know that now.

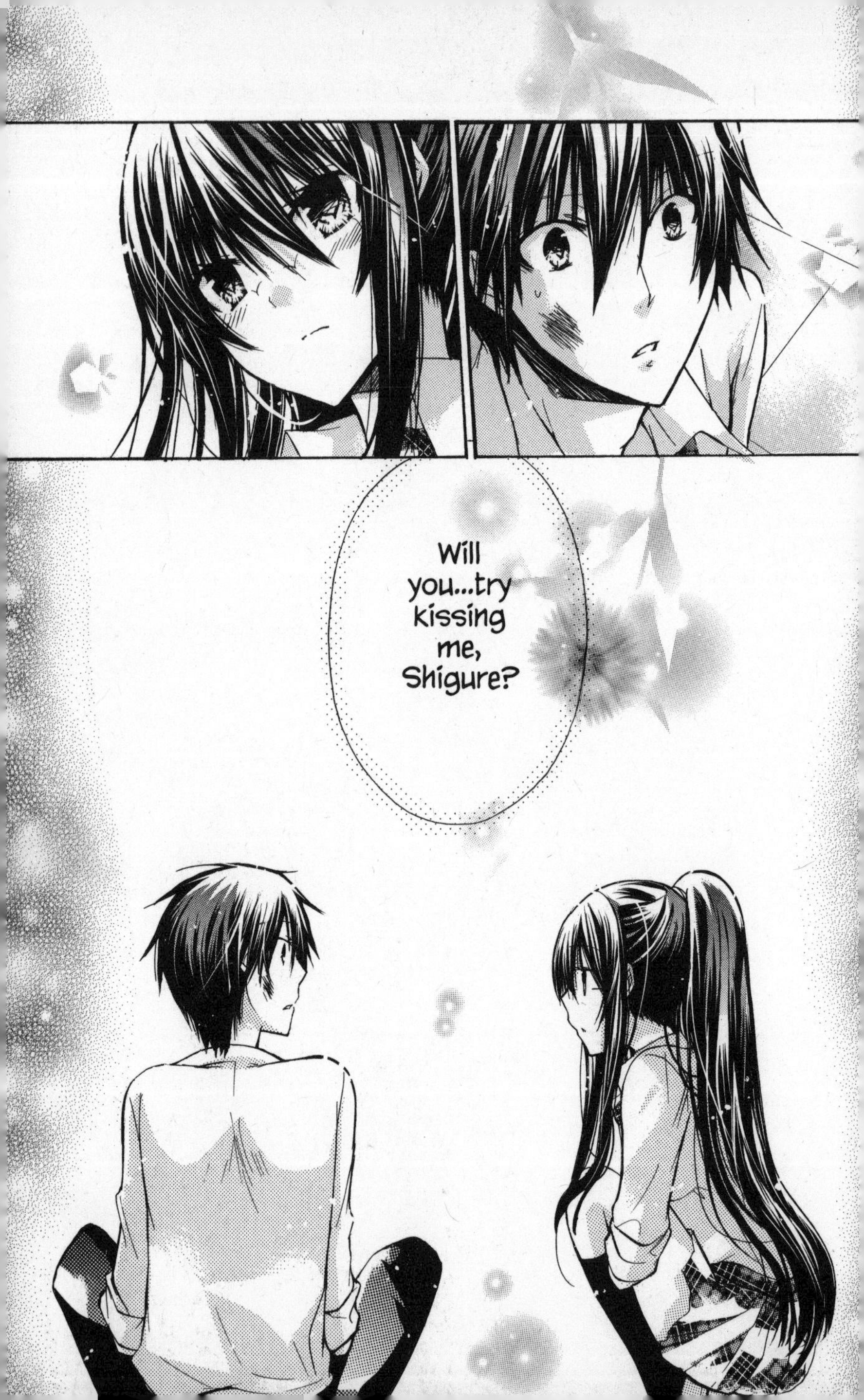
Will you...try kissing me, Shigure?

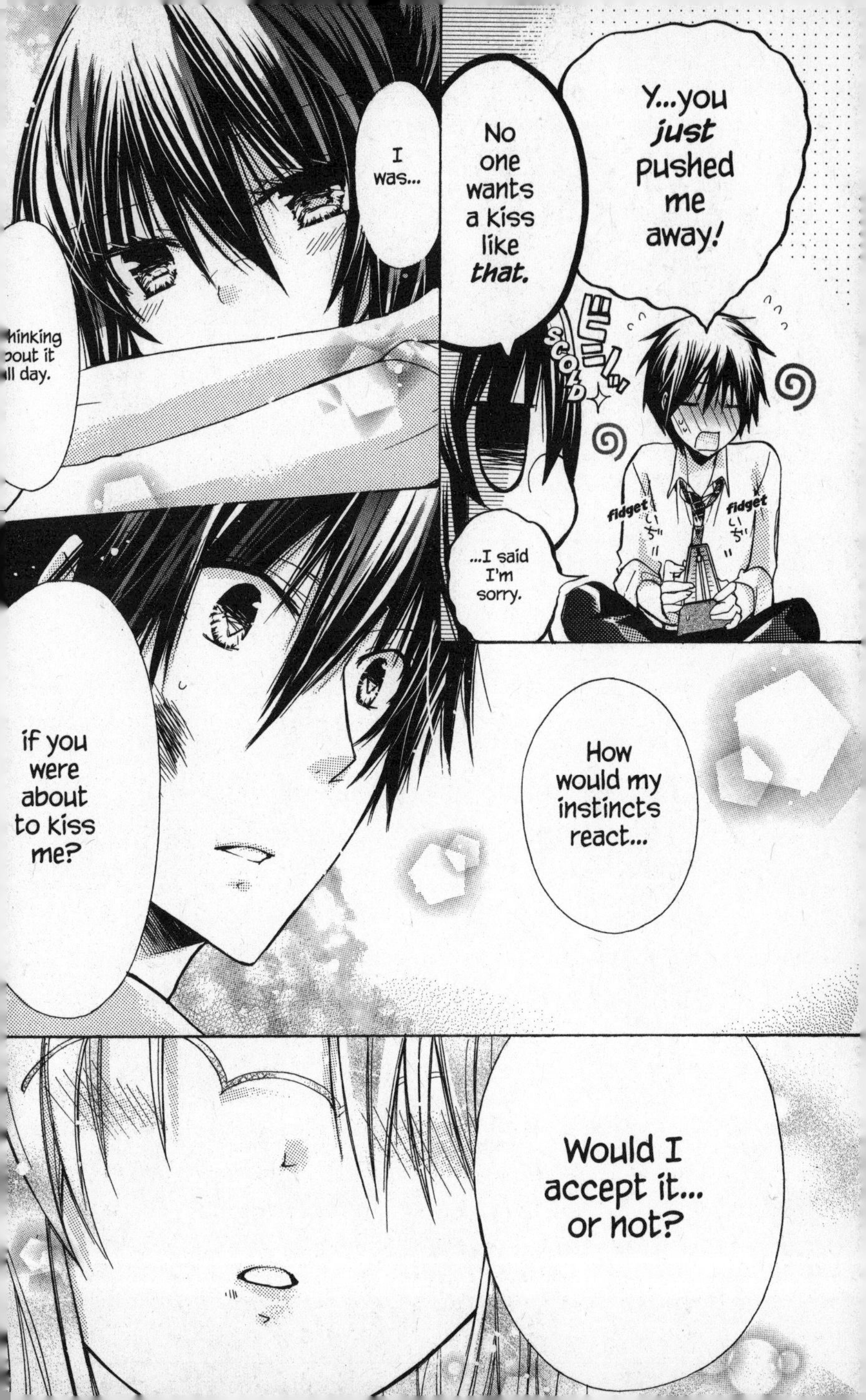
Y...you just pushed me away!
No one wants a kiss like that.
SCOLD
fidget
fidget
...I said I'm sorry.
I was...
hinking bout it ll day.
How would my instincts react...
if you were about to kiss me?
Would I accept it... or not?

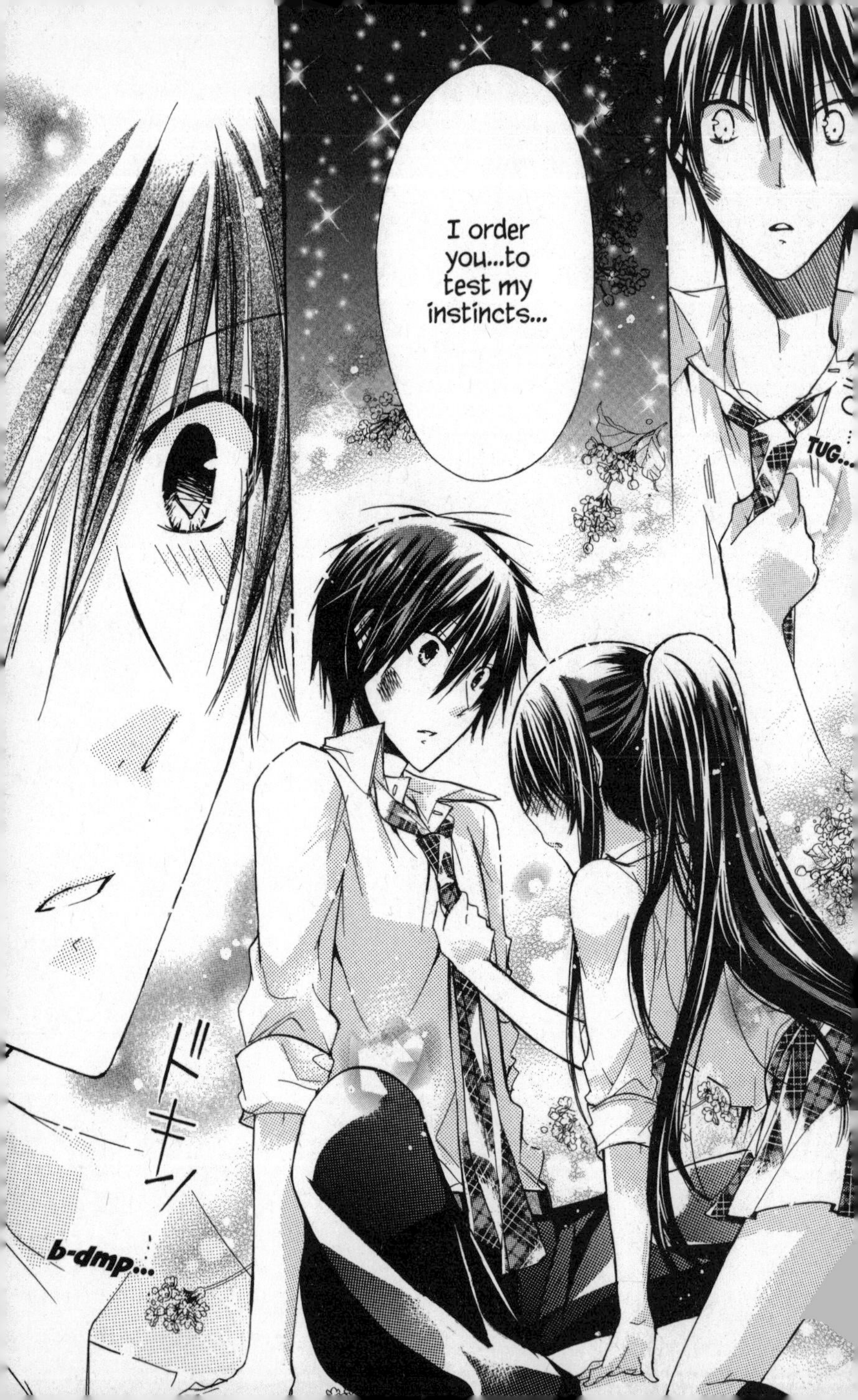
TUG...
I order you...to test my instincts...
ドキン
b-dmp...

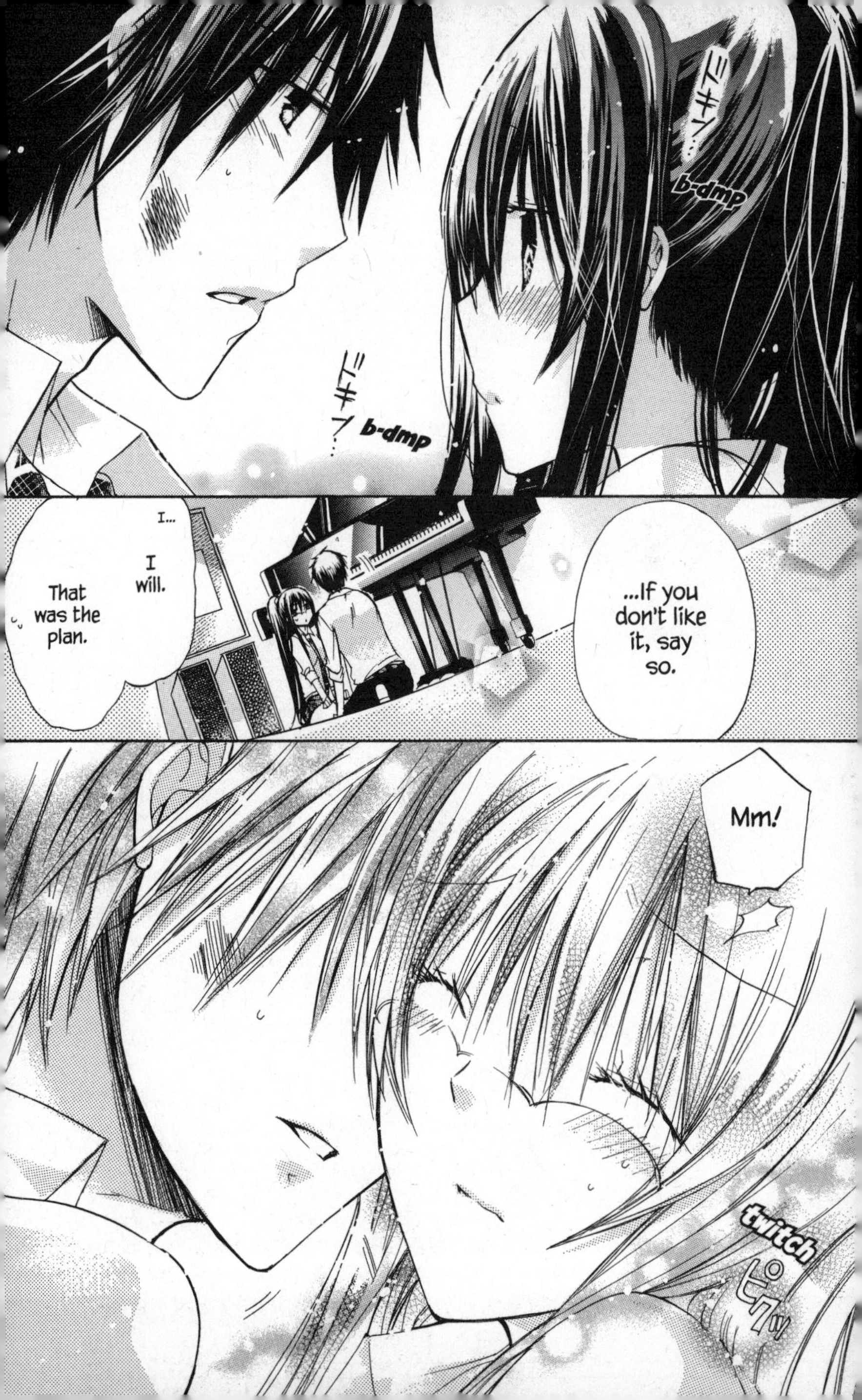
ドキン…
b-dmp
ドキン…
b-dmp
...If you don't like it, say so.
I...
I will.
That was the plan.
Mm!
twitch
ピクッ

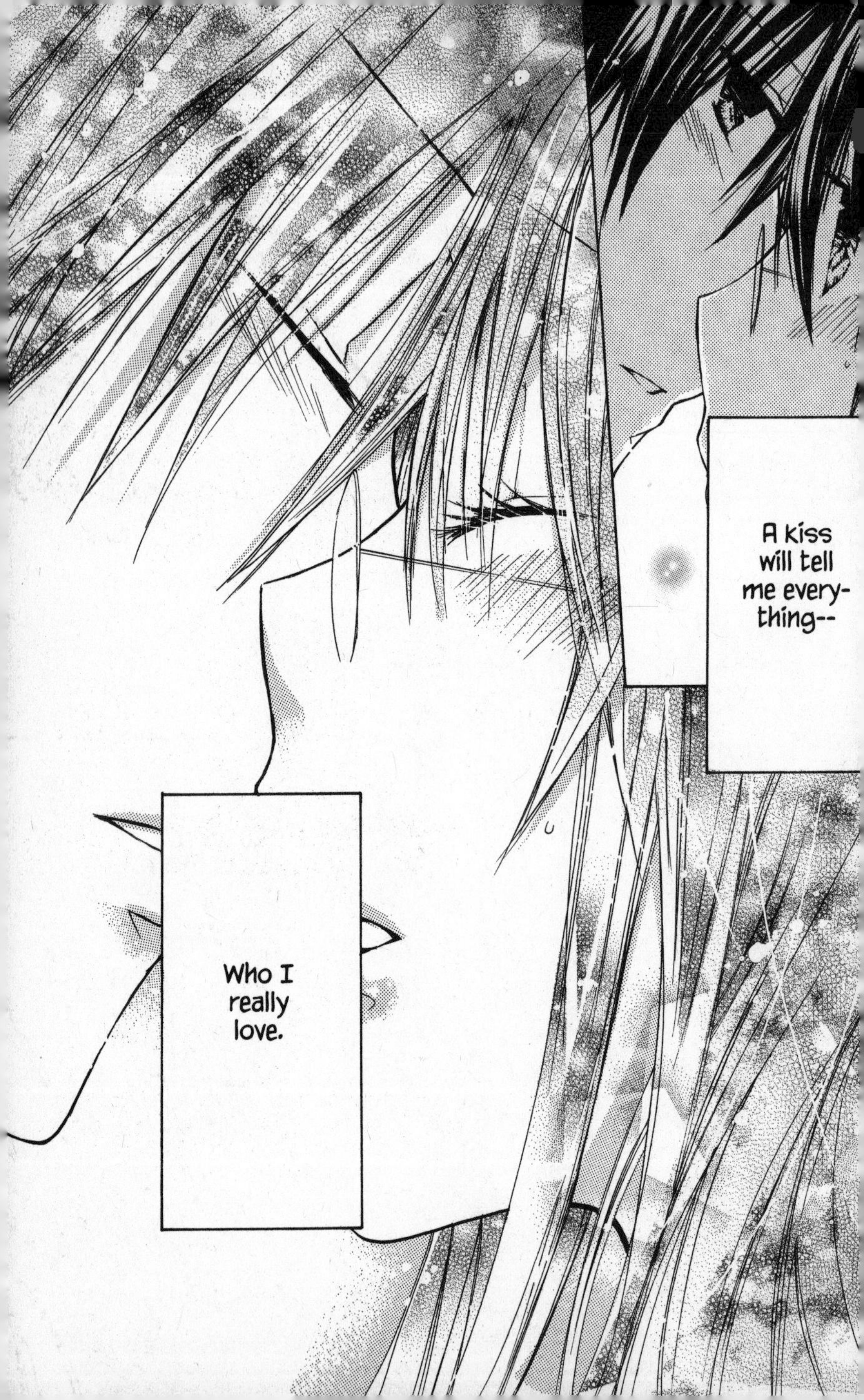
A kiss will tell me every-thing--
Who I really love.

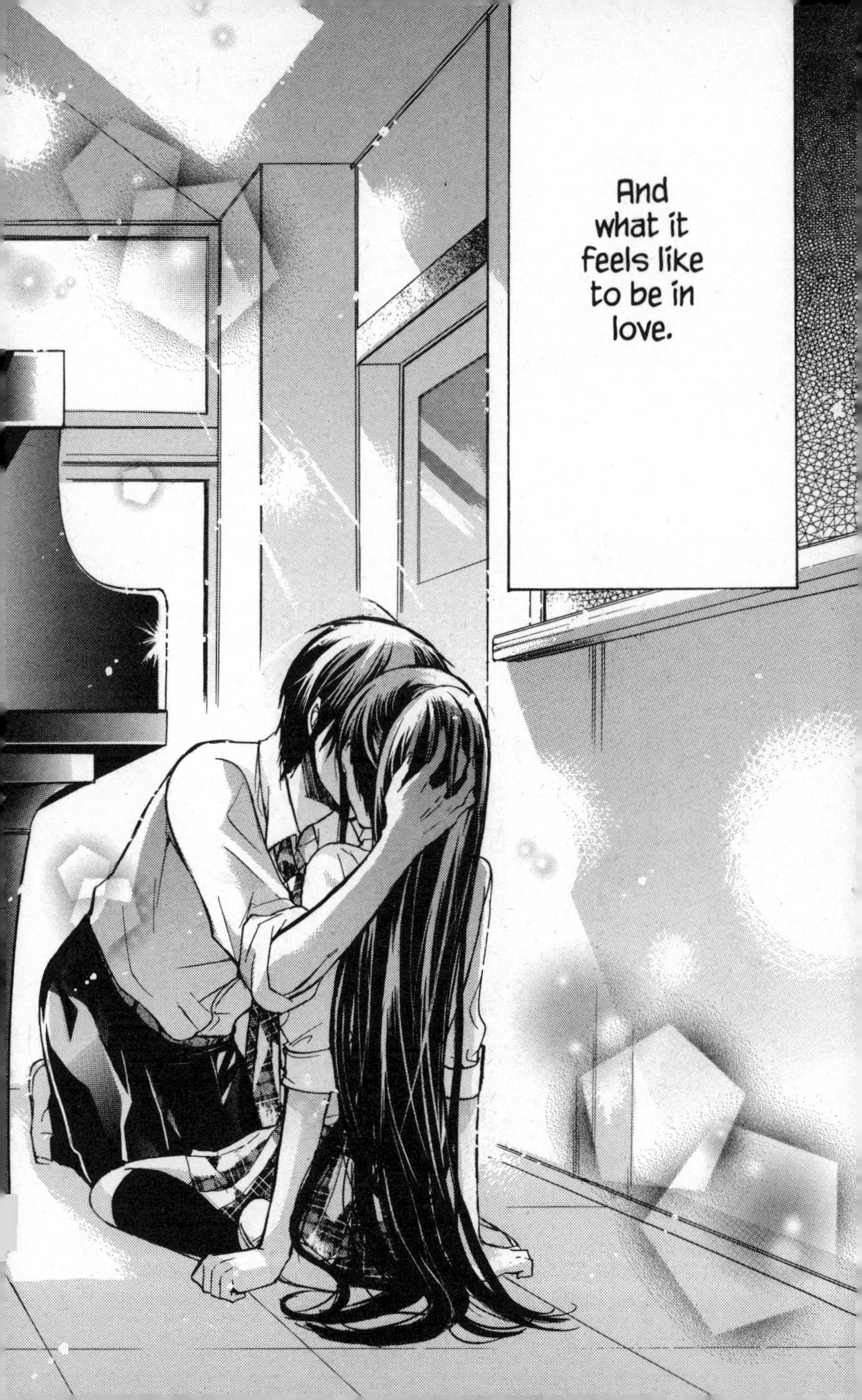
And what it feels like to be in love.

Missions of Love

**It is time for love.
Secret cell phone
novelist vs. the most
popular boy in school.
A mission of love for
absolute servitude.**

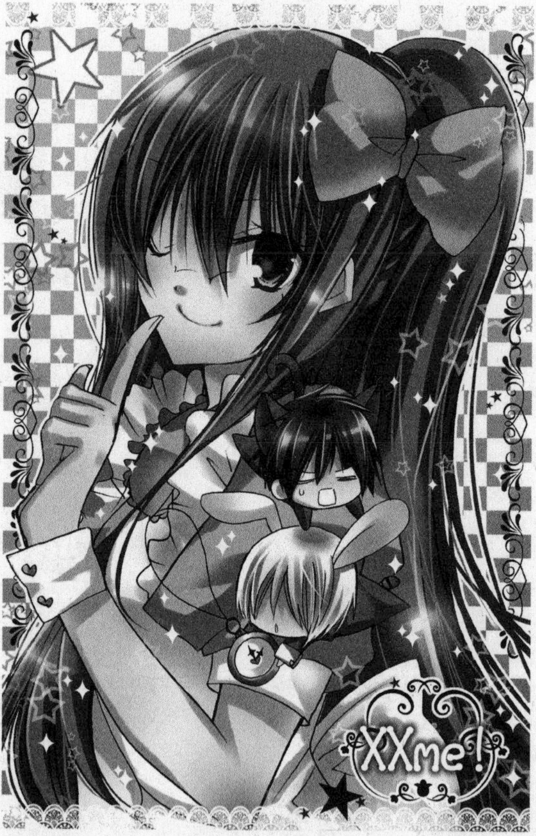
XXme!

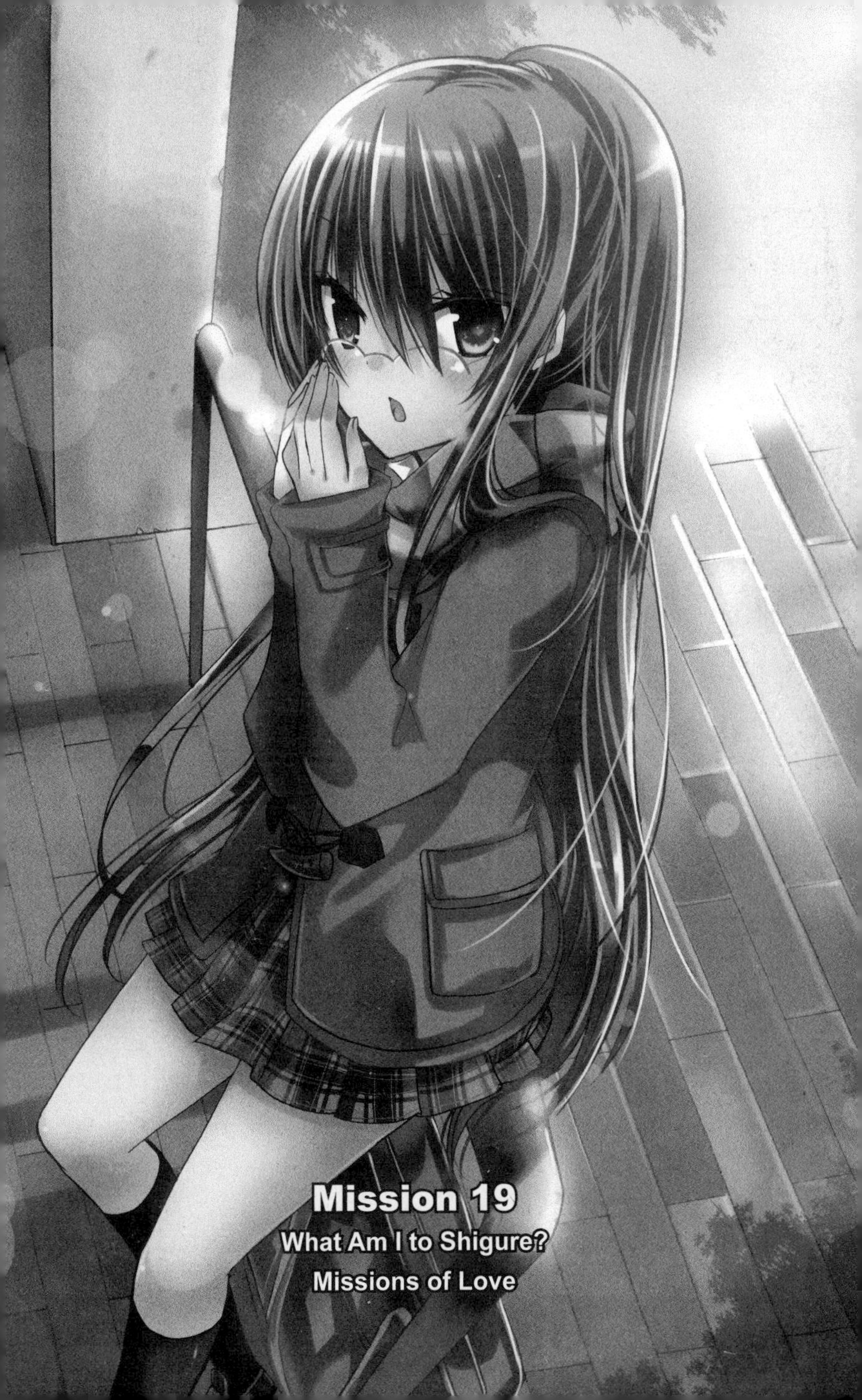
Mission 19
What Am I to Shigure?
Missions of Love

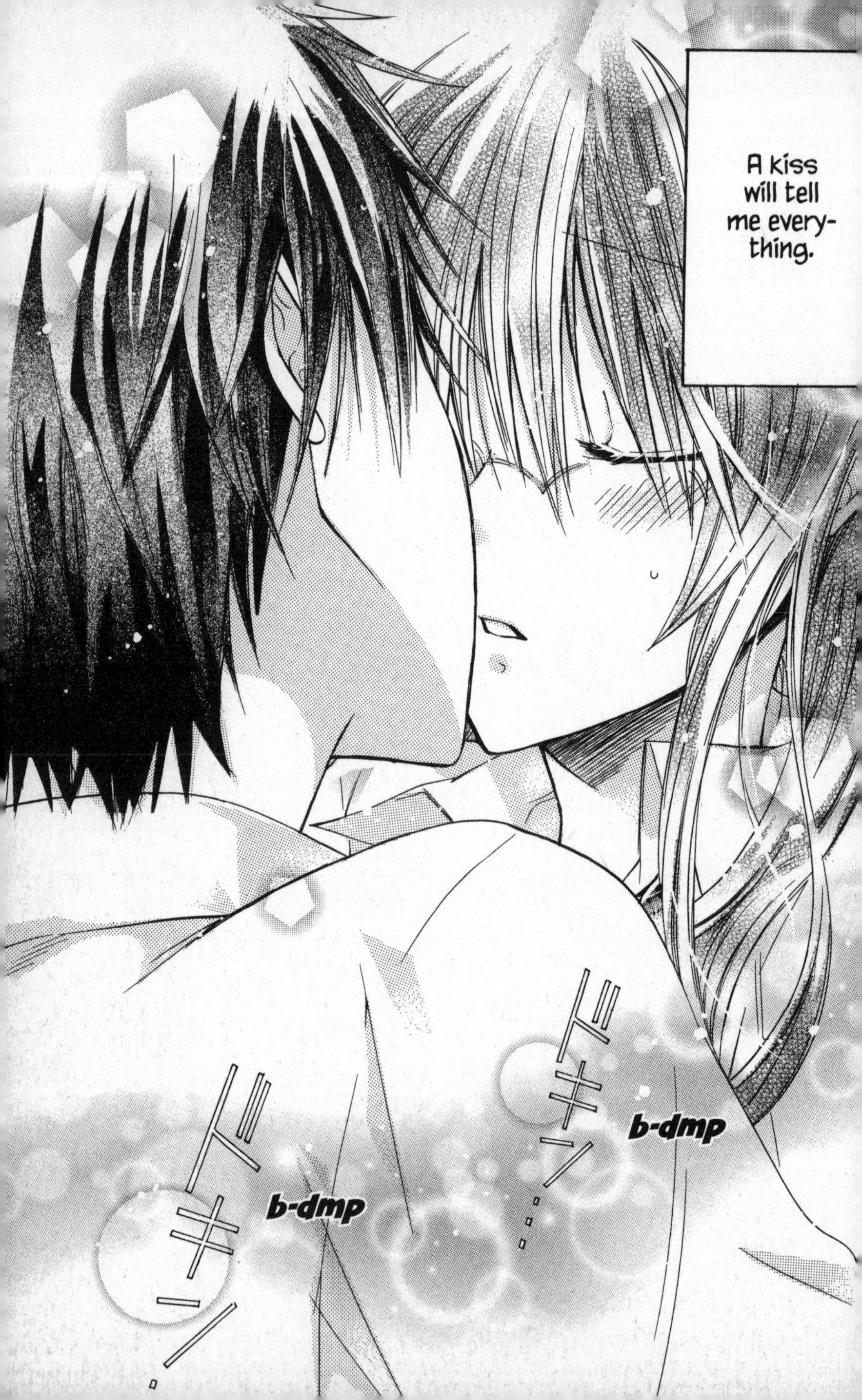
A kiss will tell me every-thing.
b-dmp
b-dmp

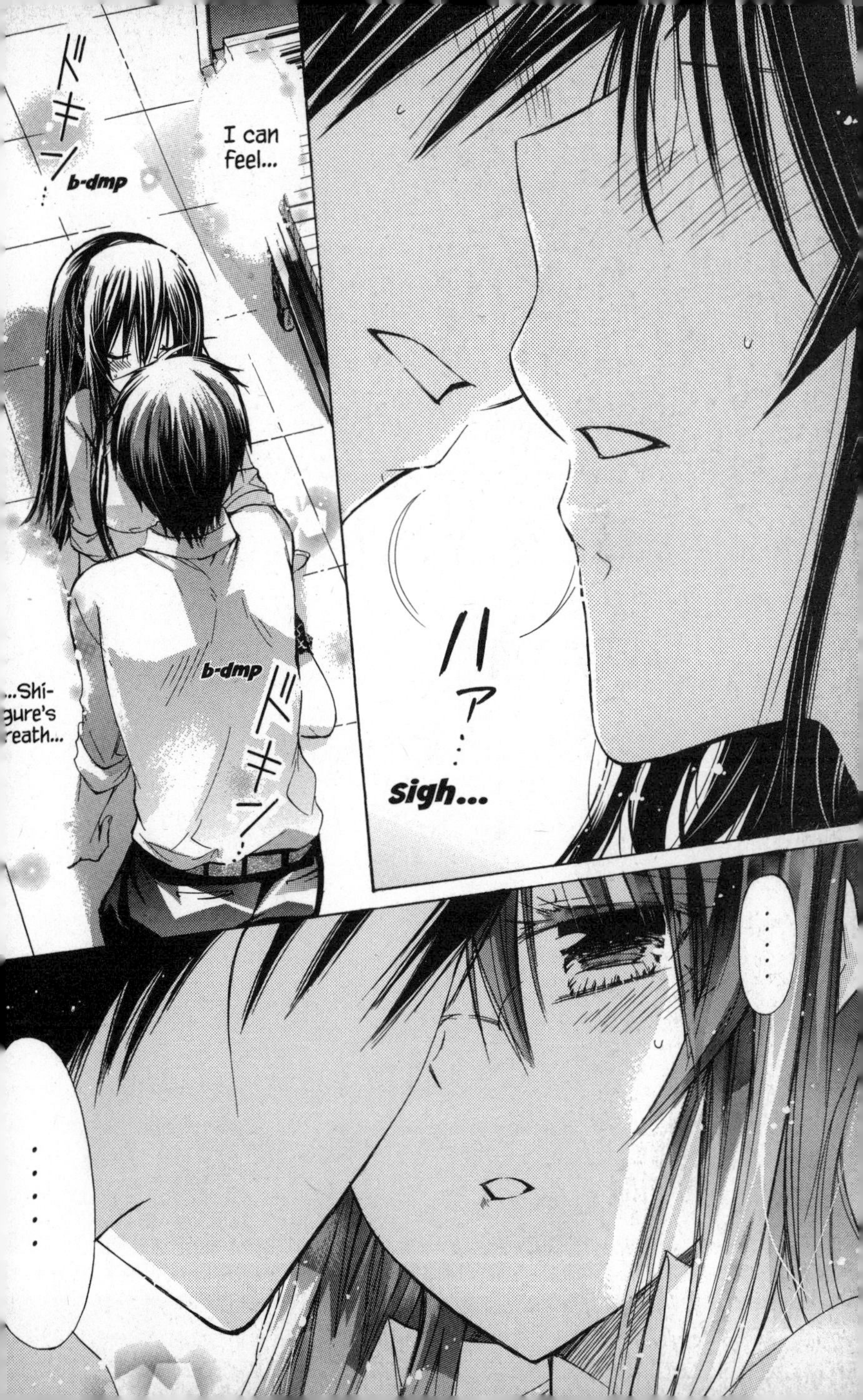
ハア…
sigh...
ドキン…
b-dmp
I can feel...
...Shi-gure's reath...
ドキン…
b-dmp
......
......

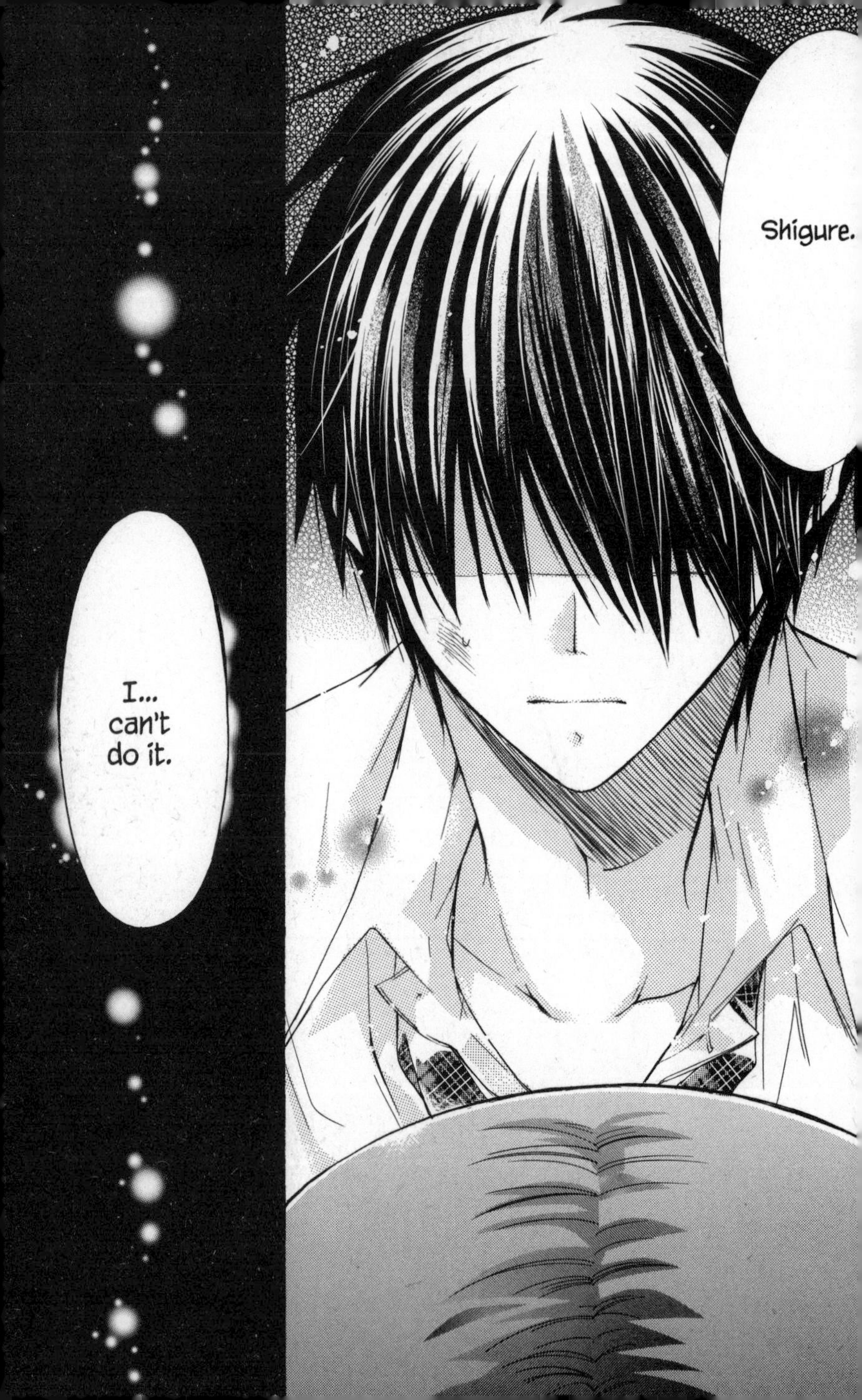
Shigure.
I... can't do it.

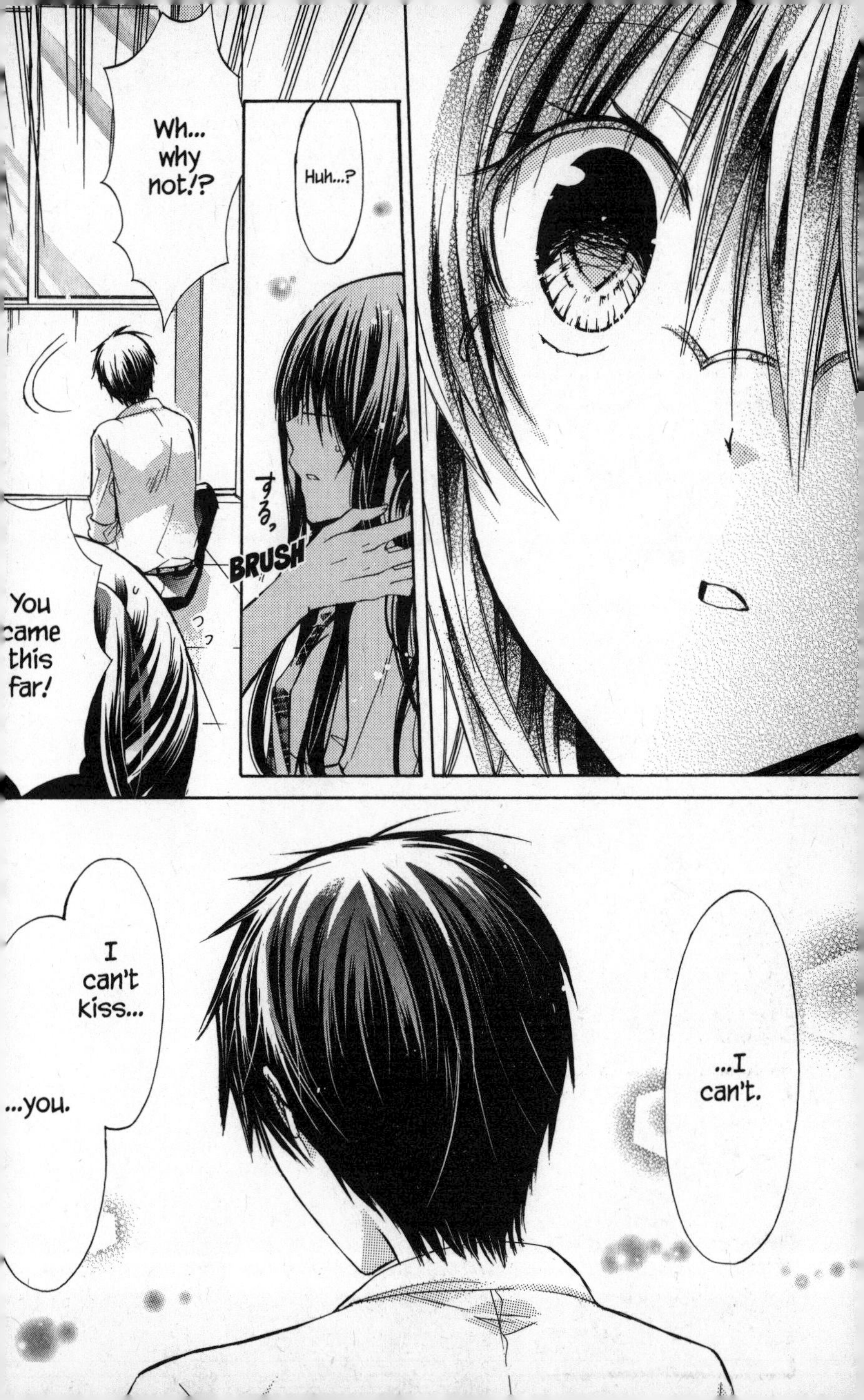

Huh...?
するっ
BRUSH
Wh... why not!?
You came this far!
...I can't.
I can't kiss...
...you.

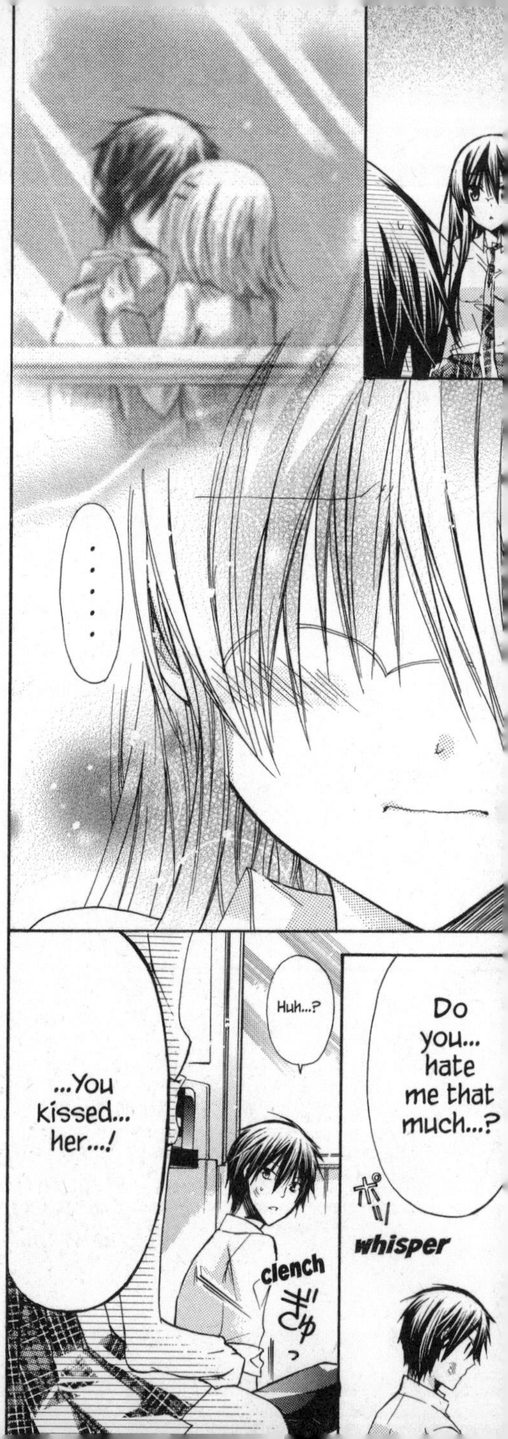
......
Do you... hate me that much...?
ポ
whisper
Huh...?
clench
ぎゅっ
...You kissed... her...!

Snow Yukina 4

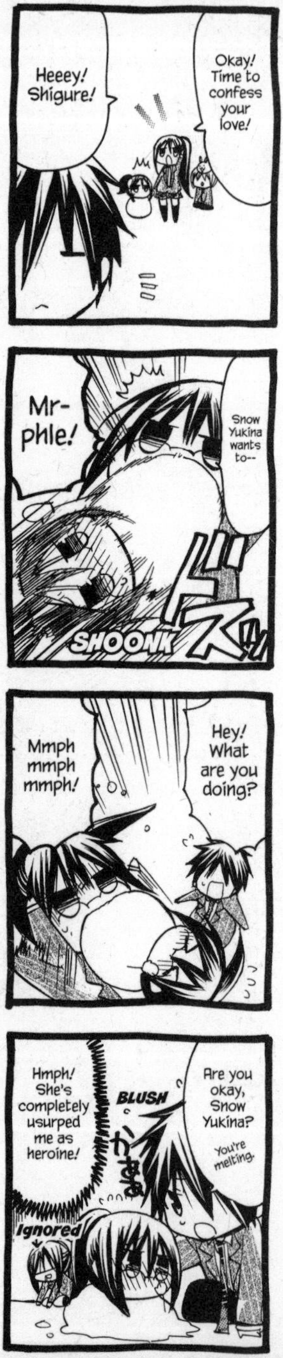
Okay! Time to confess your love!
Heeey! Shigure!
Snow Yukina wants to--
Mr-phle!
ドス!!
SHOONK
Hey! What are you doing?
Mmph mmph mmph!
Are you okay, Snow Yukina? You're melting.
BLUSH
かああ
Hmph! She's completely usurped me as heroine!
Ignored

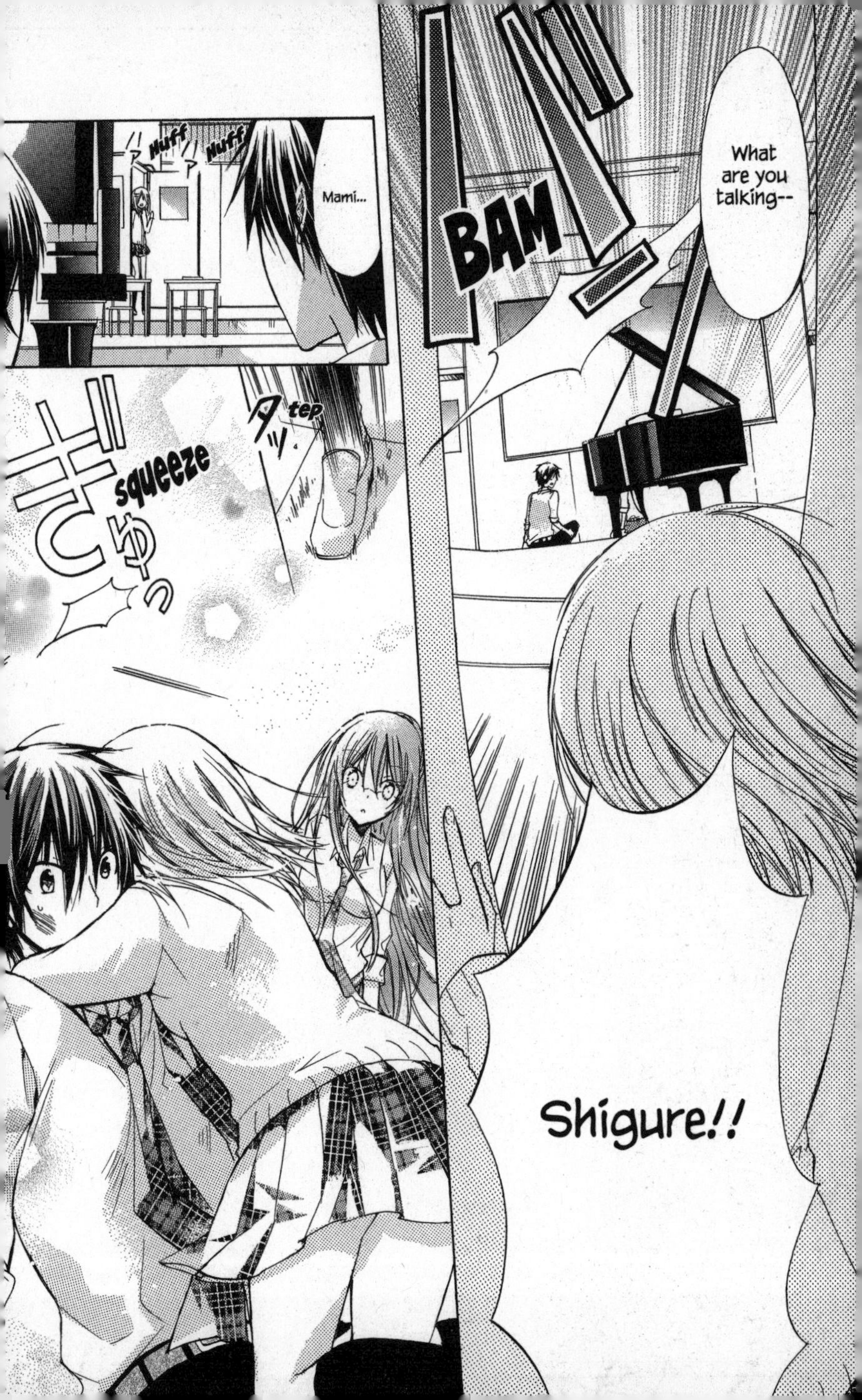

What are you talking--
BAM
Shigure!!
Huff
Huff
Mami...
タッ
tep
ぎゅっ
squeeze

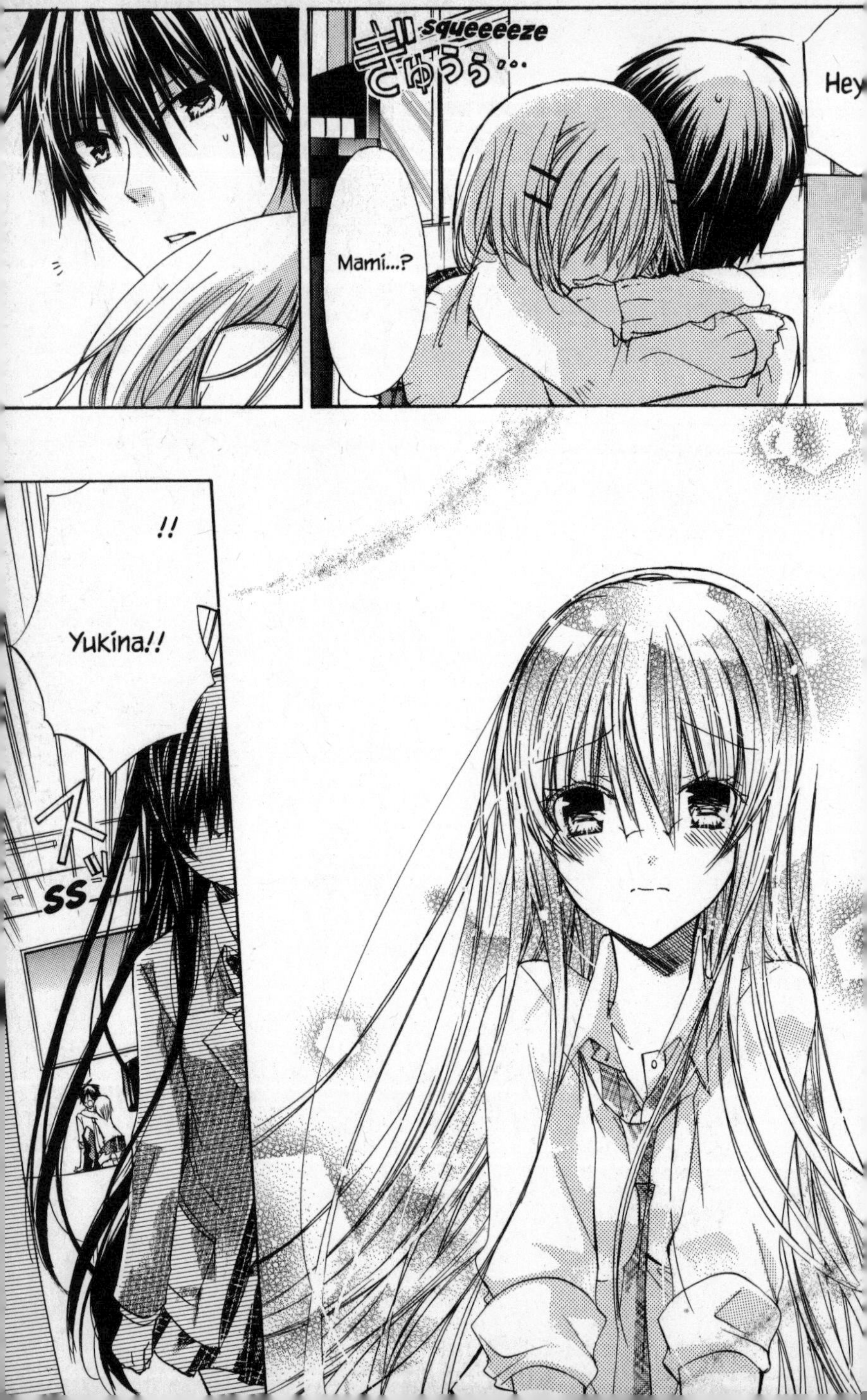

Hey
ぎゅうう…
squeeeeze
Mami...?
!!
Yukina!!
ス
SS

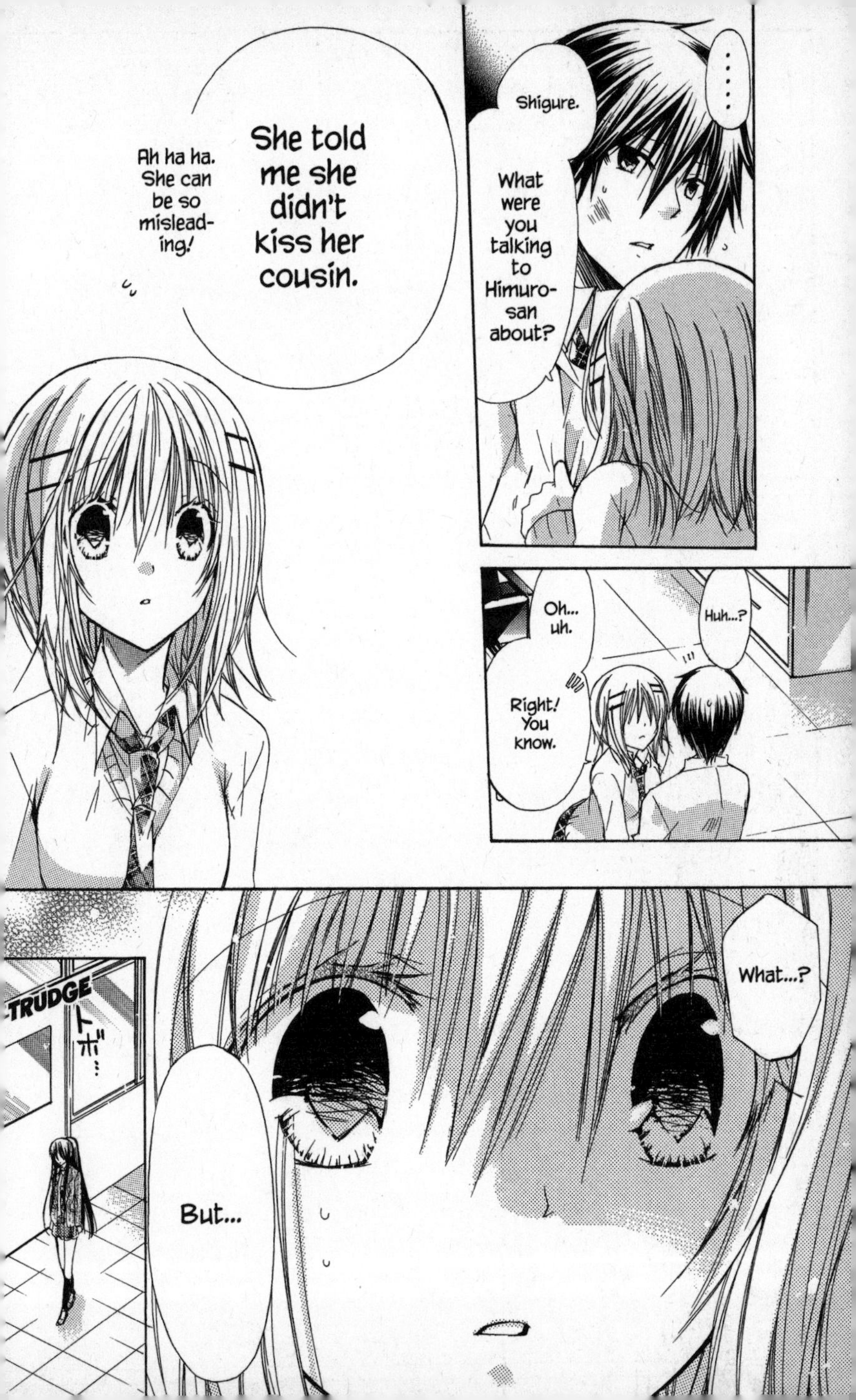
……
Shigure.
What were you talking to Himuro-san about?
Huh...?
Oh... uh.
Right! You know.
She told me she didn't kiss her cousin.
Ah ha ha. She can be so mislead-ing!
What...?
But...
TRUDGE
トボ…

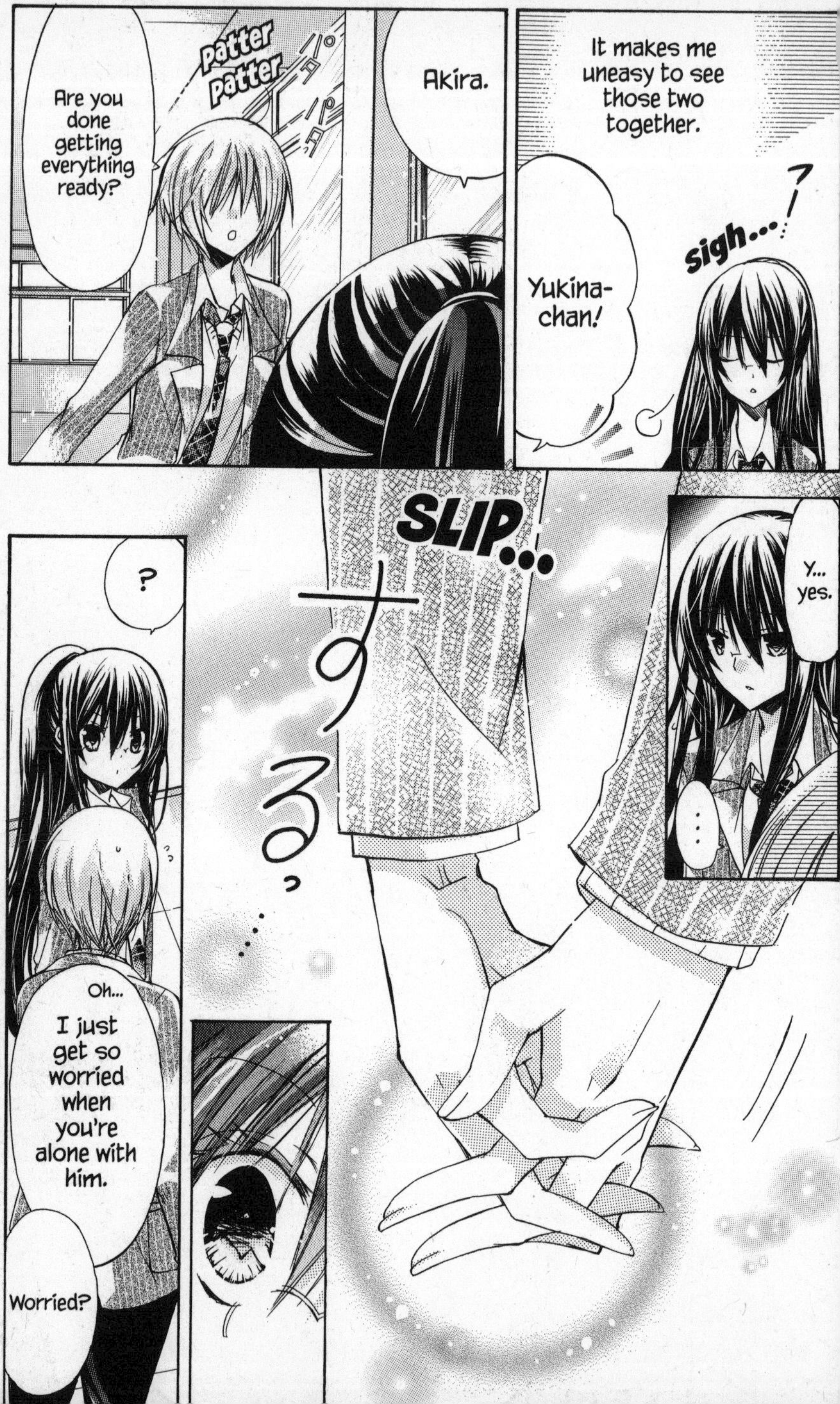
It makes me uneasy to see those two together.
Sigh...
?
Yukina-chan!
Akira.
Patter Patter
Are you done getting everything ready?
Y... yes.
...
SLIP...
?
Oh... I just get so worried when you're alone with him.
Worried?

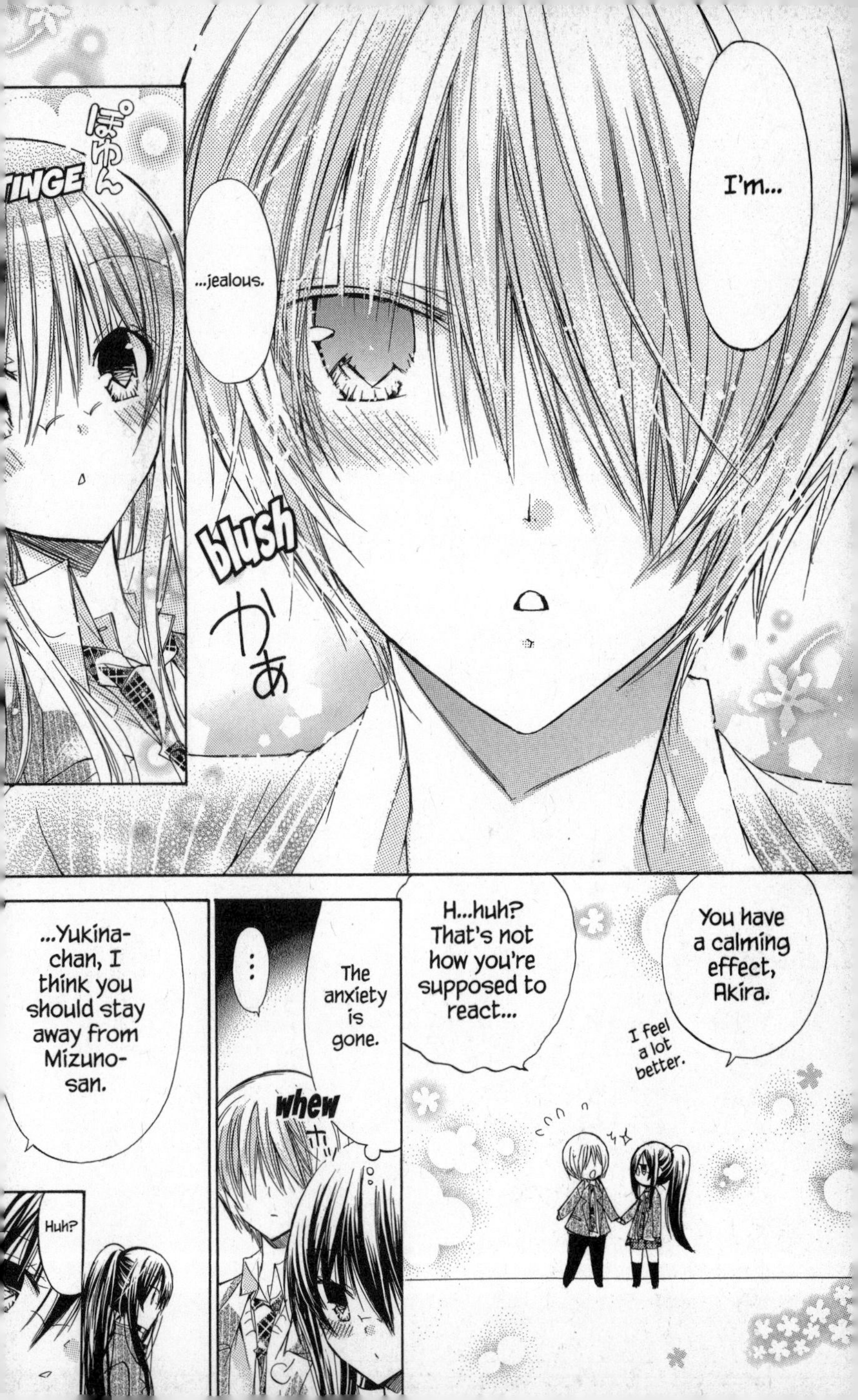

I'm...
...jealous.
blush
かあ
ぽゆん
TINGE
You have a calming effect, Akira.
I feel a lot better.
H...huh? That's not how you're supposed to react...
The anxiety is gone.
...
whew
ホッ
...Yukina-chan, I think you should stay away from Mizuno-san.
Huh?

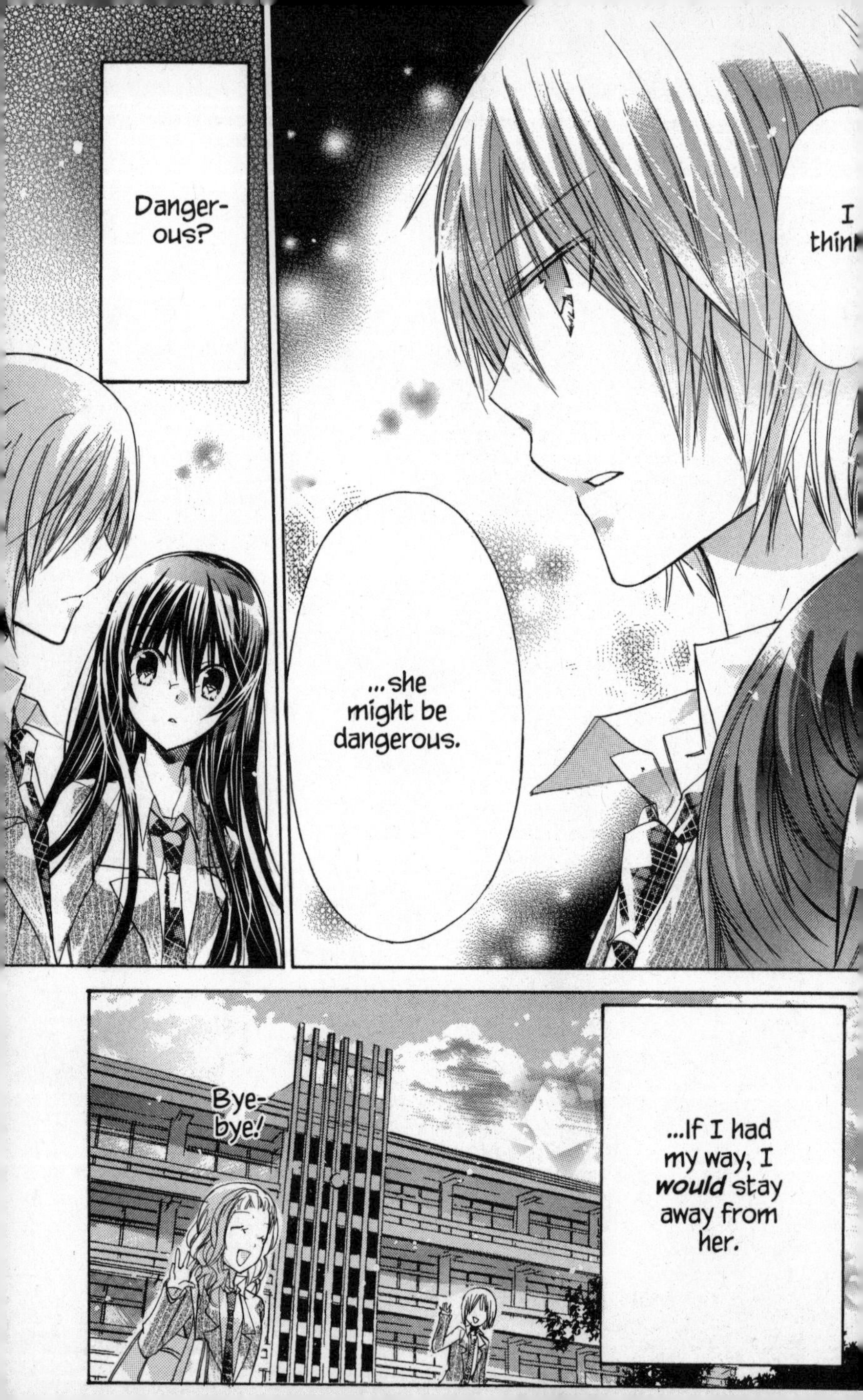
I thin
...she might be dangerous.
Danger-ous?
...If I had my way, I *would* stay away from her.
Bye-bye!

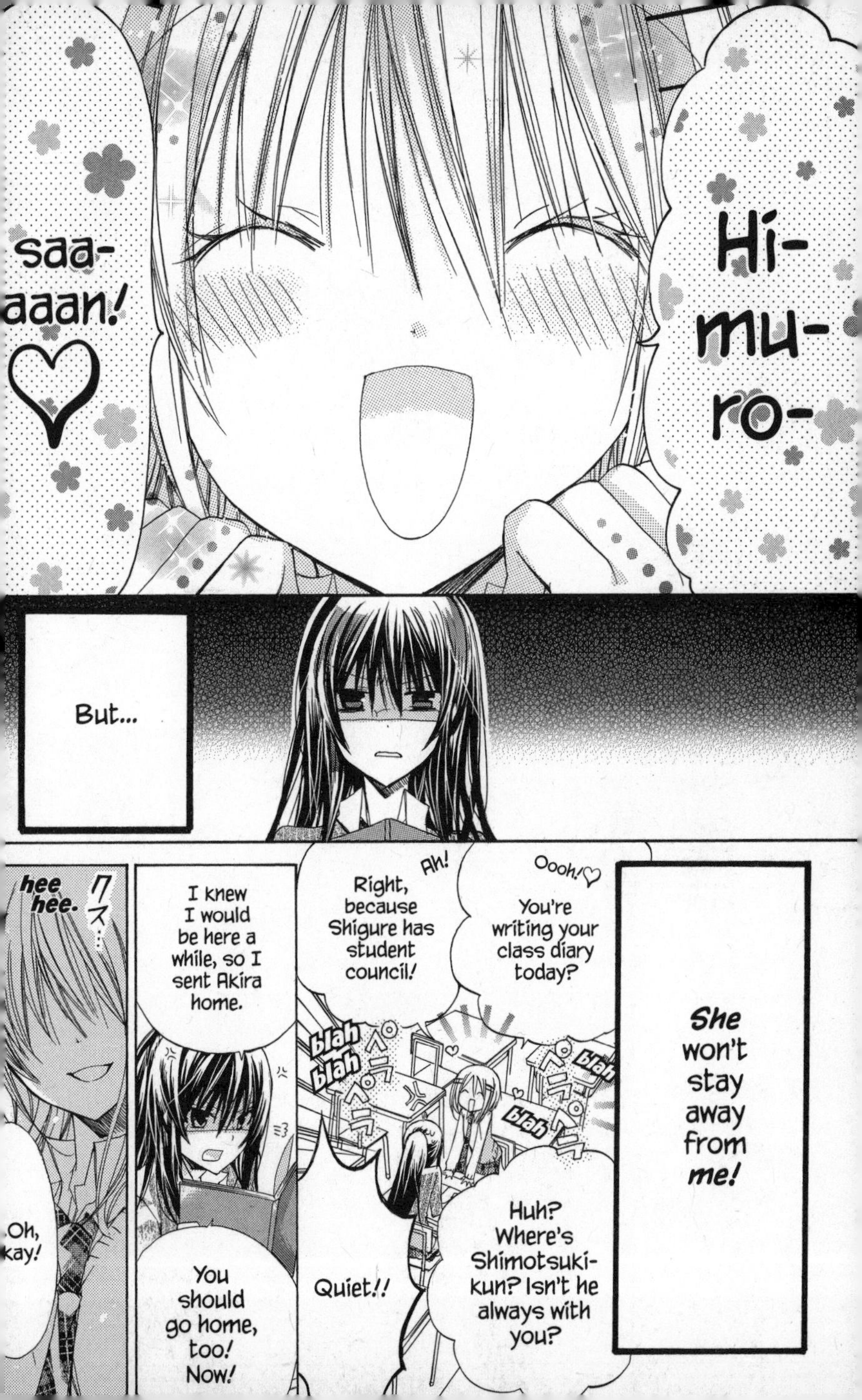

Hi-mu-ro-
saaa-aaan! ♥
But...
She won't stay away from me!
Oooh! ♡
You're writing your class diary today?
Ah!
Right, because Shigure has student council!
blah blah
blah
blah
Huh? Where's Shimotsuki-kun? Isn't he always with you?
Quiet!!
I knew I would be here a while, so I sent Akira home.
You should go home, too! Now!
hee hee.
クス…
Oh, kay!

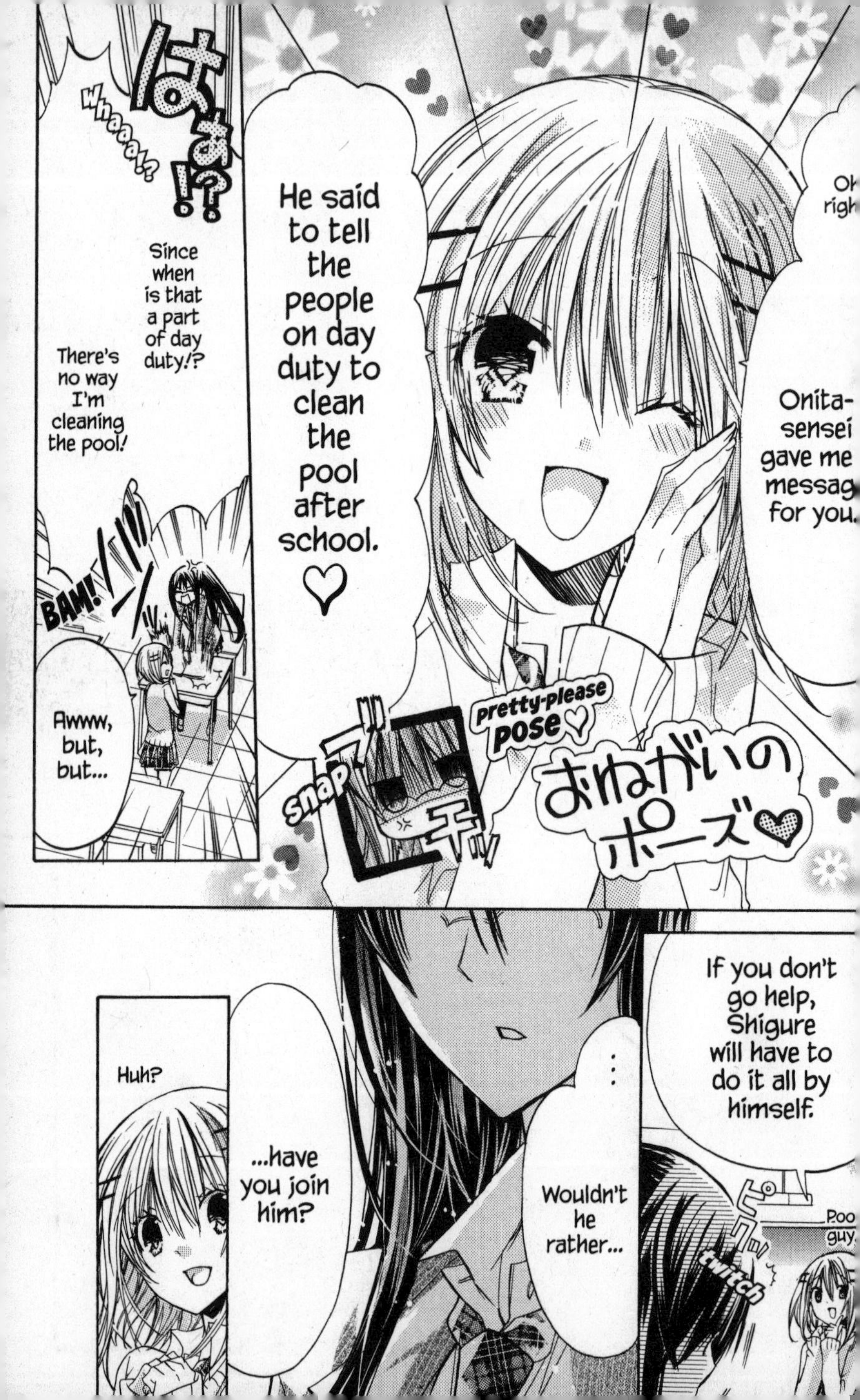

Oh righ
Onita-sensei gave me messag for you.
He said to tell the people on day duty to clean the pool after school. ♡
pretty-please POSE♡
おねがいのポーズ♥
snap
ブチッ
はあ!?
Whaaaa!?
Since when is that a part of day duty!?
There's no way I'm cleaning the pool!
BAM!
Awww, but, but...
If you don't go help, Shigure will have to do it all by himself.
ピクッ
twitch
Poo guy.
...
Wouldn't he rather...
...have you join him?
Huh?

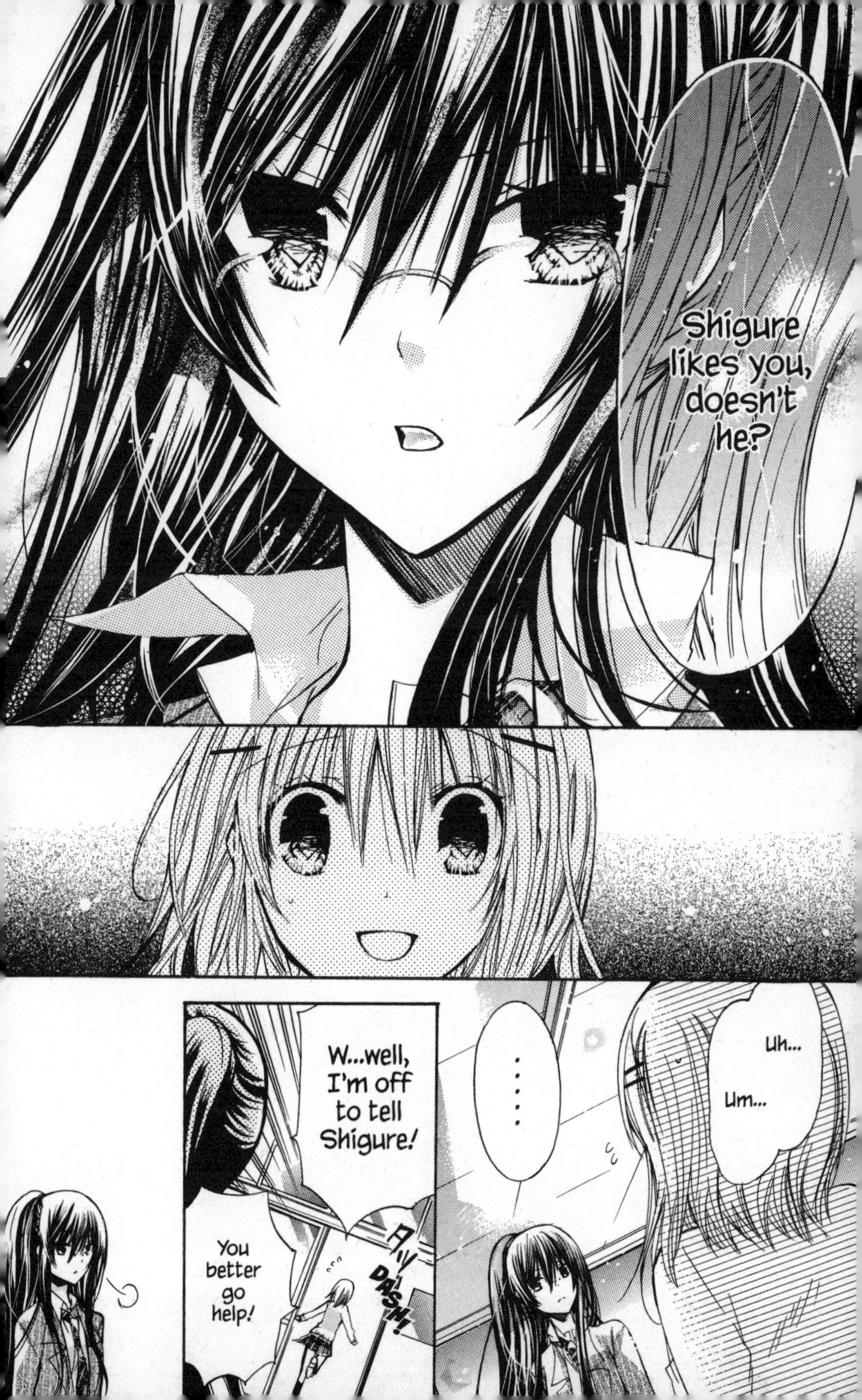
Shigure likes you, doesn't he?
Uh...
Um...
......
W...well, I'm off to tell Shigure!
DASH!
You better go help!

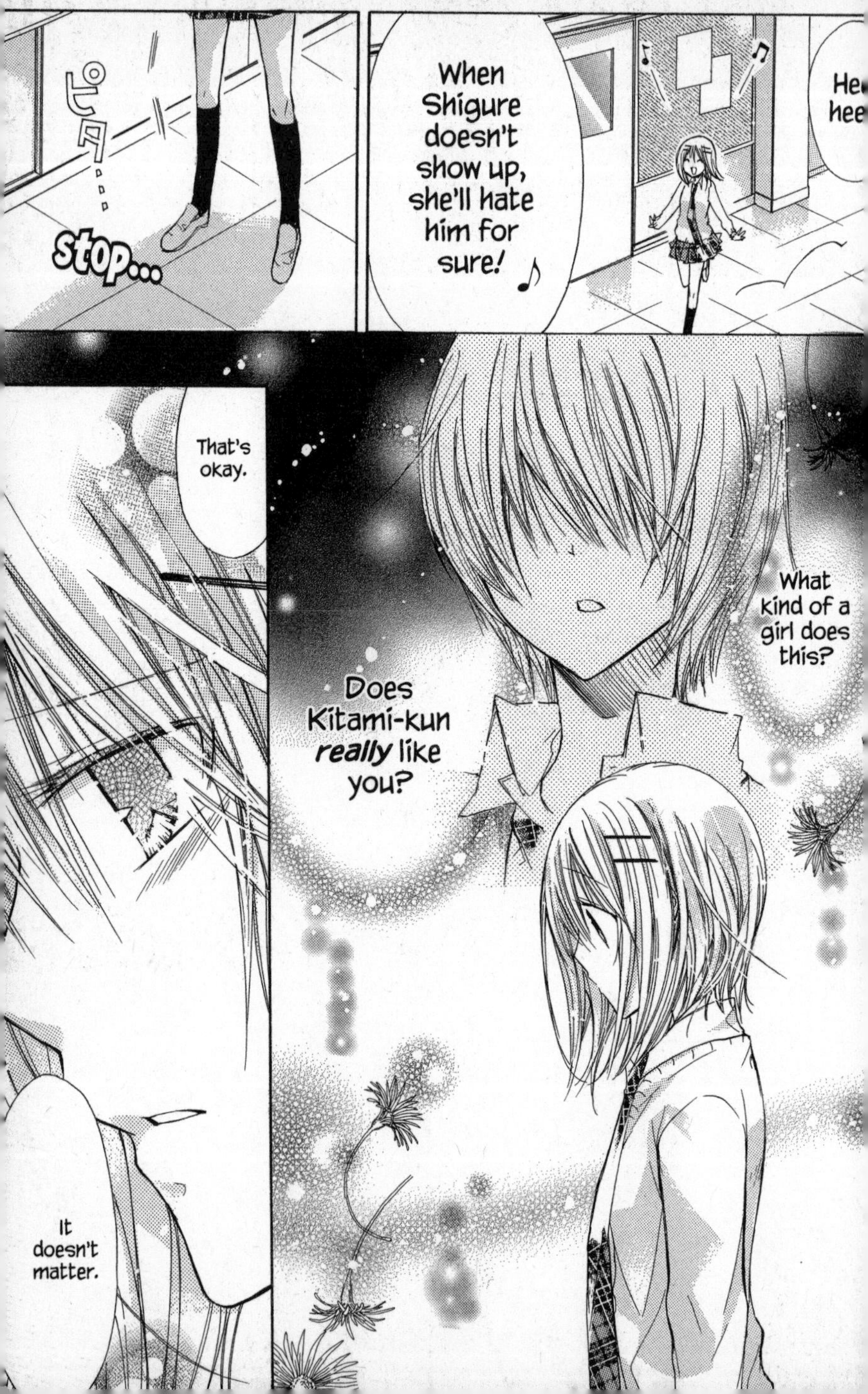
He hee
When Shigure doesn't show up, she'll hate him for sure! ♪
ピタ
stop...
What kind of a girl does this?
Does Kitami-kun *really* like you?
That's okay.
It doesn't matter.

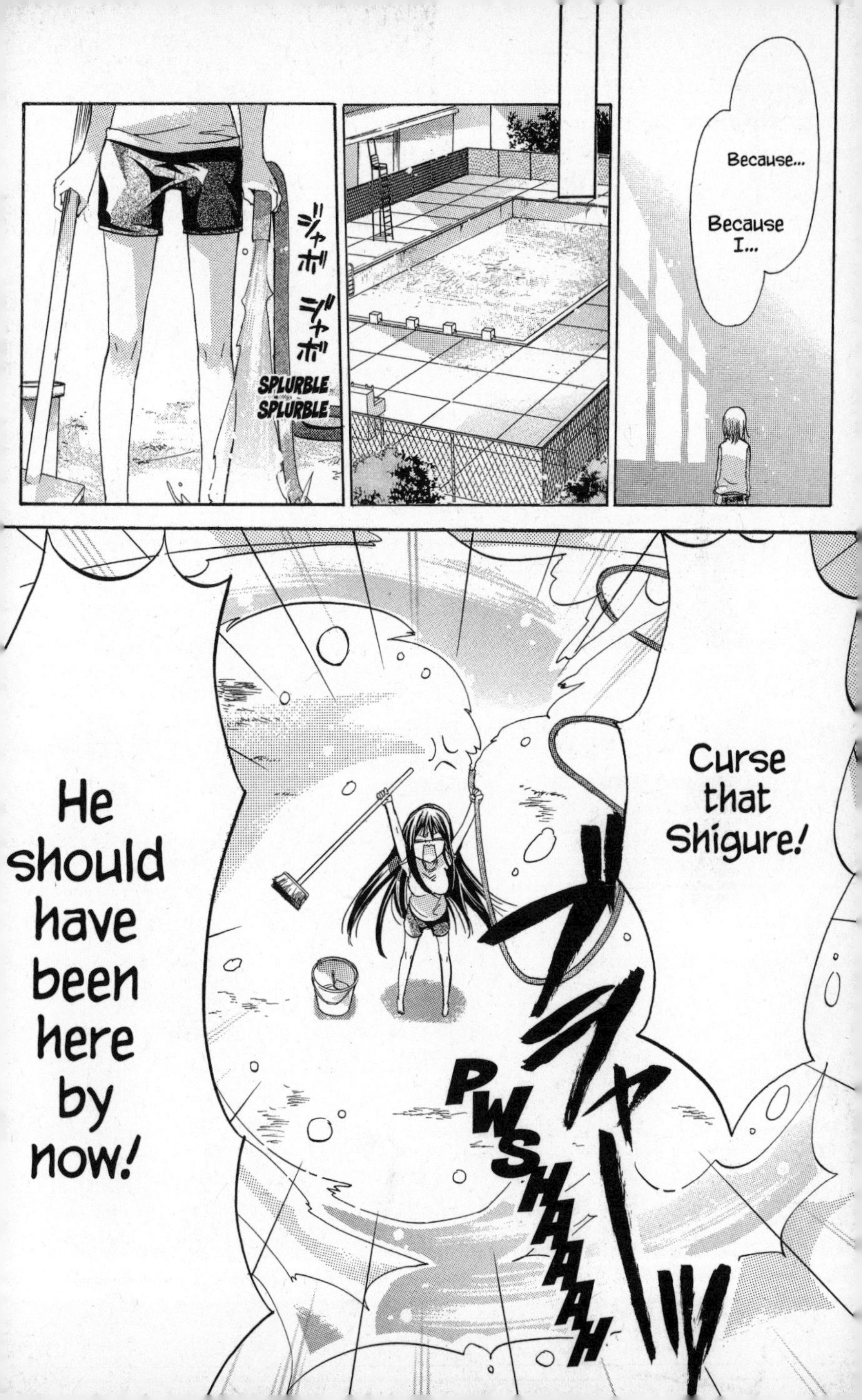
Because...
Because I...
ジャボ ジャボ
SPLURBLE SPLURBLE
Curse that Shigure!
PWSHAAAAH
He should have been here by now!

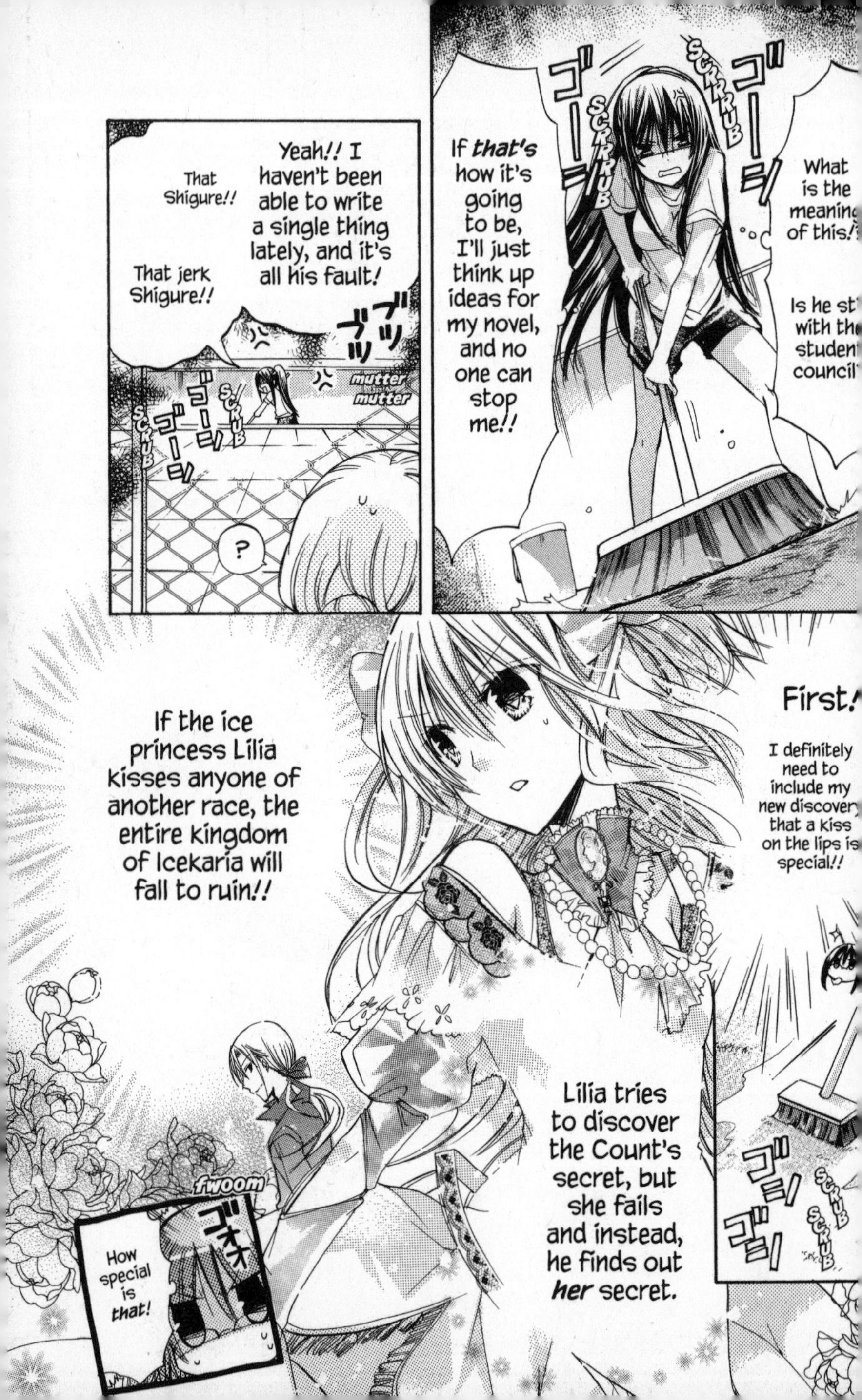
What is the meanin of this!?
SCRRRUB SCRRRUB
ゴーッ ゴーッ
Is he st with th studen council
If *that's* how it's going to be, I'll just think up ideas for my novel, and no one can stop me!!
Yeah!! I haven't been able to write a single thing lately, and it's all his fault!
That Shigure!!
That jerk Shigure!!
ブツブツ
mutter mutter
SCRUB SCRUB
ゴーッゴーッ
?
First!
I definitely need to include my new discover that a kiss on the lips is special!!
ゴシゴシ
SCRUB SCRUB
If the ice princess Lilia kisses anyone of another race, the entire kingdom of Icekaria will fall to ruin!!
Lilia tries to discover the Count's secret, but she fails and instead, he finds out *her* secret.
fwoom
ゴオオ
How special is *that!*

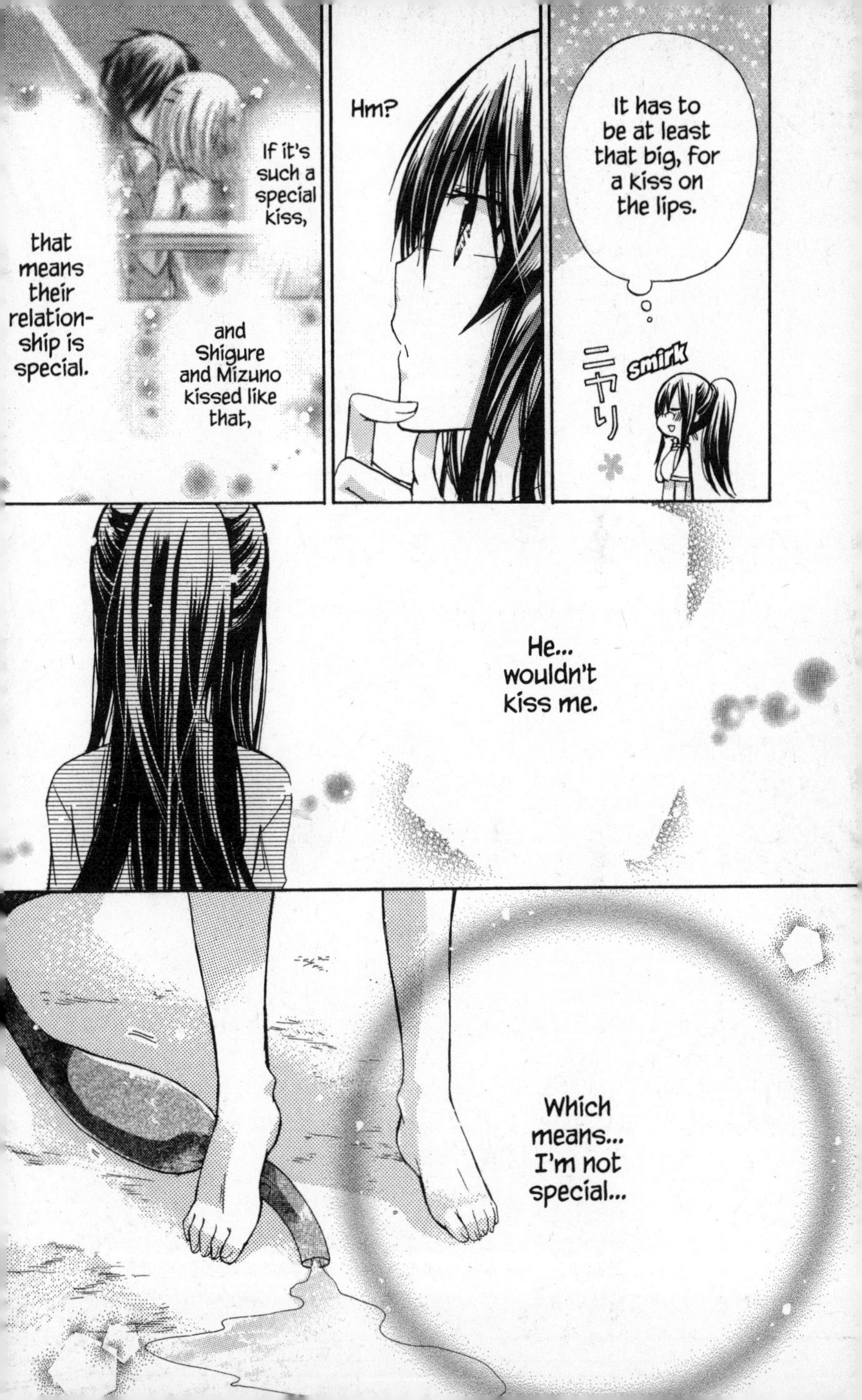

It has to be at least that big, for a kiss on the lips.
ニヤリ
smirk
Hm?
If it's such a special kiss,
and Shigure and Mizuno kissed like that,
that means their relationship is special.
He... wouldn't kiss me.
Which means... I'm not special...

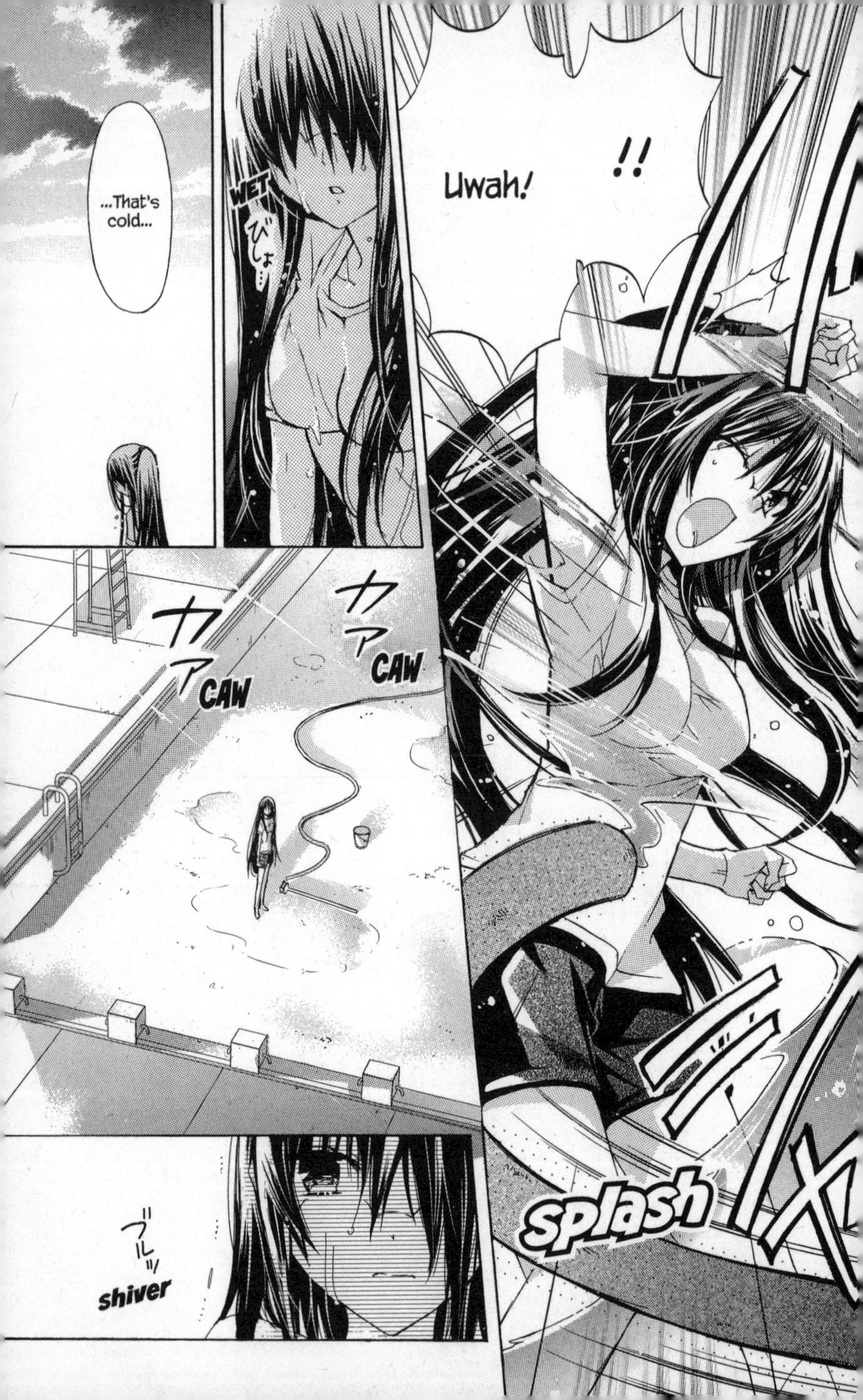

!!
Uwah!
splash
WET
びしょ…
...That's cold...
カァ
CAW
カァ
CAW
ブルッ
shiver

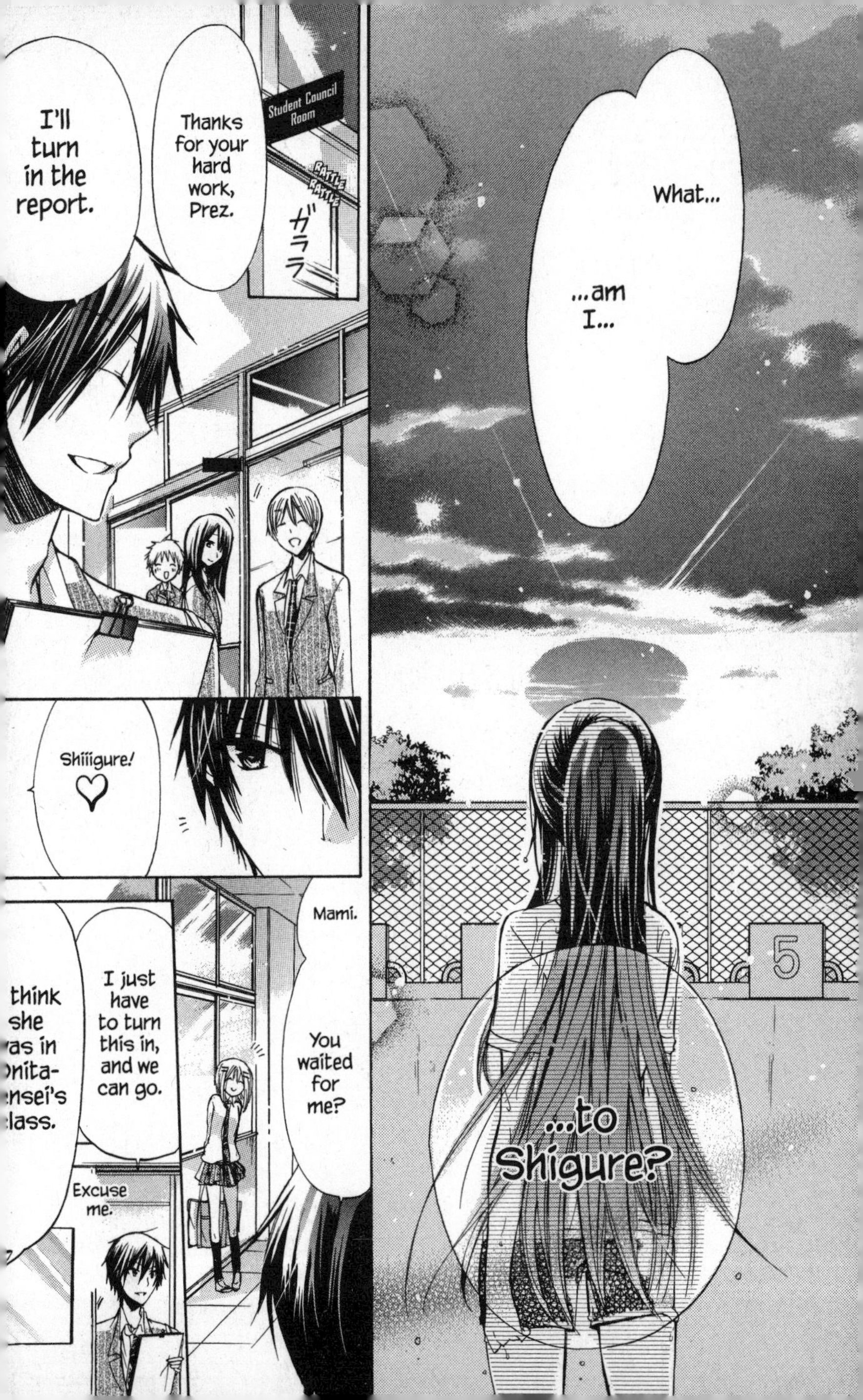
What...
...am I...
...to Shigure?
Student Council Room
RATTLE RATTLE
ガラ ラ
Thanks for your hard work, Prez.
I'll turn in the report.
Shiiigure! ♡
Mami.
You waited for me?
I just have to turn this in, and we can go.
think she vas in onita-ensei's class.
Excuse me.

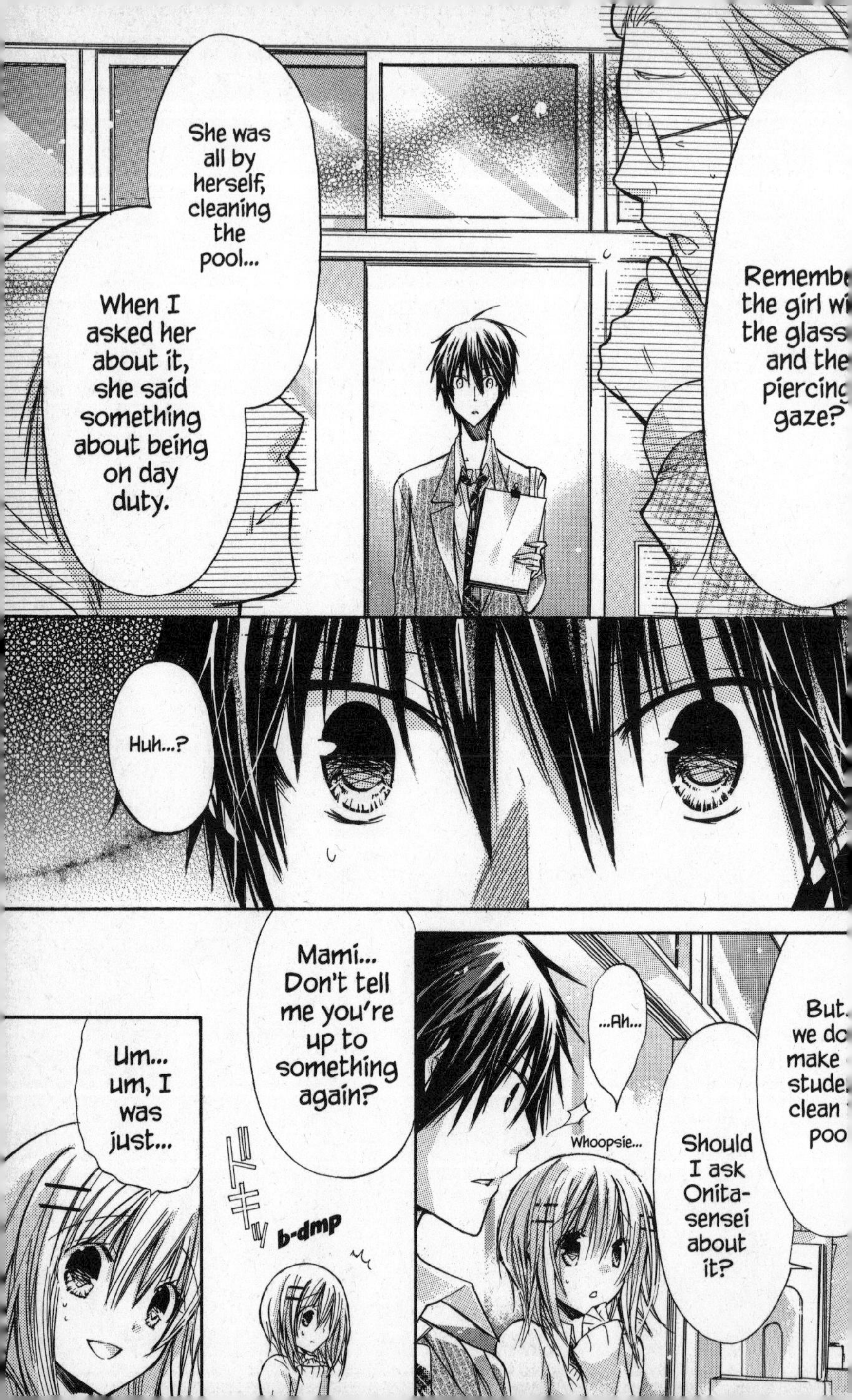
Rememb the girl wi the glass and the piercing gaze?
She was all by herself, cleaning the pool...
When I asked her about it, she said something about being on day duty.
Huh...?
But. we do make stude clean poo
Should I ask Onita-sensei about it?
...Ah...
Whoopsie...
Mami... Don't tell me you're up to something again?
b-dmp
Um... um, I was just...

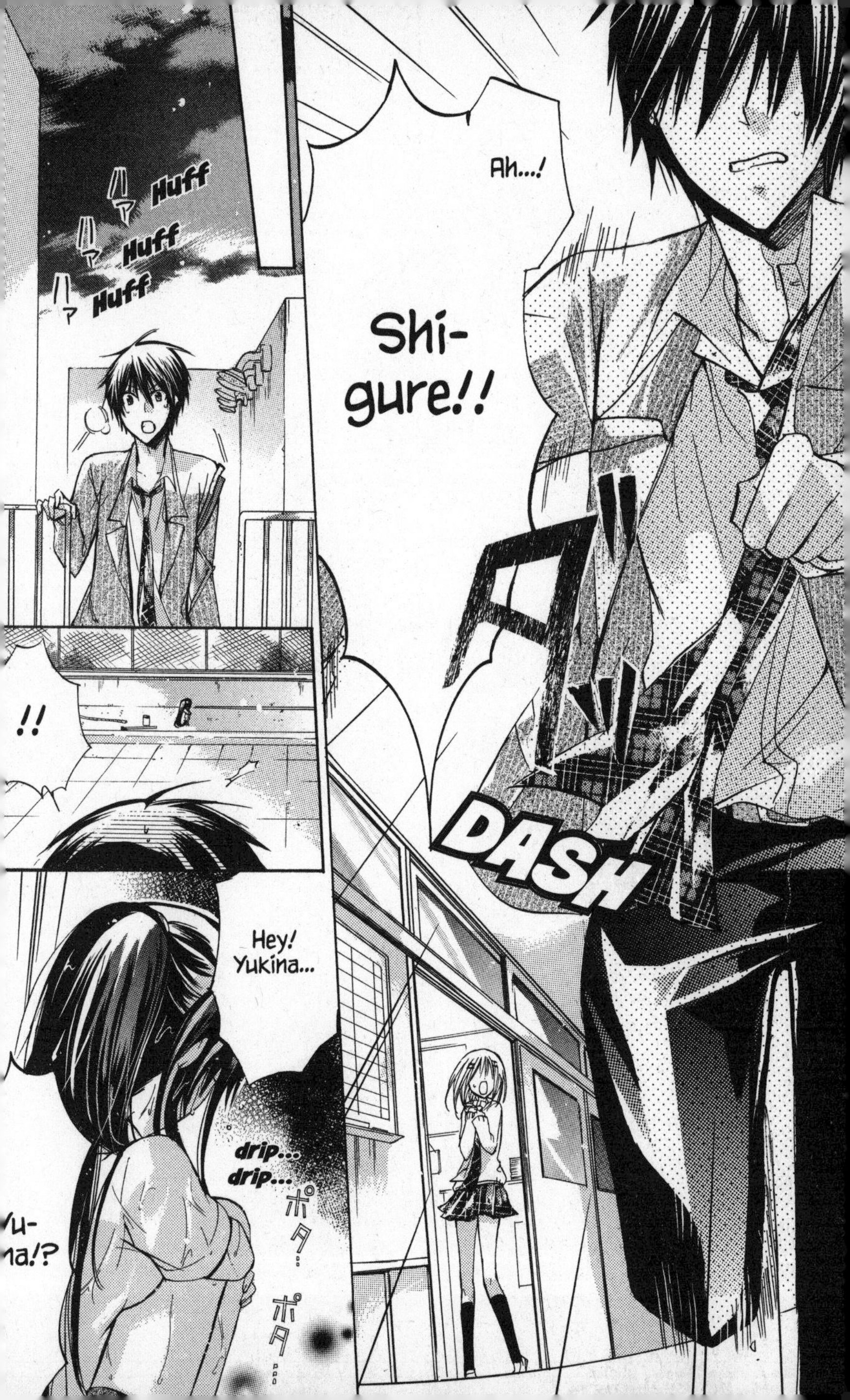

Ah...!
Shi-gure!!
DASH
ハァ Huff
ハァ Huff
ハァ Huff
!!
Hey! Yukina...
drip... drip...
ポタ
ポタ
Yu-
na!?

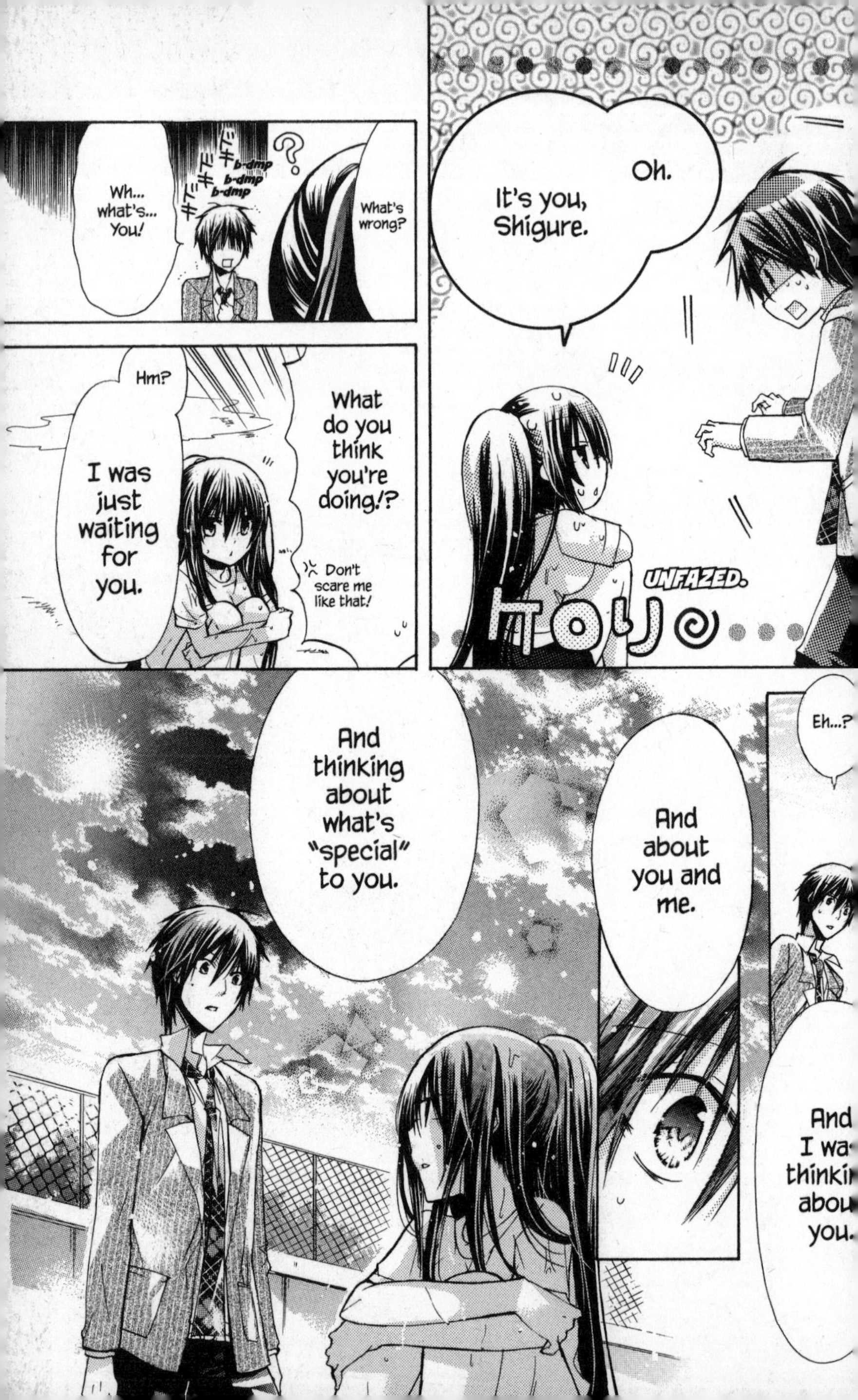
Oh.
It's you, Shigure.
UNFAZED.
What's wrong?
b-dmp b-dmp b-dmp
Wh... what's... You!
What do you think you're doing!?
Don't scare me like that!
Hm?
I was just waiting for you.
Eh...?
And I wa thinki abou you.
And about you and me.
And thinking about what's "special" to you.

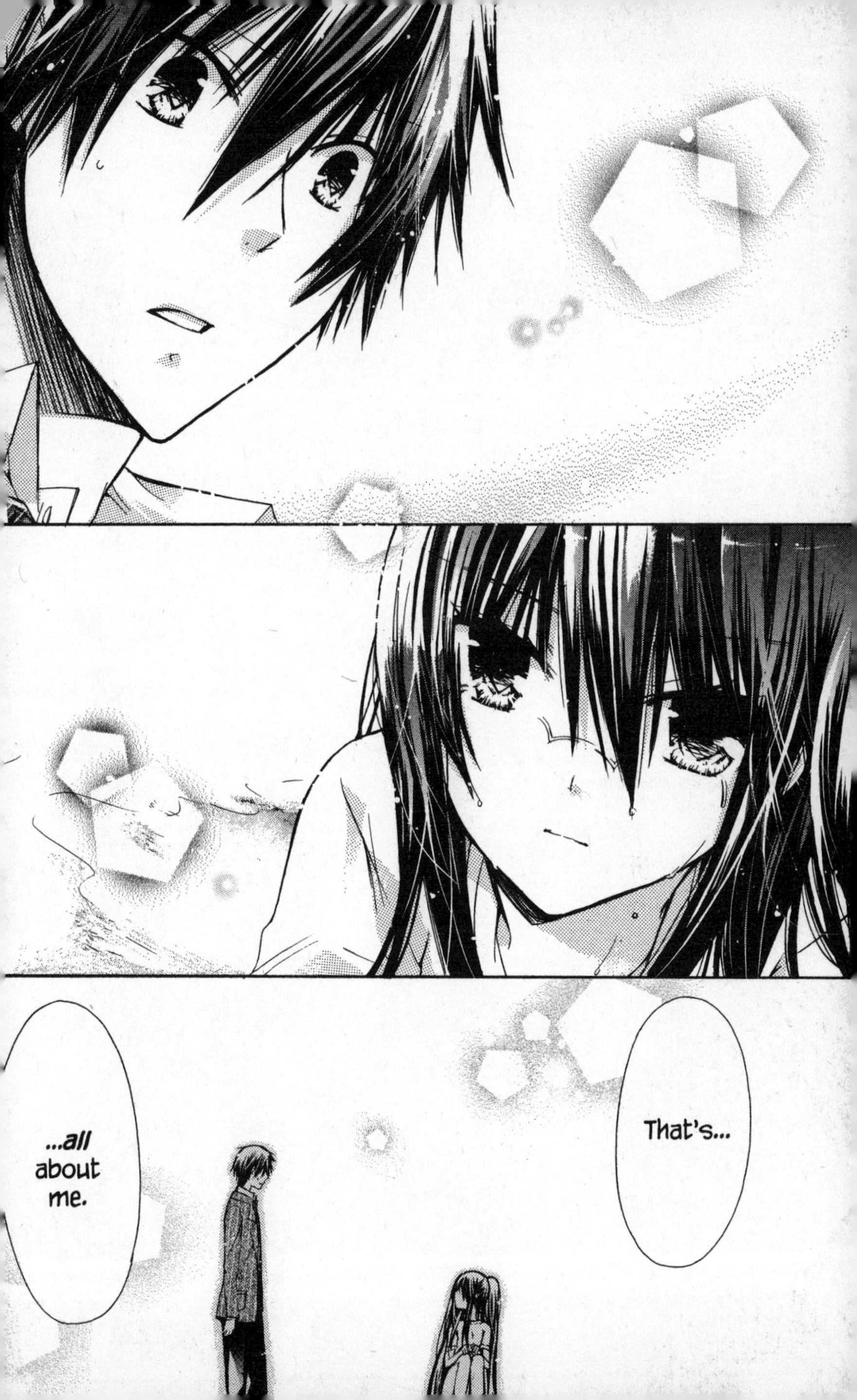
That's...
...*all* about me.

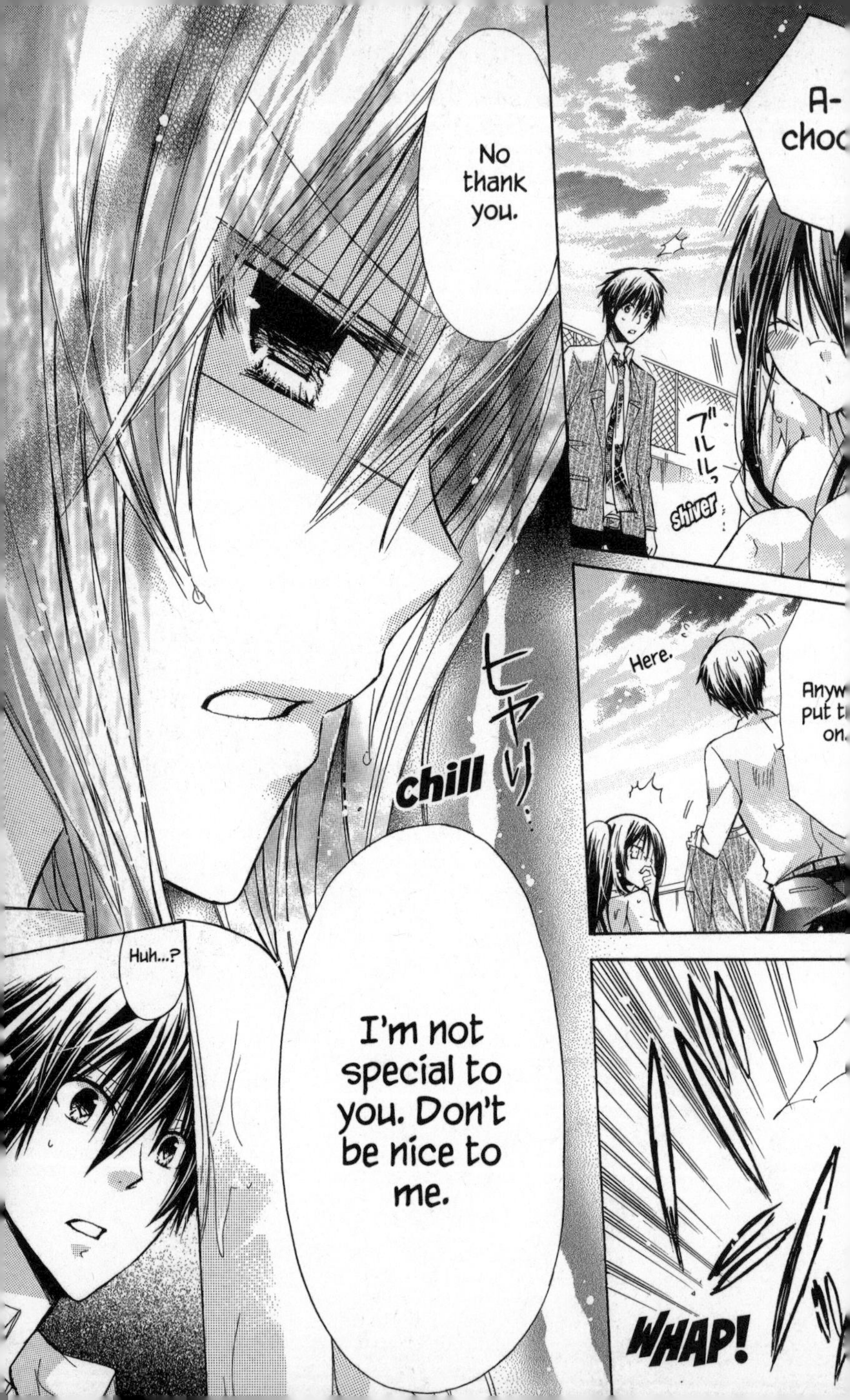
A- cho
ブルルっ
shiver
Here.
Anyw put t on.
WHAP!
No thank you.
ヒヤリ
chill
I'm not special to you. Don't be nice to me.
Huh...?

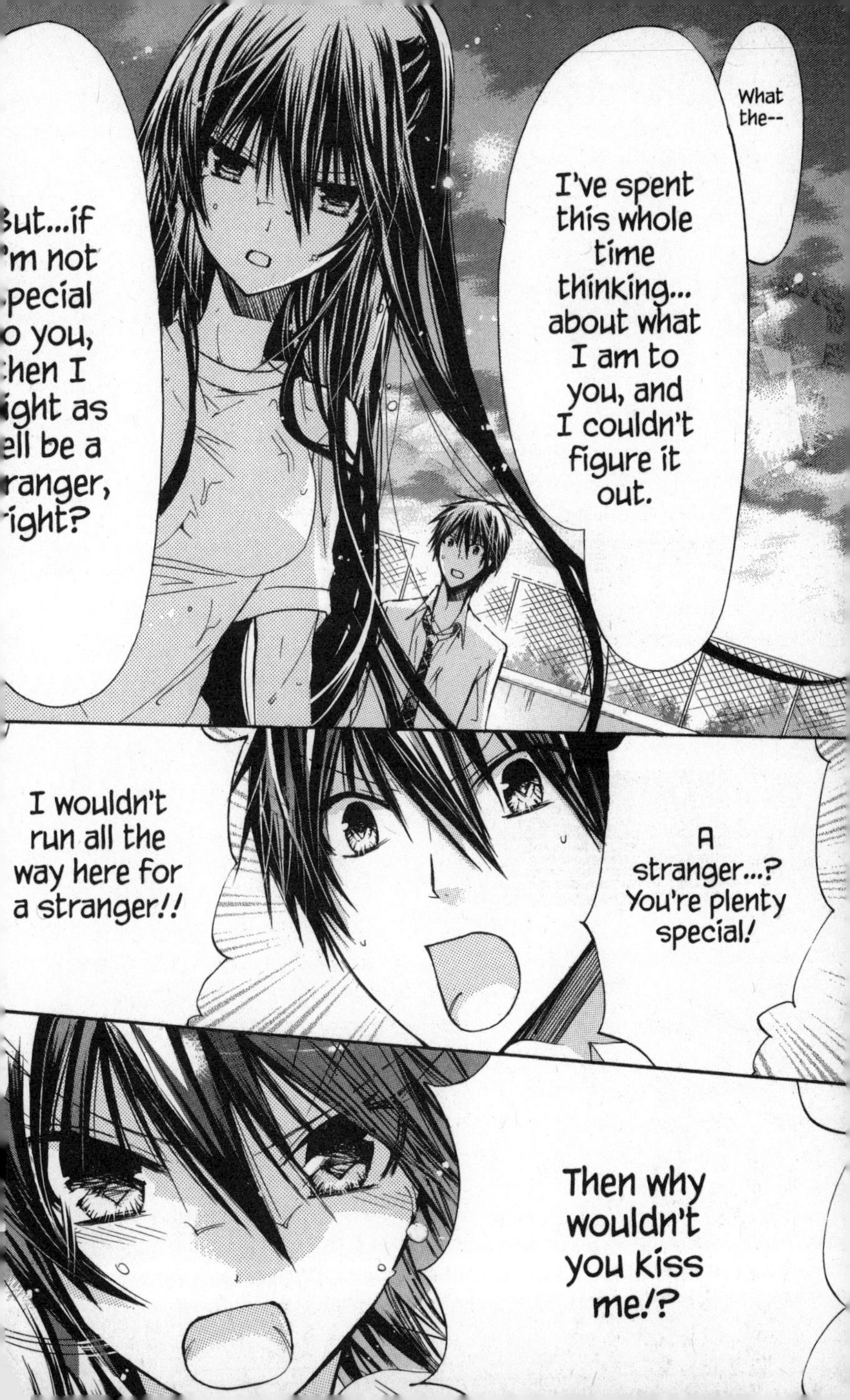
What the--
I've spent this whole time thinking... about what I am to you, and I couldn't figure it out.
ut...if 'm not pecial o you, hen I ight as ell be a ranger, ight?
A stranger...? You're plenty special!
I wouldn't run all the way here for a stranger!!
Then why wouldn't you kiss me!?

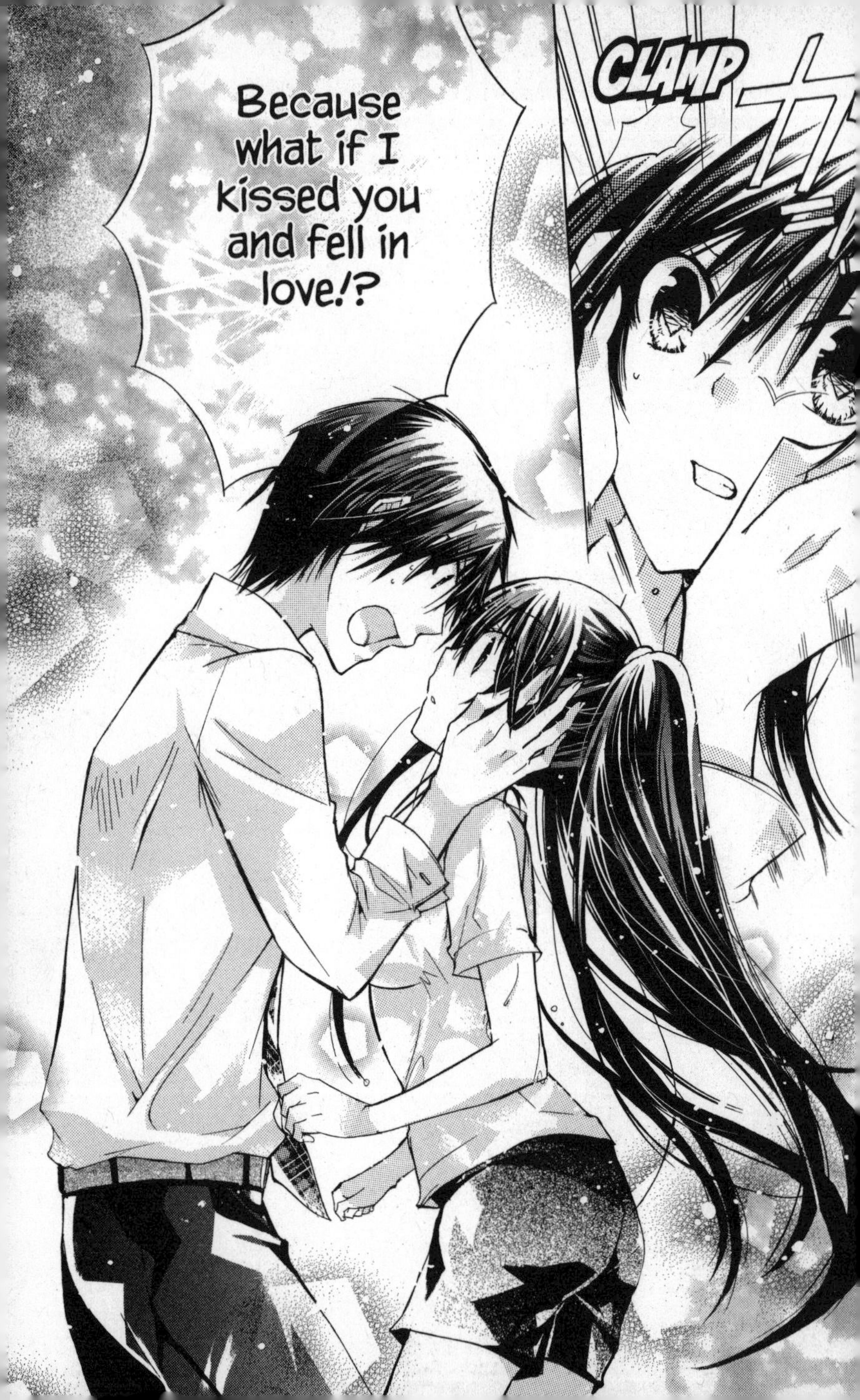
CLAMP
Because what if I kissed you and fell in love!?

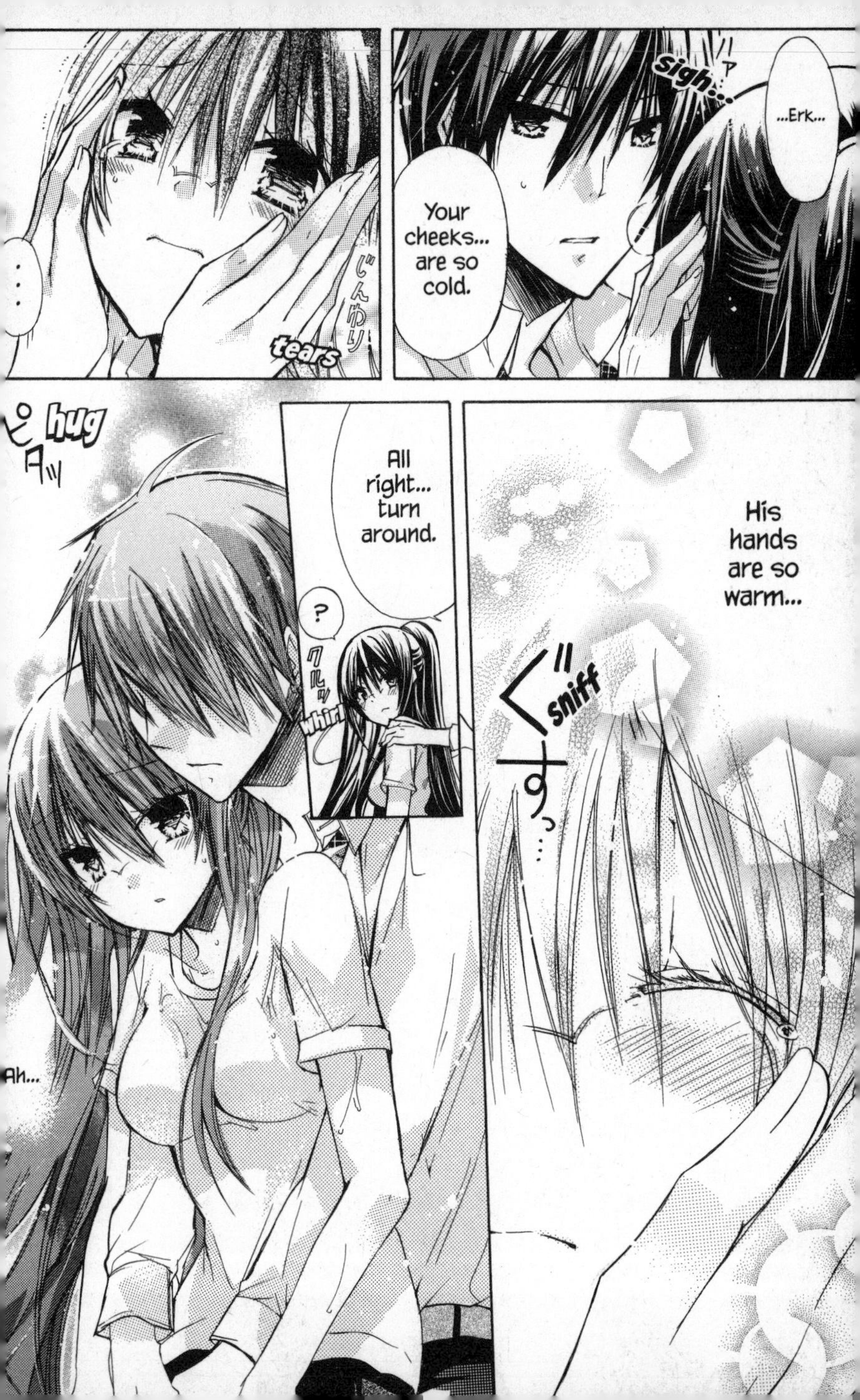

sigh...
...Erk...
Your cheeks... are so cold.
...
tears
His hands are so warm...
sniff
All right... turn around.
?
whirl
hug
Ah...

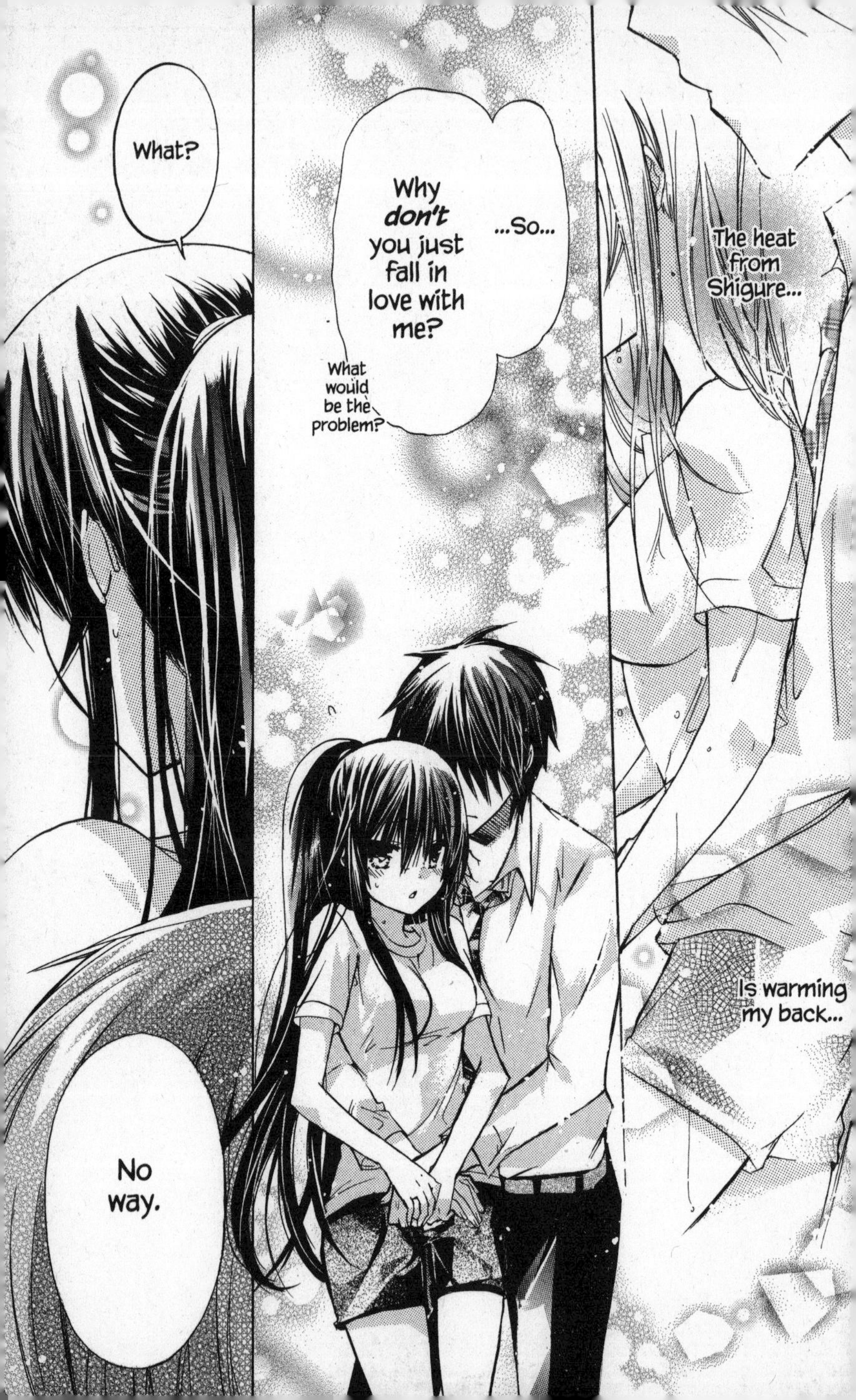
The heat from Shigure...
Is warming my back...
...So...
Why don't you just fall in love with me?
What would be the problem?
What?
No way.

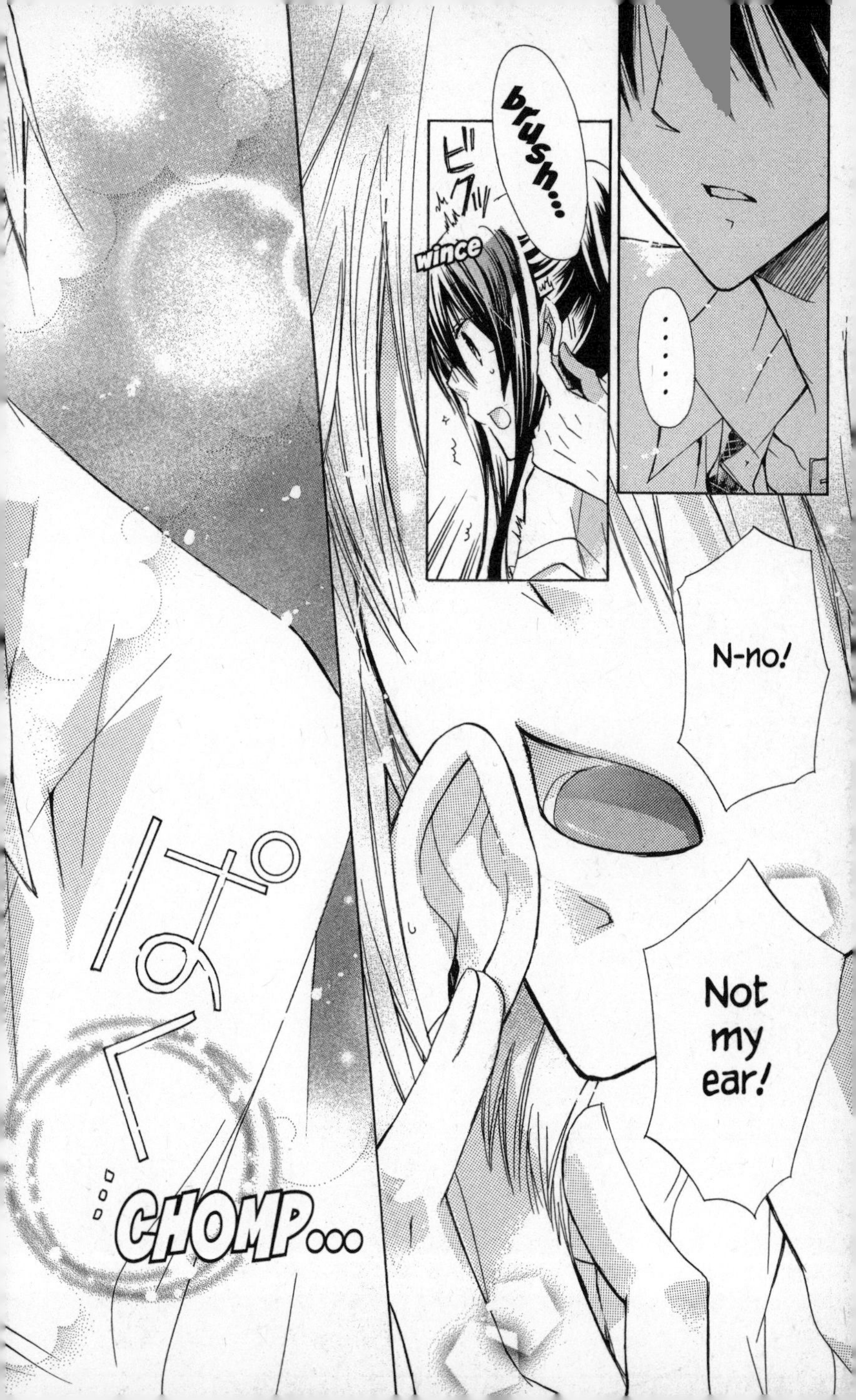

......
brush...
ビクッ
wince
N-no!
Not my ear!
ぱく
CHOMP...

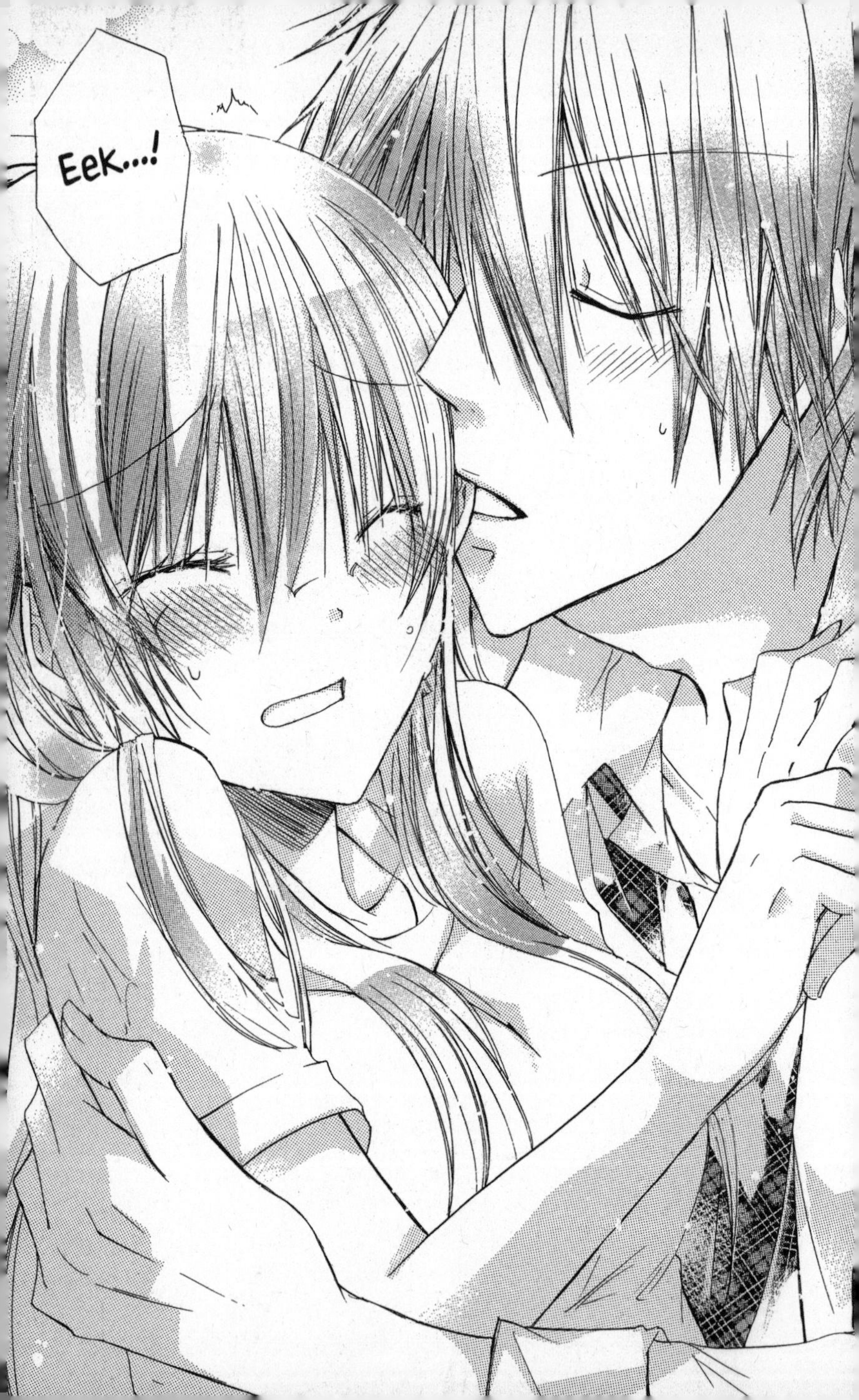
Eek...!

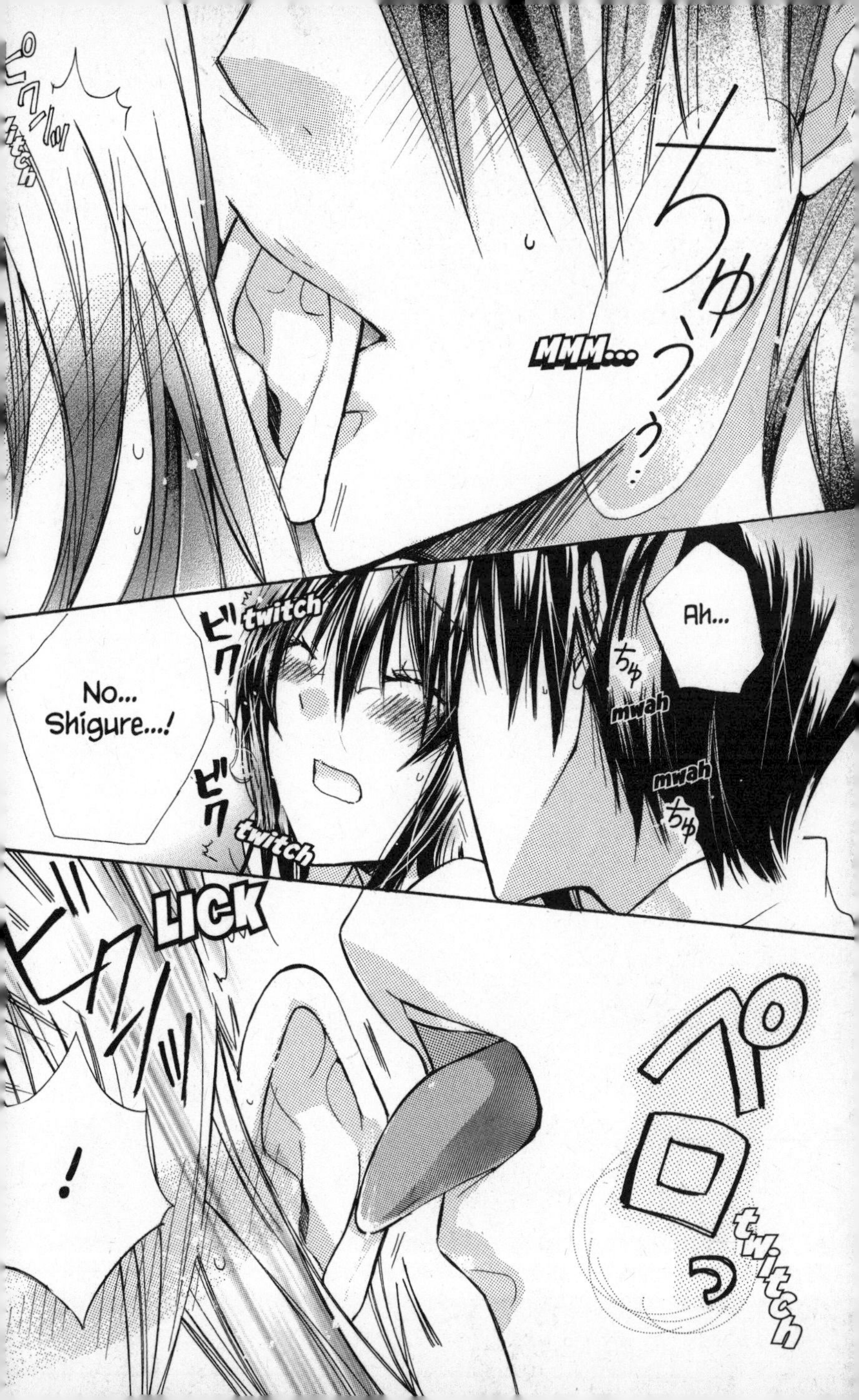
ちゅうぅ…
MMM...
ピクンッ
twitch
Ah...
ちゅ
mwah
mwah
ちゅ
ビク
twitch
No... Shigure...!
ビク
twitch
ペロっ
twitch
LICK
ビクンッ
!

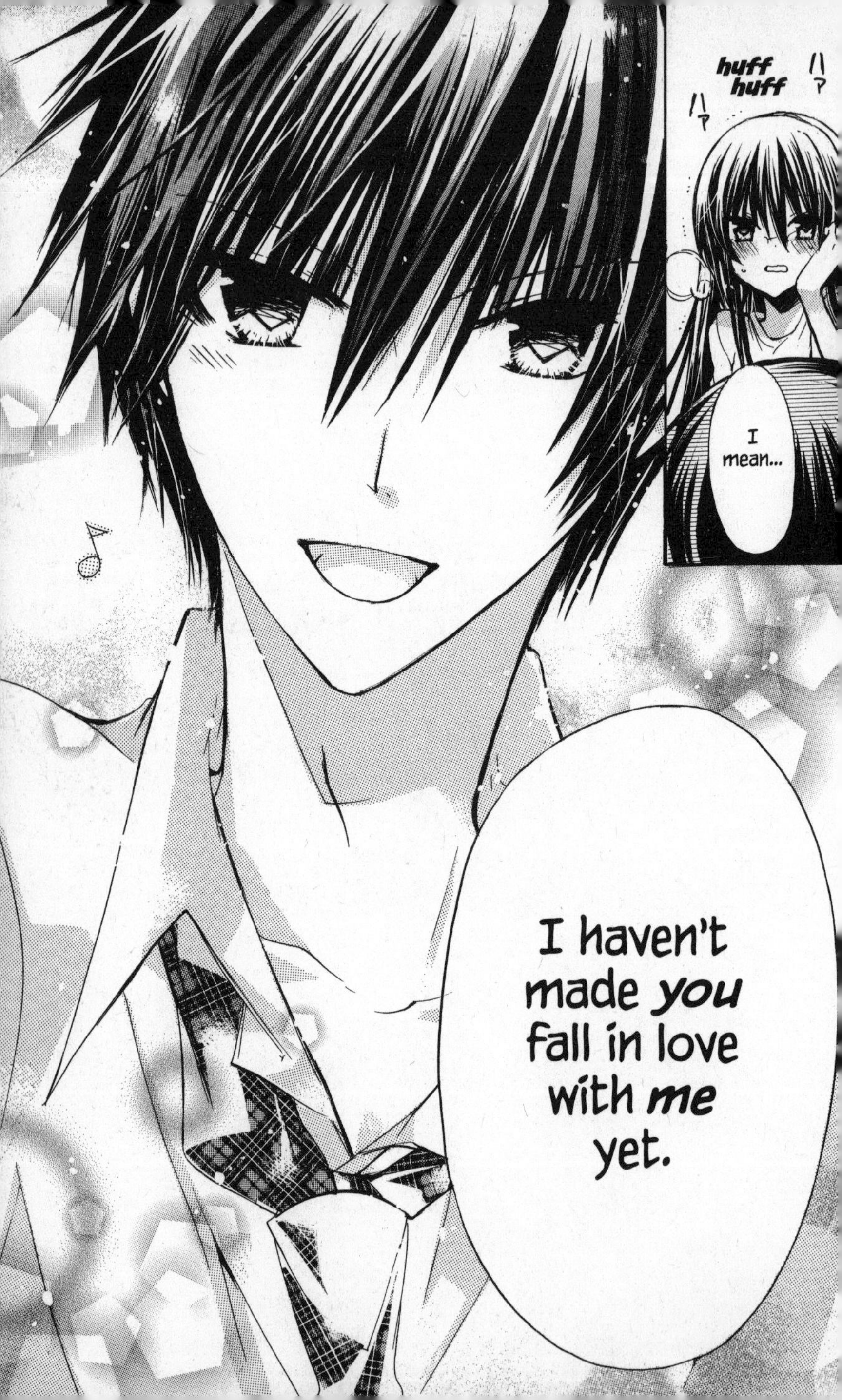
huff huff
I mean...
I haven't made *you* fall in love with *me* yet.

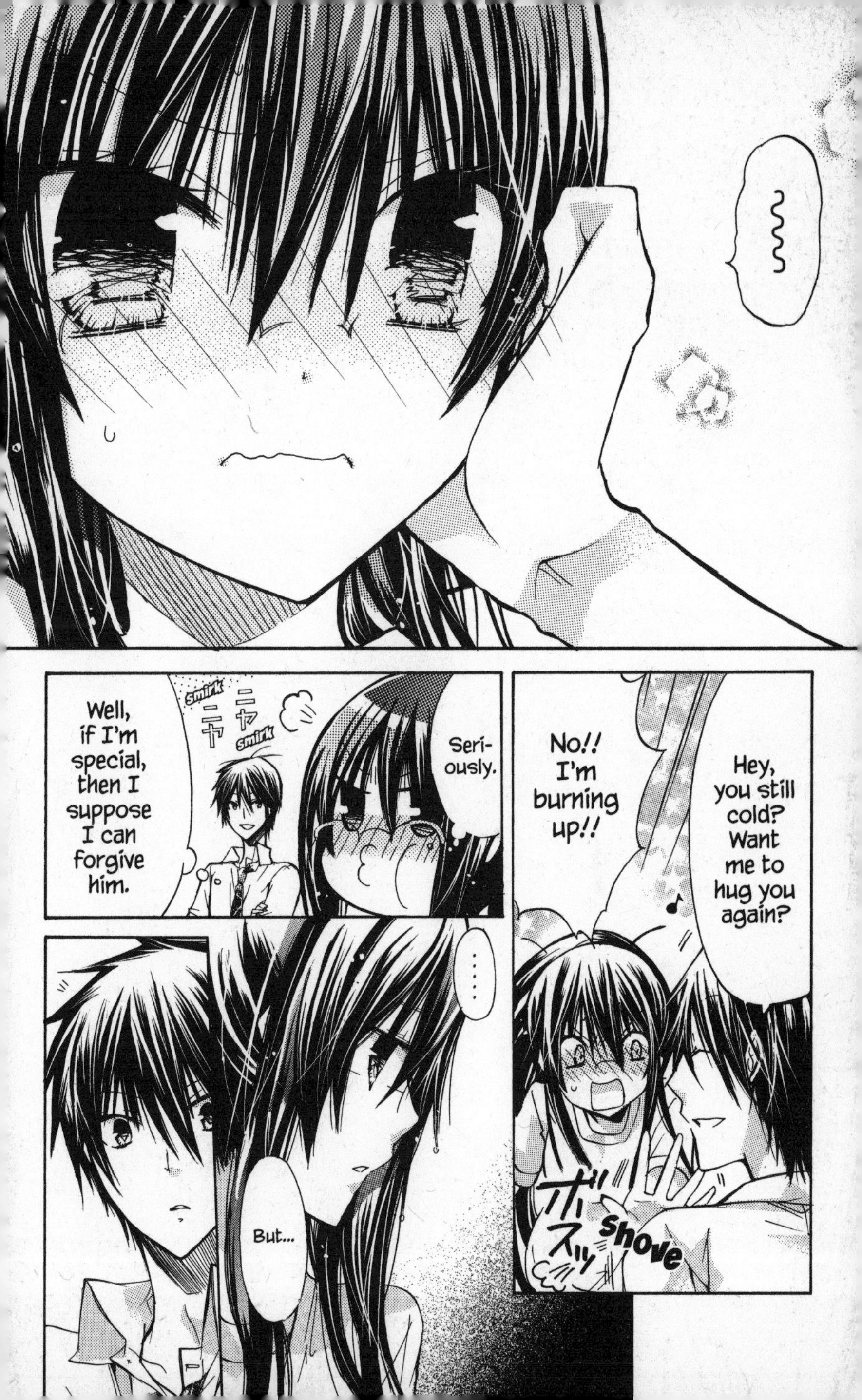
Hey, you still cold? Want me to hug you again?
No!! I'm burning up!!
ボスッ
shove
Seri-ously.
Well, if I'm special, then I suppose I can forgive him.
ニヤニヤ
smirk smirk
......
But...

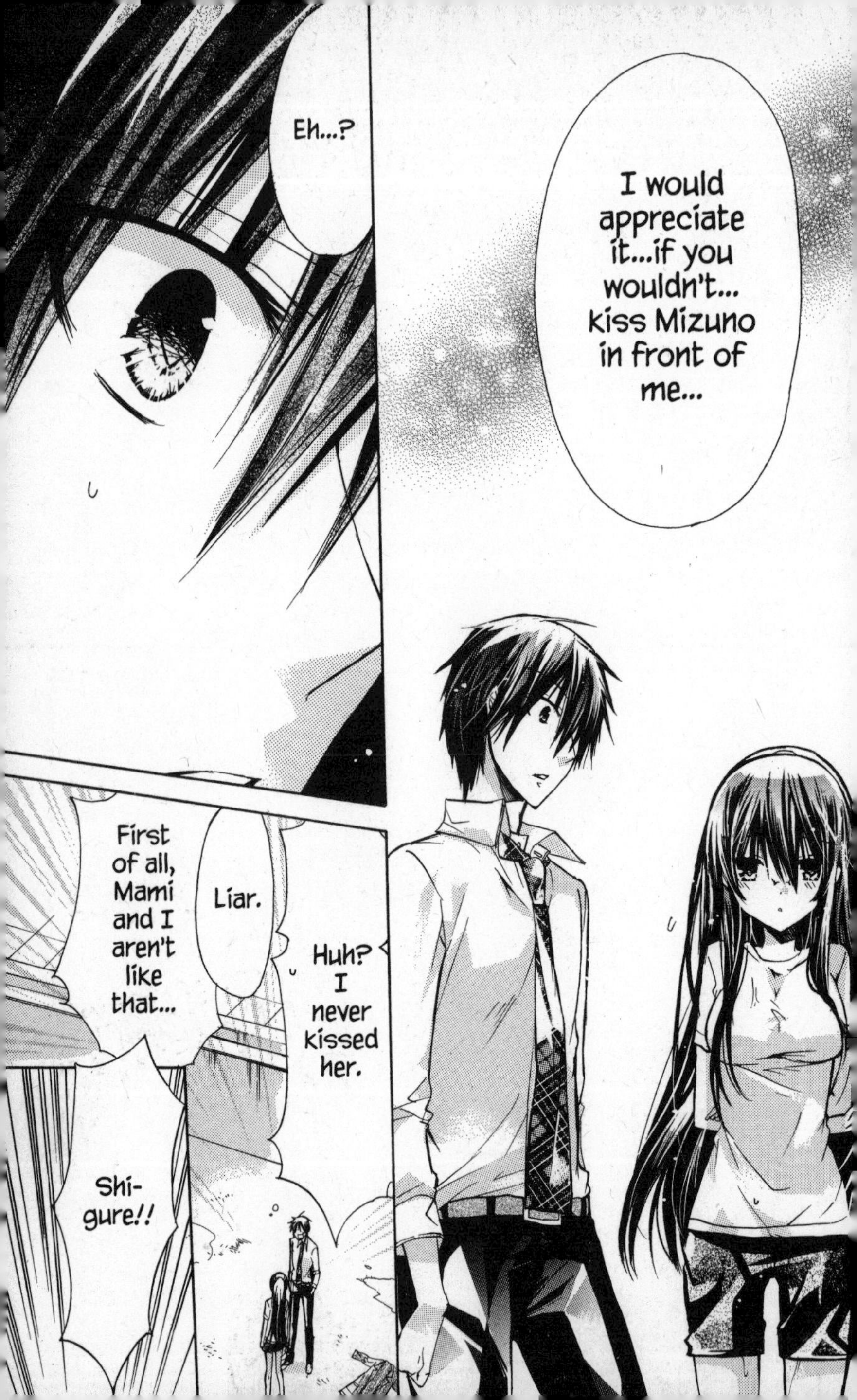

I would appreciate it...if you wouldn't... kiss Mizuno in front of me...
Eh...?
Huh? I never kissed her.
Liar.
First of all, Mami and I aren't like that...
Shi-gure!!

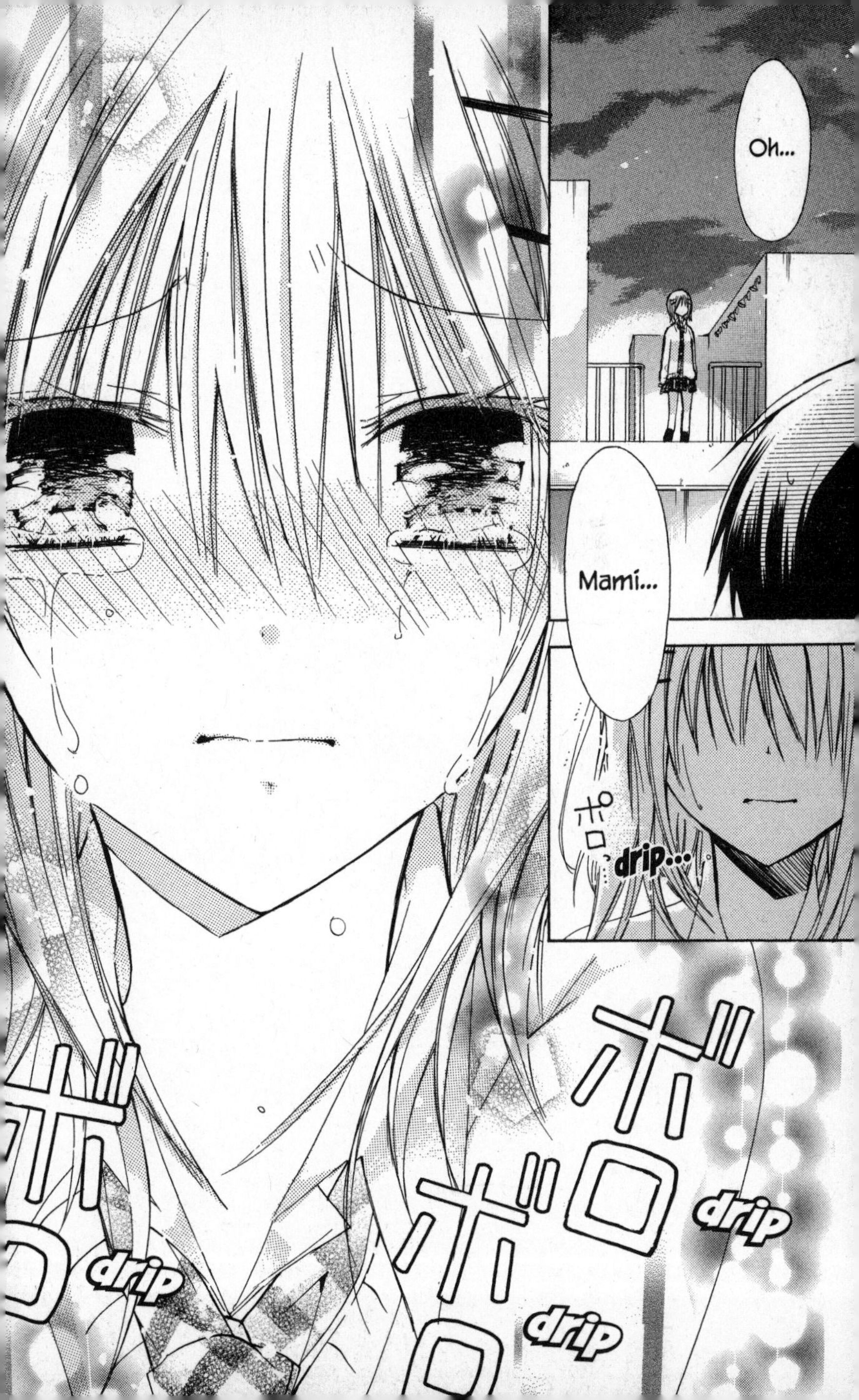
Oh...
Mami...
ポロ
drip...
ボロ
drip
ボロ
drip
ボロ
drip

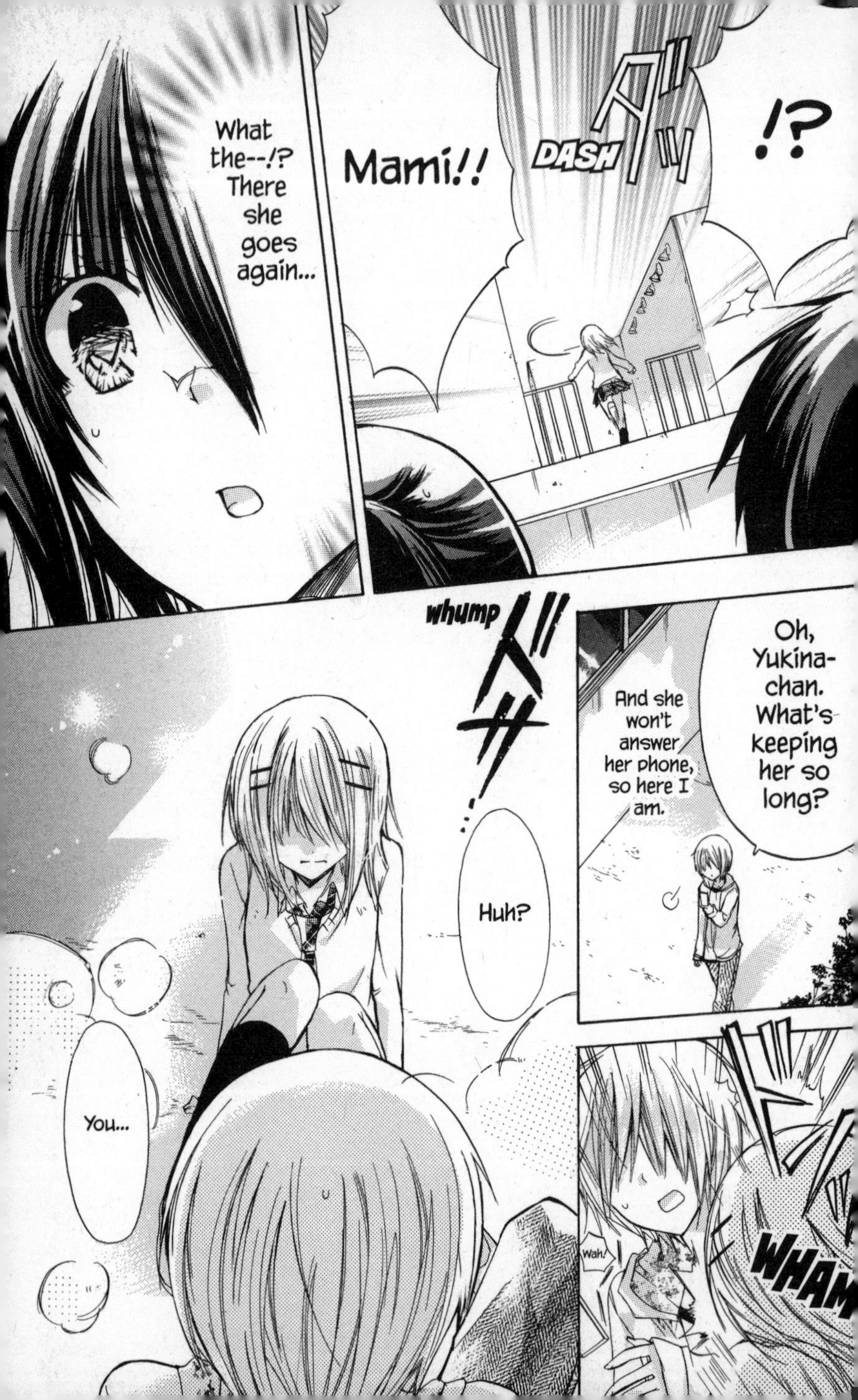
!?
DASH
Mami!!
What the--!? There she goes again...
Oh, Yukina-chan. What's keeping her so long?
And she won't answer her phone, so here I am.
WHAM
Wah!
whump
Huh?
You...

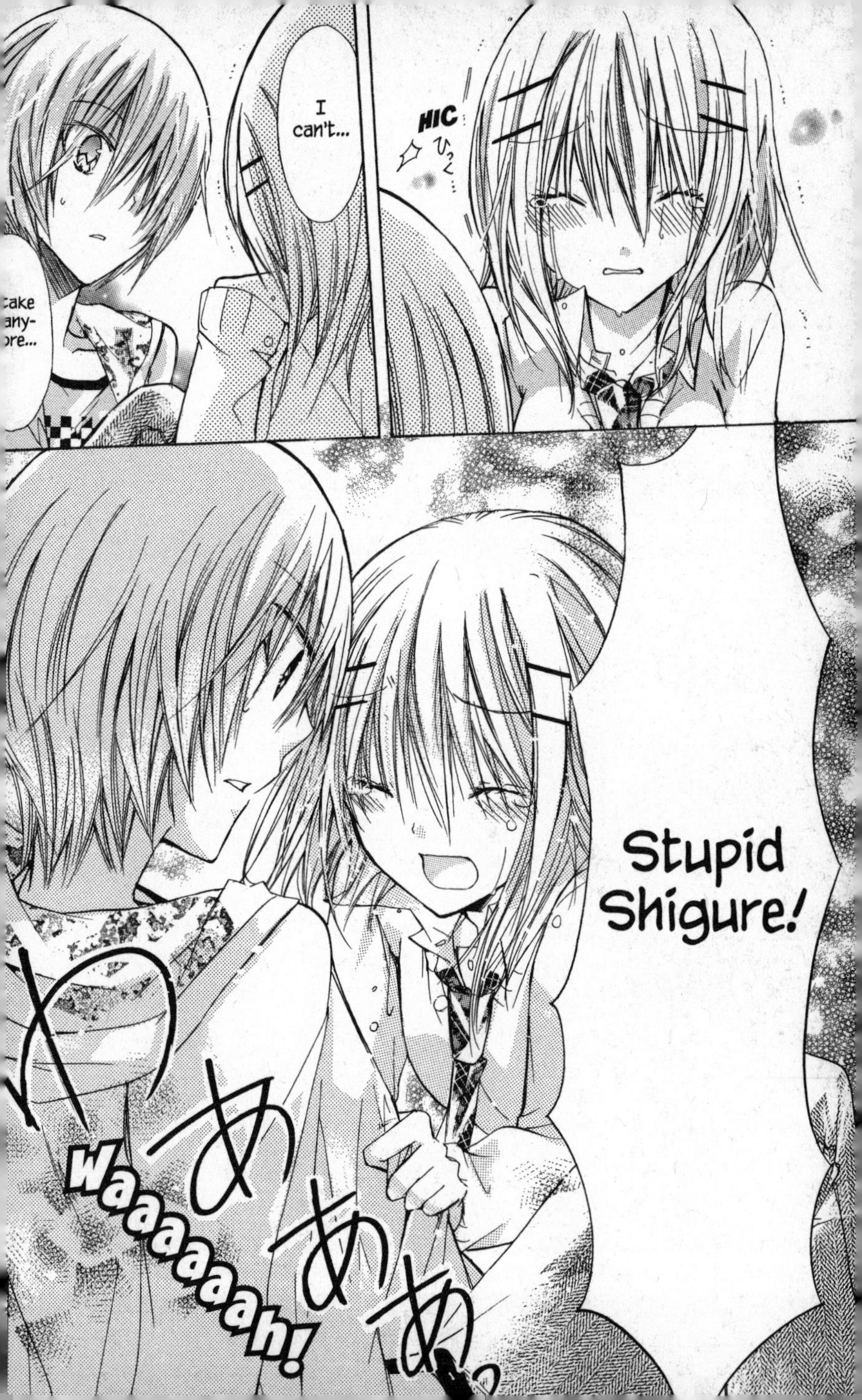
HIC
ひっく…
I can't...
cake
any-
ore...
Stupid Shigure!
やあああ
Waaaaaaah!

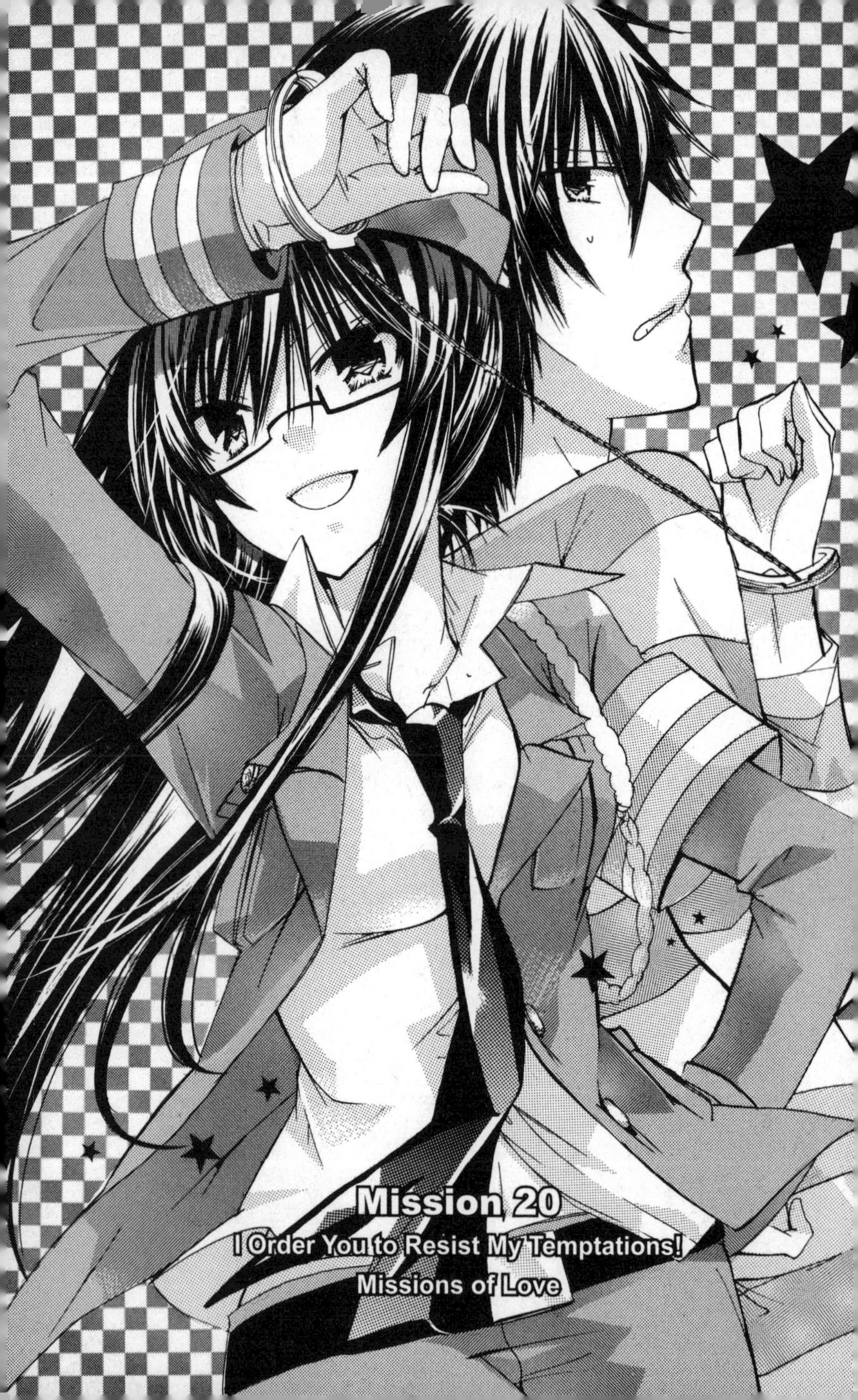
Mission 20
I Order You to Resist My Temptations!
Missions of Love

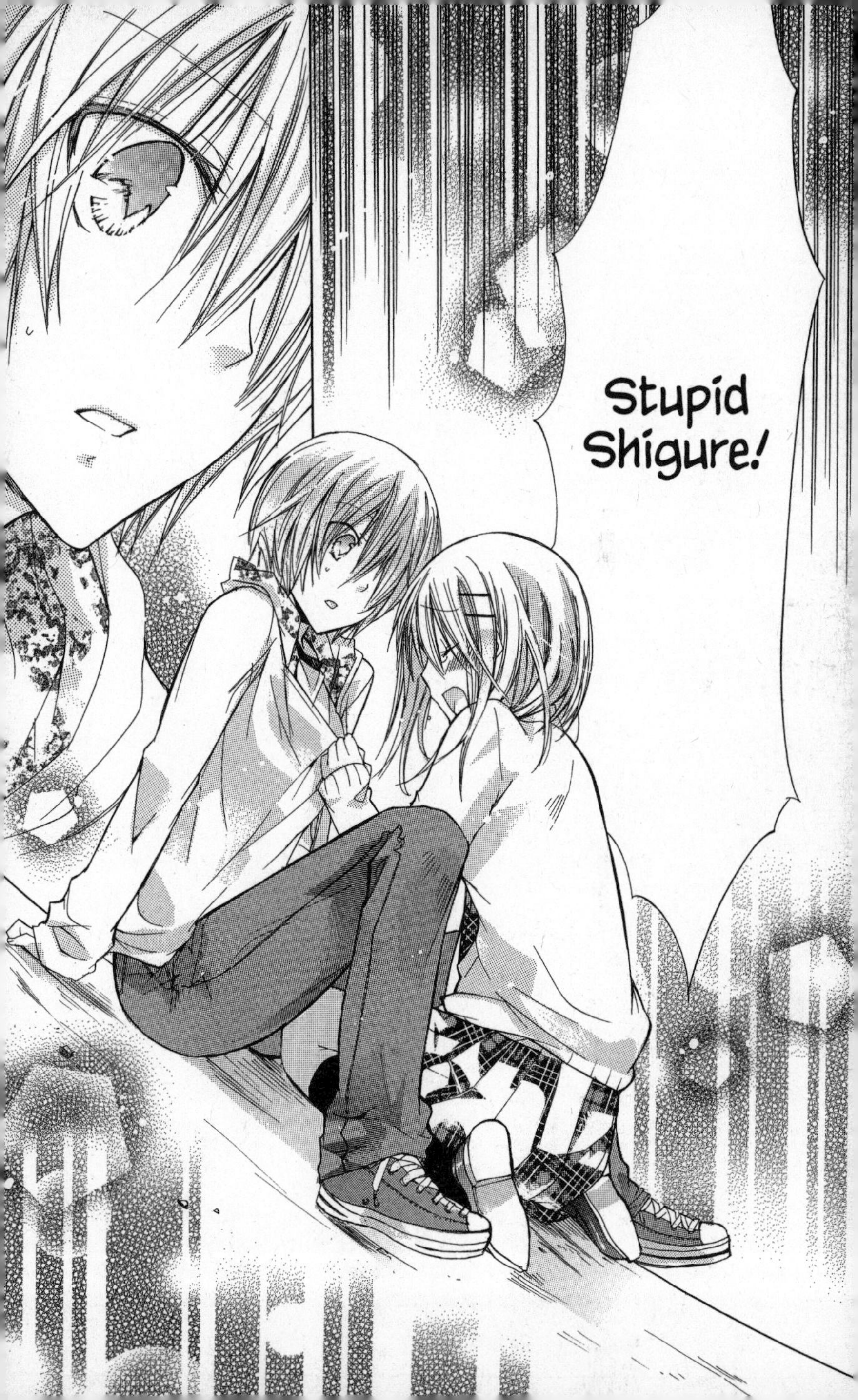
Stupid Shigure!

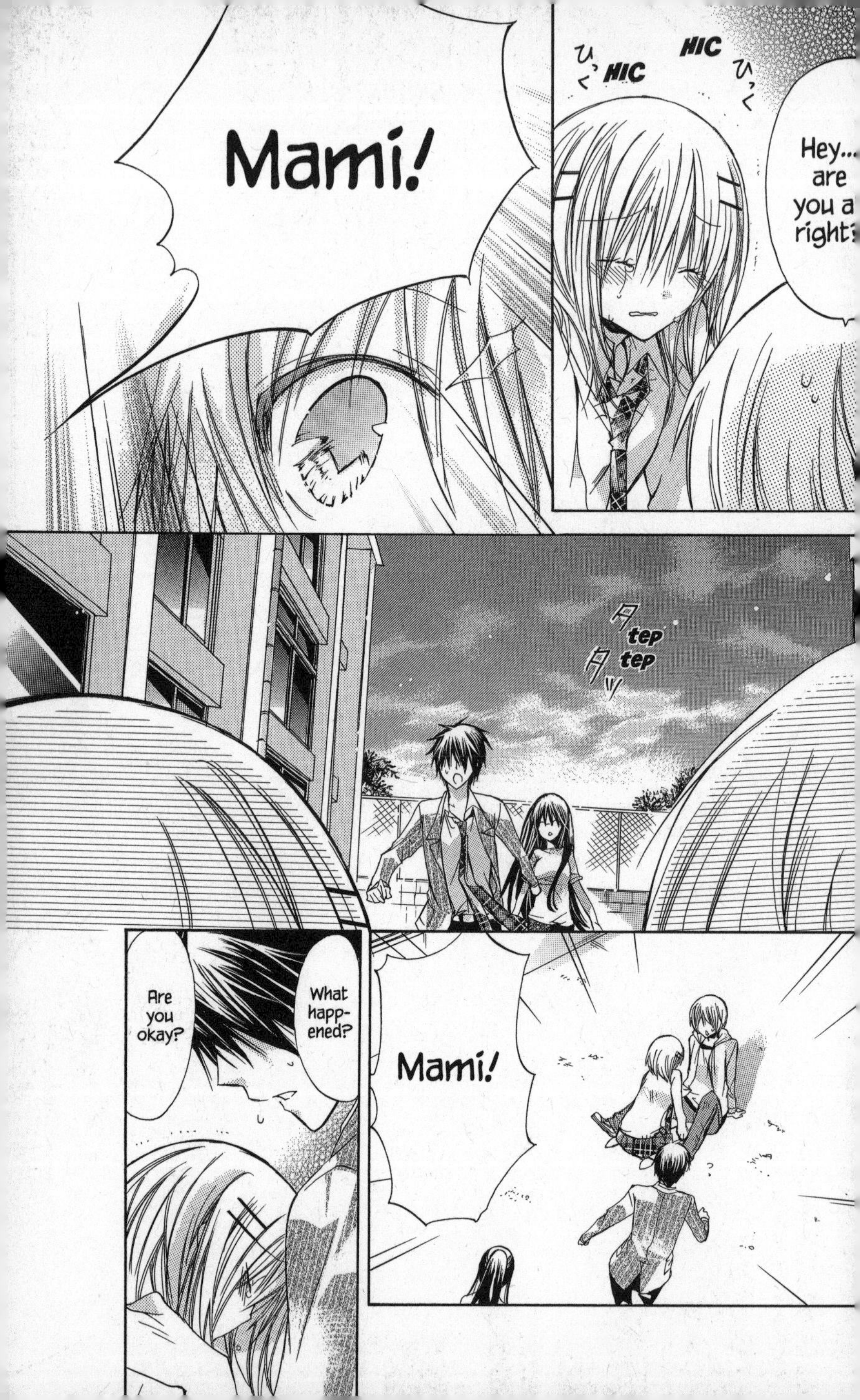
HIC ひっく
HIC ひっく
Hey... are you a right?
Mami!
タタッ tep tep
Mami!
What happ-ened?
Are you okay?

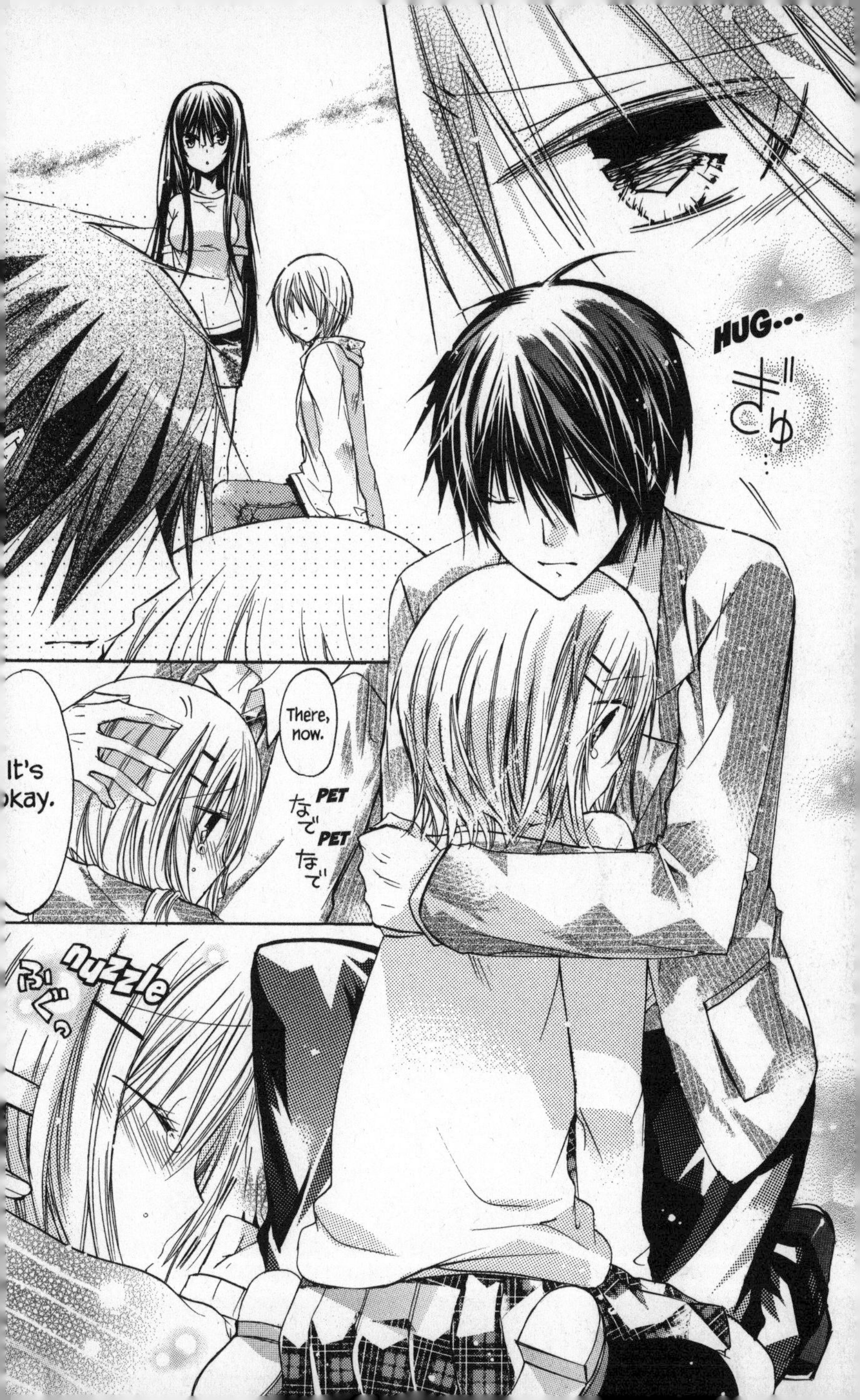
HUG...
ぎゅ…
There, now.
It's okay.
PET なで PET なで
nuzzle ふぐっ

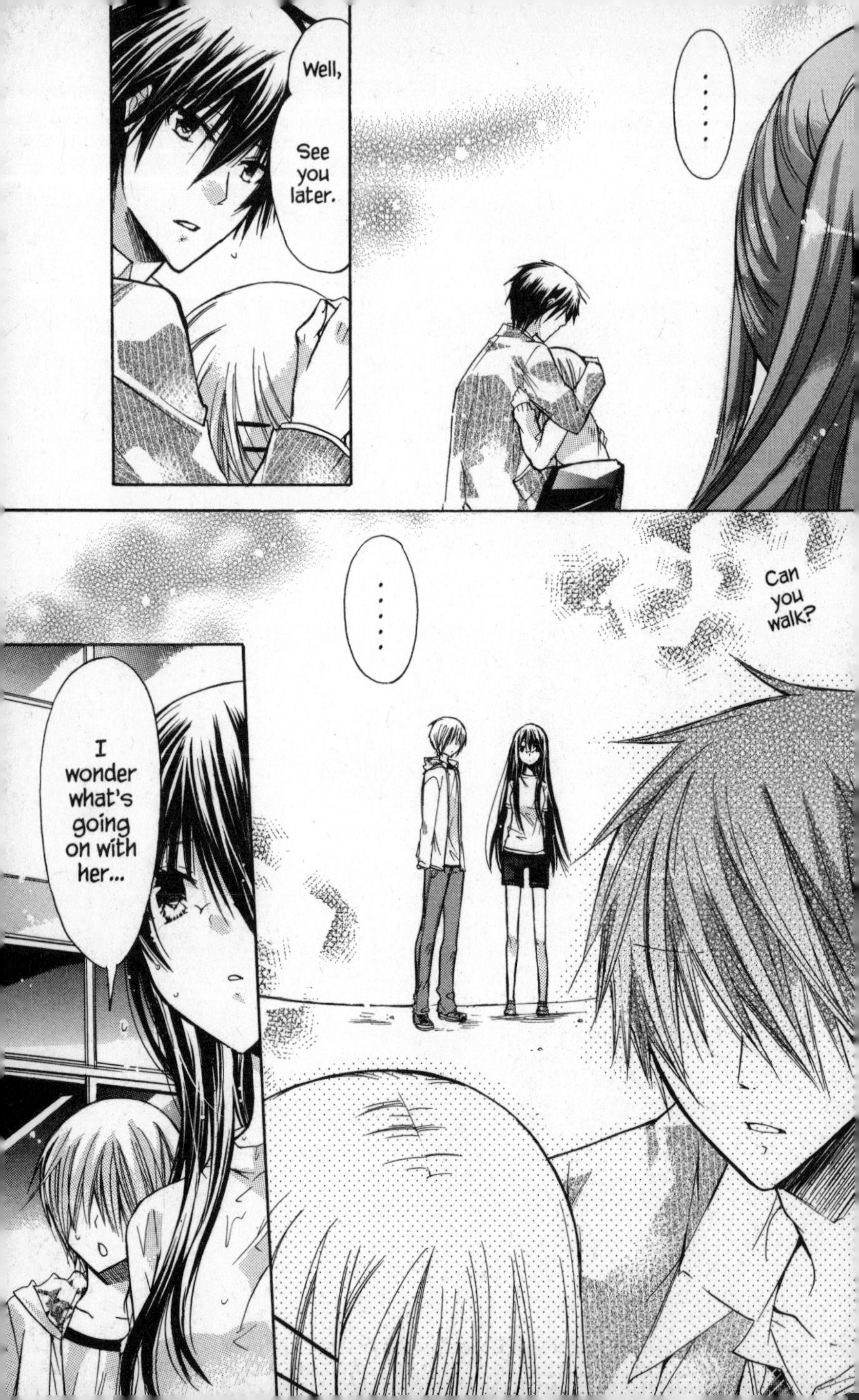
……
Well,
See you later.
Can you walk?
……
I wonder what's going on with her...

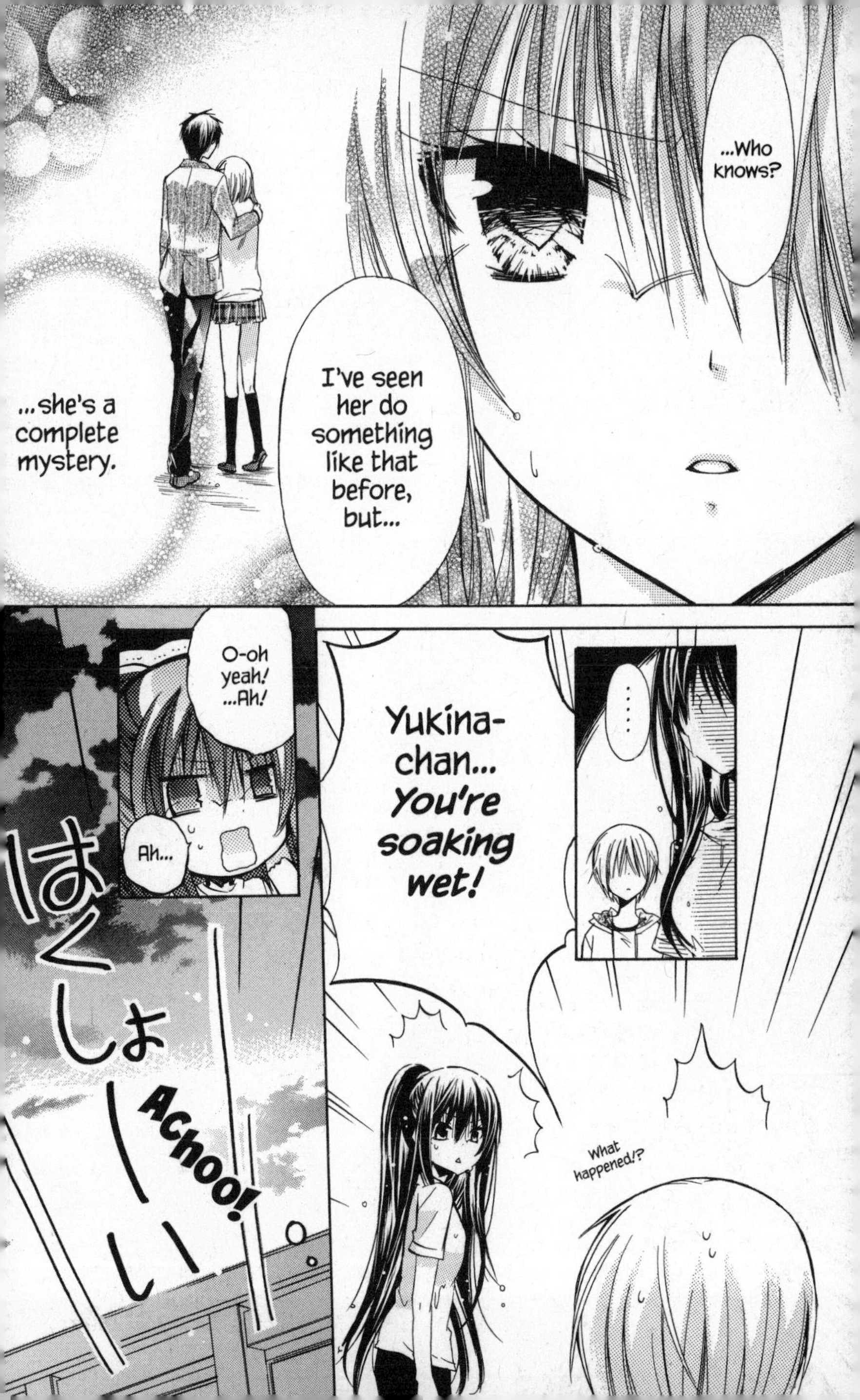
...Who knows?
I've seen her do something like that before, but...
...she's a complete mystery.
......
Yukina-chan... You're soaking wet!
What happened!?
O-oh yeah! ...Ah!
Ah...
はくしょーい
Achoo!

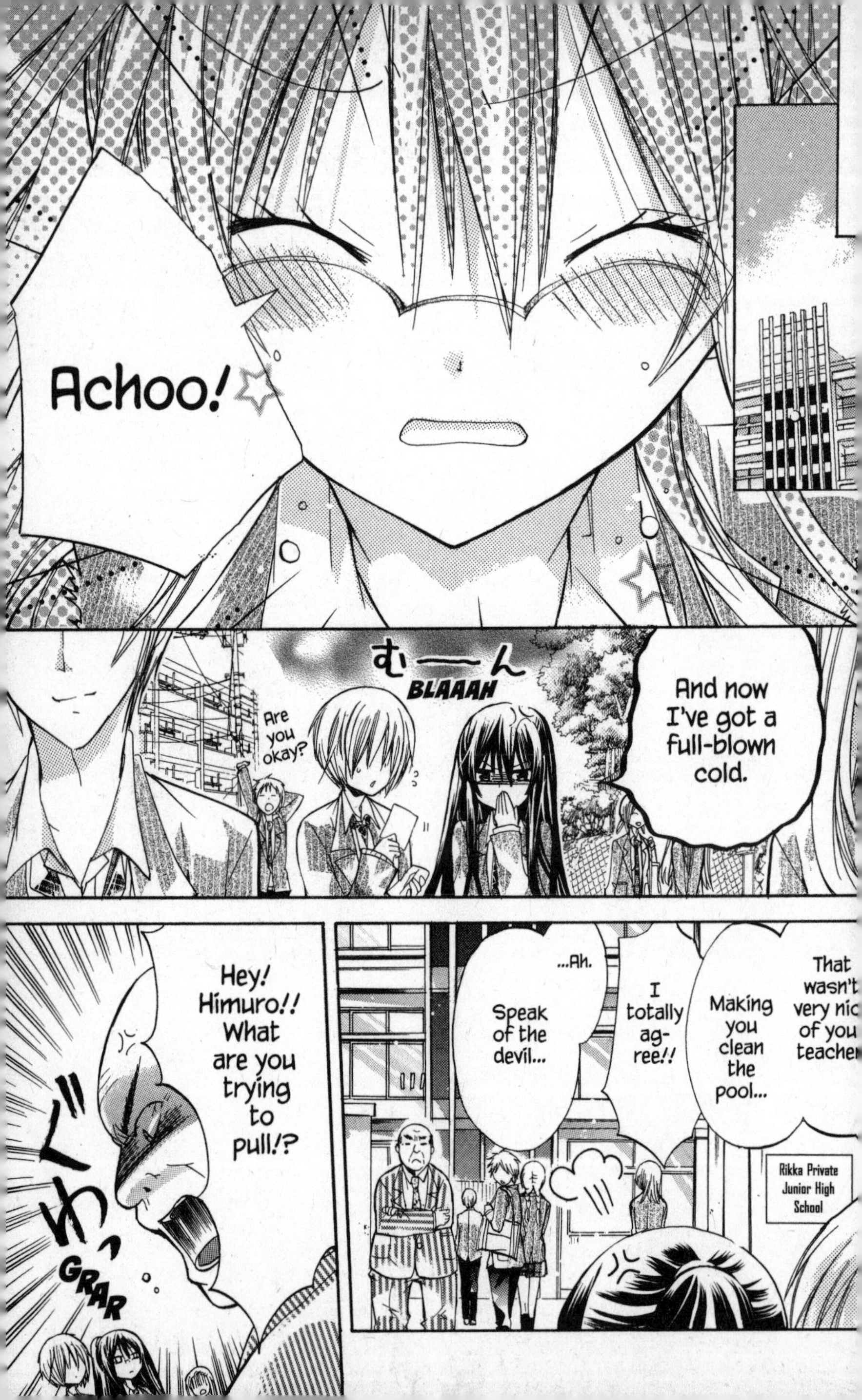
Achoo!
And now I've got a full-blown cold.
むーーん
BLAAAH
Are you okay?
That wasn't very nic of you teache
Making you clean the pool...
I totally ag-ree!!
...Ah.
Speak of the devil...
Rikka Private Junior High School
Hey! Himuro!! What are you trying to pull!?
ぐわっ
GRAR

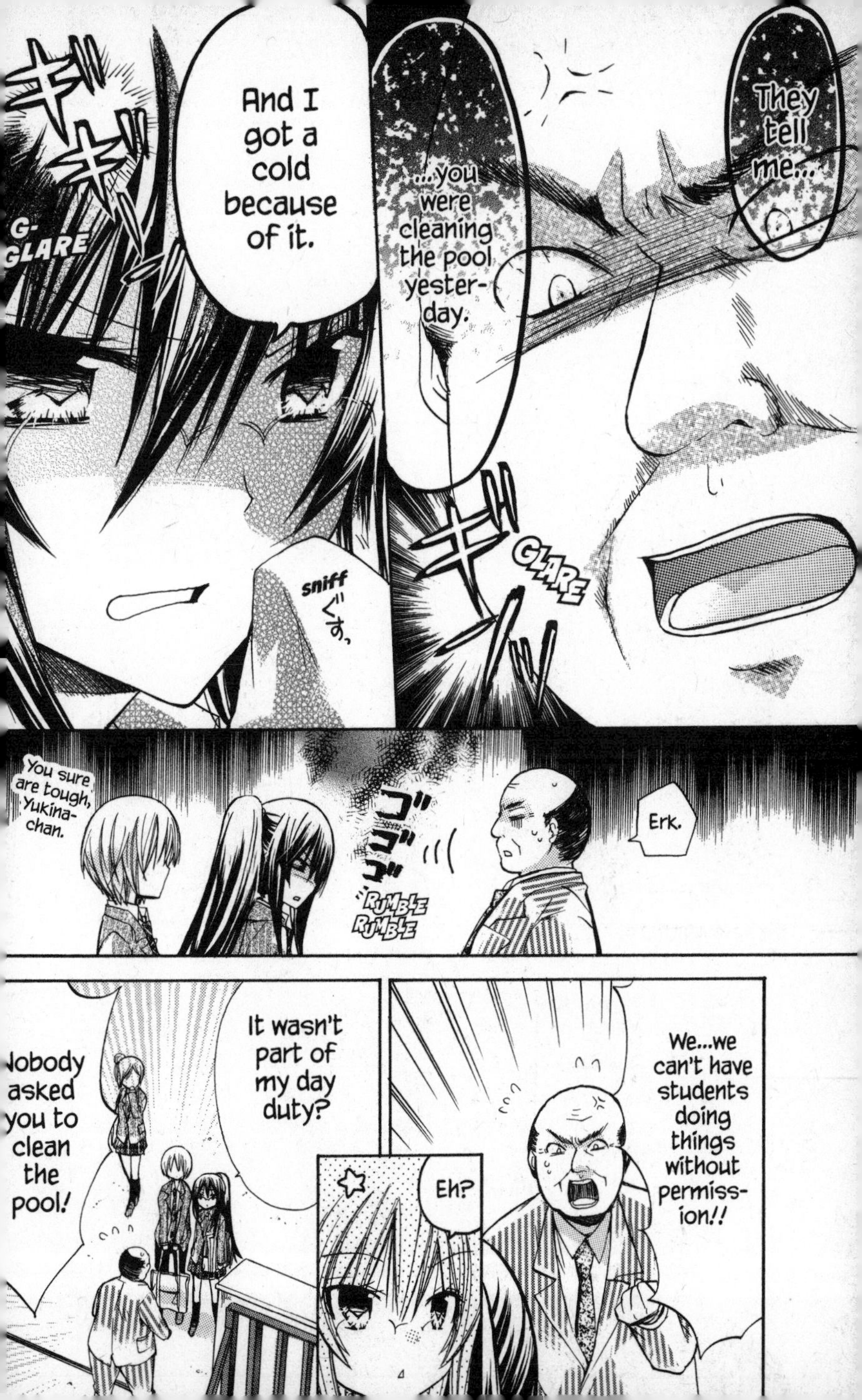
They tell me...
...you were cleaning the pool yester-day.
GLARE
And I got a cold because of it.
sniff ぐすっ
G-GLARE
Erk.
RUMBLE RUMBLE
You sure are tough, Yukina-chan.
We...we can't have students doing things without permiss-ion!!
Eh?
It wasn't part of my day duty?
Nobody asked you to clean the pool!

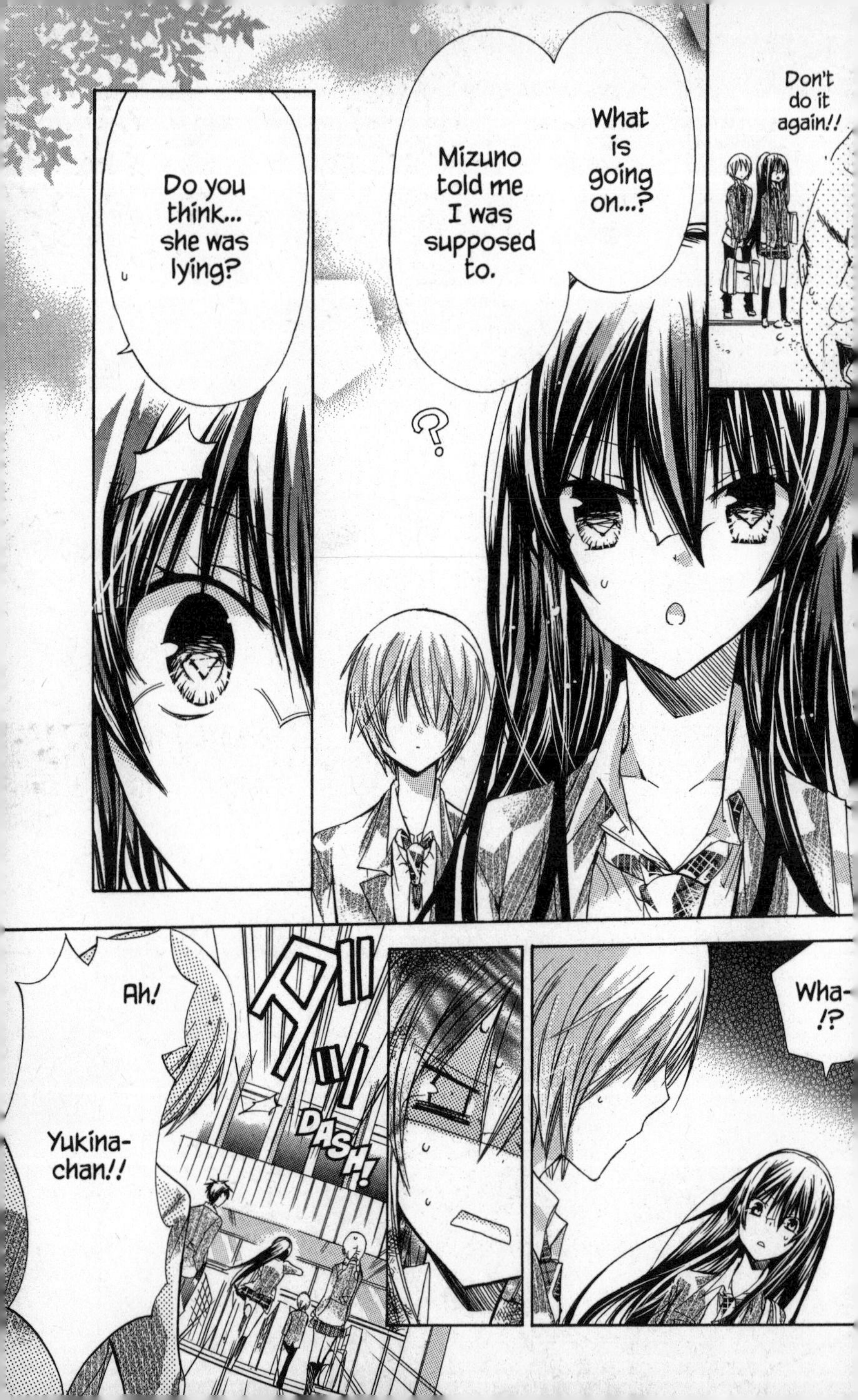
Don't do it again!!
What is going on...?
Mizuno told me I was supposed to.
?
Do you think... she was lying?
Wha-!?
Ah!
DASH!
Yukina-chan!!

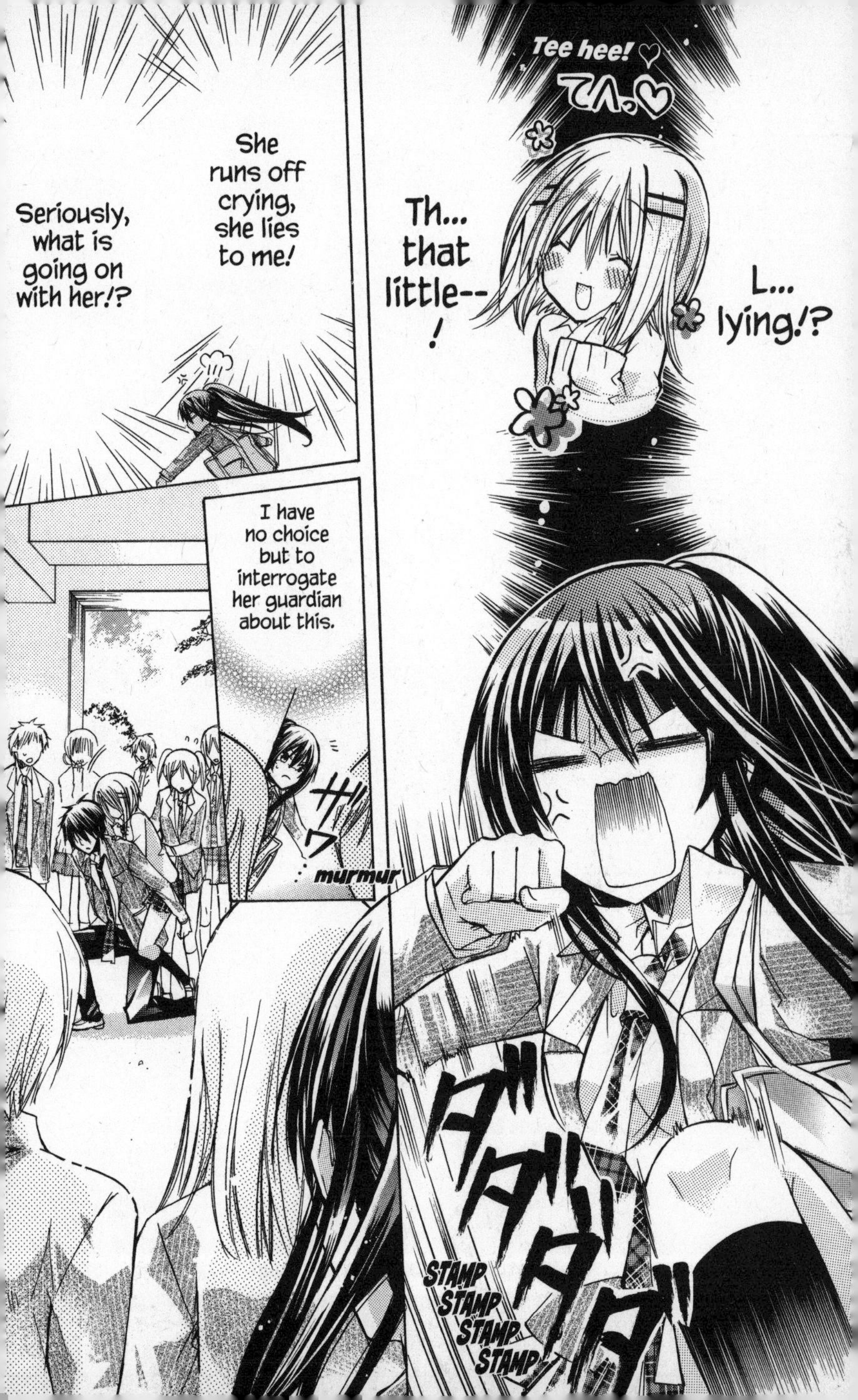

Tee hee! ♡
てへっ♡
L... lying!?
Th... that little--!
STAMP STAMP STAMP STAMP
She runs off crying, she lies to me!
Seriously, what is going on with her!?
I have no choice but to interrogate her guardian about this.
murmur

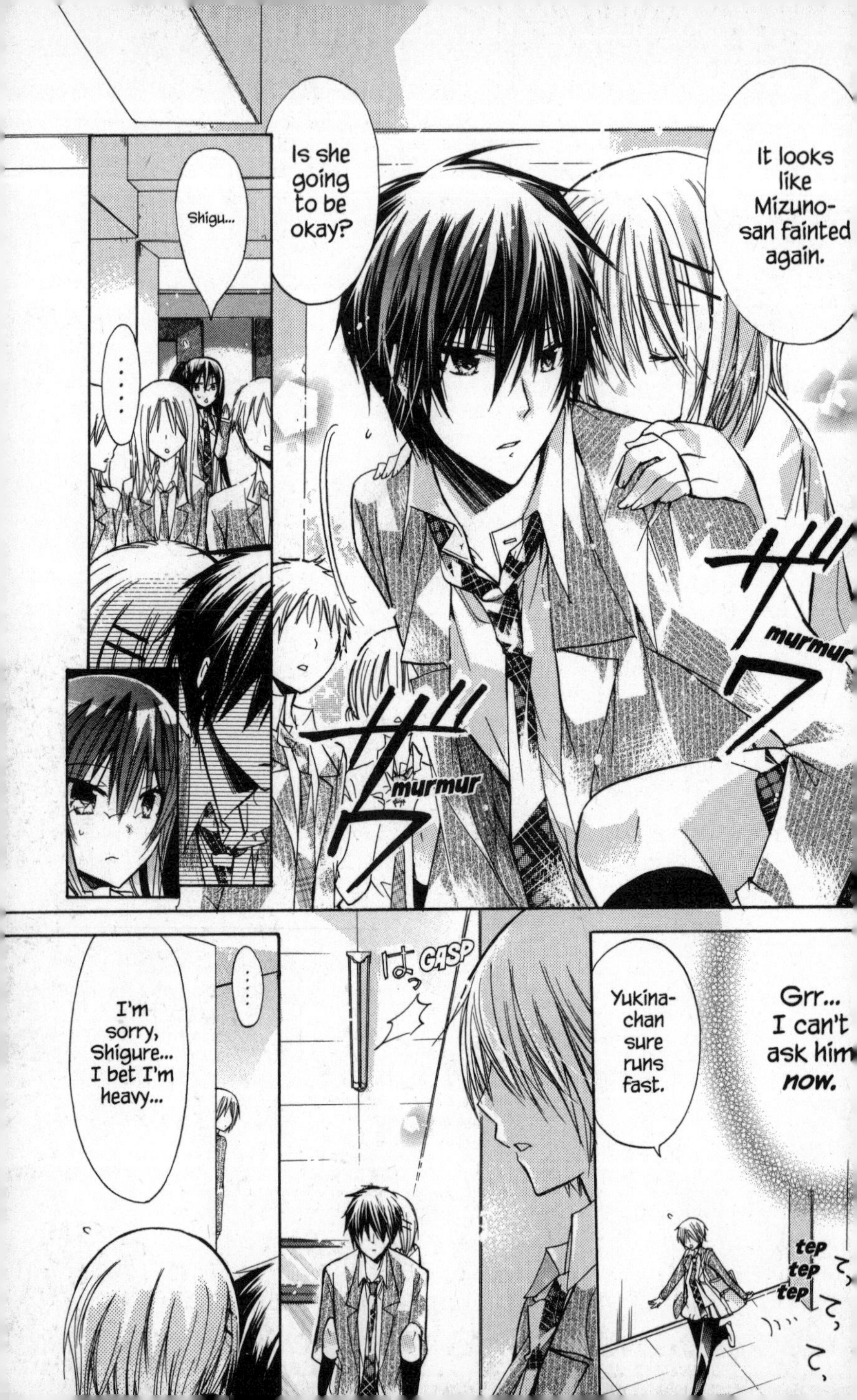
It looks like Mizuno-san fainted again.
Is she going to be okay?
ザワ murmur
ザワ murmur
Shigu...
......
Grr... I can't ask him *now*.
Yukina-chan sure runs fast.
tep tep tep
はっ GASP
......
I'm sorry, Shigure... I bet I'm heavy...

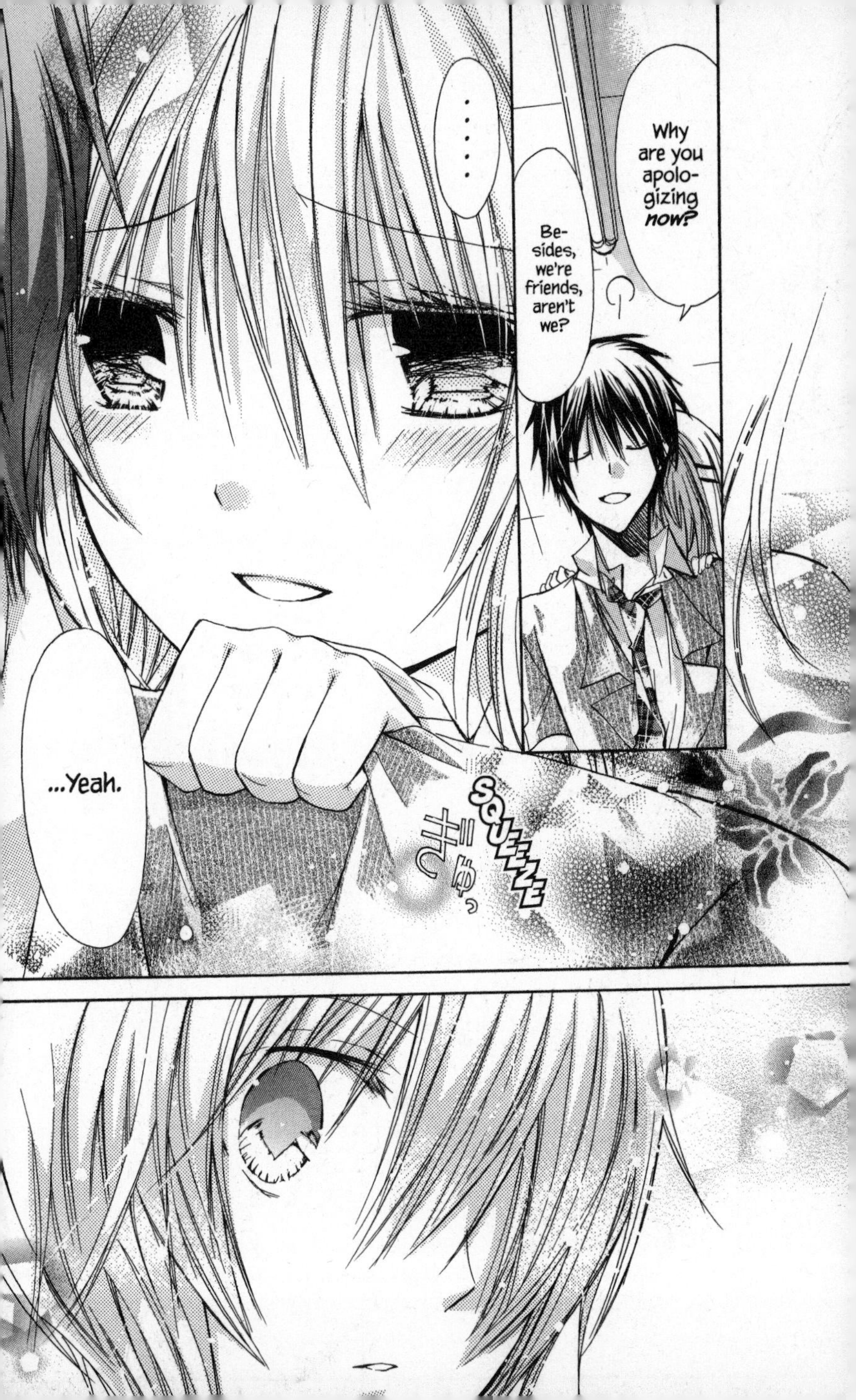
Why are you apologizing *now?*
Besides, we're friends, aren't we?
......
...Yeah.
SQUEEZE
ぎゅっ

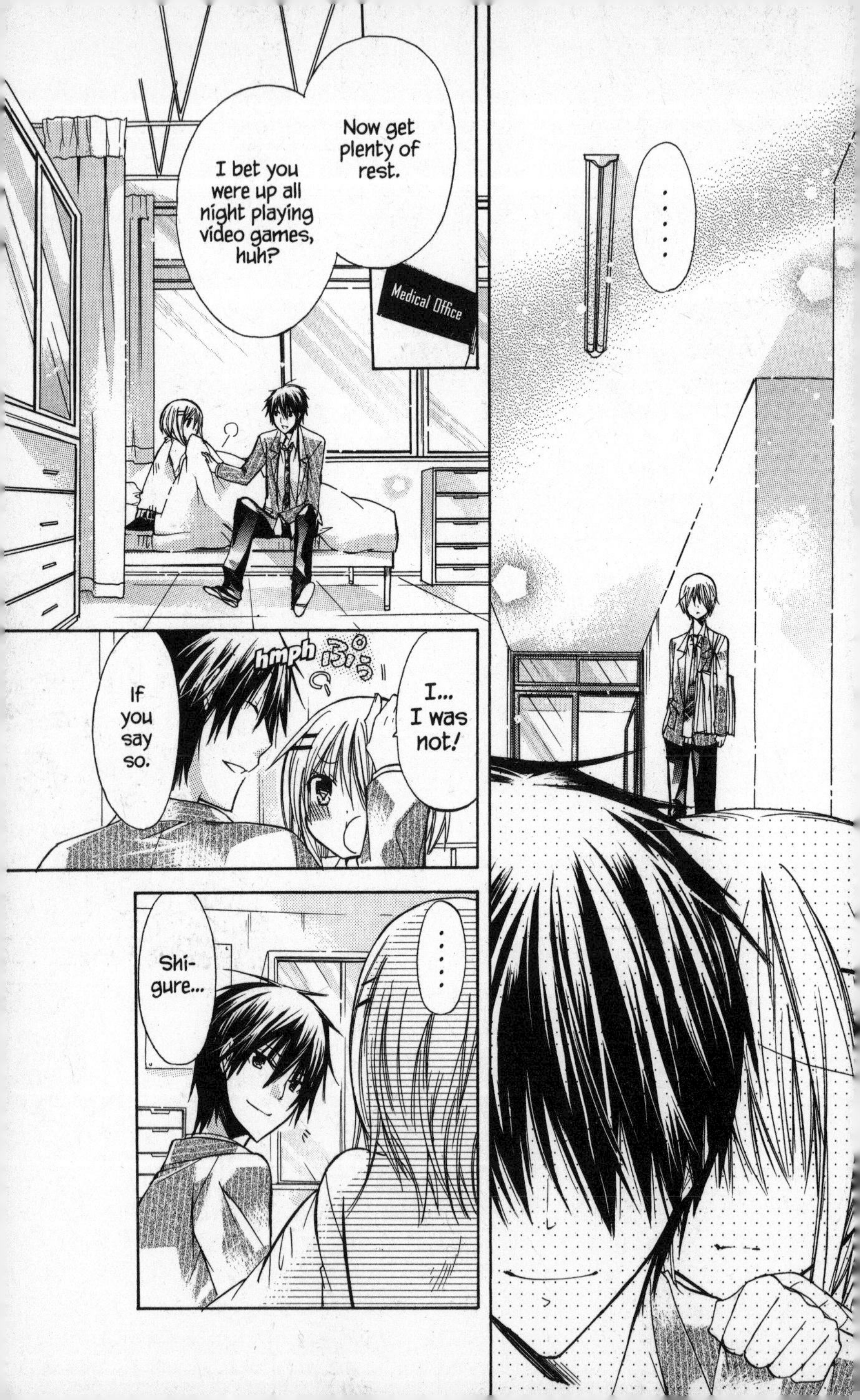
......
Now get plenty of rest.
I bet you were up all night playing video games, huh?
Medical Office
I... I was not!
hmph
If you say so.
......
Shi-gure...

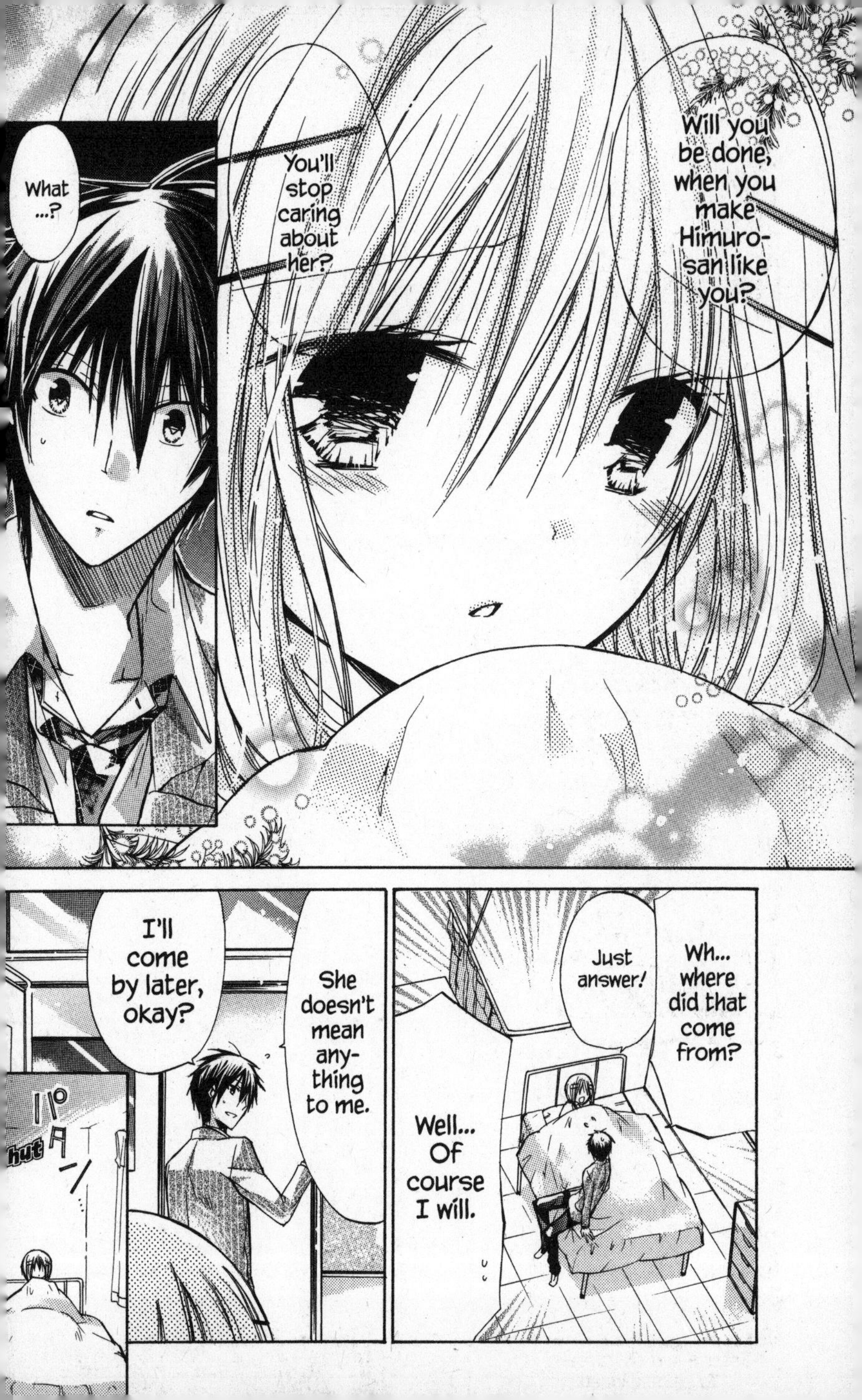
Will you be done, when you make Himuro-san like you?
You'll stop caring about her?
What ...?
Wh... where did that come from?
Just answer!
Well... Of course I will.
She doesn't mean anything to me.
I'll come by later, okay?
hut

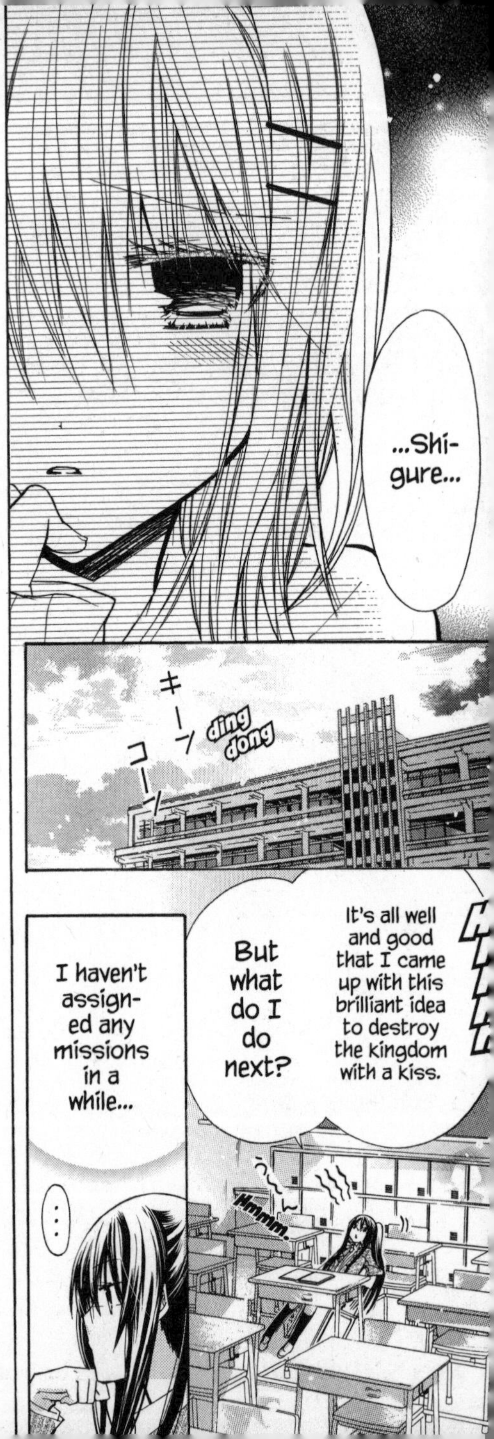
...Shigure...
ding dong
It's all well and good that I came up with this brilliant idea to destroy the kingdom with a kiss.
But what do I do next?
I haven't assigned any missions in a while...
Hmmm.
...

Snow Yukina 5

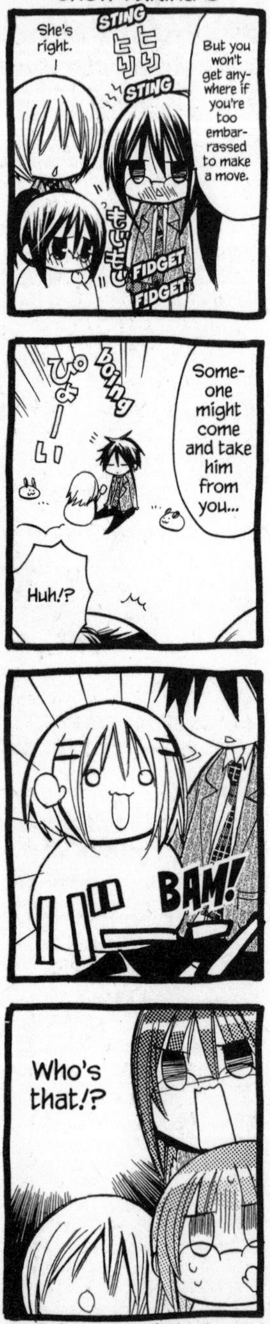
But you won't get anywhere if you're too embarrassed to make a move.
STING
STING
She's right.
FIDGET
FIDGET
Someone might come and take him from you...
boing
Huh!?
BAM!
Who's that!?

Enter a new character!! To be continued.

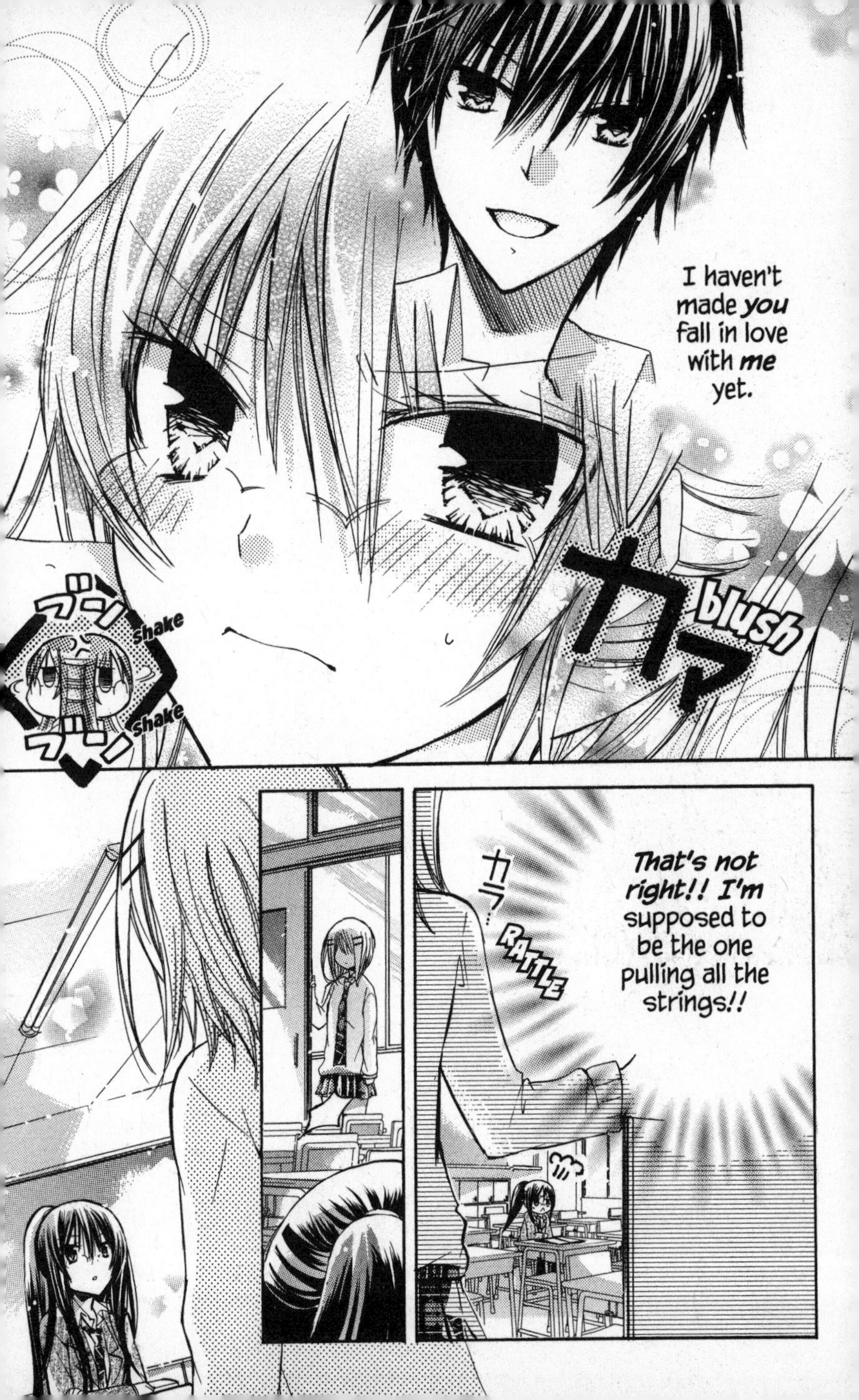
I haven't made *you* fall in love with *me* yet.
カァ
blush
shake
shake
That's not right!! I'm supposed to be the one pulling all the strings!!
カラ…
RATTLE

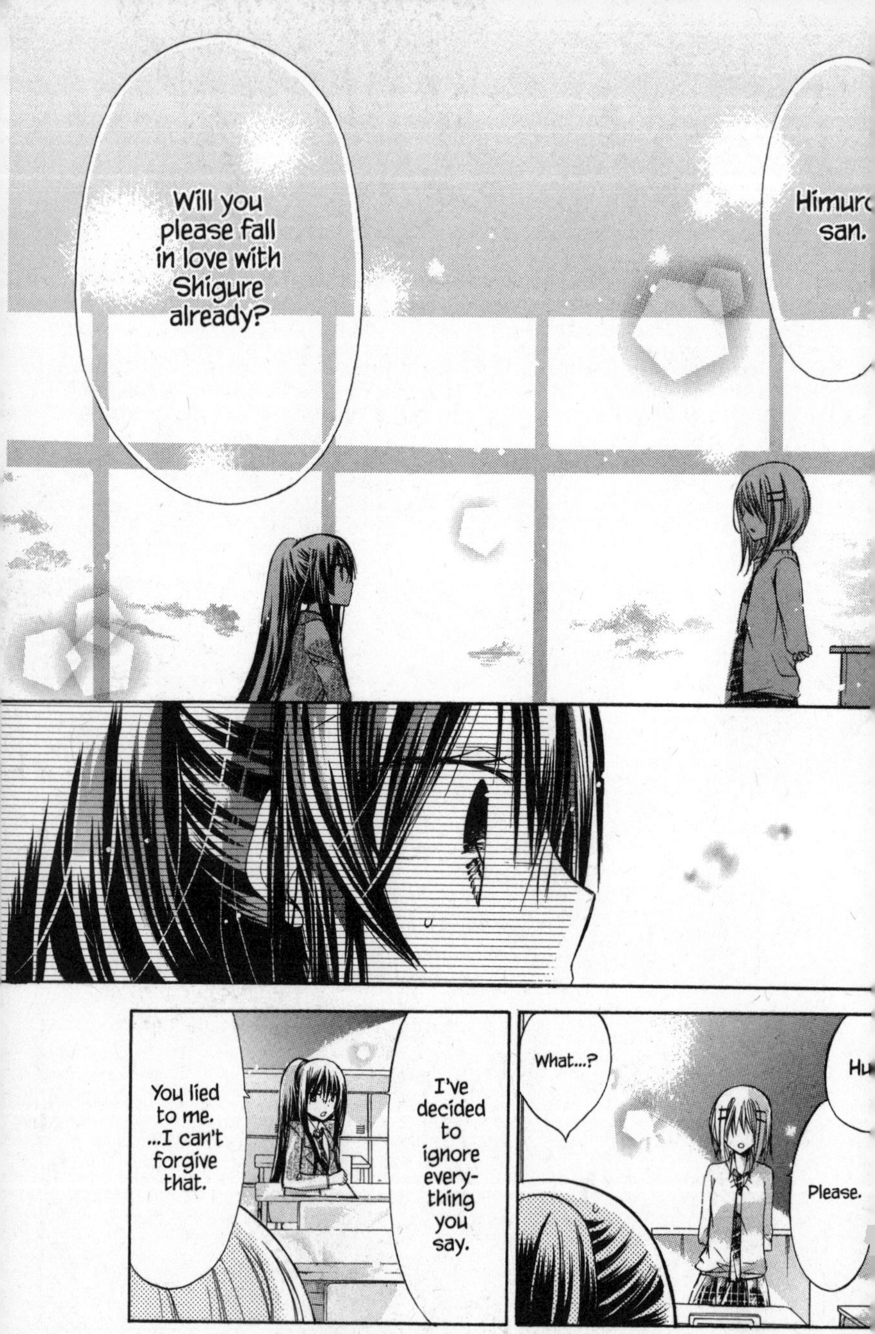
Himur
san.
Will you please fall in love with Shigure already?
Hu
What...?
Please.
I've decided to ignore every-thing you say.
You lied to me. ...I can't forgive that.

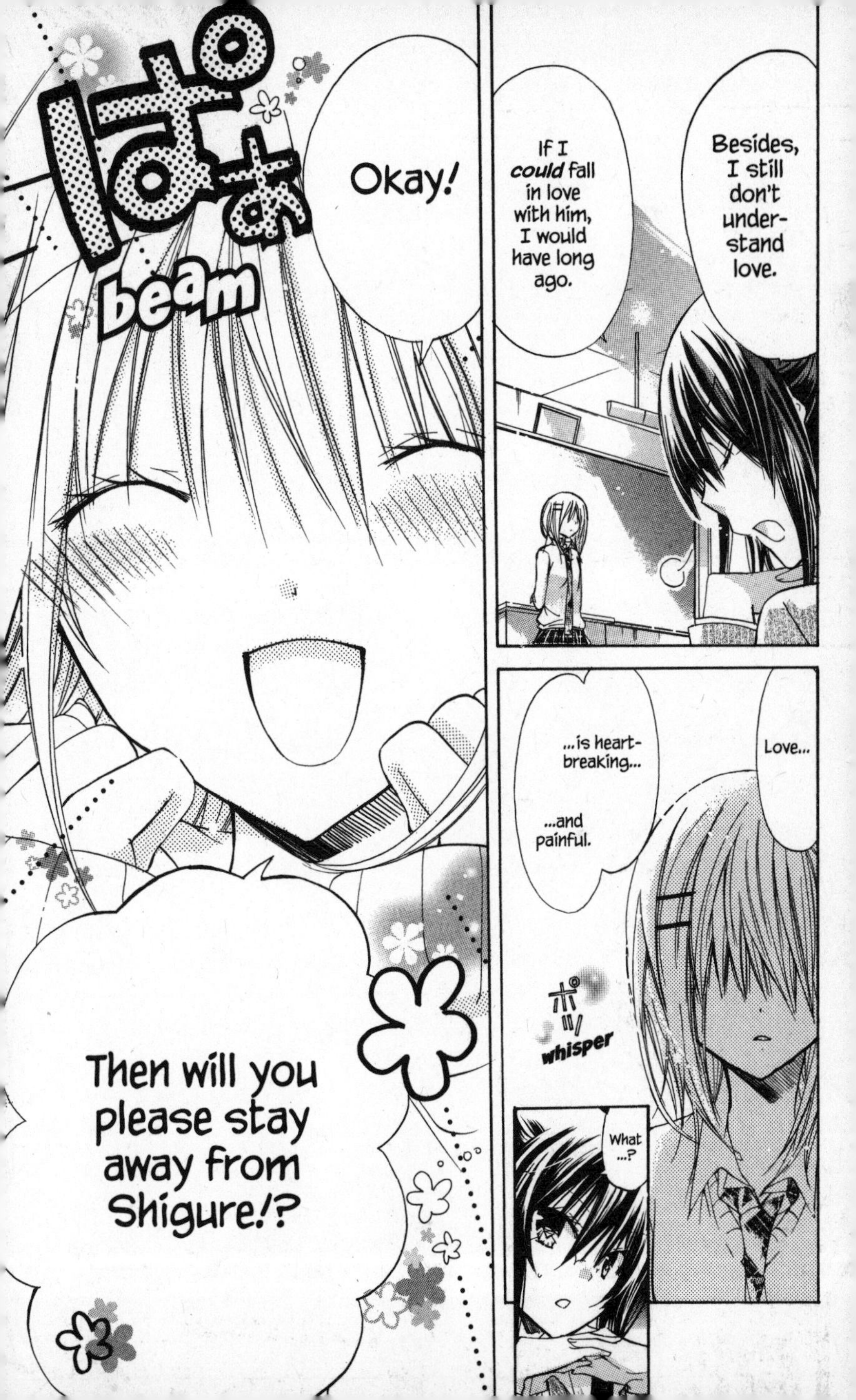
Besides, I still don't under-stand love.
If I *could* fall in love with him, I would have long ago.
Love...
...is heart-breaking...
...and painful.
whisper
What...?
beam
Okay!
Then will you please stay away from Shigure!?

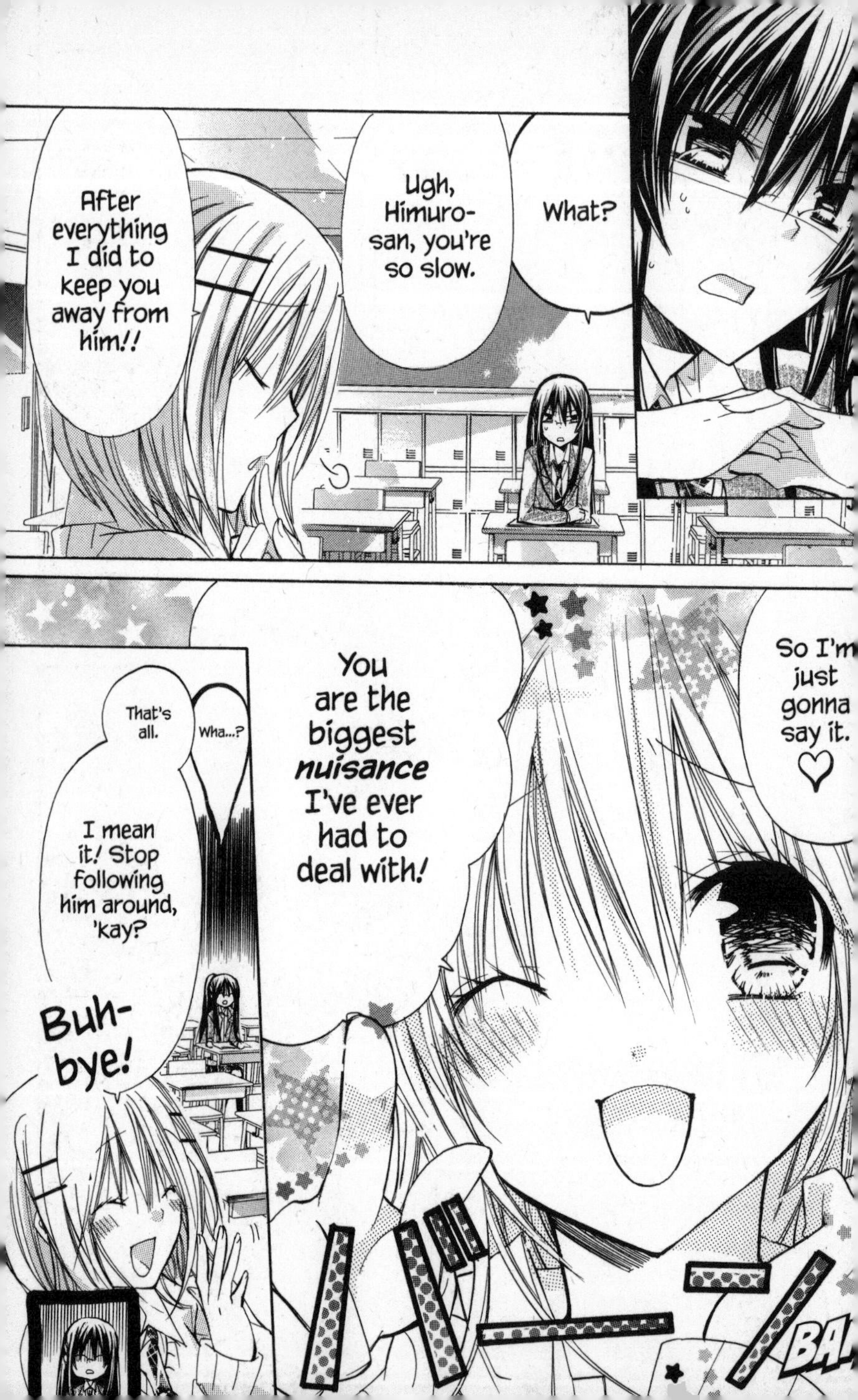
What?
Ugh, Himuro-san, you're so slow.
After everything I did to keep you away from him!!
So I'm just gonna say it. ♡
You are the biggest *nuisance* I've ever had to deal with!
Wha...?
That's all.
I mean it! Stop following him around, 'kay?
Buh-bye!

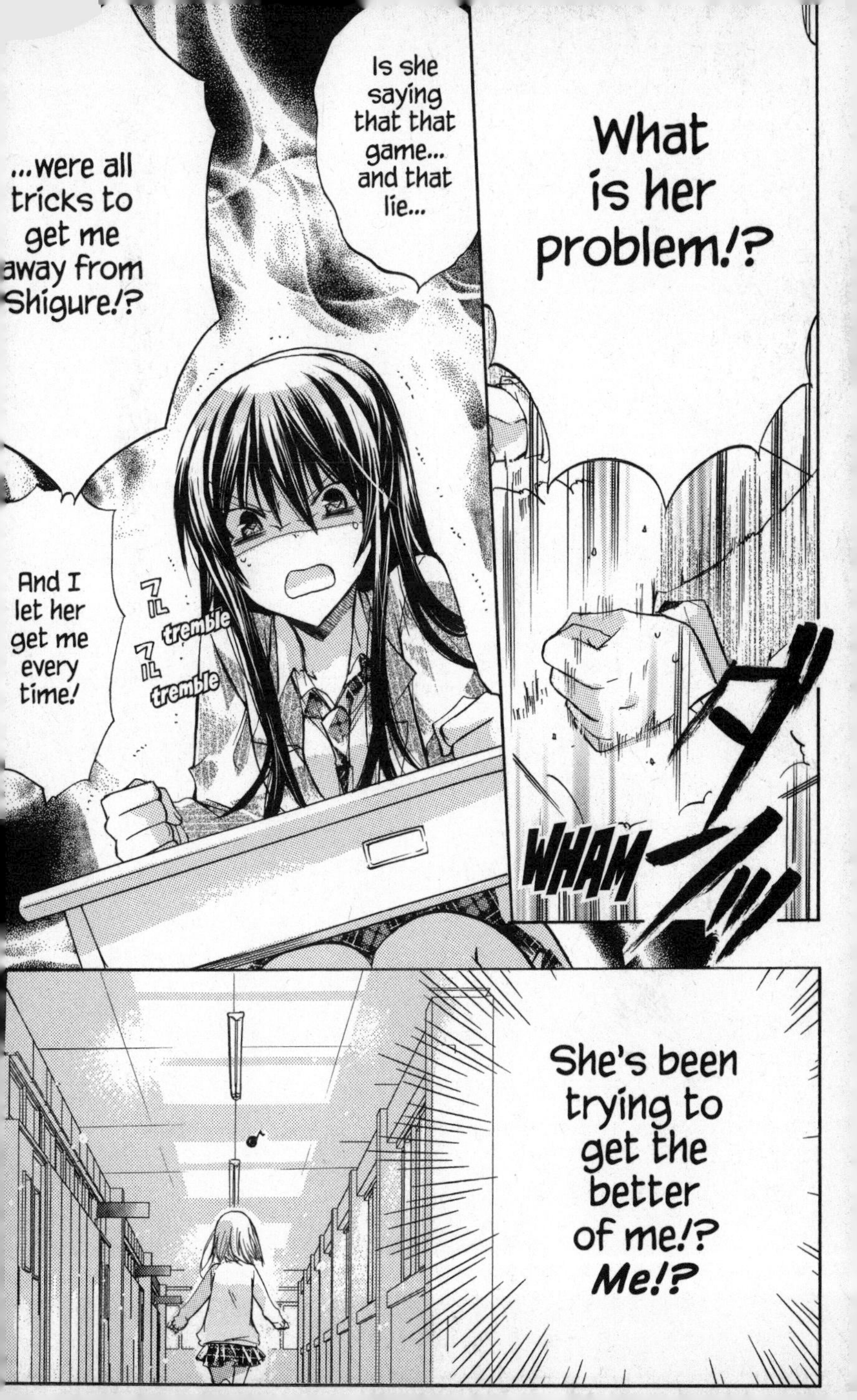
What is her problem!?
WHAM
Is she saying that that game... and that lie...
...were all tricks to get me away from Shigure!?
tremble
tremble
And I let her get me every time!
She's been trying to get the better of me!? *Me!?*

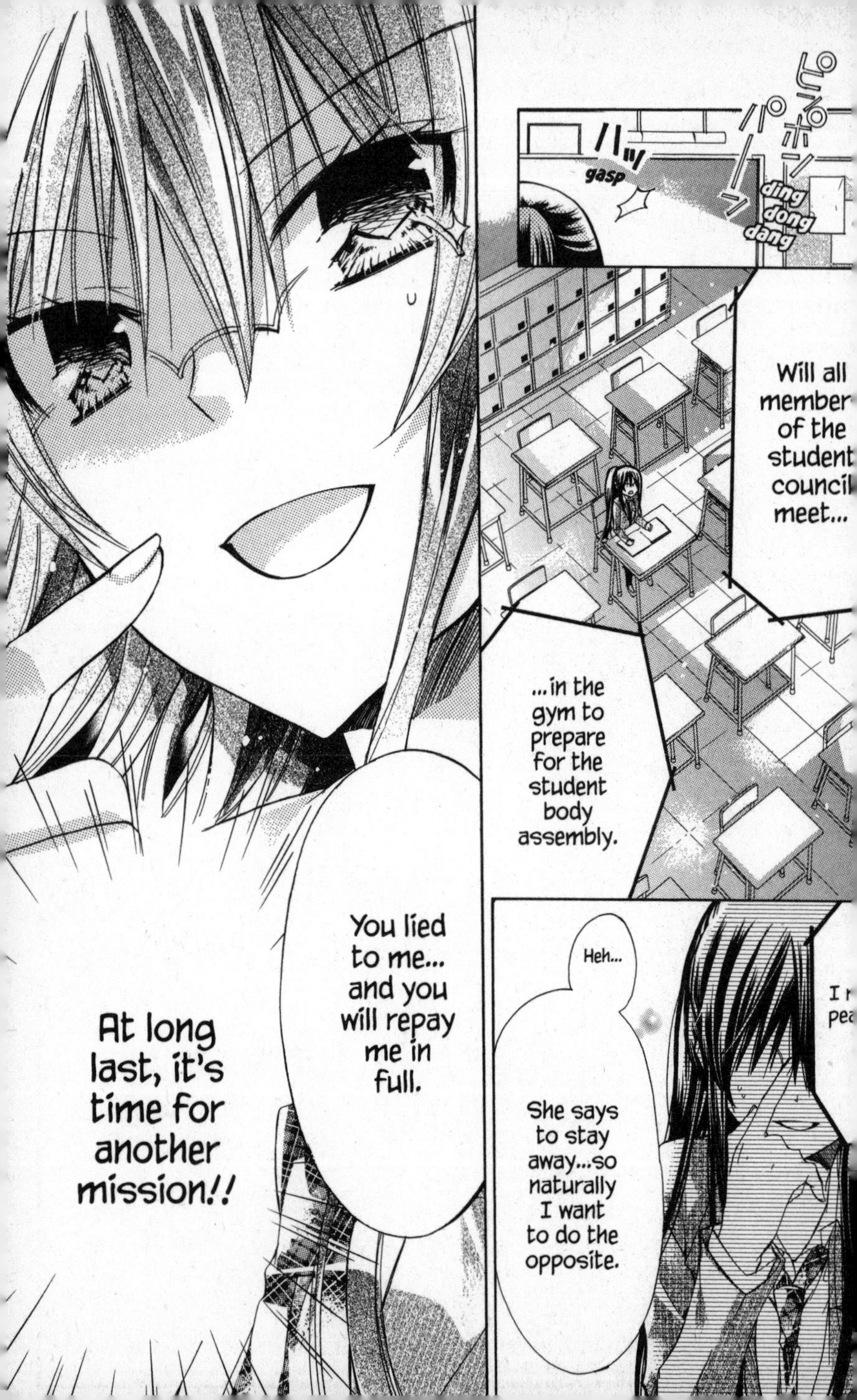
ding dong dang
gasp
Will all member of the student counci meet...
...in the gym to prepare for the student body assembly.
Heh...
She says to stay away...so naturally I want to do the opposite.
You lied to me... and you will repay me in full.
At long last, it's time for another mission!!

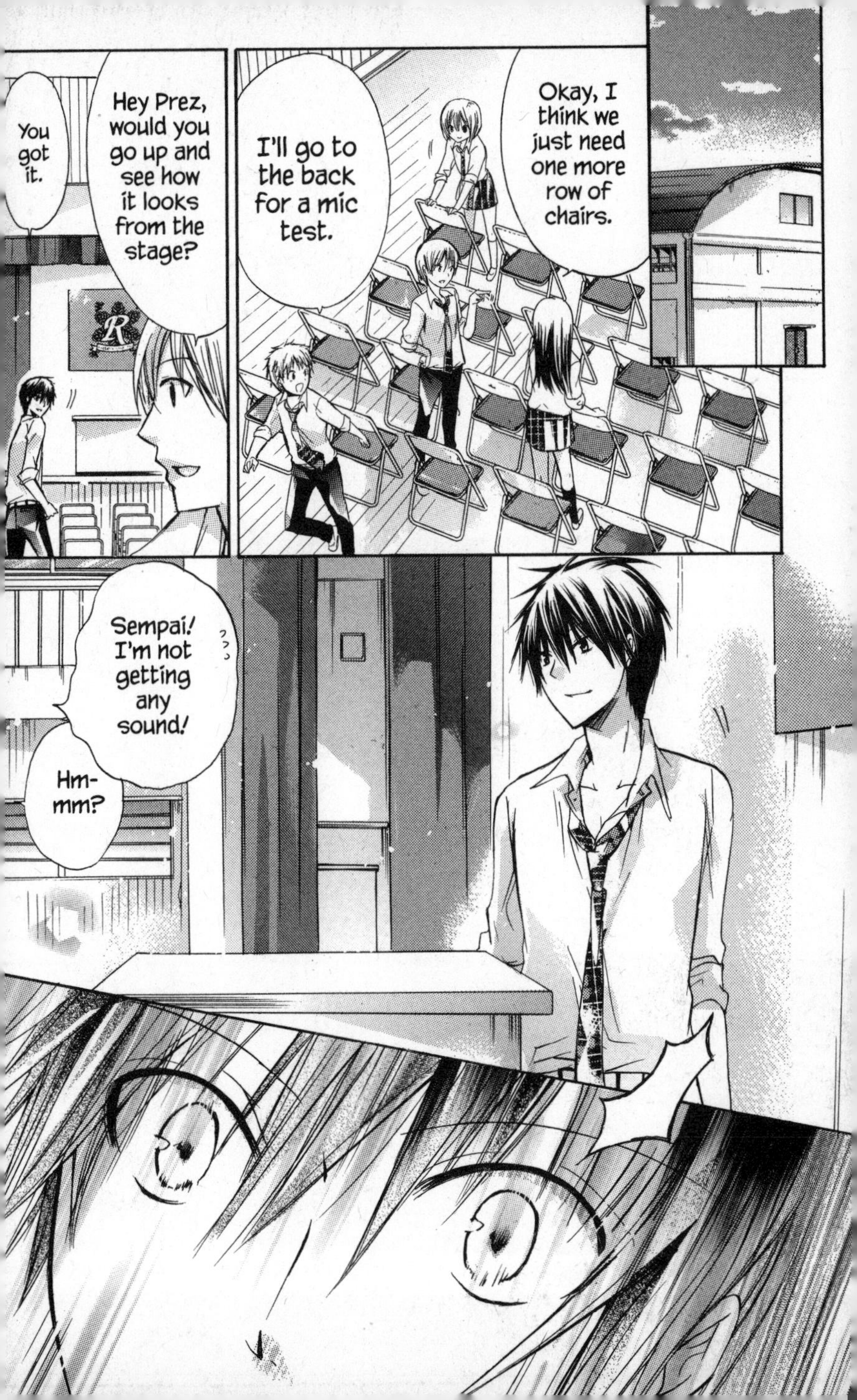
Okay, I think we just need one more row of chairs.
I'll go to the back for a mic test.
Hey Prez, would you go up and see how it looks from the stage?
You got it.
Sempai! I'm not getting any sound!
Hm-mm?

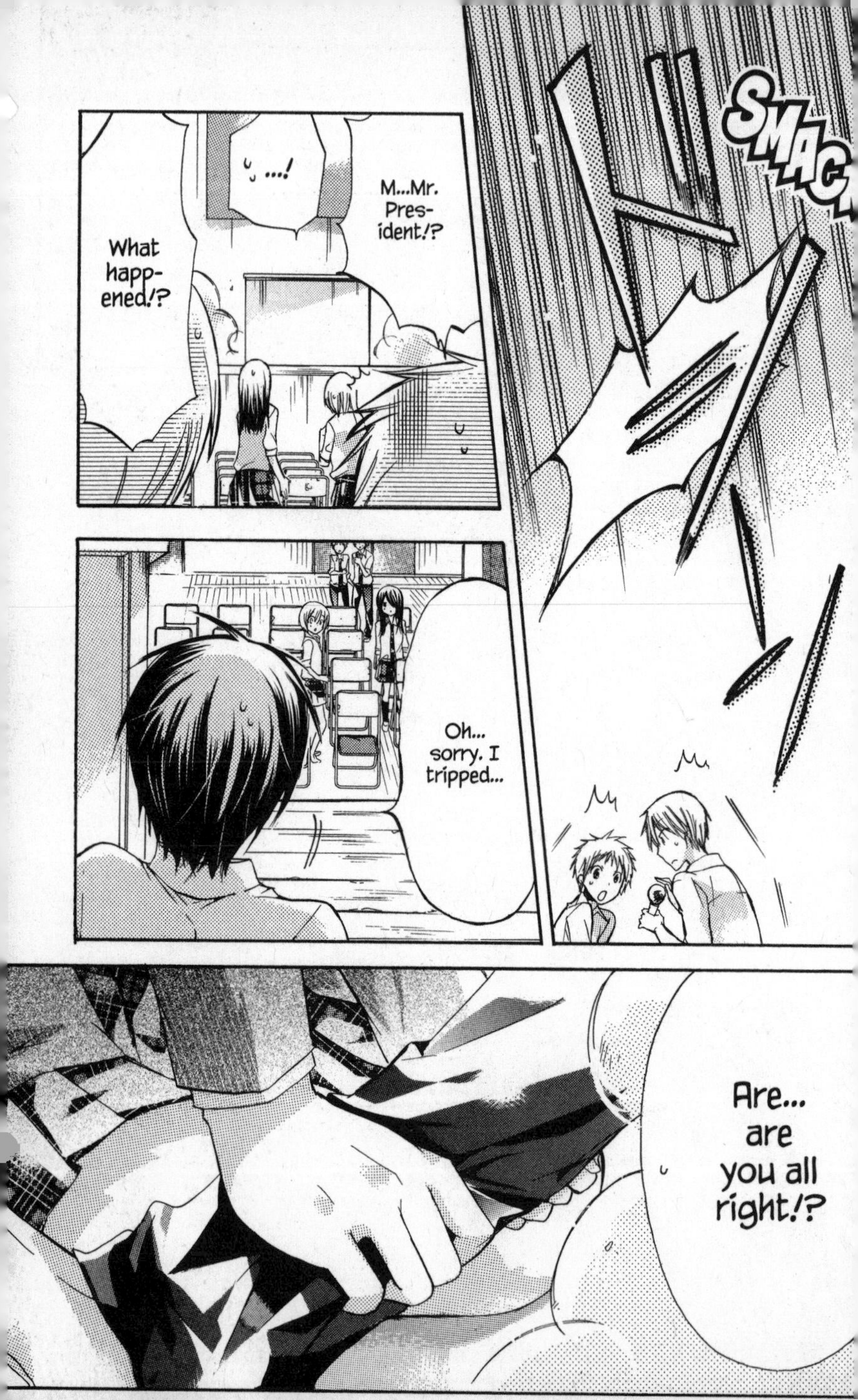

SMAC
...!
M...Mr. President!?
What happened!?
Oh... sorry. I tripped...
Are... are you all right!?

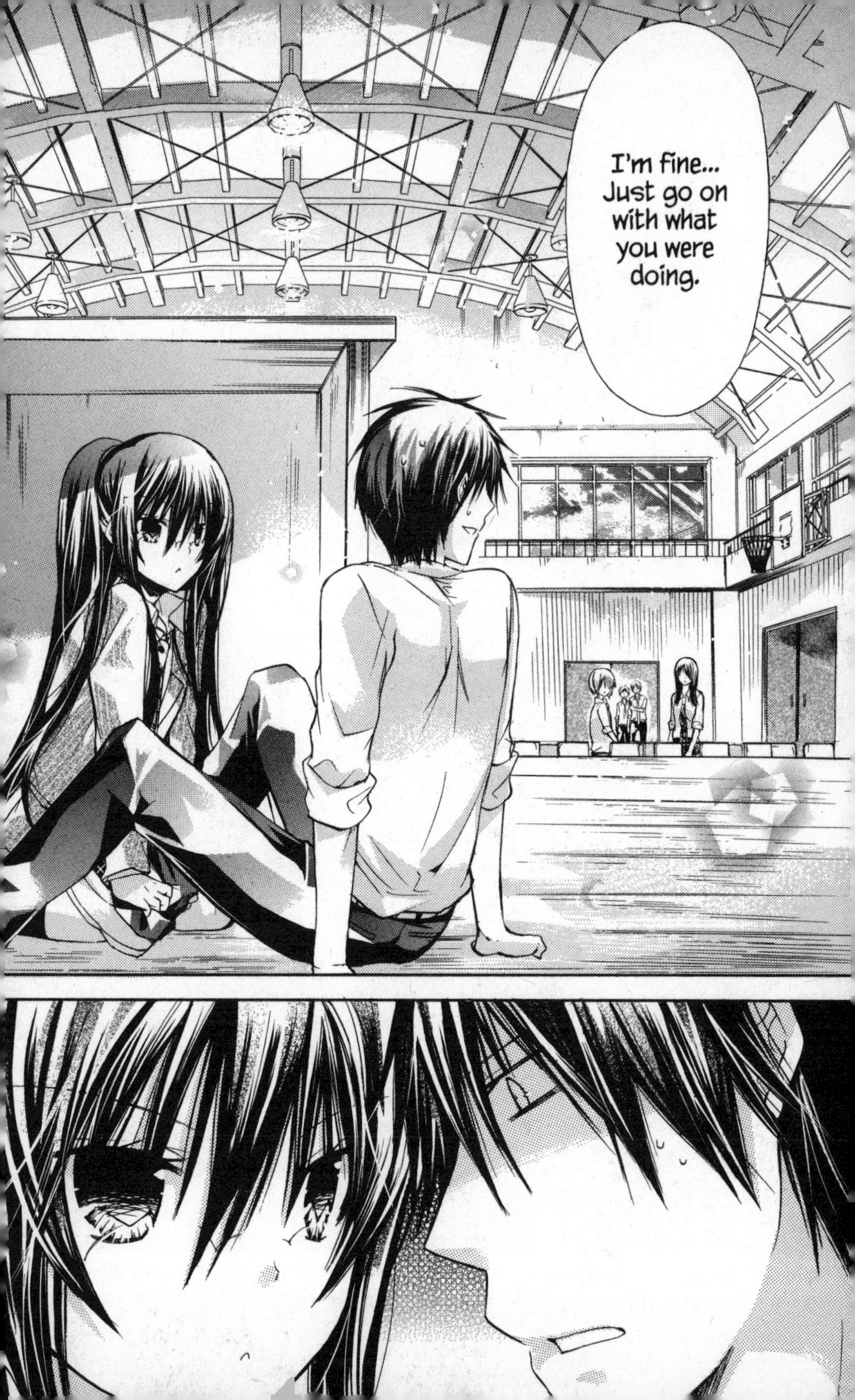
I'm fine... Just go on with what you were doing.

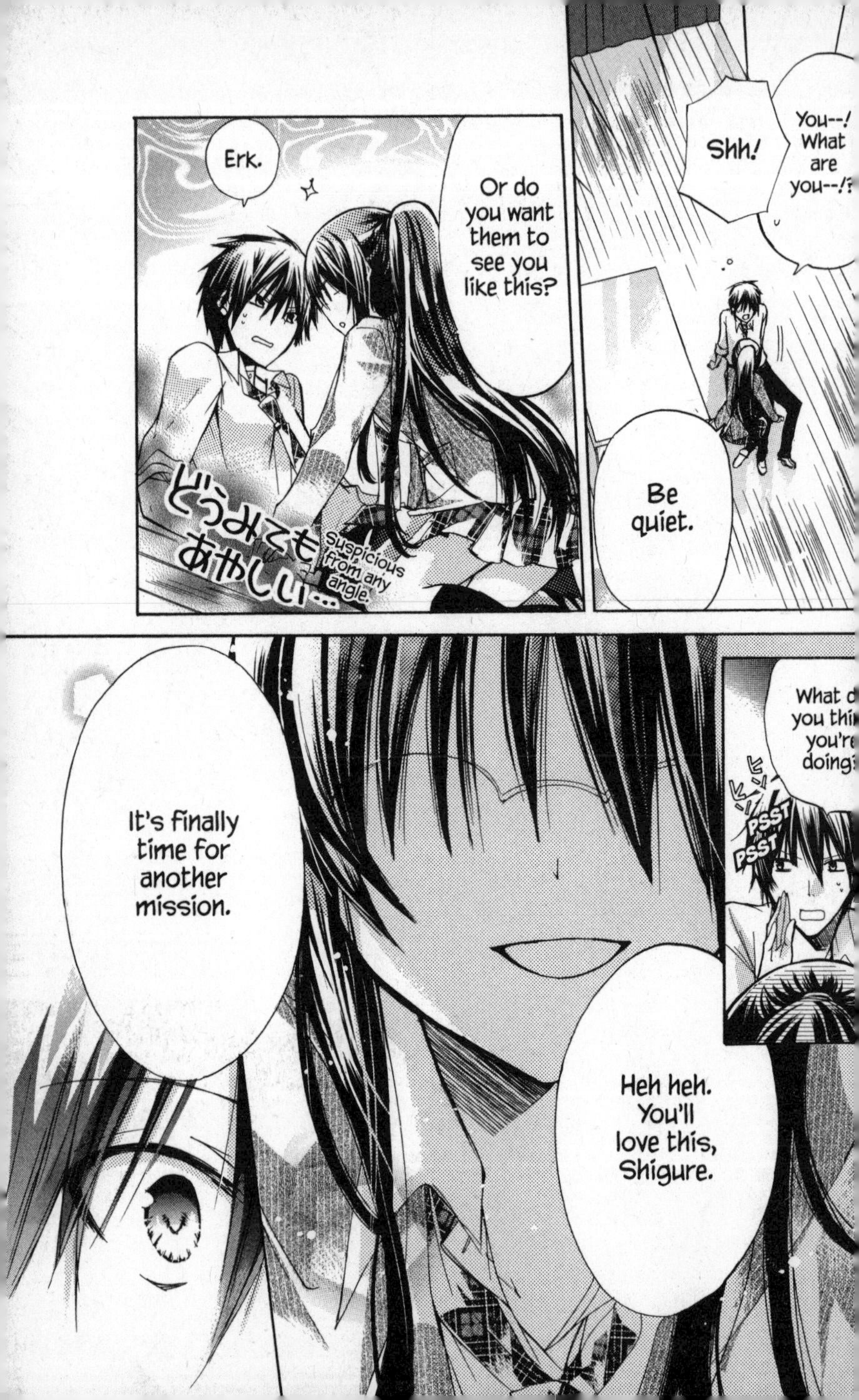
You--! What are you--!?
Shh!
Be quiet.
Or do you want them to see you like this?
Erk.
どうみてもあやしい…
Suspicious from any angle.
What d you thi you're doing
PSST PSST
It's finally time for another mission.
Heh heh. You'll love this, Shigure.

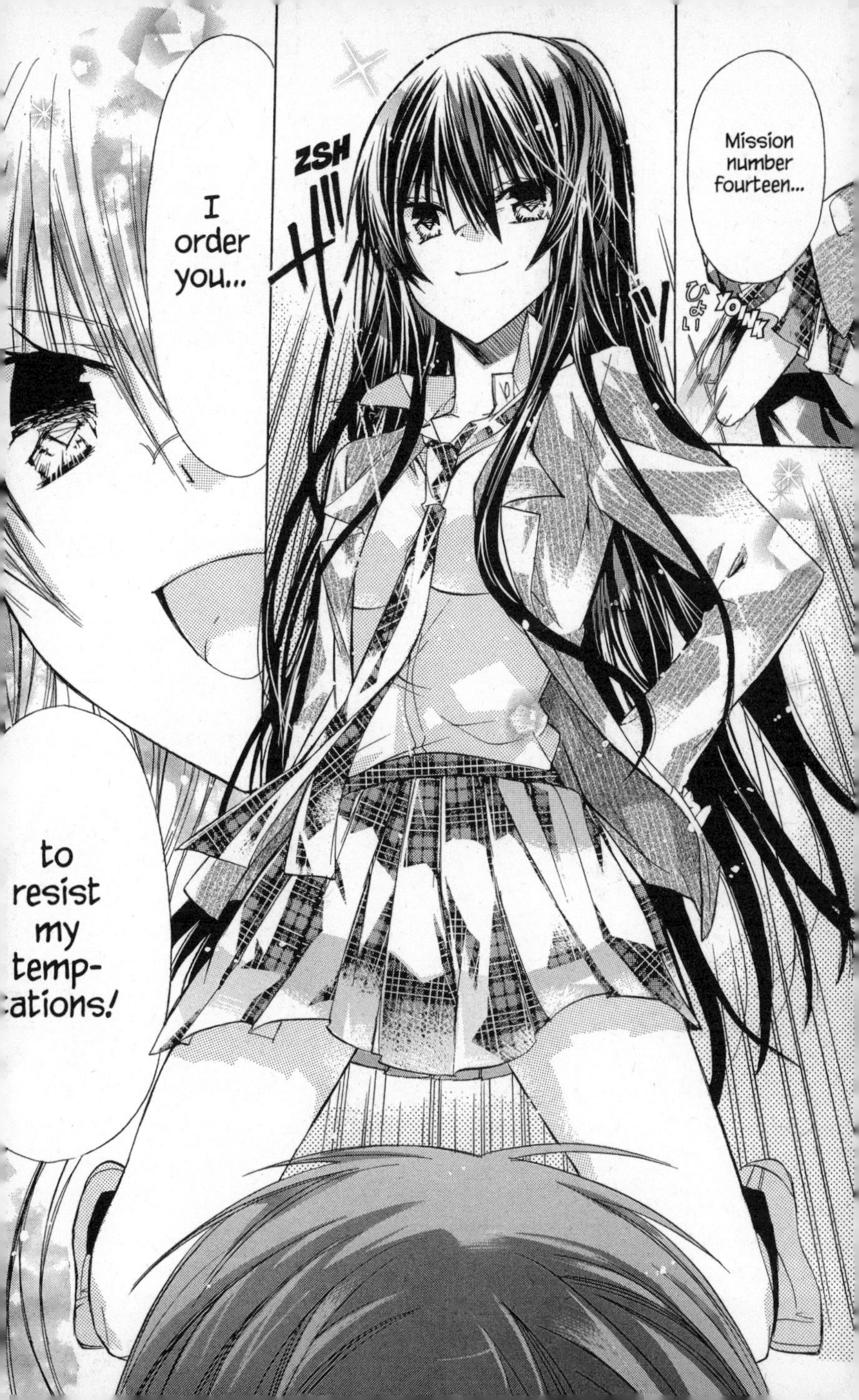
Mission number fourteen...
ひょい
YOINK
ZSH
I order you...
to resist my temp-ations!

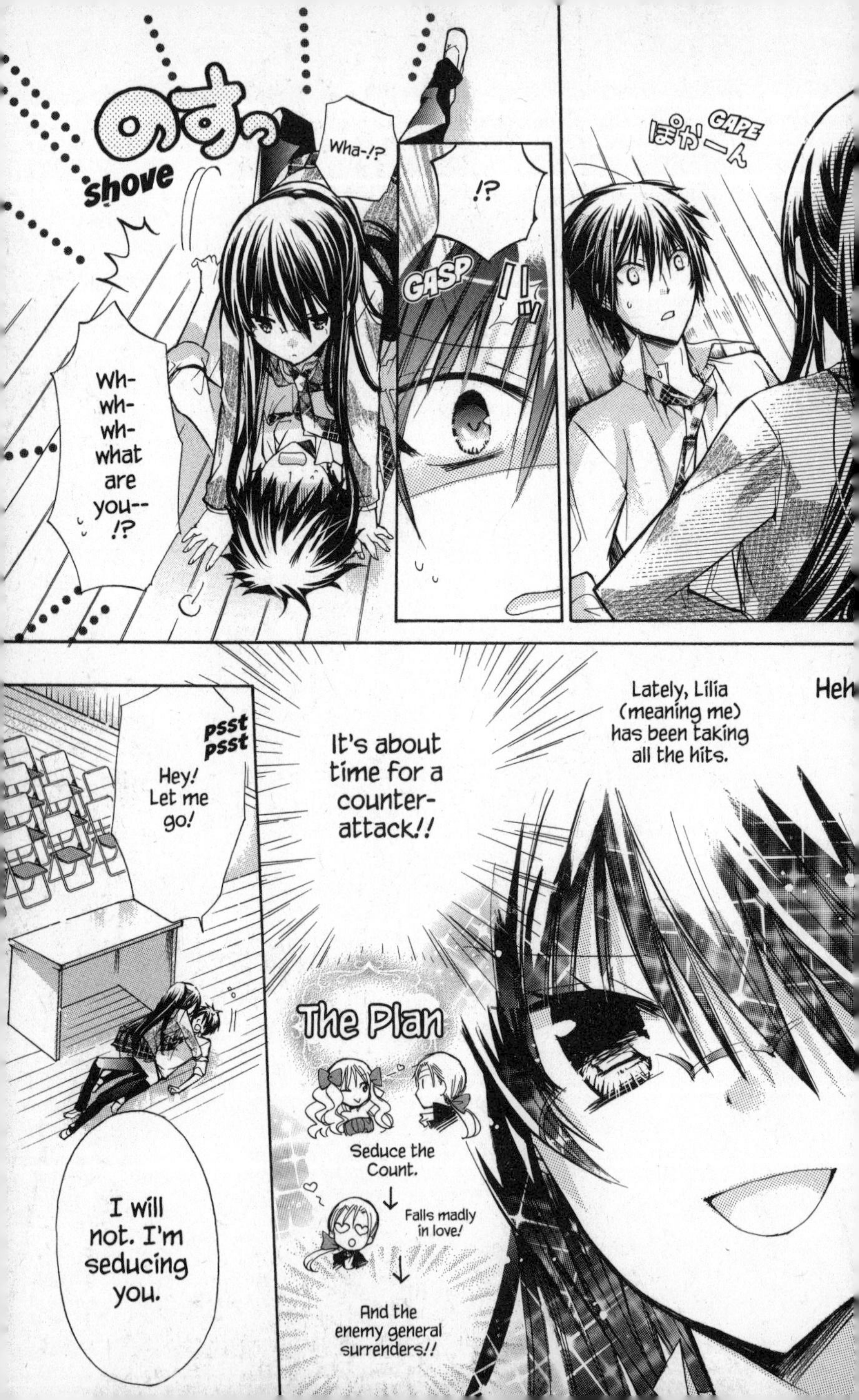
GAPE
ぽかーん
!?
GASP
Wha-!?
のすっ
shove
Wh-wh-wh-what are you--!?
Heh
Lately, Lilia (meaning me) has been taking all the hits.
It's about time for a counter-attack!!
The Plan
Seduce the Count.
Falls madly in love!
And the enemy general surrenders!!
psst psst
Hey! Let me go!
I will not. I'm seducing you.

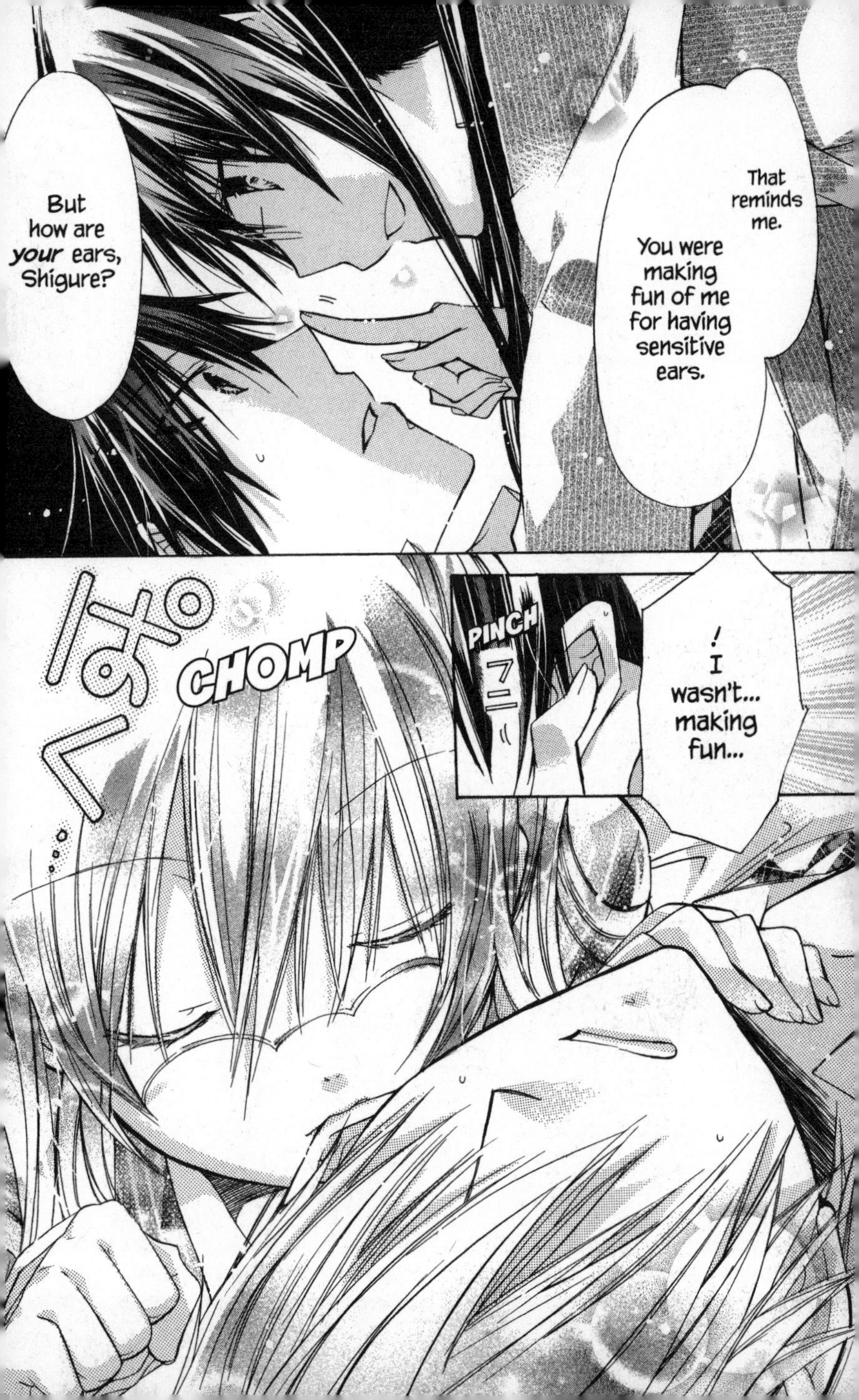
That reminds me.
You were making fun of me for having sensitive ears.
But how are *your* ears, Shigure?
! I wasn't... making fun...
PINCH
CHOMP

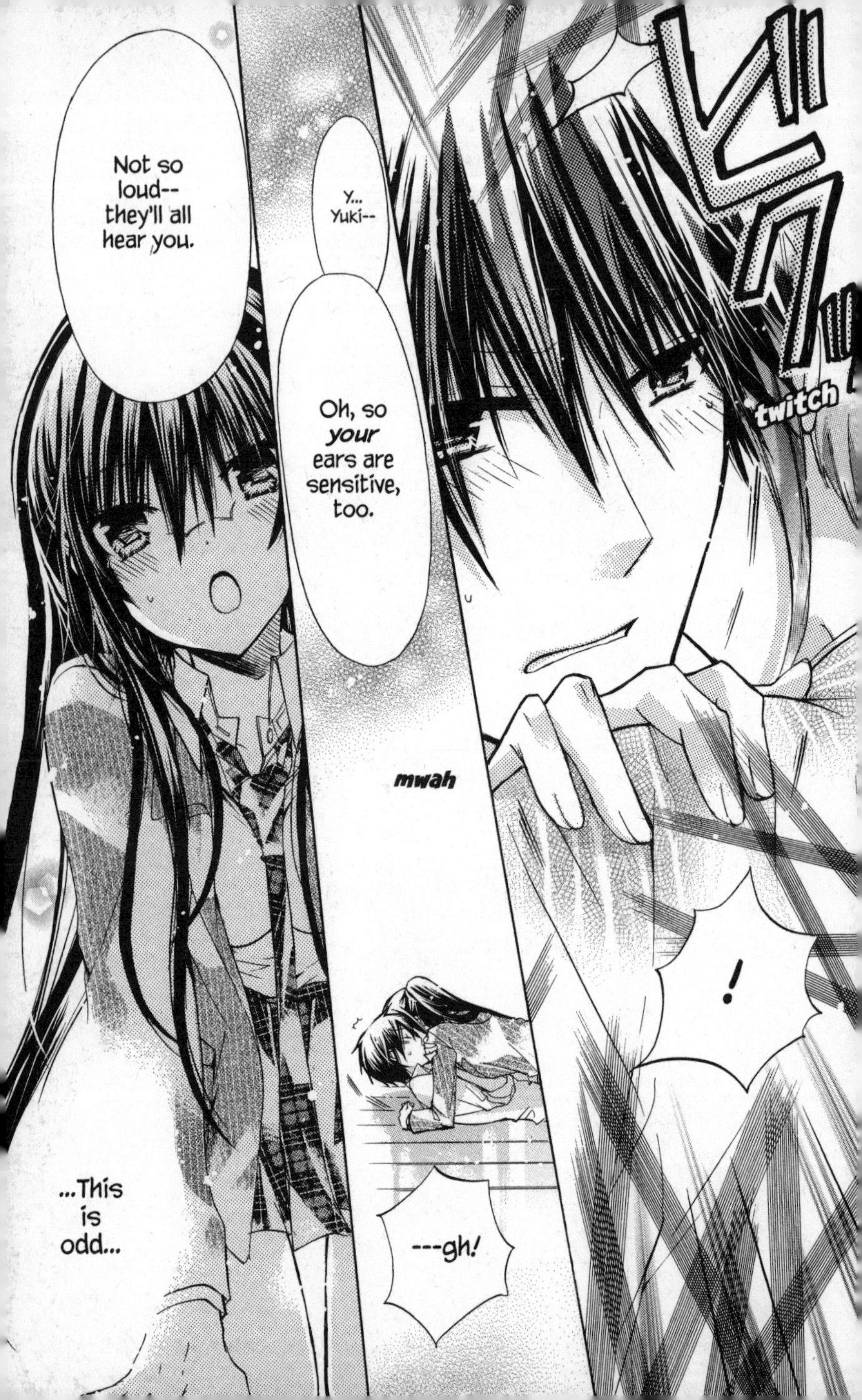
twitch
!
Y... Yuki--
Oh, so *your* ears are sensitive, too.
mwah
---gh!
Not so loud-- they'll all hear you.
...This is odd...

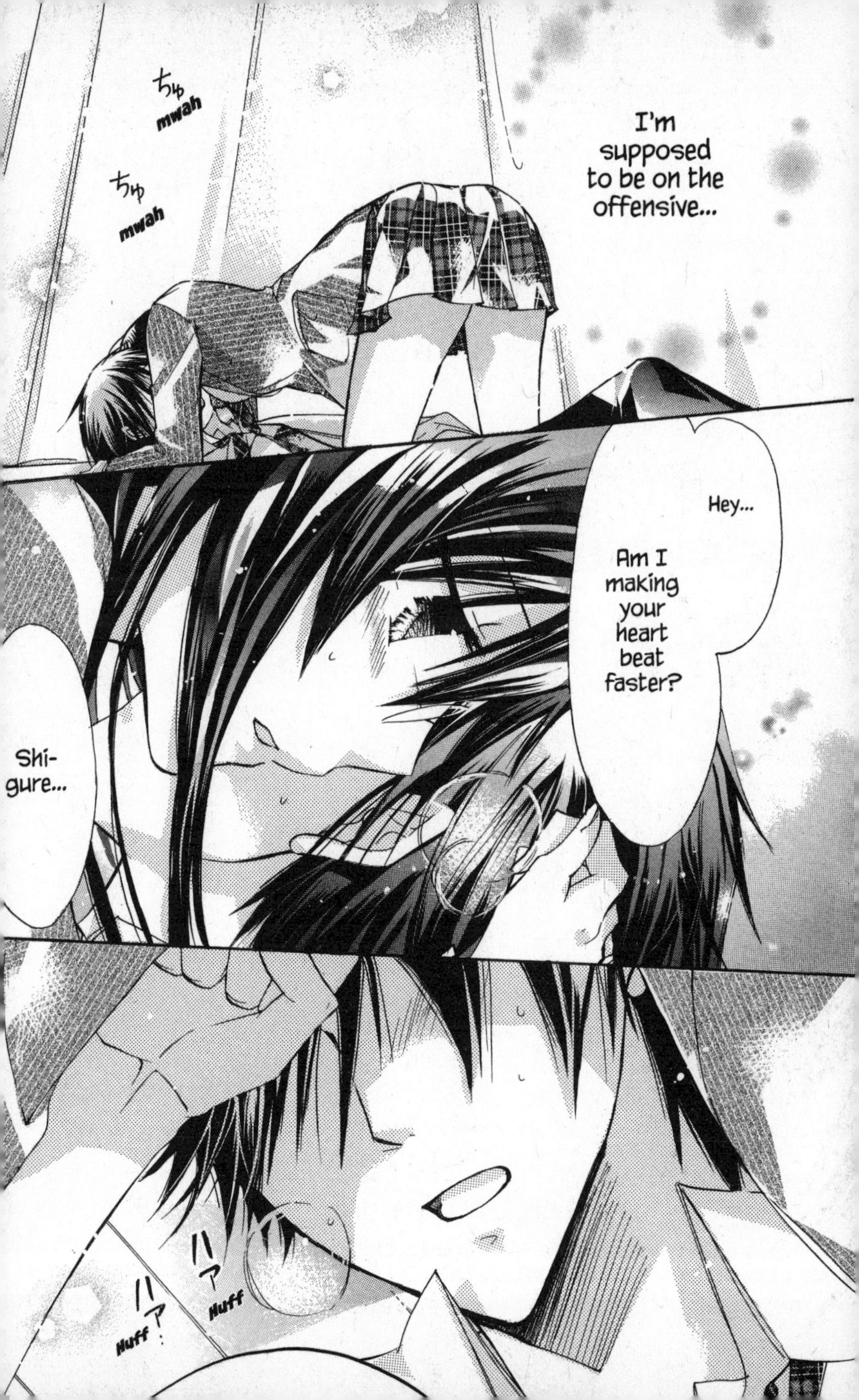
I'm supposed to be on the offensive...
ちゅ
mwah
ちゅ
mwah
Hey...
Am I making your heart beat faster?
Shi-gure...
ハァ
Huff
ハァ
Huff

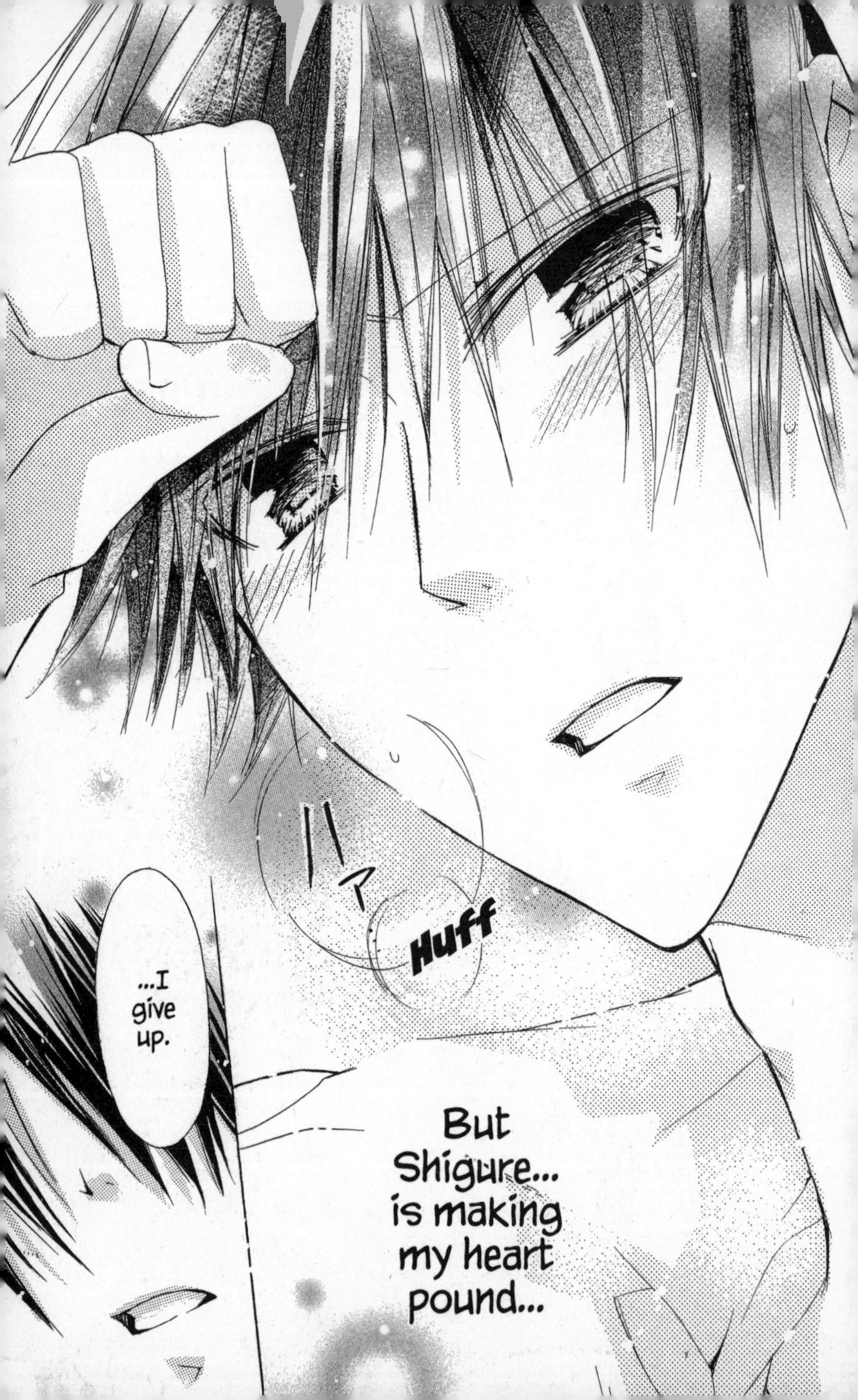
Huff
...I give up.
But Shigure... is making my heart pound...

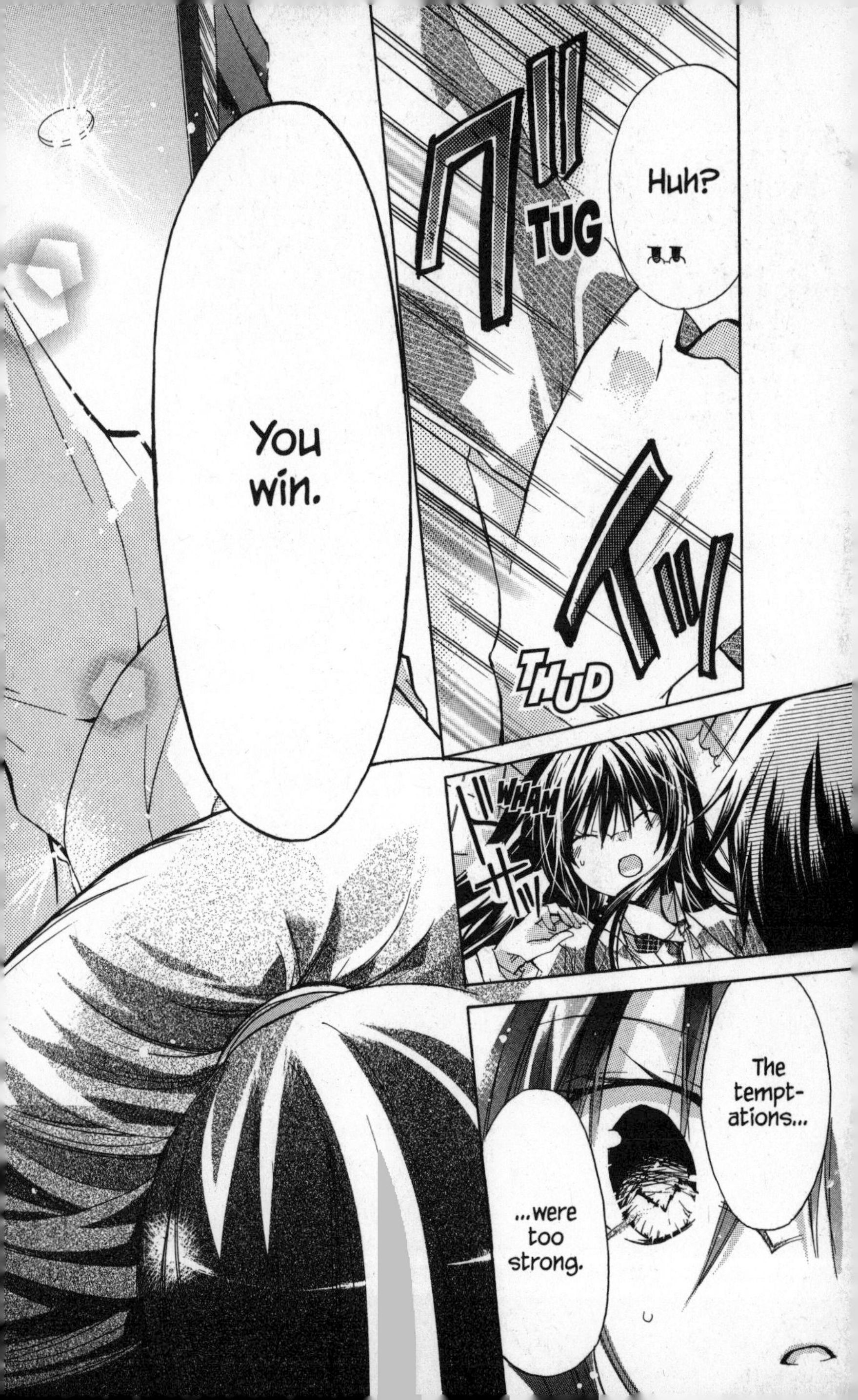
Huh?
TUG
THUD
WHAM
The temptations...
...were too strong.
You win.

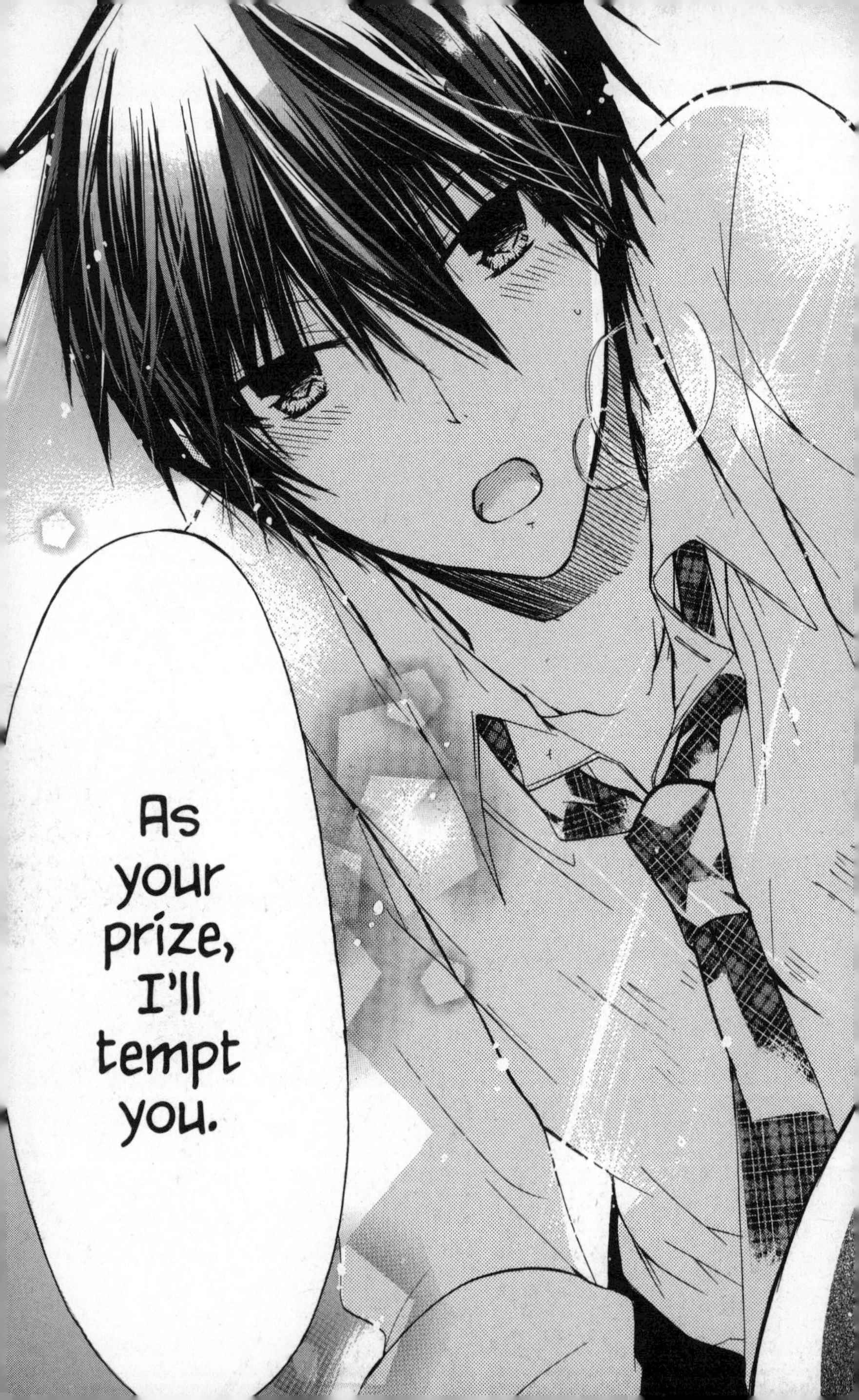
As your prize, I'll tempt you.

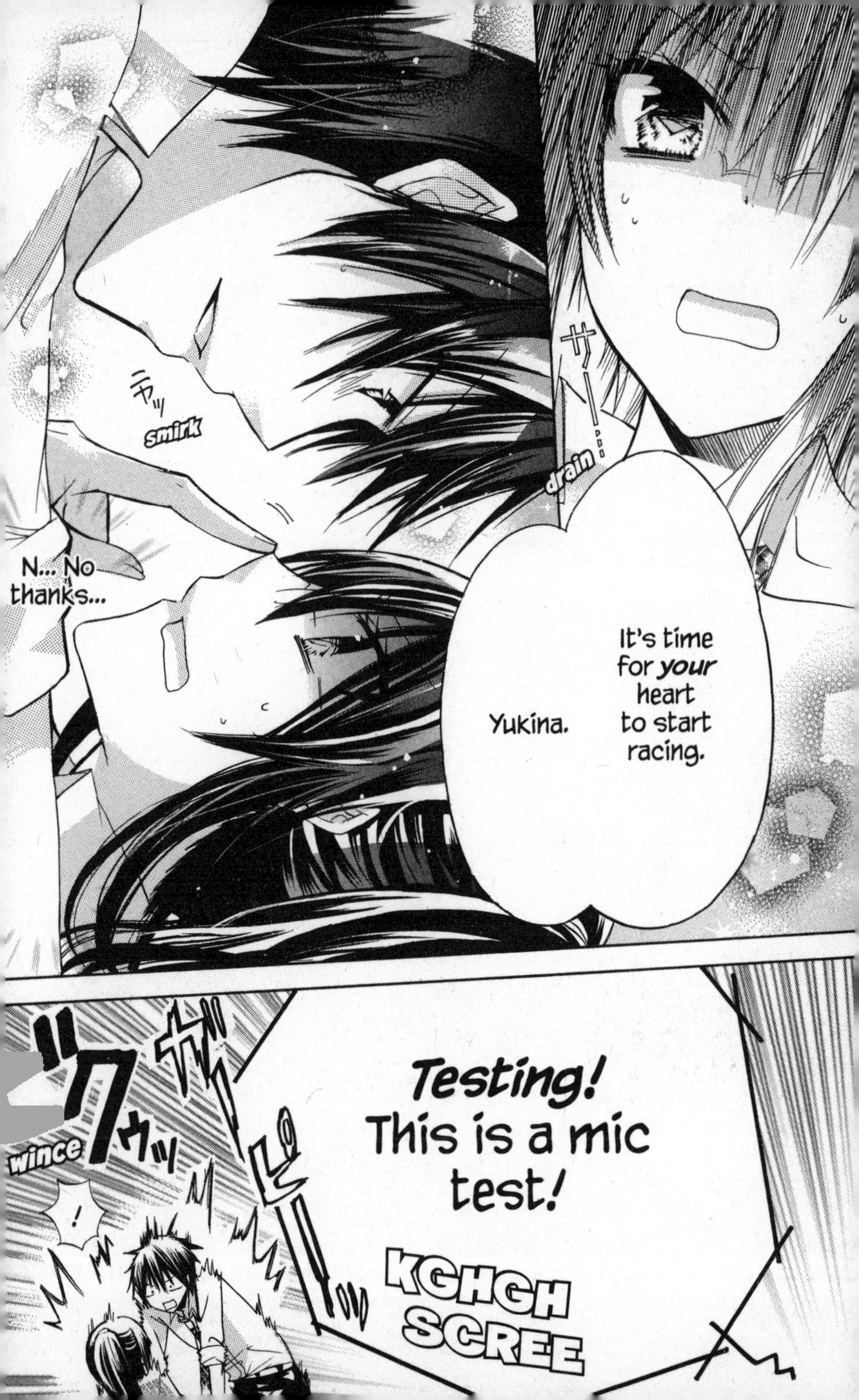

It's time for *your* heart to start racing.
Yukina.
drain
ニヤッ
smirk
N... No thanks...
Testing! This is a mic test!
KGHGH SCREE
wince
!

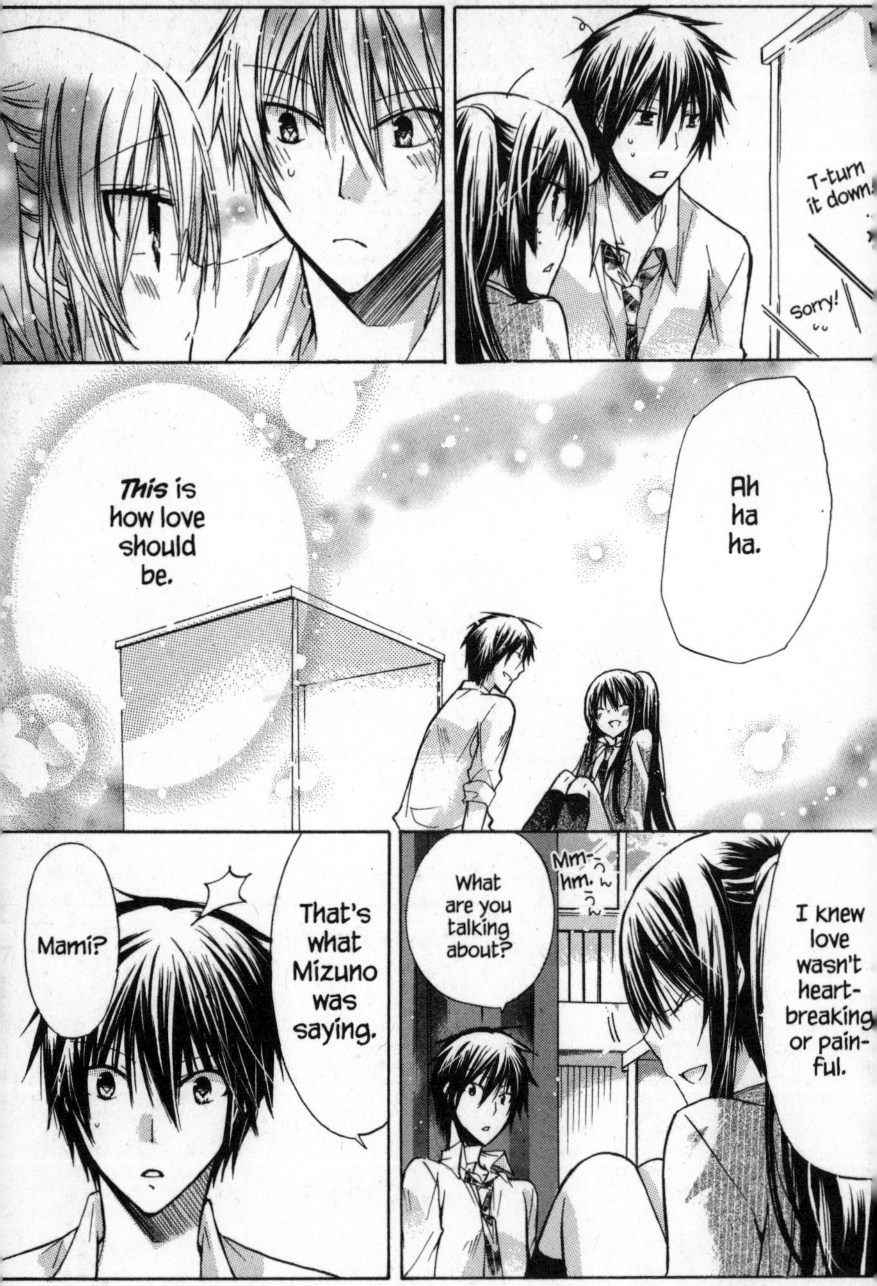
T-turn it down!
Sorry!
Ah ha ha.
This is how love should be.
I knew love wasn't heart-breaking or pain-ful.
Mm-hm.
What are you talking about?
That's what Mizuno was saying.
Mami?

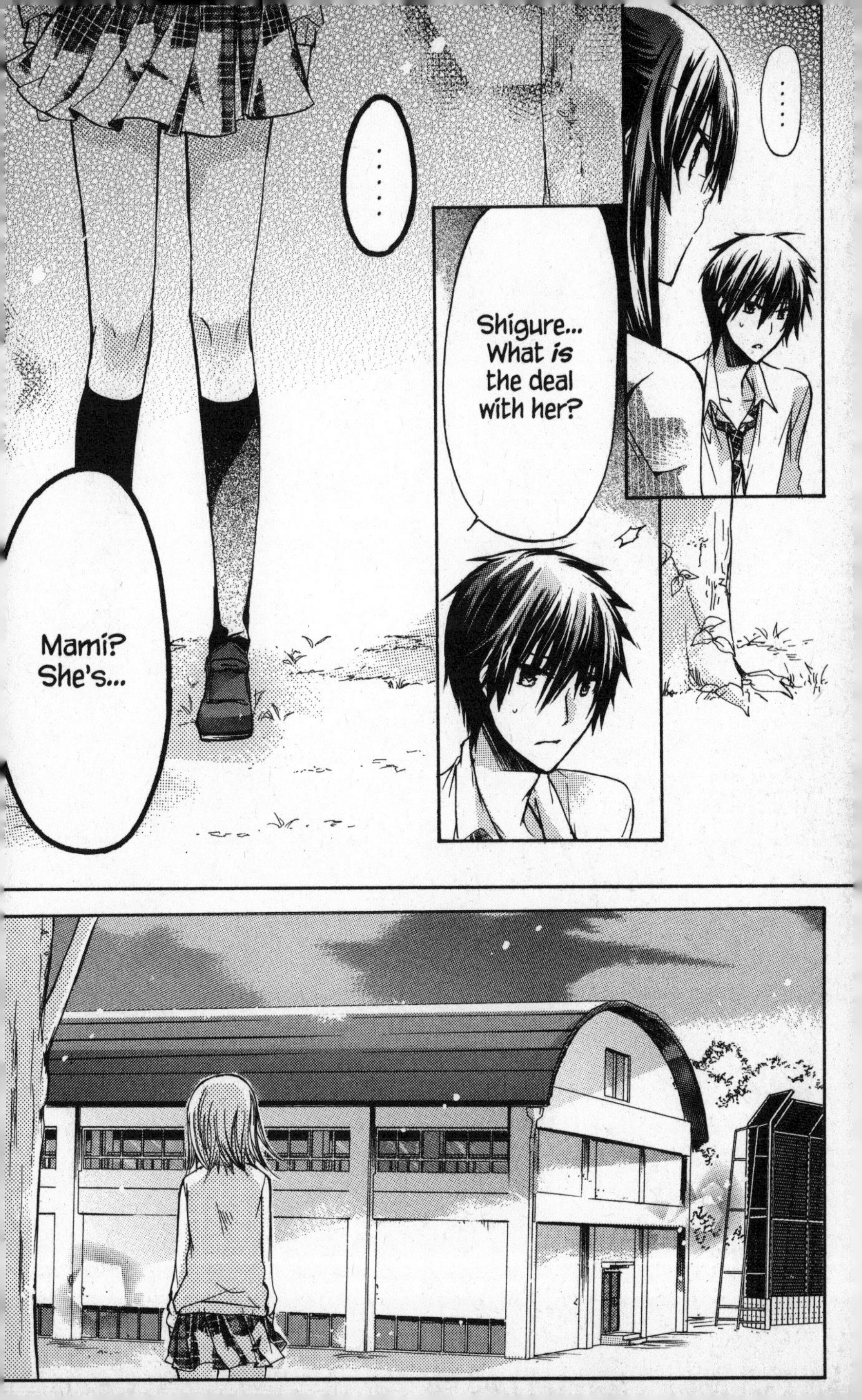
......
Shigure... What *is* the deal with her?
......
Mami? She's...

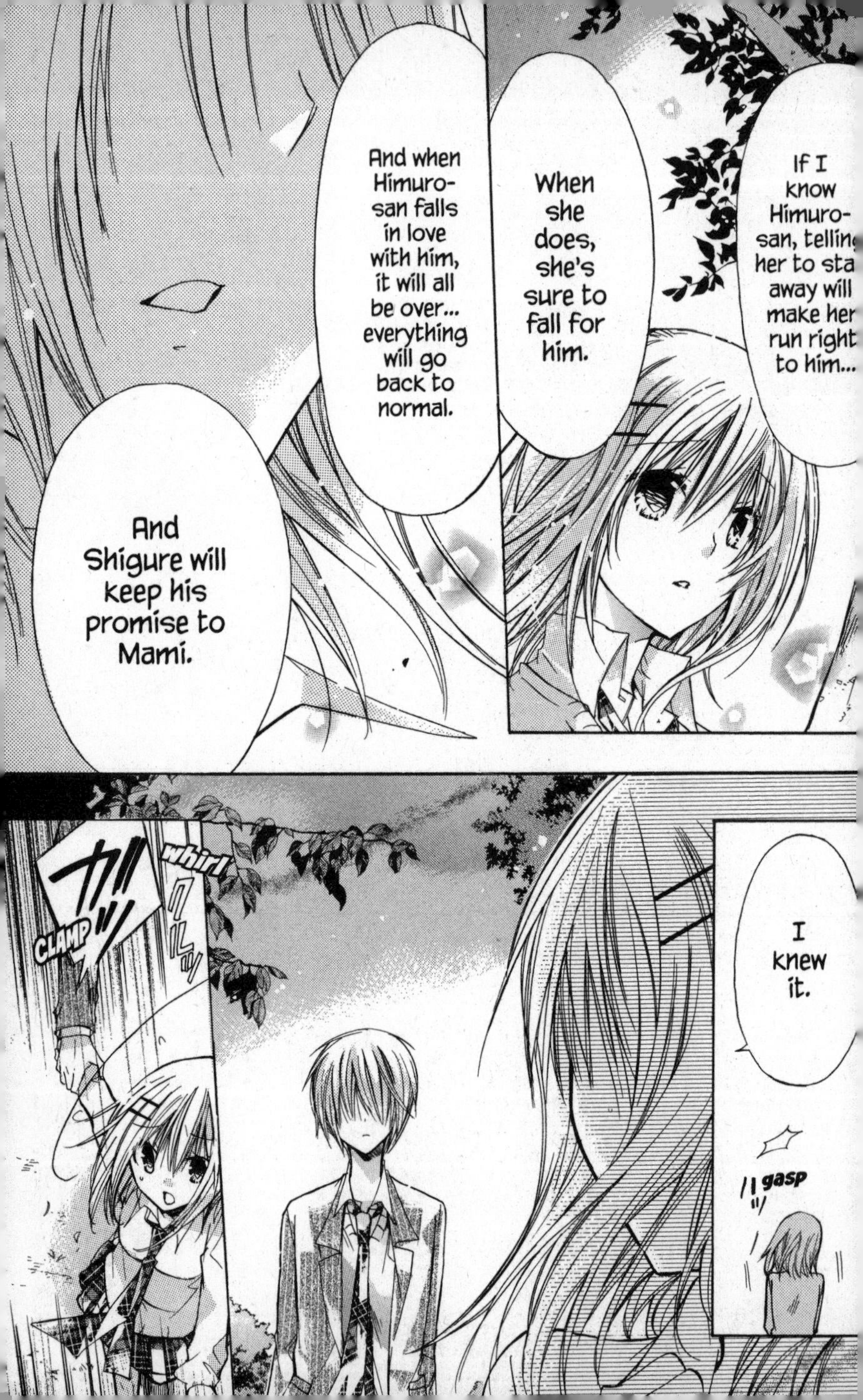

If I know Himuro-san, tellin her to sta away will make her run right to him...
When she does, she's sure to fall for him.
And when Himuro-san falls in love with him, it will all be over... everything will go back to normal.
And Shigure will keep his promise to Mami.
I knew it.
gasp
whirl
クルッ
カッ
CLAMP

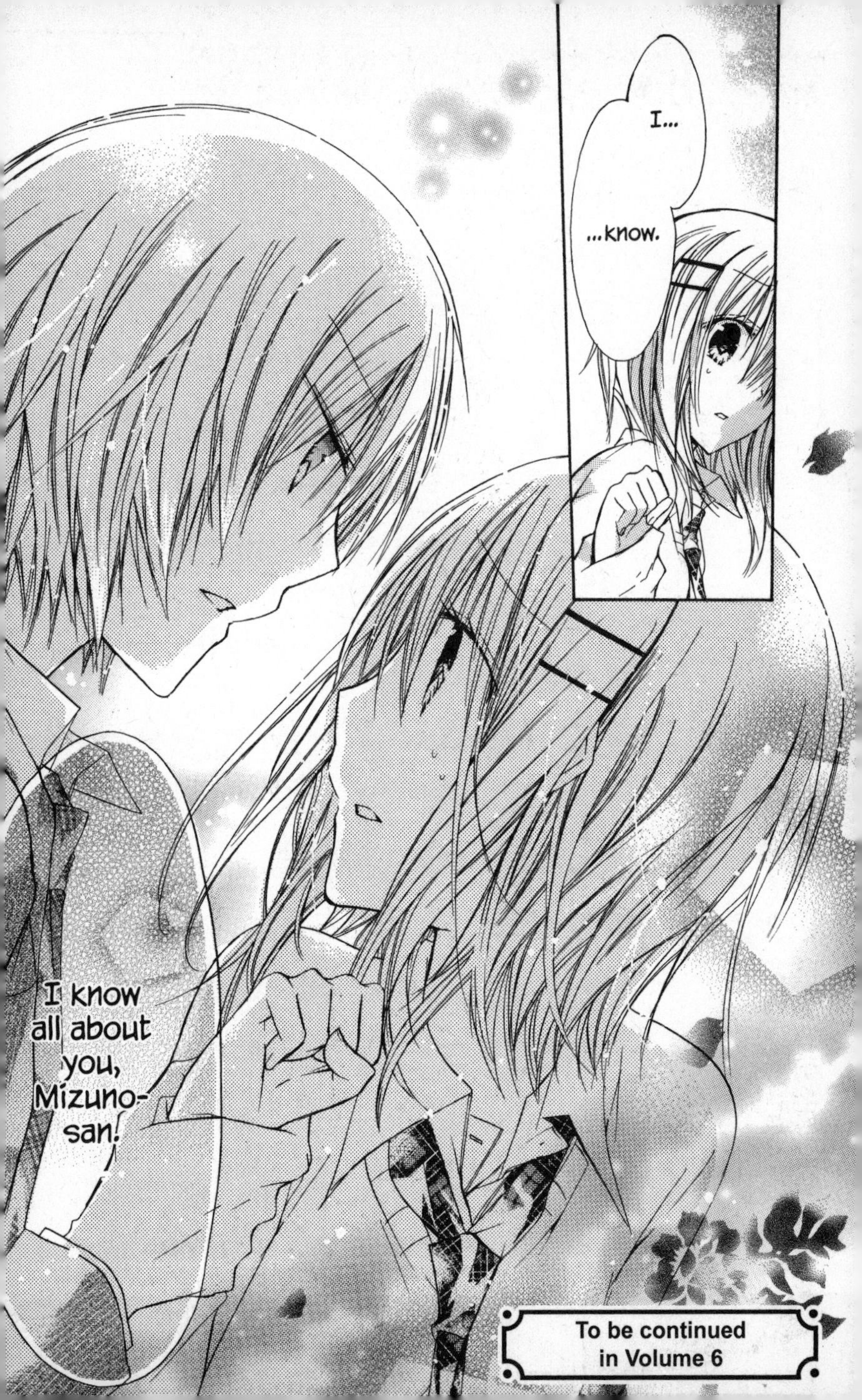
I...
...know.
I know all about you, Mizuno-san!
To be continued in Volume 6

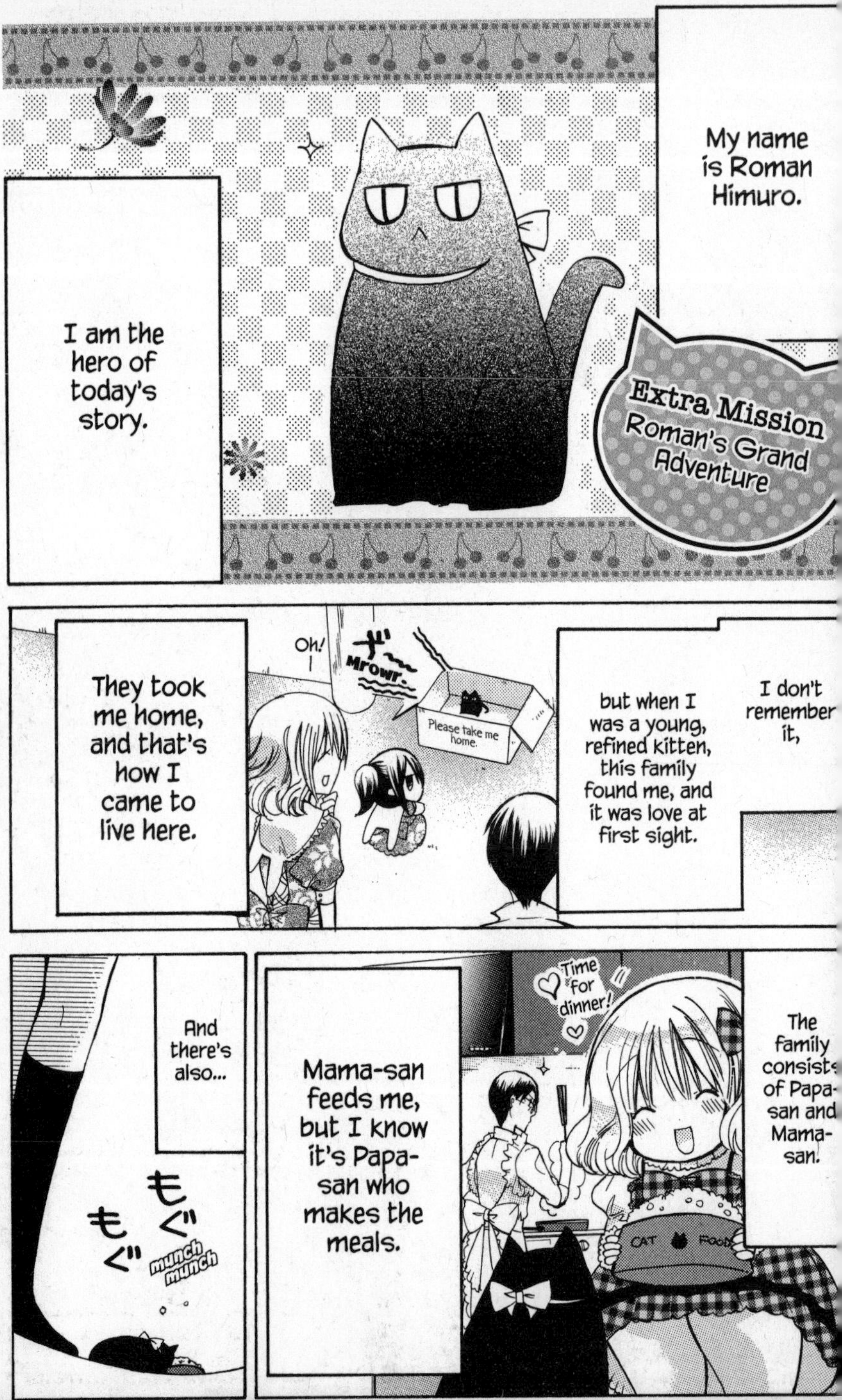

My name is Roman Himuro.
Extra Mission
Roman's Grand Adventure
I am the hero of today's story.
I don't remember it,
but when I was a young, refined kitten, this family found me, and it was love at first sight.
Mrowr.
Oh!
Please take me home.
They took me home, and that's how I came to live here.
The family consists of Papa-san and Mama-san.
Time for dinner!
CAT FOOD
Mama-san feeds me, but I know it's Papa-san who makes the meals.
And there's also...
もぐもぐ
munch munch

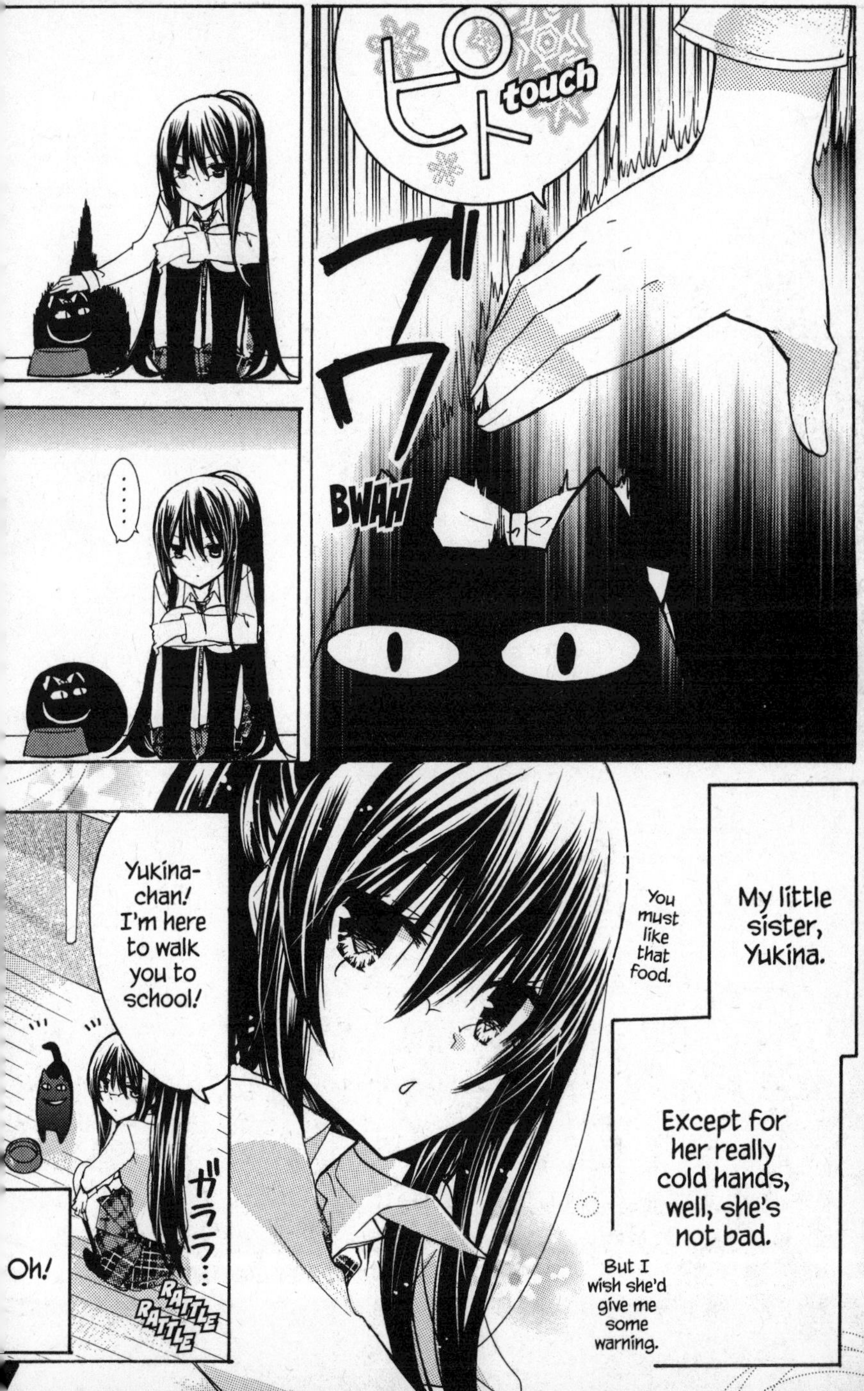

ピト
touch
ブワ
BWAH
......
My little sister, Yukina.
You must like that food.
Except for her really cold hands, well, she's not bad.
But I wish she'd give me some warning.
Yukina-chan! I'm here to walk you to school!
ガララ…
RATTLE RATTLE
Oh!

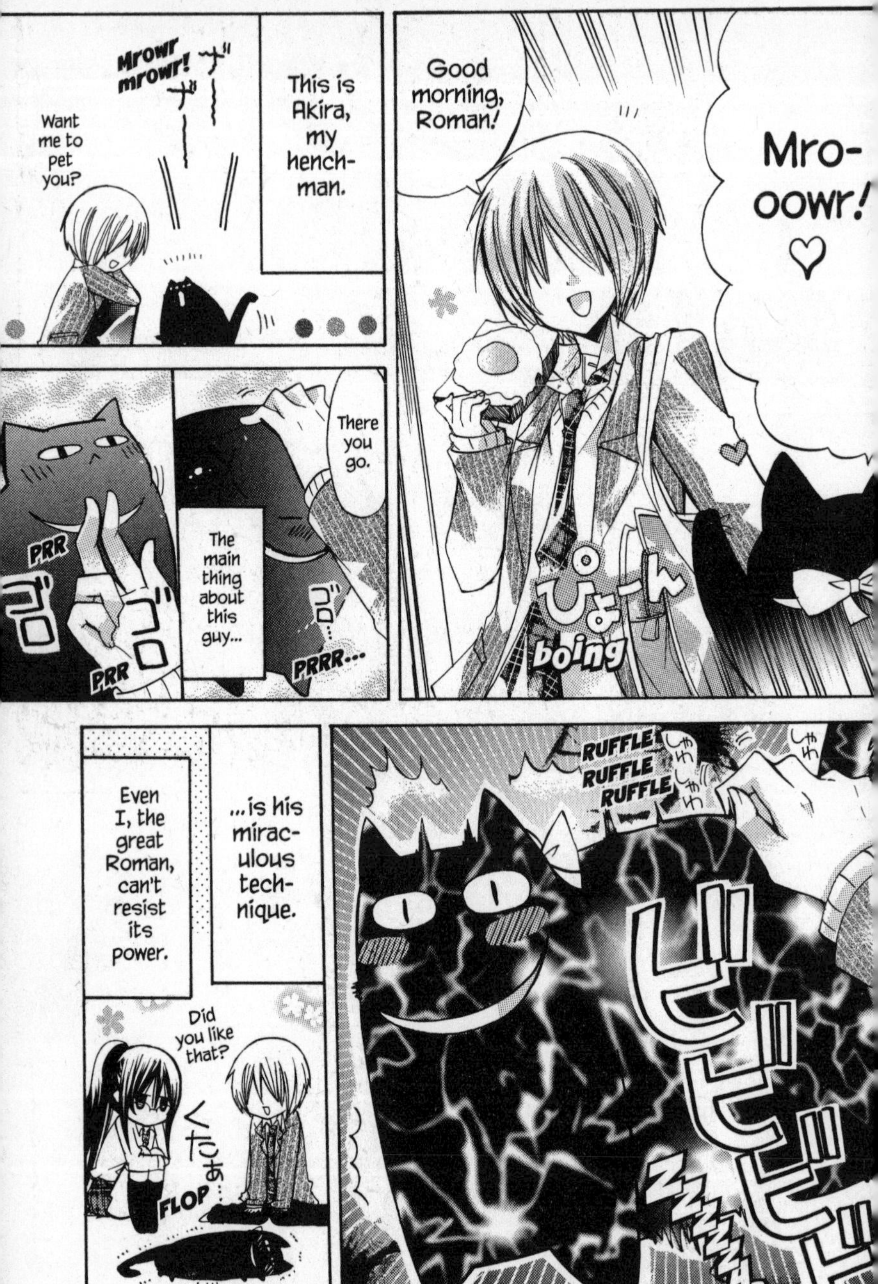
Mro-oowr! ♡
Good morning, Roman!
ぴょーん
boing
This is Akira, my hench-man.
Mrowr mrowr!
Want me to pet you?
There you go.
The main thing about this guy...
PRRR...
ゴロゴロ
PRR
PRR
RUFFLE RUFFLE RUFFLE
ビビビビ
ZZZZZAP!
...is his miraculous technique.
Even I, the great Roman, can't resist its power.
Did you like that?
くたぁ…
FLOP

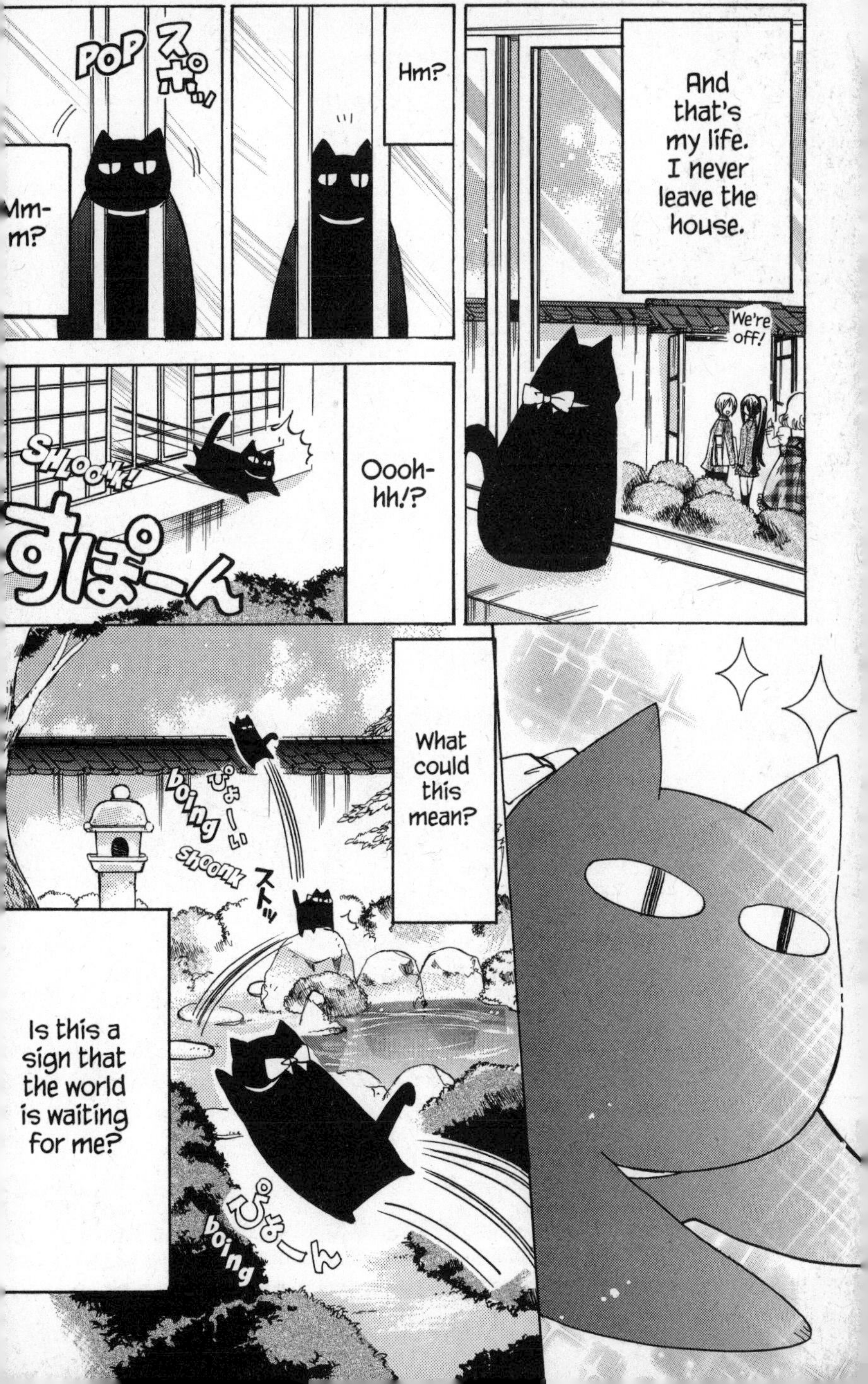
And that's my life. I never leave the house.
We're off!
Hm?
POP
スポッ
Mm-m?
Oooh-hh!?
SHLOONK!
すぽーん
What could this mean?
boing
ぴょーい
shoonk
ストッ
Is this a sign that the world is waiting for me?
ぴょーん
boing

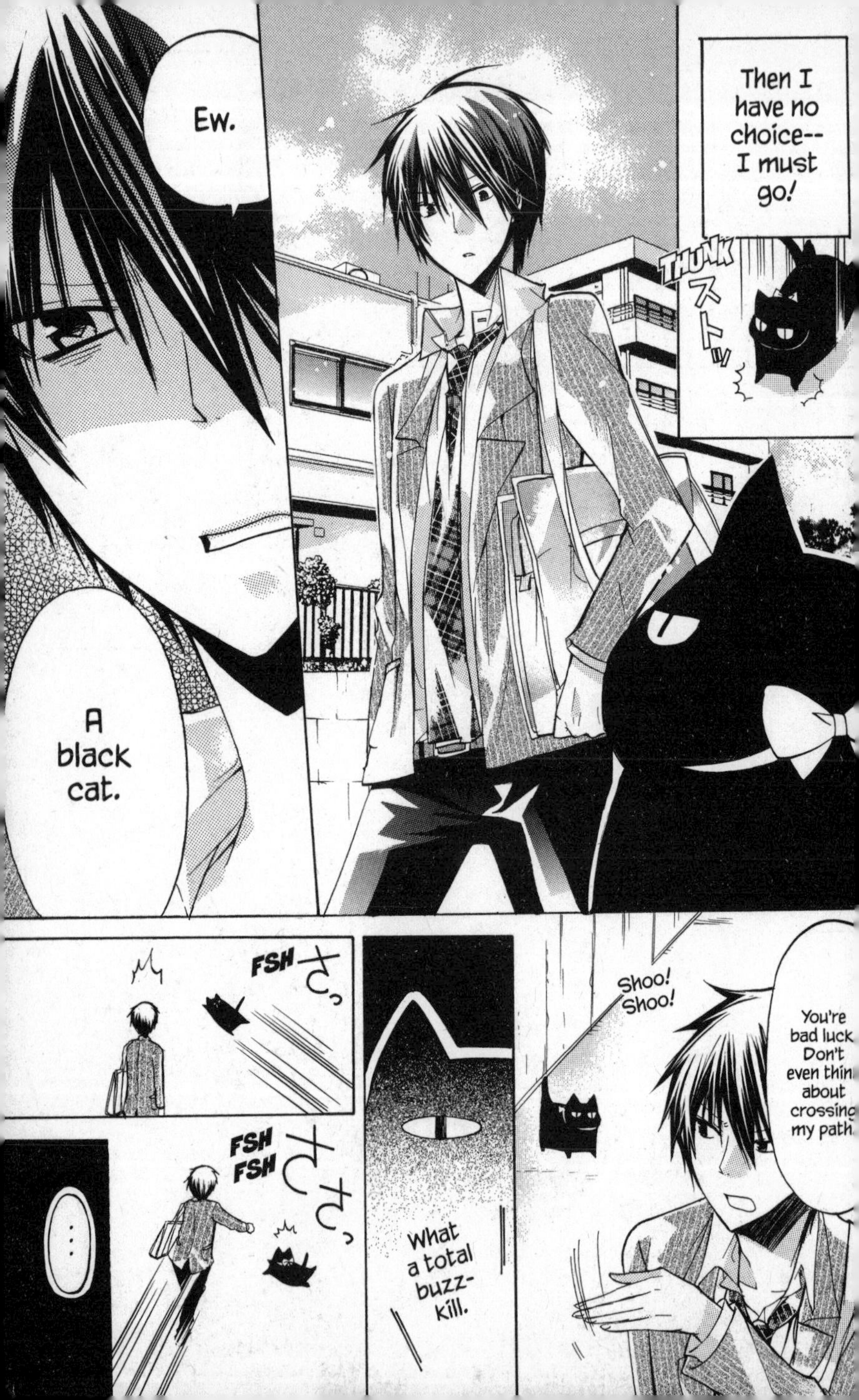
Then I have no choice-- I must go!
THUNK
ストッ
Ew.
A black cat.
You're bad luck Don't even thin about crossing my path
Shoo! Shoo!
What a total buzz-kill.
FSH
さっ
FSH FSH
さっさっ
...

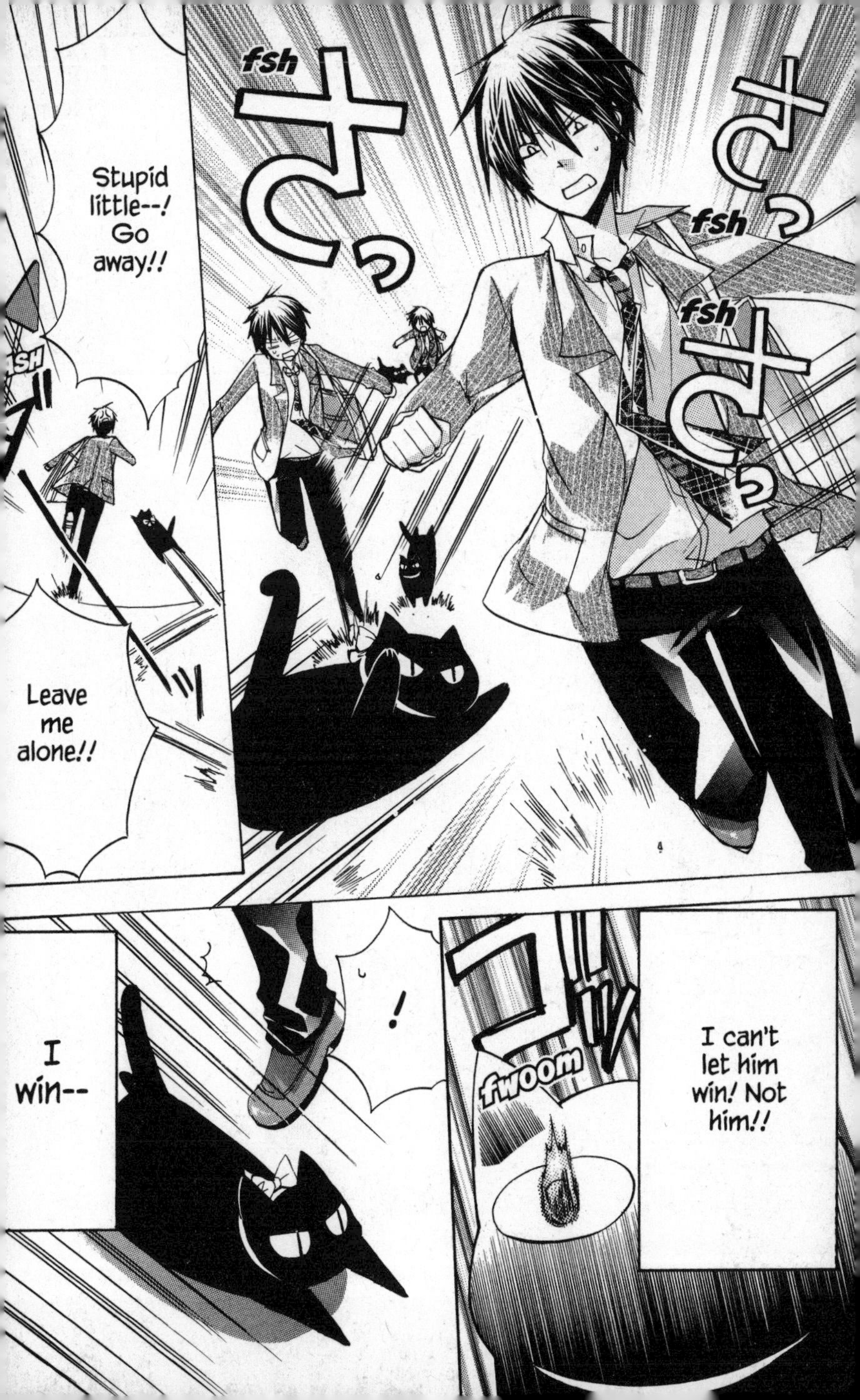
fsh
さっ
fsh
さっ
fsh
さっ
Stupid little--! Go away!!
Leave me alone!!
I can't let him win! Not him!!
fwoom
!
I win--

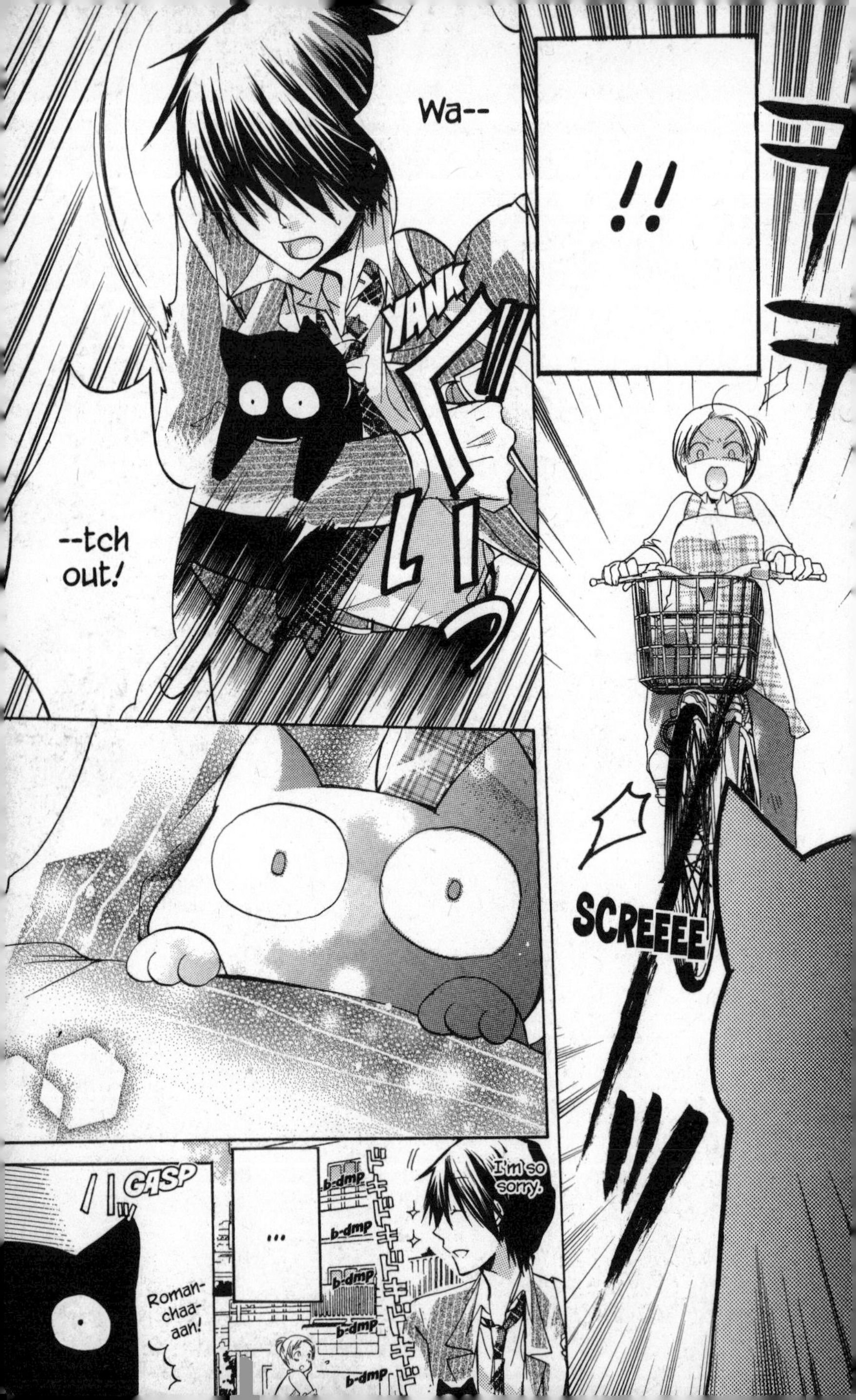
!!
SCREEEE
Wa--
YANK
--tch out!
I'm so sorry.
b-dmp
b-dmp
b-dmp
b-dmp
b-dmp
...
GASP
Roman-chaa-aan!

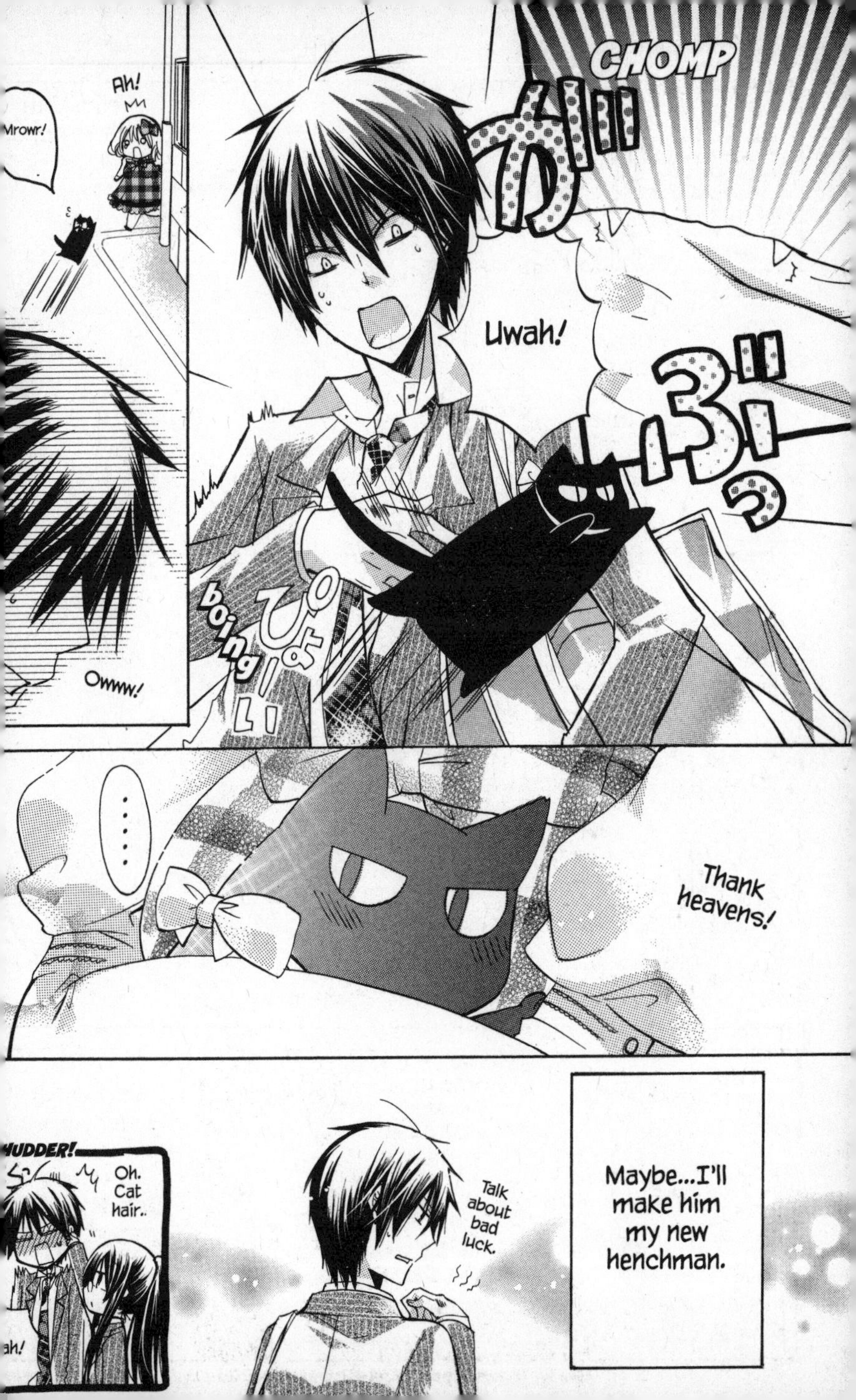
CHOMP
Uwah!
boing
Mrowr!
Ah!
Owww!
Thank heavens!
......
Maybe...I'll make him my new henchman.
Talk about bad luck.
HUDDER!
Oh. Cat hair..
ah!

Afterword

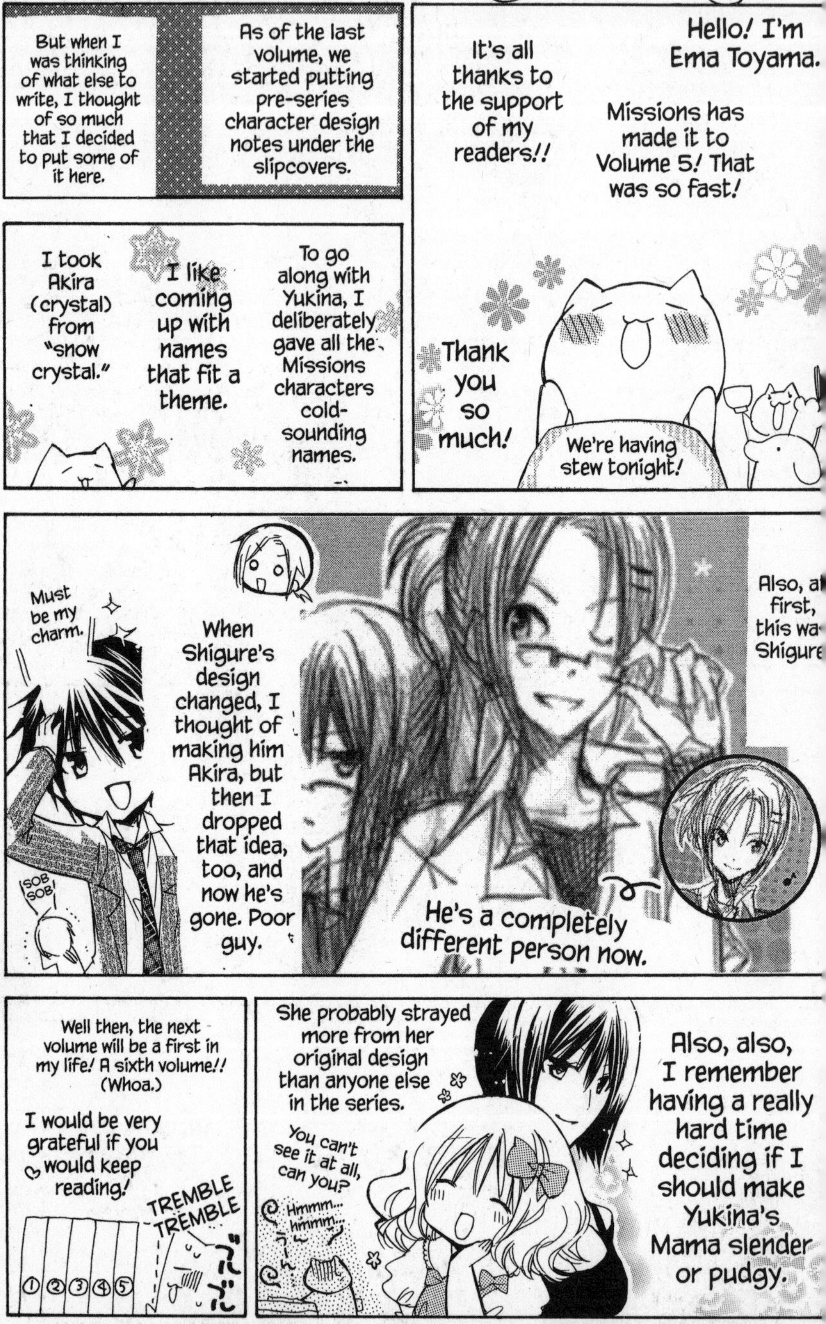
Hello! I'm Ema Toyama.
Missions has made it to Volume 5! That was so fast!
It's all thanks to the support of my readers!!
Thank you so much!
We're having stew tonight!
As of the last volume, we started putting pre-series character design notes under the slipcovers.
But when I was thinking of what else to write, I thought of so much that I decided to put some of it here.
To go along with Yukina, I deliberately gave all the Missions characters cold-sounding names.
I like coming up with names that fit a theme.
I took Akira (crystal) from "snow crystal."
Also, a
first,
this wa
Shigure
He's a completely different person now.
When Shigure's design changed, I thought of making him Akira, but then I dropped that idea, too, and now he's gone. Poor guy.
Must be my charm.
SOB SOB
Also, also, I remember having a really hard time deciding if I should make Yukina's Mama slender or pudgy.
She probably strayed more from her original design than anyone else in the series.
You can't see it at all, can you?
Hmmm... hmmm...
Well then, the next volume will be a first in my life! A sixth volume!! (Whoa.)
I would be very grateful if you would keep reading!
TREMBLE TREMBLE
① ② ③ ④ ⑤

Special Thanks: My assistants Ryo-sama and Zo-sama, my editor N-jima-sa

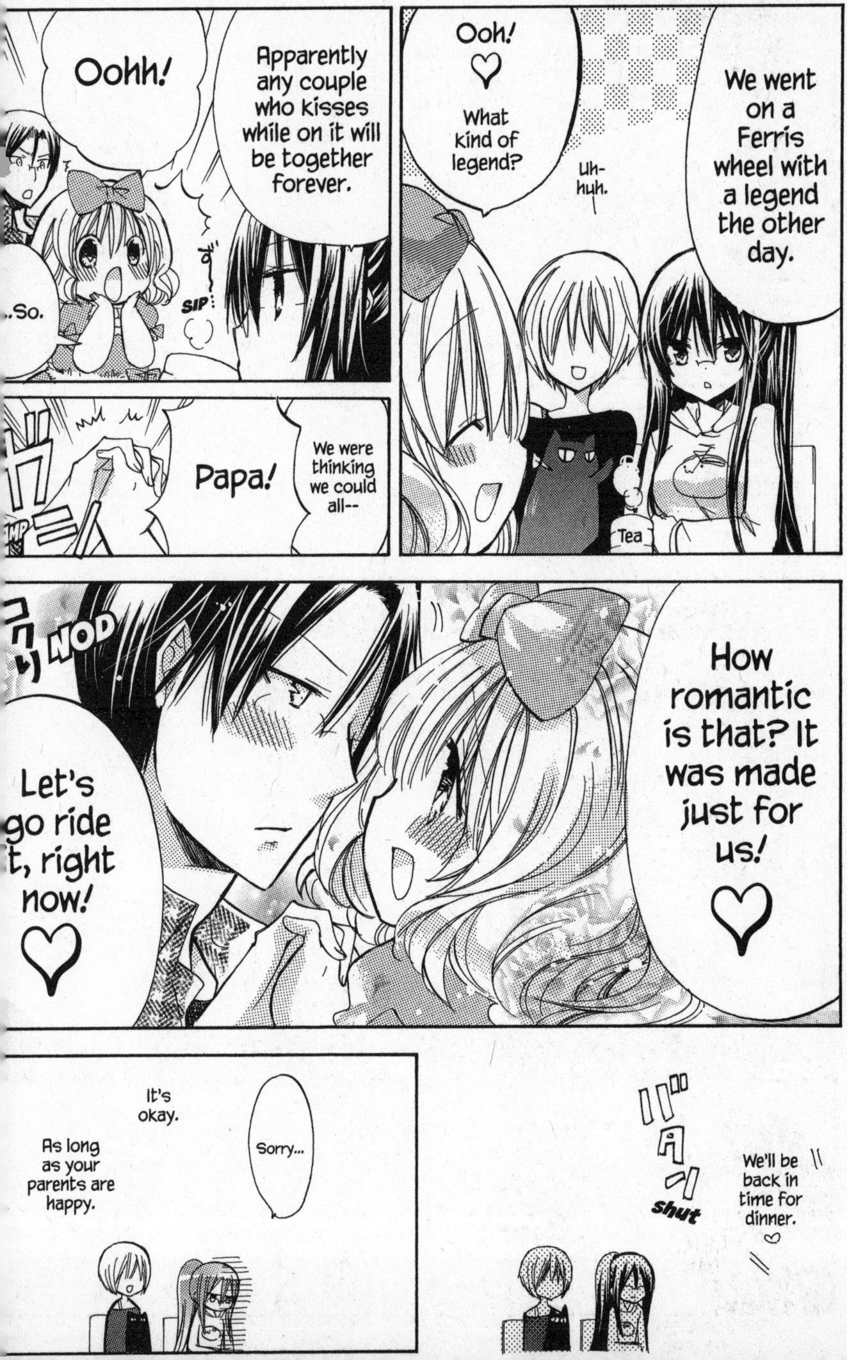
We went on a Ferris wheel with a legend the other day.
Uh-huh.
Ooh! ♡ What kind of legend?
Tea
Apparently any couple who kisses while on it will be together forever.
SIP
Oohh!
..So.
We were thinking we could all--
Papa!
How romantic is that? It was made just for us! ♡
NOD
Let's go ride t, right now! ♡
We'll be back in time for dinner.
shut
Sorry...
It's okay.
As long as your parents are happy.

And they're back

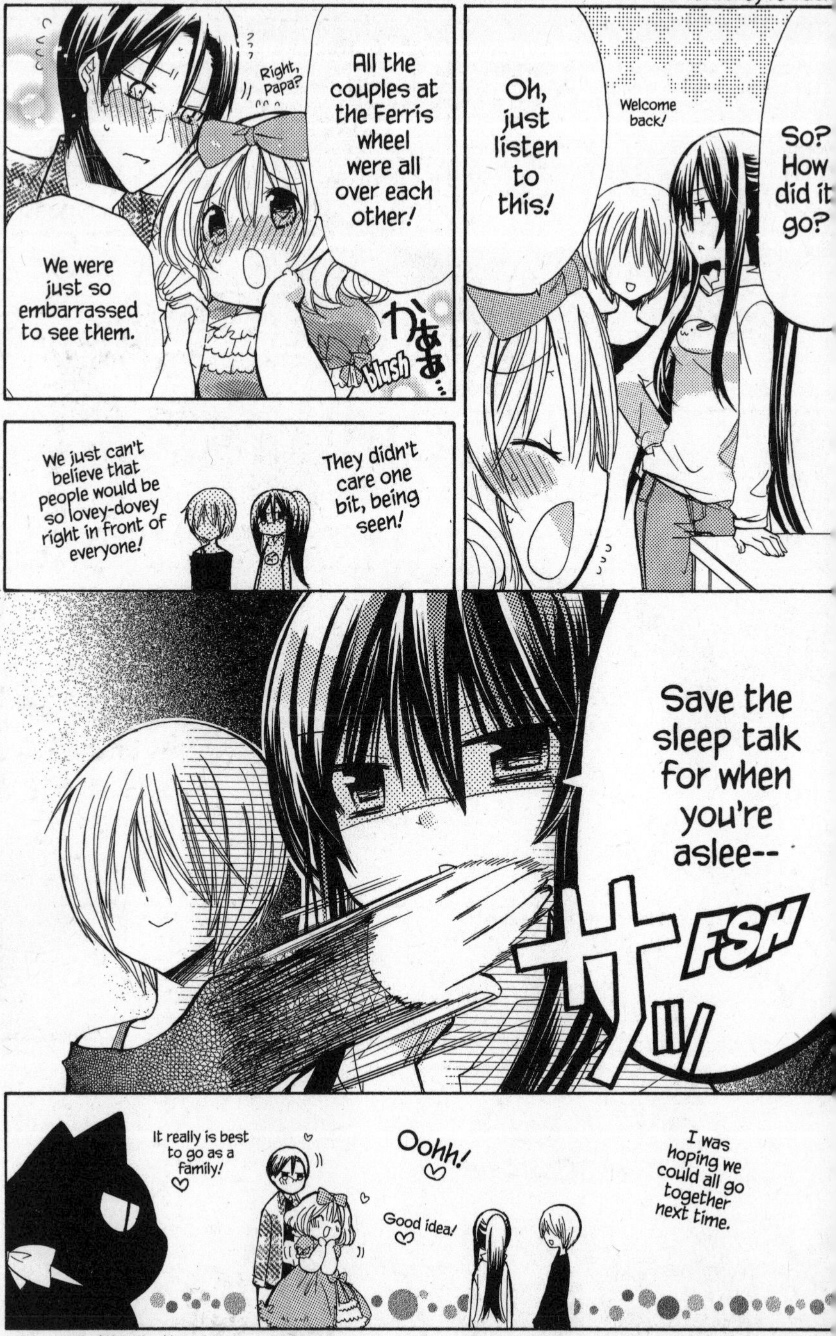
So? How did it go?
Welcome back!
Oh, just listen to this!
All the couples at the Ferris wheel were all over each other!
Right, Papa?
We were just so embarrassed to see them.
かぁぁ…
blush
They didn't care one bit, being seen!
We just can't believe that people would be so lovey-dovey right in front of everyone!
Save the sleep talk for when you're aslee--
FSH
I was hoping we could all go together next time.
Oohh!
Good idea!
It really is best to go as a family!

And they lived happily ever after.

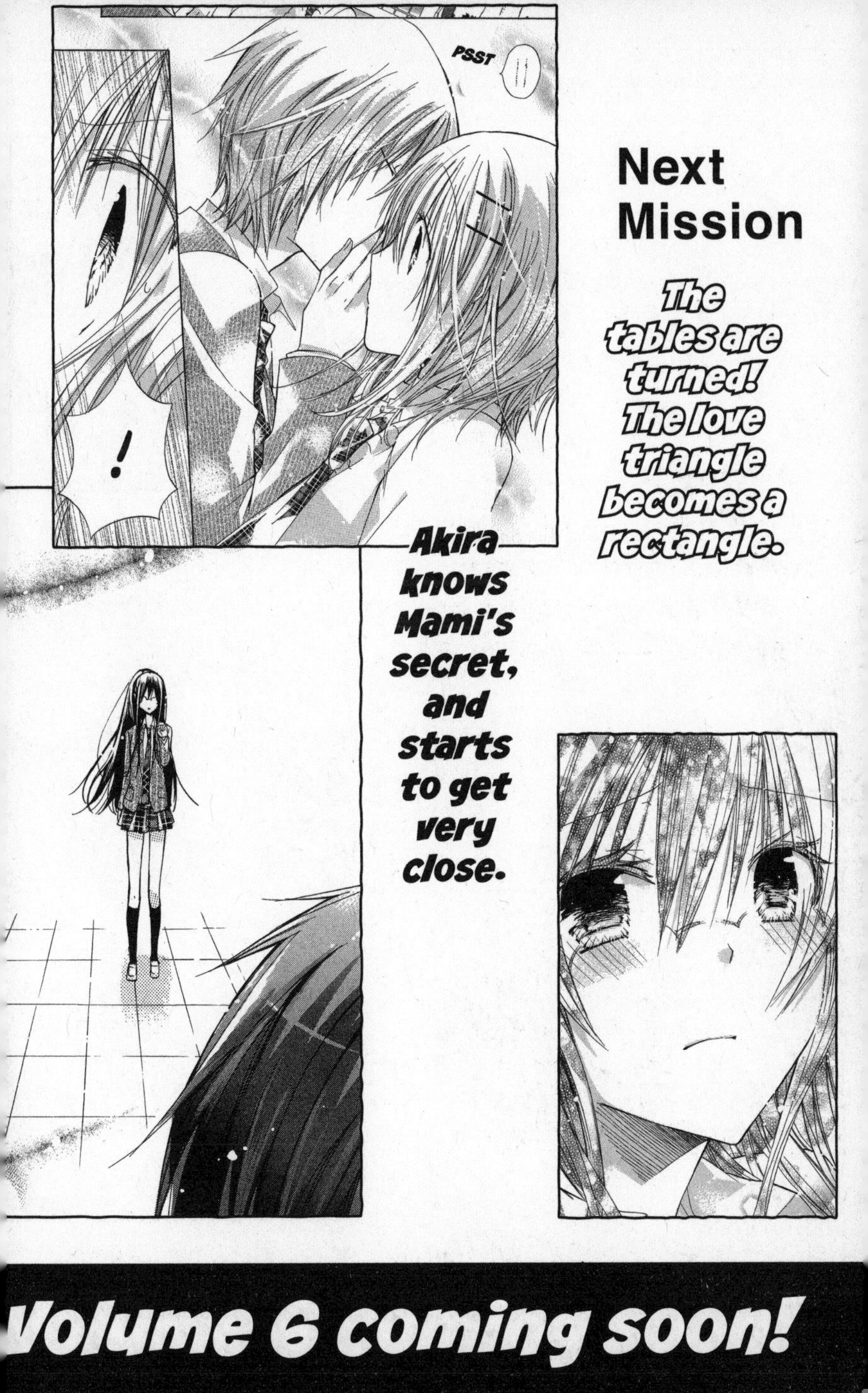
Next Mission
The tables are turned! The love triangle becomes a rectangle.
PSST
!!
!
Akira knows Mami's secret, and starts to get very close.
Volume 6 coming soon!

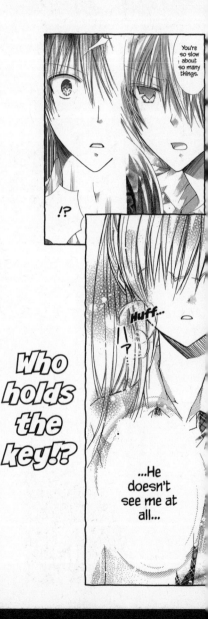

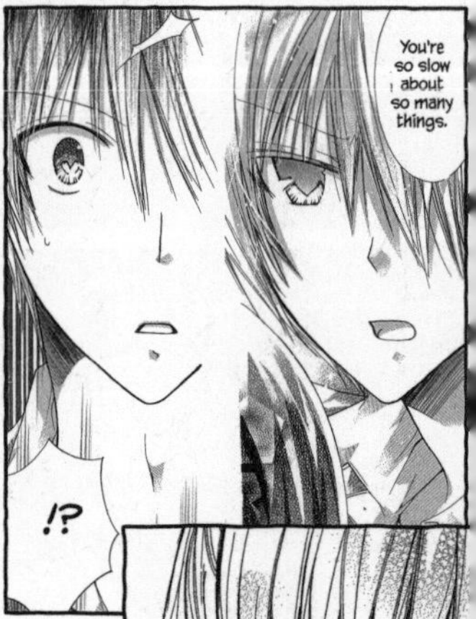
You're so slow about so many things.
!?

As Shigure worries about their relationship, Yukina's heart starts to break.

Is it all a part of Akira's plot...!?

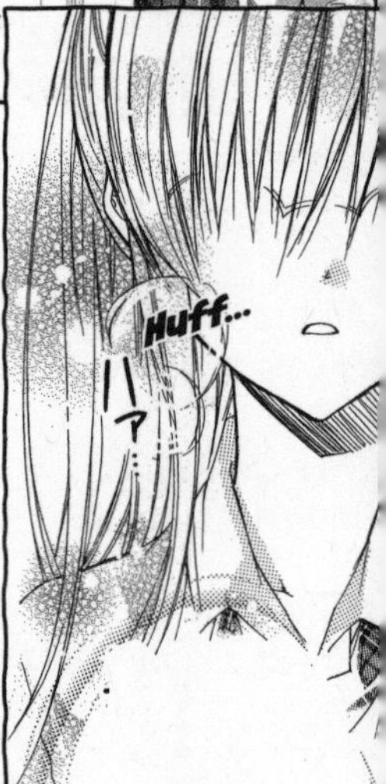
Huff...
...He doesn't see me at all...

Who holds the key!?

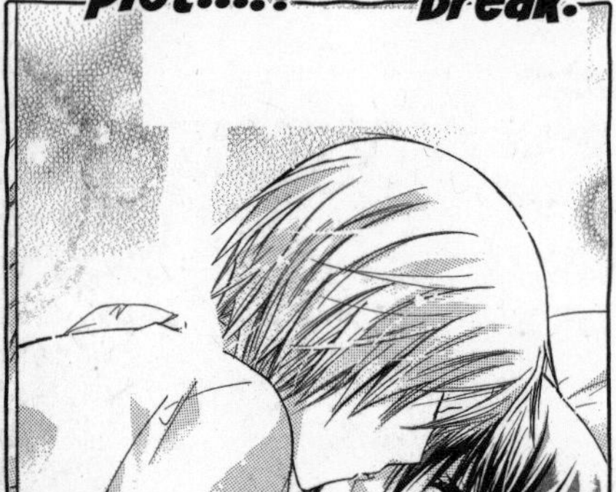

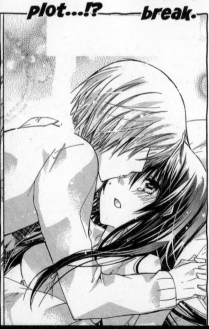

Missions of Love volume 6!

Missions of Love volume 5 is a work of
places, and incidents are the products of the author's imagination or are used fictitiously. Any resemblance to actual events, locales, or persons, living or dead, is entirely coincidental.

A Kodansha Comics Trade Paperback Original.

Published in the United States by Kodansha Comics, an imprint of Kodansha USA Publishing, LLC, New York.

Publication rights for this English edition arranged through Kodansha Ltd., Tokyo.

First published in Japan in 2011 by Kodansha Ltd., Tokyo, as *Watashi ni xx shinasai!*, volume 5.

ISBN 978-1-61262-287-3

Printed in the United States of America.

www.kodanshacomics.com

9 8 7 6 5 4 3 2 1

Translator: Alethea Nibley and Athena Nibley
Lettering: Paige Pumphrey